Correction Symbols

Page numbers in parentheses refer to specific discussions in the text.

Abr Abbreviation needed (or in error)

Agr Agreement error
1. pronoun and antecedent (140)
2. subject and verb (140)

Apos Apostrophe needed (or in error)

Awk Awkward phrasing

Cap Capital needed (427–30)

CR ⌃ Comma required
1. with conjunction between clauses (132–34)
2. after opening clause or verb phrase (435)
3. in series (125–27)
4. with nonrestrictive modifier (68–71, 79–81, 435)

CS Comma splice (132–34)

CU Comma unnecessary
1. between sentence slots (19–20)
2. between compound pair (125–26)
3. with restrictive modifier (68–71, 79–81)

Dang Dangling verb phrase
1. gerund (102–3)
2. infinitive (14)
3. participle (73–75)

Dic Inappropriate level of diction (199–202)

Div Error in word division (refer to dictionary)

Doc Documentation needed (472–73)

Emph Emphasis misplaced (376–80)

Fall Fallacy in argument (327–30)

Frag Sentence fragment (112)

Gl/mp *See* Glossary of Mechanics and Punctuation (423–50)

Gl/us *See* Glossary of Usage (251–63)

Hy Hyphen needed (or in error) (63, 440–41)

Ital Italics (underline) (442)

lc Lower case needed

Met Mixed or ineffective metaphor (205)

MM Misplaced modifier (92–97)

Num Numeral needed (or in error) (443–45)

Pass Ineffective passive voice (55–57, 402–3)

Ref Pronoun referent unclear (187–88, 385–88)

Rep Unnecessary repetition

Sp Spelling error (215, 235)

Spec Specific details needed

Sub Subordination needed (or in error) (412–18)

Trans Missing or awkward transition (369–73)

Vb Verb form or tense in error (40–43)

W Wordiness

WW Wrong word (refer to dictionary)

✔ Good point!

∧ Omission in sentence

// Faulty parallelism

¶ Paragraph break needed

No ¶ Paragraph break not needed

\# space

⌒ close up

— dash

; semicolon

: colon

... ellipses

! exclamation point

' apostrophe

" " quotation marks

' ' single quotations

? question mark

( ) parentheses

A Handbook and Rhetoric

Language and Composition

Martha Kolln

The Pennsylvania State University

Macmillan Publishing Company • NEW YORK
Collier Macmillan Publishers • LONDON

*To my Penn State colleagues, from whom
I am constantly learning about language and
composition: Betsy, Betty, Gus, Jack, Jim,
John, Judy, Louie, Marie, Nancy,
Ron, and, of course, Wilma.*

Macmillan Publishing Company
866 Third Avenue, New York, New York 10022

Collier Macmillan Canada, Inc.

Library of Congress Cataloging in Publication Data

Kolln, Martha.
  Language and composition.

  Includes index.
  1. English language—Grammar—   . 2. English
language—Rhetoric. I. Title.
PE1112.K65 1984   808'.042   83-9887
ISBN 0-02-365860-6

Printing: 2 3 4 5 6 7 8   Year: 4 5 6 7 8 9 0 1 2

ISBN   0-02-365860-6

Acknowledgments

Permission to reprint excerpts from the works of the authors listed below has been given as indicated:

Hal Borland, "The Katydid," from *Sundial of the Seasons* (N.Y.: Lippincott, 1964). Reprinted by permission of Barbara Dodge Borland. Copyright © 1964 by Hal Borland.

William Faulkner, "Barn Burning," from *Collected Stories of William Faulkner*. Reprinted by permission of Random House, Inc. Copyright © 1956 by William Faulkner.

Susan Holden, "Why Television Is Fattening," *Nutrition Action*, May 1982, p. 9. *Nutrition Action* is available by membership from the Center for Science in the Public Interest, 1755 S Street, N.W., Washington, D.C. 20009.

Roger Tory Peterson, *The Birds*, Life Nature Library. Reprinted by permission of Time-Life Books, Inc. Copyright © 1963 Time, Inc.

Thomas Rogers, *At the Shore*. Copyright © by Thomas Rogers. Reprinted by permission of Simon & Schuster, Inc.

Carl Sagan, *Broca's Brain*. Reprinted by permission of Random House, Inc. Copyright © 1980 by Carl Sagan.

Preface

Language and Composition: A Handbook and Rhetoric, as its subtitle announces, is indeed both a handbook and a rhetoric. The handbook includes a practical and thorough description of sentence grammar, using traditional and contemporary methods of analysis. The step-by-step explanations make the system of expanding sentences and punctuating them meaningful for student writers. The rhetoric describes in detail the stages in the writing process, with special attention throughout given to the three components of every writing situation: topic, purpose, and audience. It includes a complete chapter on each of the traditional rhetorical modes; it recognizes invention and revision as ongoing processes; and it offers practical advice on paragraphs, style, editing, and library research.

The Emphasis on Language

The word *language* was chosen for the title to reflect the book's special emphasis. In one sense, of course, language is the emphasis of every handbook and rhetoric; and learning to use language effectively is the goal of every composition course. My choice of the word, however, affirms the book's emphasis on the structure—the grammar—of English and on the ways in which knowledge of grammar can influence the composing process. An important message of the book is that the writer who understands the structure of language, who can manipulate sentences with genuine control, will be a better writer.

Rhetorical Grammar

Rhetoric, too, gets special emphasis throughout the book, even in the chapters about grammar. Part I, "The Grammar of Sentences," deals with what I call *rhetorical grammar*, a description of grammar that aims to give writers control over their sentences. For too long we have thought of grammar as subject matter only for remedial purposes—a kind of band-aid for helping students patch up the cuts and bruises that blemish the surface of their sentences. But to consider grammar in this limited way is to miss its most important contribution to composition: its usefulness as a rhetorical tool.

Picture, instead, the study of grammar as a continuum, ranging from remedial to rhetorical:

REMEDIAL GRAMMAR   RHETORICAL GRAMMAR

At the remedial end of the scale, the teacher is indeed concerned with errors of subject–verb and pronoun–antecedent agreement, of dangling and misplaced modifiers. Learning to recognize and correct errors is a part of the value of studying grammar; the lessons here will certainly help students with these tasks. But understanding grammar is, or should be, so much more than error correction. At the other end of the continuum is the rhetorical value of understanding grammar. Rhetorical grammar is a means of illuminating the choices available for composing and revising; rhetorical grammar is a way of examining the options for modification in the noun phrase, for adding adverbial information to sentences, for compounding sentences and their parts, for shifting stress, for improving style.

The sentence-building chapters in Part I do not simply *prescribe* rules and give examples; they *describe* the grammar of English in a systematic way, emphasizing the importance of the rules that speakers of the language know in a subconscious way. The grammar lessons begin with a description of six sentence patterns that underlie nearly all of our sentences in English; they go on to describe the expansions through modification, subordination, and coordination in a systematic way. Each step in the process includes the relationship of the grammar system to the conventions of punctuation.

The study of rhetorical grammar certainly need not dominate the composition class—not at all. If time is a problem—and it usually is—students can be assigned parts of the sentence grammar to study on their own, outside of class, so that class time can be spent on rhetorical applications of grammar to writing. Numerous exercises at each step will help to reinforce the students' understanding of the concepts. That understanding will certainly help students approach their own writing with enhanced confidence and sensitivity. Familiarity with the grammar system will also enhance the value of the book as a reference tool. When questions of usage and grammar and punctuation come up, not only will students understand the questions, they will know where to go for answers.

Words

The study of sentences provides a framework for the study of words in Part II. The classification of words into parts of speech uses the sensible categories of the structural linguists: form classes, structure classes, and pronouns. As in the study of sentence grammar, students will come to appreciate how much they know about language when they realize how much they know about words. The four chapters of Part II include insights from semantics and psycholinguistics, discussions of usage, including ways of avoiding sexism in writing, and a chapter that offers both hope and help for students with spelling problems.

Rhetoric and the Essay

The whole essay is studied in detail in Parts III and IV, again with a genuine rhetorical emphasis. The three components of the writing situation—topic, purpose, and audience—are central to the discussions of invention, of arrangement, and of the rhetorical modes. In fact, all the suggested assignments in the chapters on description, narration, and exposition include the rhetorical framework of purpose and audience.

The importance of all three components of the writing situation is also emphasized throughout the discussions in Part IV on planning and writing the essay. Instruction in the paragraph includes three patterns of development, with special attention focused on reader expectation. The system of grammar studied in Part I will illuminate the discussion of paragraph coherence, based on current research in grammatical, semantic, and lexical cohesion. A chapter on revision and style explains revision as an ongoing part of the composing process; here the emphasis is on the importance of developing a personal voice and learning to listen to that voice. This chapter, with its specific suggestions on what to listen and look for in revising an essay, also uses the writer's understanding of grammar. Included are checklists for editing and proofreading.

Library Research

Part V presents a case study of a student using the library, including detailed information on the library's resources and on documentation. Chapter 20 includes both a rough and a final draft of the student's research paper. Chapter 21 offers practical advice for special writing situations: the essay examination, the business letter, and the résumé.

Glossaries

Three clearly marked glossaries give the book further practical value as a reference tool: definitions of grammatical terms, an explanation of common diction errors, and a thorough summary of mechanics and punctuation. Because the conventions of writing grow out of the system of rules underlying our language—that is, out of the grammar—these glossaries of usage and punctuation include numerous references to the discussions of sentence grammar and words in Parts I and II.

Teaching Aids

Supplementing the book is a detailed *Instructor's Manual*, which includes diagnostic tests with answers, answers to the exercises, sample syllabi, and other suggestions for using the text. Also available is a workbook, *Language and Composition: A Workbook*, which contains further instruction and exercises on sentence grammar, punctuation, the paragraph, and the essay. The workbook can be used as a supplement to the text, or it can be used independently.

Because the workbook places special emphasis on sentences and paragraphs, it would be ideal as the text for a basic skills course.

Acknowledgments

It is impossible, of course, for me to acknowledge all of the sources that have contributed to this book. For years I have been reading about and hearing about and talking to others about and, of course, teaching language and composition. I have been inspired by convention addresses and influenced by conference sessions; I have learned from books and essays dealing with theory and practice in composition and linguistics and speech and education. I have argued with and learned from colleagues, worked on committees to plan courses and prepare syllabi. I have taught courses for basic, intermediate, and advanced writers in composition, grammar, and English as a second language; I learn continually from those students. In short, the ideas in this book spring from many sources.

Some of the sources I can easily name. My understanding of grammar has come from the scholarly descriptive work of pioneers like Otto Jesperson and George Curme and more recently from the detailed descriptions of Randolph Quirk and Sidney Greenbaum. My understanding of new theories of grammar has come from the work of Noam Chomsky, Charles Fillmore, Charles C. Fries, Paul Roberts, and James Sledd, among others. I have learned a great deal from Wayne Booth, James Britton, Kenneth Burke, Francis Christensen, Edward Corbett, Wilma Ebbitt, Jeanne Fahnestock and Marie Secor, Linda Flower and John Hayes, M. A. K. Halliday and Ruqaiya Hasan, William Irmscher, James Kinneavy, Richard Larson, Mina Shaughnessy, Joe Williams, Richard Young, and others who have researched and written about rhetoric and composition and teaching.

My colleagues have been especially helpful in my work on this book. Special thanks go to Betsy Brown, John Harwood, and Betty Johnson, all of Penn State, and to Jeanne Fahnestock, of the University of Maryland, all of whom read parts of the manuscript at various stages and raised critical questions. I owe a special debt to Beverly Renford, a dear friend and a talented librarian, who understands the questions that student researchers ask. Beverly laid out the format for the library chapters; she supplied a great deal of expertise and information about library resources; and she has been more than generous with her time, critiquing many parts of the book and encouraging me through all of its stages. Thanks go also to Paul Hutchison, whose library adventure and research paper resulting from it are recorded in Part IV, and to Beth Strange, for her careful proofreading and valuable help with the index.

Many people at Macmillan have made the job of writing this book not only possible but pleasurable. First, I appreciate the careful comments of Macmillan's manuscript reviewers, particularly, Richard L. Larson, Jean G. Pival, Walter E. Meyers, John T. Harwood, Francesca Tillonq, and Joyce Stith. I very much appreciate the careful work of Bob Hunter, who guided the book through the details of production; the expertise of my editor, Eben Ludlow, who helped me say what I wanted to say and managed to keep me feeling optimistic; and the friendship and welcome words of Tony English.

Finally, I wish to thank my family for their encouragement and patience—especially Tiger Jack, without whom . . .

M. K.

Contents

Part I
The Grammar of Sentences

1. Sentence Patterns   5

  1.1   The Two-Part Sentence   5
  1.2   The Six Basic Patterns   9
      The Basic Transitive-Verb Pattern   9
      Other Transitive-Verb Patterns   10
        The Objective Complement   10
        The Indirect Object   11
      The Optional Slots   12
        The Dangling Infinitive   14
      The Intransitive-Verb Pattern   16
      The Linking-Verb Patterns   17
  1.3   Punctuation and the Sentence Slots   19
  1.4   Punctuation of Sentence Openers   20
  1.5   Summary   22
      Sentence Practice   23

2. Expanding the Verb   25

  2.1   The Verb Forms   26
  2.2   The Expanded Forms   28
  2.3   The System of Expansion   29

2.4   Subject–Verb Agreement   31
       Errors in Subject–Verb Agreement   32
2.5   Addition of Tense to the Verb String   34
2.6   The Modal Auxiliaries   35
2.7   The Moods of the Verb   37
       The Subjunctive Mood   38
2.8   Summary of Verb Forms   40
       Verb Practice   42
2.9   The Irregular Verbs   43

3. *The Passive Voice*   47
3.1   A Three-Step Transformation   47
       Other Passive Sentences   50
3.2   Transformation of Expanded Verbs   51
3.3   Use of the Passive Voice   53
3.4   Misuse of the Passive Voice   55

4. *Expanding the Noun Phrase: Adjectivals*   59
4.1   The Determiner   60
4.2   The Headword   61
4.3   The Prenoun Modifiers   61
       Adjectives and Nouns   61
4.4   The Postnoun Modifiers   64
       The Prepositional Phrase   65
       The Participial Phrase   66
         Punctuation of Participial Phrases   68
         The Movable Participle   71
         The Dangling Participle   73
         The Prenoun Participle   75
       The Relative Clause   75
         Indefinite Relative Pronouns   77
         Relative Adverbs   78
         Punctuation of Relative Clauses   79
       The Appositive   81
         The Movable Appositive   82
         The Punctuation of Appositives   83
         The Colon with Appositives   84
         Dashes with Appositives   86

Compound Sentences with Colons	88
Punctuation Errors with the Colon	89
Multiple Modifiers	92
Misplaced Modifiers	92
Sentence Practice	93

5. *Nominals and Sentence Modifiers*   99

5.1	Nominals	99
	Gerunds	99
	The Subject of the Gerund	100
	Functions of the Gerund	101
	The Dangling Gerund	102
	Infinitives	103
	Clause Nominals	104
	Punctuation of Nominal Clauses	107
	A Tricky Punctuation Problem	107
5.2	Sentence Modifiers	110
	The Subordinate Clause	111
	Punctuation of Subordinate Clauses	112
	Elliptical Subordinate Clauses	113
	The Absolute Phrase	115
	The Relative Clause	118
	Sentence Practice	119

6. *Coordination*   *123*

6.1	Coordination Within the Sentence	124
	Punctuation of Coordinated Parts	125
	Parallel Structure	127
	Subject–Verb Agreement with Compound Subjects	128
	And	129
	Or, Nor	129
6.2	Coordination of Complete Sentences	129
	The Coordinate Sentence with *But*	131
	Punctuation of the Compound Sentence	132
	The Comma-plus-Conjunction	132
	The Semicolon	133
	The Semicolon with a Conjunctive Adverb	134
	The Semicolon with a Conjunction	135
	Sentence Practice	136

Glossary of Grammatical Terms   *139*

Part II
Words

7. The Parts of Speech   *153*

    7.1 Morphemes   155
              Derivational and Inflectional Affixes   157
    7.2 The Form Classes   158
              Nouns   158
              Noun Derivational Suffixes   159
              Noun Inflectional Suffixes   160
              Other Noun Classes   160
              Noncountable Nouns   160
              Plural-only Forms   161
              Collective Nouns   162
              Verbs   163
              Verb Derivational Affixes   163
              Verb Inflectional Suffixes   164
              Adjectives   165
              Adjective Derivational Suffixes   165
              Adjective Inflectional Suffixes   166
              Subclasses of Adjectives   168
              Adverbs   169
              Adverb Derivational Suffixes   169
              Adverb Inflectional Suffixes   170
    7.3 The Structure Classes   172
              Determiners   172
              Auxiliaries   173
              Qualifiers   175
              Prepositions   176
              Simple Prepositions   177
              Phrasal Prepositions   178
              Conjunctions   178
              Interrogatives   179
              Expletives   180
    7.4 Pronouns   181
              Personal Pronouns   182
              Pronoun Errors   184
              Reflexive Pronouns   185
              Intensive Pronouns   186
              Reciprocal Pronouns   187
              Demonstrative Pronouns   187
              Indefinite Pronouns   188
              Relative Pronouns   189
              Interrogative Pronouns   190

8. Using Words Effectively 191

8.1	The Meaning of Words	191
8.2	Denotation and Connotation	192
8.3	Categories of Meaning	194
8.4	Levels of Diction	199
8.5	The Writer's Attitude	202
8.6	Figurative Language	203
8.7	Euphemism	208
8.8	Predictability and Redundancy	209

9. Spelling 215

9.1	Spelling Rules	218
	Rule 1: ie/ei	220
	Rule 2: Doubling Consonants	221
	Rule 3: The Silent *e*	222
	Rule 4: *-ize/-ise*	223
	Rule 5: *-eed/-ede*	223
	Rule 6: Regular Noun Plurals	223
	Rule 7: Irregular Noun Plurals	224
	Rule 8: The Possessive Case	227
	Possessive Case of Pronouns	228
	Rules 9 and 10: Pay Attention!	230
	Rule 9: Be Observant	230
	Rule 10: Think About Pronunciation: Listen	232
9.2	Spelling Tricks	232
9.3	Frequently Misspelled Words	233

10. What Is "Good English"? 237

10.1 Is It Good English to End a Sentence with a Preposition?	239
10.2 Is It Good English to Split an Infinitive?	242
10.3 In Good English Do Pronouns Like *Everyone* and *Everybody* Always Have Singular Referents?	245
10.4 Is It Good English to Use *He* in Reference to a Person of Unknown Gender or Is That Usage Sexist?	246

Glossary of Usage 251

Part III
The Whole Theme

11. The Writing Situation: Topic,
Audience, and Purpose   267
  11.1 Defining the Writing Situation   269
  11.2 Finding a Topic   270
  11.3 Establishing Purpose and Audience   273
  11.4 Writing the Thesis Statement   274
  11.5 A Summary of the Writing Situation: Six Steps 276

12. The Modes of Composition: Description   279
  12.1 The Descriptive Essay: The Writing Situation   280
  12.2 Arrangement   281
  12.3 Point of View   281
  12.4 Word Choice   282
       Writing Exercises   284

13. The Modes of Composition: Narration   287
  13.1 The Components of Narration   288
  13.2 The Narrative Essay: The Writing Situation   289
  13.3 Point of View   290
       First Person   290
       Third Person   290
  13.4 The Beginning Point   291
  13.5 The Use of Quotations   293
  13.6 Summary   295
       Writing Exercises   296

14. The Modes of Composition: Exposition   297
  14.1 Process   298
       Writing Exercises   299
  14.2 Division (or Analysis)   300
       Writing Exercises   302

14.3 Comparison/Contrast 303
Writing Exercises 305
14.4 Classification 307
Writing Exercises 309
14.5 Definition 310
Writing Exercises 312

15. The Modes of Composition: Argumentation 313

15.1 Topics for Argument 314
15.2 The Argumentation Orbit 315
15.3 The Parts of the Argumentative Essay 316
　　Background 317
　　Evidence 317
　　Refutation 317
15.4 The Appeals of Argument 318
　　Ethical Appeals 318
　　Emotional Appeals 320
　　Logical Appeals 321
　　　　Definition 321
　　　　Cause and Effect 322
　　　　Likenesses and Differences 323
　　　　External Arguments 325
15.5 How Arguments Go Wrong 327
　　Writing Exercises 332

Part IV
The Writing Process

16. Planning and Writing the Essay 339

16.1 Exploring the Topic 339
16.2 Exploring Attitudes 340
16.3 Planning the Essay 341
16.4 Establishing the Point of View 343

16.5 Writing the Essay   345
  The Beginning: Four Criteria   345
  The Middle   349
    Paragraph Blocs   350
  The Ending   351
16.6 The Title   354

17. *Writing Effective Paragraphs*   *355*
17.1 General-to-Specific Paragraphs   355
  The Opening Sentence   356
17.2 Specific-to-General Paragraphs   358
17.3 Reader Expectation   360
17.4 The Example Paragraph   361
17.5 Must Every Paragraph Have a Topic
        Sentence?   363
17.6 Development of the Paragraph   364
  Levels of Generality   364
  Writing Exercises   367
17.7 Coherence in Paragraphs   369
  Semantic Cohesion   370
    Transition Devices   371
  Writing Exercise   372
  Grammatical Cohesion   373
    Parallelism   373
    Known Information   374
    Sentence Stress   376
    The Passive Voice   380
    Other Sentence Transformations   381
  Lexical Cohesion   384
    Pronouns   384
    Problem Pronouns   385
    Vocabulary Choice   388
17.8 In Summary: Ten Questions to Consider   389

18. *Revision and Style*   *391*
18.1 What Is Revision?   391
18.2 What Is Style?   392
18.3 Learn to Listen   393
18.4 The Use of Your Personal Voice   394

18.5 The Grammar of Your Personal Voice 397
Nominalization 398
The Passive Voice 401
18.6 The Use of Your Voice to Revise 404
18.7 Grammar and Sentence Style 407
Word Order Variation 407
Ellipsis 408
The Coordinate Series 409
The Introductory Appositive Series 410
Sentence Practice 411
18.8 Grammar and Revision: Some Questions to Ask 412
Question 1: Is *And* Effective and Accurate? 412
The Misuse of Plus 414
Question 2: Is the Subordinate Clause Effective? 415
Question 3: Is *But* Accurate? 417
18.9 In Summary: Ten Questions to Consider 420
18.10 Six Proofreading Questions 421

Glossary of Mechanics and Punctuation *423*

Part V
Research

19. Using the Library *453*
19.1 Step One: Identifying the Sources of Information 454
Summary 455
19.2 Step Two: Finding the Information 456
19.3 Step Three: Using the Resources 466

20. Writing the Research Paper *469*
20.1 The First Step: Focusing 469
20.2 The Informal Outline 471

20.3 Acknowledgment of Sources   473
     A Word About Plagiarism   474
20.4. The Typing of the Final Draft   474
20.5 Documentation, Footnotes and Endnotes   475
20.6 Documentation: Bibliography   479
20.7 Two Draft's of Paul's Essay   482

21. *Special Writing Situations*   *507*
    21.1 The Essay Examination   508
    21.2 The Business Letter   511
    21.3 The Résumé   516
      Step One: Analyzing Yourself   516
      Step Two: Condensing and Organizing Your Data   517
      Summary   519

Index   *521*

Part I

The Grammar of Sentences

Just imagine a sentence-producing computer capable of printing out sentences day after day, year after year, without ever producing the same sentence twice. The language area of your brain is like that. Human language capacity is such that, theoretically, you could produce an infinite number of different sentences. Not only that, you can create original ones. At this very moment, in fact, you could come up with a grammatical, well-formed sentence that has never been seen or heard before. Here's one that probably qualifies:

I understand that the really sophisticated field mice of Wisconsin prefer their cheddar cheese well aged and served at room temperature.

And another:

This book contains only one sentence about the cheese preferences of Wisconsin's really sophisticated field mice.

It's easy to come up with original sentences; we do it every day, whenever the need arises. Of course, many of the things

we say are common and fairly predictable: "How are you?"
"Have you eaten yet?" "It's been a rough day." "I can't find my
gloves." "Please pass the salt." But whether our sentences are
originals or old standards, long or short, we speak them easily,
automatically, and usually without error.

If you're a native speaker of English, you've known how to
produce such sentences for years. No one is quite certain how
or why it happened, but when you were only one or two years
old, you began to invent—yes, invent—sentences. You heard
conversation spoken around you and to you, and soon you
started talking, too, using your own, invented, version of
English: Baby cookie; Daddy car; No sit there. *Before long*
your sentences began to sound like those of the adults in your
life; and by the time you started school, you could talk in long,
complicated sentences filled with coordinate structures and
subordinate structures and modifiers. All that talk has been
going on now for years.

It's possible, however, that even after all these years of
speaking grammatical sentences, you still don't know how to
discuss them. Your teachers may have tried through the years
to explain sentence completeness and the parts of speech and
the rules connected with them. But if you weren't listening—or
if you've forgotten all those language-arts lessons—you may
not be very articulate on the subject of sentence grammar.
Consequently, you probably don't appreciate how much you,
as a native speaker, actually do "know." In this first part of the
book, we will look at the sentences you speak every day;
perhaps you'll discover that you know more about grammar
than you thought you did.

You may also discover that a conscious understanding of
sentence grammar will make writing easier. Unlike speaking,
which we do automatically, writing is a conscious activity; it is
a skill we begin to learn many years after we begin to speak.
Even for the experienced professional writer, the act of writing
is far from automatic. It requires deliberate choices of words
and phrases, as well as careful attention to the details of style
and punctuation; it requires thoughtful revising and editing.

Because the act of writing is a conscious behavior, a clear understanding of sentence structure can help the writer make choices in the most effective way. The more clearly and precisely you can think about writing, the more clear and precise your writing performance will be.

1

Sentence Patterns

Even though the number of possible sentences that a speaker can produce is indeed infinite, the number of basic sentence forms, or patterns, is decidedly finite—in fact, the total is very small. Only six general patterns will account for the underlying skeletal structure of almost all of the possible grammatical sentences in English. The patterns are much simpler than most of the sentences that we actually produce in both speech and writing, but to understand how we write those more complicated sentences, we must first understand the simple skeletons that underlie them.

1.1 The Two-Part Sentence

An efficient way to organize the details of the sentence patterns is to think of a sentence as a series of slots filled by various structures. Your intuition will often be sufficient for figuring out the slot boundaries. For example, if you were asked to divide each of the following sentences into its two basic parts, where would you draw the line?

Crowds of excited students went to the game on Saturday.
The fans cheered wildly.

1.1

Chris finished his math assignment during the game.

A fired-up Lion squad defeated the Panthers.

The players were ecstatic.

If you divided those sentences like this,

Crowds of excited students / went to the game on Saturday.

The fans / cheered wildly.

Chris / finished his math assignment during the game.

A fired-up Lion squad / defeated the Panthers.

The players / were ecstatic.

—and chances are good that you did—then you have recognized the two basic parts of every sentence pattern, the subject and the predicate:

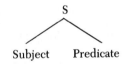

S

Subject   Predicate

The terms *subject* and *predicate* name the functions of those two slots: The **subject**,[1] as its name implies, is the topic of the sentence; the **predicate** is the comment made about it.

Another way to describe the sentence slots is according to the form of the structure that fills them. The subject slot is generally filled by a **noun phrase** (NP), and that's exactly what these five subjects are:

Crowds of excited students

The fans

Chris

A fired-up Lion squad

The players

(We say "generally" filled by a noun phrase rather than "always" because, as we will see later, there are other structures, such as verb phrases and clauses, that can also fill subject slots.) In each of the five

---

[1] The words in boldface are defined in the Glossary of Grammatical Terms, beginning on page 139.

sentences, the predicate is a **verb phrase** (VP) in form—and that's what the predicate *always* is:

went to the game on Saturday
cheered wildly
finished his math assignment during the game
defeated the Panthers
were ecstatic

Here, then, is a branching diagram with labels that describe the sentence in terms of form rather than function:

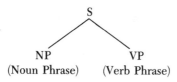

NP   VP
(Noun Phrase)   (Verb Phrase)

This two-part structure underlies all of our sentences in English—even those in which the two parts may not be apparent at first glance. In questions, for example, the subject is buried in the verb phrase. You have to recast the question as a statement to discover the two branches:

Q: Have the new neighbors finished moving in?

NP	**VP**
The new neighbors	have finished moving in.

Q: Which dress did Jenny decide to wear?

NP	**VP**
Jenny	did decide to wear which dress.

Another sentence transformation that changes word order is known as the ***there*** transformation.

There's a fly in my soup.

NP	**VP**
A fly	is in my soup.

1.1

(Note that the word *there* is not a part of the basic sentence. Such added words are known as **expletives**.) In the **imperative** sentence, or command, one of the parts has been deleted altogether: The subject is "understood."

NP	VP
(you)	Help!
(you)	Sit down.
(you)	Come with me to the party.

By recognizing the underlying subject–predicate relationship, you can often avoid the problems of **subject–verb agreement** that tend to crop up in such transformations:

*Which version of the third act has the author and the director decided to use?[2]

NP	VP
The author and the director	*have* decided . . .

*There's a little girl and two little boys on the porch dressed like ghosts.

NP	VP
A little girl and two little boys	*are* on the porch . . .

EXERCISE 1

Identify the two basic parts of the following sentences.

1. Who are all those people in the Post Office?
2. My roommate from last term is taking a leave of absence.
3. There are a great many steelworkers unemployed now.
4. Where are you going this weekend?
5. I plan to stay on campus to finish my term paper for biology.
6. There's a meeting of our PTA finance committee tomorrow.
7. Come over tomorrow after your meeting.
8. Why haven't more people signed up for the committee?

---

[2] An asterisk indicates an ungrammatical or questionable sentence.

1.2 *The Six Basic Patterns*

All of the sentence patterns include the two parts we have just described. The differences among the six occur in the predicate—in the verb itself and in the number and the kind of slots that follow the verb. These variations are determined by the class of the verb, whether transitive, intransitive, or linking.

The Basic Transitive-Verb Pattern

In two of the sample sentences on page 6, the verbs are **transitive:**

Chris finished his math assignment during the game.
A fired-up Lion squad defeated the Panthers.

We can recognize these as transitive because the slot that follows the verb answers the question of *what* or *whom,* the test of a **direct object;** and only transitive verbs take direct objects:

Chris finished *what?*
A fired-up Lion squad defeated *whom?*

In this, the basic transitive verb pattern, the subject is the actor, the "doer" or cause of the action, sometimes called the **agent:** The Lions are doing the defeating; Chris is doing the finishing. The direct object is traditionally labeled the *receiver of the action,* but probably a more accurate label is *objective* or *goal.* The underlying relationship in this *subject–verb–direct object* sentence is generally that of *agent–action–goal.* Following is a formula that describes the three slots of this pattern according to their form:

Pattern 1: NP_1 V NP_2

(**Note:** The numbers attached to the noun phrases stand for their referents. *Referent* means the reality—the thing, person, event, concept, and so on—that the word stands for. The numbers of the subject and the direct object are different because their referents are different.)

Here are some further examples of Pattern 1 sentences:

John Irving wrote *The World According to Garp.*
Enjoy the movie.
Jenny fixed the spaghetti sauce.
Robin made the salad.
The old couple next door drives a 1936 Chevrolet.

Other Transitive-Verb Patterns

The transitive-verb patterns can be distinguished by the presence of at least one **complement,** or "completer," in the slot following the verb. Most of the transitive sentences are like the samples we have just seen, with only one required slot—the direct object—following the verb. However, there are a handful of transitive verbs, fairly common ones, that have an additional slot containing either an objective complement or an indirect object.

The Objective Complement. Certain verbs, such as *make* and *consider*, often take either an adjective or a noun phrase following the direct object; that structure is called an **objective complement** (a completer of the object):

The football team made the coach *proud.*
I consider my parents *a happily divorced couple.*

Without the objective complement, neither of these sentences would make sense:

*The football team made the coach.
*I consider my parents.

With some verbs, the sentence is grammatical without the objective complement, even though the information is less complete:

We elected Ronald Reagan *president.*
We elected Ronald Reagan.

The objective complement, then, either renames (if a noun phrase) or describes (if an **adjective**) the direct object; and it completes the idea of the verb.

Pattern 2: NP_1 V NP_2 $\begin{Bmatrix} NP_2 \\ Adj \end{Bmatrix}$

                             Direct   Objective
                             Object   Complement

Notice that in this pattern the direct object and the objective complement have the same number because the two noun phrases have the same referent. Incidentally, the braces around the objective complement indicate a choice: Either a noun phrase or an adjective may fill that slot.

At this point, you may be wondering how you can recognize an objective complement or a Pattern 2 sentence when you're not sure what an adjective is. To solve this problem, look for a word that will fill both slots in the following frame:

The _____ NOUN is very _____.

Only an adjective will fit. When we insert the word *proud* into both slots of the frame, we recognize the resulting sentences as grammatical:

The *proud* coach is very *proud.*
The *proud* parents are very *proud.*

Try some others:

The *dull* movie is very *dull.*
The *happy* couple is very *happy.*

There are a few adjectives that don't fit both slots—only one or the other—but most adjectives do; and any word that does fit both is unquestionably an adjective.

The Indirect Object.   When the main verb is *give*—or a verb close in meaning, such as *present* or *award*—we commonly include the recipient of the giving as the **indirect object:**

1.2

The professor gave *the class* a tough assignment.

She assigned *us* six chapters.

The judges for the ice-sculpture contest awarded *our sorority* the grand prize.

Other verbs, such as *tell* and *teach* and *show,* may also include an indirect object:

Show *me* your new car.

The director taught *the marching band* a new routine.

The indirect object, then, is a noun phrase or a pronoun that comes between the verb and the direct object; it names the recipient of the direct object. Notice that in the formula all of the noun phrases—subject, indirect object, and direct object—have different referents.

Pattern 3: NP_1 V NP_2 NP_3

Indirect   *Direct*

Object   *Object*

To describe the sentence patterns as formulas is not to suggest that we somehow use formulas when we write—as we might use a formula to compute the year's interest on a loan. The purpose of describing sentences in this way is simply to reveal the forms of the various slots and thus to demonstrate the simple skeletal structures that underlie all of our sentences—even the long and complex ones.

The Optional Slots

Before taking up the remaining sentence patterns, we will look briefly at optional elements that are commonly found in all of the patterns.

We can think of the three or four slots in the basic patterns we have seen as sentence "requirements," the elements needed for sentence completeness. But notice that the previous sentence about Chris includes an additional, optional, structure: *during the game.*

We call it *optional* because the sentence would be complete without it, a grammatical Pattern 1 sentence:

> Chris finished his homework.

Such optional elements in the form of adverbs, prepositional phrases, clauses, verb phrases, and noun phrases can be added to any sentence to answer such questions as *where, when, why, how, how much,* and *how many.* We call the answers to these questions *adverbial information,* and we call the structures that provide those answers **adverbials.**

Here are some further examples of adverbial information provided by various forms:

Adverbs

> *Slowly* the TV camera panned the crowd. (How?)
> The storm should stop *soon.* (When?)

Prepositional Phrases

The prepositional phrase, one of our most common adverbial forms, is a two-part structure consisting of a **preposition**—a word like *in, out, up, down, over, under, for,* or *from*—and a noun phrase, known as the *object of the preposition.*

> Chris finished his math assignment *during the game.* (When?)
> The Lions meet the Bulldogs *in the Sugar Bowl.* (Where?)
> *In 1980* we elected Ronald Reagan president. (When?)

Noun Phrases

> I tossed and turned *last night.* (When?)
> *Friday morning* I'll have my last exam. (When?)

Verb Phrases

The verb phrase that functions adverbially is usually an **infinitive** in form—the base form of the verb preceded by *to.*

> *To keep in shape,* Jan walks to work. (Why?)
> Mike worked hard *to finish his homework before the weekend.* (Why?)

1.2 Sometimes *-ing* verbs (participles) function adverbially:

> I spent the whole evening *cleaning house*. (How?)

Subordinate Clauses

The subordinate clause is a sentence in form, here introduced by the subordinator *when*. The **subordinator** is a word or phrase that signals a connection between two sentences. Other subordinators are *if, because, although,* and *since*. (See also pages 111–113.)

> *When the rain stops*, we'll get back to our game. (When?)

An important characteristic of many adverbials is their movability. Notice that they appear at both the beginning and the end of sentences. All of the opening adverbials could be shifted to the end of their sentences; and some, but not all, of the closing adverbials could be shifted to the beginning. Some are more movable than others:

> The TV camera panned the crowd *slowly*.
> *Last night* I tossed and turned.
> We'll get back to our game *when the rain stops*.

The flexibility that this kind of shifting offers is important for writers to understand and to take advantage of. As the examples show, adverbials can act as sentence openers, not only providing variation from the standard subject opener but also changing the rhythm and stress of the sentence when needed.

The Dangling Infinitive. In the two examples of adverbial infinitives in the preceding section, you'll notice that the subject of the sentence is also the subject of that infinitive:

> *To keep* in shape, Jan walks to work.

> Mike worked hard *to finish* his homework before the weekend.

When that subject–verb relationship is not the case, the infinitive is said to "dangle," as in the following sentences, where the infinitive phrases have no stated subject:

> *To keep farm machinery in good repair*, a regular maintenance schedule is necessary.
>
> For decades the Superstition Mountains in Arizona have been explored in order *to find the fabled Lost Dutchman Mine.*

1.2

Certainly the problem with these sentences is not a problem of communication; no one is likely to misinterpret their meaning. But in both cases a kind of fuzziness exists that can be cleared up with the addition of a subject for the infinitive:

> *To keep* farm machinery in good repair, *a farmer* needs a regular maintenance schedule.
>
> For decades *people* [or *adventurers* or *prospectors*] have explored the Superstition Mountains in Arizona *to find* the fabled Lost Dutchman Mine.

EXERCISE 2

Underline any adverbials in the following sentences; identify their form; test their movability.

1. Luckily, we had two spare tires with us.
2. The fans cheered wildly.
3. Kevin wore his new three-piece suit to make a good impression.
4. He spent the night sleeping in his car.
5. Last night the sky was filled with falling stars.
6. We hiked two miles.
7. When winter comes, I will spend all of my free time on the ski slopes.
8. I am always depressed when the computer refuses to follow my orders.

EXERCISE 3

Identify the required and the optional slots in the following sentences. Identify the pattern of each sentence.

1. Students in my journalism class interviewed several visiting celebrities after the concert.
2. My parents give my little sister a hard time when she comes home late.

1.2

3. Last weekend our neighborhood held a block party to celebrate the end of winter.
4. The English majors named their newly established literary club Tex Libris.
5. My office partner bought her son a pet snake for his birthday.
6. At the homecoming celebration, sparks from the bonfire burned several students.
7. A hard gust of wind spread the sparks very suddenly.
8. After our victory over Nebraska, the sportswriters called the game the upset of the season.

The Intransitive-Verb Pattern

Two of our earlier sample sentences have no complement slots following the verb; they have only adverbials, those structures that tell *how* and *where* and *when* and so on:

The fans cheered *wildly*.
Crowds of excited students went *to the game on Saturday*.

Verbs in basic sentences that are complete without a following adjective or noun phrase are known as **intransitive verbs.** Such verbs are generally action words, such as *cheered* and *went;* however, there is no "receiver of the action" or goal, no direct object, as there is for the transitive action verbs.

In general we can think of the intransitive sentence as having only two required slots, the subject and the verb:

NP	V
The fans	cheered.
The baby	slept.

Admittedly, such sparse sentences are uncommon, but they are grammatical, and, in fact, they can be quite effective in a paragraph filled with long sentences. But some verbs, such as *go* and *live*, rarely occur without an adverbial:

The students went (to the game).
The Penobscot Indians live (in Maine).

In the formula for the intransitive-verb pattern we will include the adverbial, but we will put it in parentheses as a reminder that it is optional in most sentences.

Pattern 4:   NP   V   (Adv)

The Linking-Verb Patterns

The last sample sentence illustrates our third verb class, the **linking verbs:**

> The players were ecstatic.

In this sentence the main verb is *were*, a form of *be*, which is our most common linking verb. *Be* can be followed by either an adjective, such as *ecstatic*, or a noun phrase:[3]

> The players were *the happiest people in the stadium.*

The adjective or noun phrase following any form of *be* is called a **subjective complement;** it describes or renames the subject (just as the *objective* complement in Pattern 2 describes or renames the direct *object*). Here are some further examples of *be* as a linking verb:

> Summer is my favorite season.
> Autumn in New England is spectacular.
> Everyone was happy after the game.
> This has been a wonderful evening.

Other verbs that commonly act as linking verbs are *seem*, *become*, and *remain*, along with verbs of the senses, such as *taste*, *feel*, *smell*, and *look:*

> The room seems hot.
> I feel drowsy.
> The speaker became tiresome.
> Margie and I have remained good friends.

---

[3] When *be* is followed by an adverbial, it is classified as an intransitive verb: The teacher is *in the library.* (Where?)

1.2

The pizza smells delicious.

It tastes wonderful.

Gary became a lawyer.

We will divide the linking verbs into two patterns, with forms of *be* in one pattern and the others in the second:

Pattern 5: NP_1 *be* $\left\{ \begin{matrix} NP_1 \\ Adj \end{matrix} \right\}$

Pattern 6: NP_1 V $\left\{ \begin{matrix} NP_1 \\ Adj \end{matrix} \right\}$

Like the objective complement in Pattern 2, the subjective complement in the linking-verb patterns can be either a noun phrase or an adjective. When it is a noun phrase, the two NPs—the subject and the subjective complement—have the same referent.

EXERCISE 4

Identify the sentence pattern of each of the following sentences; identify the slot boundaries and the form of the structure that fills each slot.

1. On Saturday the fans went crazy after every touchdown.
2. The hikers walked slowly up the hill.
3. My neighbor's stereo drives me crazy when I'm trying to study.
4. The spring flowers along the mall make the campus really beautiful.
5. Those pesky gnats are everywhere this summer.
6. For twenty years Professor Mauner has been head of the Music Department.
7. We smelled the pizza a block away.
8. Mary's brother finally took the law board exam.
9. Cut me a piece of your birthday cake.
10. The visitors from Denver arrived on schedule yesterday morning.

FOR CLASS DISCUSSION

1. Here are some pairs of sentences that look alike. Identify their patterns by analyzing the slots that follow the verb: What is the

form of the structure that fills each slot? What is its relationship to the other structures?

1.3

a. The teacher made the test hard.
   The batter hit the ball hard.
b. The kids grew fast during the summer.
   The cattle grew fat on their high-protein diet.
c. My husband made me a chocolate cake.
   My husband made me a happy woman.

2. The following sentences are ambiguous; that is, they have more than one possible meaning. Explain the ambiguity by identifying more than one sentence pattern that each could belong to:

   a. Henry found his mechanic a good helper.
   b. Liz called her mother.
   c. The detective looked hard.

1.3 Punctuation and the Sentence Slots

There is an easy punctuation lesson to be learned from the sentence patterns with their two or three or four slots:

DO NOT PUT COMMAS BETWEEN THE REQUIRED SLOTS.

That is, never separate

- the subject from the verb
- the verb from the direct object[4]
- the direct object from the objective complement
- the indirect object from the direct object
- the verb from the subjective complement.

---

[4] The one exception to this rule occurs when the direct object is a direct quotation following a verb like *say:*

He said, "I love you."

Here the punctuation convention calls for a comma before the quoted words. This topic is discussed further on page 107.

For example, in the following sentences there is simply no place for commas:

> The sportswriters considered the game between the Lions and the Panthers one of the truly great games of the collegiate football season.
> The local women's club gave all the guests at the Marion County Home for the Aged decorated Christmas trees for their rooms.
> All of the discussion groups I took part in during Orientation Week were extremely helpful for the incoming freshmen.

So even though the noun phrases that fill the slots may be long, the slots are never separated by commas. A pause for breath does not signal a comma. In Chapter 4, where we will take up the expanded noun phrase, we will encounter sentences in which punctuation is called for *within* a noun phrase slot, but even in those situations the rule stated above still applies:

NO PUNCTUATION BETWEEN THE REQUIRED SLOTS.

1.4 *Punctuation of Sentence Openers*

In some of the sentences with opening adverbials, the adverbial structure is set off by commas—but not always. The choice is often up to you, the writer, and sometimes you will make your decision based on the number of other commas in the sentence or simply on your judgment of whether or not the comma will help the reader.

Here are some rules of thumb to help you make the decision:

1. The comma is a signal to the reader that a particular unit of meaning has ended; if the beginning of the new unit is not obvious without the comma, then the comma is called for. The following examples are confusing; they need the comma:

   > During the winter vacation days are especially welcome.
   > In the middle of the night winds from the north brought subzero temperatures and the end of Indian summer.

2. Often the opening phrase is parenthetical—more clearly a comment on the whole sentence or a transition device than a

straightforward adverbial structure telling *when* or *where* or *how*.
Such phrases call for a comma:

1.4

> On the other hand, not everyone was surprised at the outcome of
> Saturday's game.
>
> Luckily, no one was hurt.
>
> As a matter of fact, a great deal of so-called junk food is quite
> nourishing.

Incidentally, such parenthetical comments are sometimes placed
in the middle of a sentence—usually between the subject and the
predicate—where they have the effect of interrupting the pace of
the sentence:

> My own parents, on the other hand, have always been willing to let me
> make decisions for myself.

Such interrupters are always set off by commas, both before and
after.

3. Opening subordinate clauses and verb phrases are *always* set off
by commas:

> When the sun went down, we packed up our gear and headed home.
>
> To have the evening free for dinner with Judy, Chris finished his math
> assignment during the game.

(For the punctuation of subordinate clauses at the end of the
sentence, see page 112.)

4. Short opening phrases or single words of time and place and
manner are usually not set off:

> Saturday morning we all pitched in and cleaned the garage.
>
> By noon we were exhausted.
>
> Hastily they gathered their books and left the room.

5. Longer phrases may or may not be set off:

> In the middle of the night we heard a strange noise.
>
> At the top of the hill the hikers sat down to rest.
>
> At the end of a long and exhausting morning, we all collapsed.

(**Note:** The first two sentences would be equally acceptable with
the comma; the third would be acceptable without.)

1.5

FOR CLASS DISCUSSION

1. Punctuation often makes a difference in meaning. Sometimes only the writer knows for sure if the punctuation is correct. How does the meaning of the following sentence change with the addition of the comma?

> He did not tell me the whole story clearly.
> He did not tell me the whole story, clearly.

2. Add punctuation to the following sentences, if necessary:

   a. In 1747 a physician in the British Navy conducted a controlled experiment to discover a cure for scurvy.
   b. Dr. James Lind fed six groups of scurvy victims six different remedies.
   c. The group that ate oranges and lemons every day recovered miraculously.
   d. Although it took fifty years for the British Admiralty Office to recognize Lind's findings they finally ordered a daily dose of fresh lemon juice for every British seaman.
   e. Interestingly Lind's discovery also affected the English language.
   f. The British called lemons "limes" two hundred years ago.
   g. As a result of the British sailors' new diet people began calling sailors *limeys*.

1.5 Summary

The six basic sentence patterns you have read about in this chapter describe the skeletal framework of nearly every sentence in English. That description includes

1. A basic subject–predicate structure;
2. One or two slots following the verb, depending on the class of the verb;
3. Optional slots at the beginning or end of the sentence that contain adverbial or parenthetical information.

In subsequent chapters you will learn that these six patterns form the underlying framework for many sentence expansions, too, including participles, gerunds, infinitives, subordinate clauses, noun

clauses, and adjective clauses. A thorough understanding of the
sentence patterns and their expansions can put you in control when
you sit down to write. The time you spend developing that understanding will be time well spent.

1.5

In Chapter 2 we will take a closer look at the verb slot.

SENTENCE PRACTICE
    In this exercise you are to (1) write a basic sentence for each of the
verbs provided with the patterns, and (2) then expand each sentence
by inserting adverbials in either the opening or the closing position,
or both. Think of words and phrases and clauses that provide
adverbial information. Some suggestions are listed on page 24; use
these or any other structures that are appropriate in your sentence.
(You'll find the lists of prepositions on pages 177 and 178 useful in
constructing adverbials.)

Pattern 1: NP_1 Verb NP_2

    Verbs: *find, explain, create, enjoy, demolish*

    (**Note:** Do not limit yourself to this base form of the verb; use any
    expansion you wish. Some of the possible expansions are listed on
    page 29).

Pattern 2: NP_1 Verb NP_2 $\begin{Bmatrix} NP_2 \\ Adj \end{Bmatrix}$

    Verbs: *make, consider, find, prefer, elect*

Pattern 3: NP_1 Verb NP_2 NP_3

    Verbs: *hand, award, pass, assign, grant*

Pattern 4: NP_1 Verb

    Verbs: *work, sleep, travel, relax, hike*

Pattern 5: NP_1 *be* $\begin{Bmatrix} NP_1 \\ Adj \end{Bmatrix}$

    Verb: *be*

Pattern 6: NP_1 Verb $\begin{Bmatrix} NP_1 \\ Adj \end{Bmatrix}$

    Verbs: *seem, become, sound, appear, taste*

ADVERBIALS

1.5

Time:

yesterday	at noon	last night
often	between five and six on	each week
soon	Friday	every summer
	during intermission	this morning

when the noise stopped
after we said grace
by the time I get to Phoenix
as soon as they could
since you left

Place:

here	in the computer center
there	near the park
everywhere	behind the door
upstairs	above his head

Manner:

carefully	without complaining
quickly	by working hard
extravagantly	with the best of intentions
skillfully	through sheer determination
carelessly	according to a plan
	as if it were going of out of style

Reason:

for a good reason
out of spite
in connection with the assignment
in order to keep them happy   (to keep them happy)
because the noise was driving me crazy

2

Expanding the Verb

In this chapter you will learn about **verbs** and about the way they are used with **auxiliaries** to produce a wide variety of meaning. Even though the verb expansion system may seem complicated at first, you'll probably discover that you know more than you thought you did. You'll also find that the understanding of verbs you gain from studying this chapter will enhance your writing ability. To be a good writer is to be verb-conscious. All good writers select their verbs with care; they pay attention to the effects that different verbs and different forms of the same verb can convey.

It's not true, of course, that a writer stops after the subject of every sentence to ponder the verb that's coming next. We don't do that in speech either; we speak sentences easily, without conscious effort. In fact, we can talk all day with our friends without once thinking about the form of verbs. But as a writer you do have to make certain conscious decisions about which verb form would be the most effective one in a particular passage:

The rain *beat* steadily against the windshield as they drove through the unfamiliar streets.

The rain *was beating* steadily against the windshield . . .

For an hour the rain *had been beating* steadily . . .

For an hour the rain *had beaten* steadily . . .

In the rewriting and editing stages especially, you must read and listen carefully for both meaning and rhythm to be sure that your choice is the most effective.

In Chapter 1 most of the verbs used in the sample sentences are of the one-word variety: *is, cheered, went, defeated.* We call these the simple **present** and simple **past tenses.** But the verbs we use in our everyday speech and writing are often expanded forms that include additional words called **auxiliaries:**

The students *have been* diligent.

John *may become* a scholar.

The teacher *has given* us too much homework.

The students *should elect* Helen president.

The rain *has been beating* steadily against the windshield for an hour.

In this chapter we will look at the system for expanding the verb in order to understand all of its possible forms and to recognize the differences in meaning that those forms convey.

2.1 *The Verb Forms*

First, let's look at the variations in the verb itself. Compared with those of other languages, English verbs are simple: We have only five forms. Following is an example of a **regular** verb (*walk*) and an **irregular** one (*eat*):

walk	*eat*	**base form** (PRESENT TENSE)
walks	*eats*	*-s* **form** (also PRESENT TENSE)
walked	*ate*	*-ed* **form** (PAST TENSE)
walking	*eating*	*-ing* **form** (PRESENT PARTICIPLE)
walked	*eaten*	*-en* **form** (PAST PARTICIPLE)

Most verbs in English are regular verbs, those in which both the *-ed* (*walked*) and the *-en* (*walked*) forms are alike and are formed by the addition of *-ed* (sometimes *-t*). Only a small number, one hundred or so, are irregular, although they are among the verbs we use most frequently. Here are some further examples of verb forms: The first two are regular verbs; the last four are irregular. (For a more complete list of irregular verbs, see section 2.9.)

2.1

Base form	-s	-ed	-ing	-en
decide	decides	decided	deciding	decided
help	helps	helped	helping	helped
drive	drives	drove	driving	driven
give	gives	gave	giving	given
go	goes	went	going	gone
hit	hits	hit	hitting	hit

In discussing verbs, we will use labels that describe their forms. The *-s* form and the *-ing* form are always recognizable, whether the verb is regular or irregular. (In fact, if a word has no *-s* or *-ing* form, it's simply not a verb.)

In regular verbs the *-ed* form, the past tense, is actually written *ed*, but in many irregular verbs it is not, as the previous examples show. The *-en* form takes its name from irregular verbs like *eaten* (and *driven, taken, given,* and so on), but in most verbs the form does not actually have the letters *en;* in regular verbs, like *help* and *walk,* the *-en* form is identical to the past tense.

The only verb in English with more than these five forms is *be,* which has eight, including the base form, or infinitive, which is different from the present tense. *Be* is the only verb in English with a separate infinitive.

be	**base form** (INFINITIVE)
am *are* *is*	**present tense**
was *were*	**-ed form** (PAST TENSE)
being	**-ing form** (PRESENT PARTICIPLE)
been	**-en form** (PAST PARTICIPLE)

Note also that *be* is the only verb with more than one past-tense form—a separate past for third-person singular subjects (*was*)—and the only one with a separate form for the first-person singular in the present tense (*am*).

2.2

EXERCISE 1

Don't think of irregular verbs as unfamiliar or difficult. Most of them are common words that you began using—and using grammatically—as a small child. Fill in the blanks with the forms called for. To think of the -ed form, say a sentence with yesterday (Yesterday I went home); to think of the -en form, say a sentence with the auxiliary have (I have gone already). (You can check your answers with the list in section 2.9.)

Base Form	-s	-ed	-ing	-en
bet	_____	_____	_____	_____
bleed	_____	_____	_____	_____
cost	_____	_____	_____	_____
dive	_____	_____	_____	_____
drink	_____	_____	_____	_____
fall	_____	_____	_____	_____
hide	_____	_____	_____	_____
hold	_____	_____	_____	_____
hurt	_____	_____	_____	_____
lay	_____	_____	_____	_____
lie	_____	_____	_____	_____
rid	_____	_____	_____	_____
set	_____	_____	_____	_____
sit	_____	_____	_____	_____
slay	_____	_____	_____	_____
speed	_____	_____	_____	_____
stink	_____	_____	_____	_____
sweat	_____	_____	_____	_____
tread	_____	_____	_____	_____
wet	_____	_____	_____	_____

2.2 *The Expanded Forms*

Now let's look at the way we use the simple and expanded forms of the verb in everyday situations:

1. I *eat* an apple every day.
2. I *ate* one this morning.

3. My sister *eats* the seeds and all.
4. I *have eaten* an apple every day this week.
5. I *had eaten* all the grapes by the time you arrived.
6. I *am eating* a peach at this very moment.
7. I *was eating* both candy and pretzels last night.
8. I *have been eating* junk food all evening.

There's nothing at all complicated about these verbs. We use them with and without auxiliaries almost unconsciously, and we do so in a systematic way.

2.3 *The System of Expansion*

Let's analyze what the expansion system is by studying the foregoing list of sentences. First, you'll notice that three of the sentences (4, 5, and 8) include a form of *have* as an auxiliary. The word that follows *have* in all three cases is the *-en* form:

*have **eaten**, had **eaten**, have **been** eating.*

There are no instances of *have* without a following *-en* word, so we'll describe this part of the system as a unit:

(have + -en)

Next you'll discover that three of the sentences (6, 7, and 8) include a form of *be* as an auxiliary. In all of these cases the word that follows *be* is the *-ing* form:

*am **eating**, was **eating**, have been **eating**.*

And notice that there are no *-ing* forms without a form of *be;* so we'll describe this part of the system as a unit:

(be + -ing)

Let's stop to summarize what we have found so far:

1. When the auxiliary is a form of *have*, the verb or auxiliary that follows is the *-en* form:

   (have + -en)

2. The *-ing* form of the verb is always preceded by the auxiliary *be*, that is, a form of *be:*

   (be + -ing)

   Now let's add a verb to the auxiliary unit:

   have + -en + eat

The *-en* of the unit "have + -en" represents the form of the verb, as we saw in the list of sentences; in other words, the *-en* gets attached to whatever follows:

   have + -en + eat = have eaten
   have + -en + walk = have walked

The *-ing* works in the same way, attaching itself to the verb:

   be + -ing + eat = is (or *am* or *are*) eating
   be + -ing + walk = is walking

(**Note:** The subject of the sentence will, of course, determine whether we use *is* or *am* or *are*.)

Can we use both *have* and *be* as auxiliaries in the same verb string? Look at sentence 8 in the list:

   I have been eating junk food all evening.

Remember, the *-en* and *-ing* endings get attached to whatever follows, in this case producing *been* and *eating:*

   have + -en + be + -ing + eat = have been eating

Our system requires that *have + -en* come before *be + -ing*. Try it the other way!

*be + -ing + have + -en + eat = *is having eaten

Let's back up again. What exactly are we doing, manipulating verb strings like this, with formulas and arrows and such? What we are doing is discovering the system that underlies our ability to put auxiliaries and verbs together automatically. Believe it or not, there are over fifty different forms of the verb—not just the eight in our list of sentences; there are over fifty ways of combining auxiliaries with the verb, which we know and use automatically. So what we are doing is describing a formula that accounts for that ability, a formula that, if we were to make a rather simple computer program of it, would result in all those variations. We call this formula the **verb-expansion rule.** Understanding the system and recognizing how simple it is will help you realize how much you know about verbs; it will also help you make conscious choices when you use the various forms in your writing.

EXERCISE 2

Figure out the resulting verb string from each of the following formulas. Assume that the subject is Fred.

1. have + -en + try =
2. be + -ing + dream =
3. have + -en + break =
4. be + -ing + try =
5. have + -en + be + -ing + work =

2.4 *Subject–Verb Agreement*

In Exercise 2 the instructions for figuring out the verb forms specify that the subject be *Fred.* The reason for including this detail is to make sure that everyone comes up with the same answer. If you

2.4

had used a plural subject, the form of the auxiliary verb in each case would have been different:

> Fred and Linda *have* tried. (not *has*)
> They *are* trying. (not *is*)

The singular subjects *I* and *you* would also take different auxiliaries:

First person:
> I *have* tried.   I *am* trying.

Second person:
> You *have* tried.   You *are* trying.

Only a third-person singular subject takes the *-s* form:

Third person:
> Fred *has* tried.   He *is* trying.
> Linda *has* tried.   She *is* trying.
> The cat *has* tried.   It *is* trying.

The term *third-person singular subject*, then, refers to a noun or noun phrase that can be replaced by the pronoun *he* or *she* or *it*.

From these examples you can figure out what the term **person** means. You'll encounter it again in discussions about the writer's point of view, with references to the use of *I* or *we* as first person, to the use of *you* as second person, and to the use of *he*, *she*, *it*, or *they* as third person. You'll also read about person in connection with personal pronouns.

Errors in Subject–Verb Agreement

Errors in subject–verb agreement occur in the present tense when the *-s* ending is used in error (with *I* or *you* or a plural subject) or when it is omitted with a third-person singular subject:

> *The *instructions* on my tax form *drives* me crazy.
> *The *book* of rules showing a hundred ways to play solitaire simply *amaze* me.

Subject–verb agreement errors may also occur when the subject is a pair of singular nouns:

2.4

> *The sidewalk in front of the house and the driveway was* in need of repair.

Here the subject of the sentence would be replaced by the plural pronoun *they*, not the singular *it*, so the correct verb form is *were:*

> *They were* in need of repair.

This trick of substituting a pronoun in the NP slot will also help avoid the problem with transformed sentences like those we saw in Chapter 1:

> *Which version of the third act *has the author and the director* decided to use?

Remember, the only subjects that take the *-s* form of the verb are those that can be replaced by a singular pronoun: *he, she,* or *it.*

Another situation that sometimes causes confusion about **number**—that is, whether the subject is singular or plural—occurs with subjects that include a phrase introduced by "as well as" or "in addition to":

> *The sidewalk, in addition to the driveway, need to be repaired.
> *The piano player, as well as the rest of the group, usually join in the singing.

These additions to the subject are parenthetical; they are not treated as part of the subject. To make the subject compound—to include them—the writer should use a coordinating conjunction, such as *and:*

> The sidewalk *and* the driveway *need* to be repaired.
> The piano player *and* the rest of the group usually *join* in the singing.

(For further discussion of subject–verb agreement in sentences with compound subjects, see page 128.)

2.5 | 2.5 *Addition of Tense to the Verb String*

Here again are the verbs from our earlier list of eight sentences:

1. eat	4. have eaten	7. was eating
2. ate	5. had eaten	8. have been eating
3. eats	6. am eating	

You'll notice that the first auxiliary is not always the present tense of *have* or *be*. In verbs 5 and 7 it is the past tense: *had* and *was*. In every sentence, the first word of the verb string indicates **tense,** either present or past: *have eaten / had eaten; am eating / was eating*. That rule also applies when there is no auxiliary, as in verbs 1, 2, and 3. We'll add this choice of tense marker to our string of units, using the symbol T. So far, we can describe the units in terms of a formula, beginning with T, because the tense marker always applies to the first word in the string:

$$T + (have + -en) + (be + -ing) + \text{VERB}$$

You'll notice that in writing out the formula, we have put the auxiliary units with *have* and *be* in parentheses. You'll recall from the sentence pattern formulas that parentheses designate a structure that is optional. In other words, these auxiliaries are not required; a verb is grammatical without an auxiliary, as verbs 1, 2, and 3 demonstrate. Only the tense marker and the verb itself are required:

pres + eat = eat (verb 1)
past + eat = ate (verb 2)
pres + eat = eats (verb 3)

Now let's try out the complete formula. Remember that tense, either present or past, marks the first word in the string; the *-en* form follows *have;* the *-ing* form follows *be:*

pres + have + -en + walk = have walked
past + have + -en + walk = had walked
pres + have + -en + drive = have driven

past + be + -ing + sleep = was (or were) sleeping

pres + be + -ing + feel = is (or are or am) feeling

You can see that it would be fairly easy to program a computer to produce these expanded verbs; your brain's linguistic computer follows the formula with little difficulty. Once in a while, in the case of an irregular verb, you may hear a deviation from the system. For example, you might hear someone say (or you might say yourself), "I've already ate." That speaker is using the *-ed* form of *eat* with the auxiliary *have* when the rule calls for the *-en* form. But this variation is understandable: In most cases the two forms (the *-en* and the *-ed*) are identical:

I walked home yesterday. (the *-ed* form)

I have walked home every day this week. (the *-en* form)

EXERCISE 3

What verb does each of the following strings produce? Write a sentence for each of them.

1. pres + have + -en + find =
2. past + be + -ing + work =
3. past + study =
4. pres + have + -en + be + -ing + play =
5. pres + help =
6. past + be + -ing + have =
7. pres + be + -ing + have =
8. pres + have + -en + have =
9. past + have + -en + have =
10. past + have + -en + be + -ing + be =

2.6 *The Modal Auxiliaries*

As we mentioned earlier, the eight sentences listed at the beginning of this chapter do not show all of the ways in which we use the verb *eat*. Here are some others:

2.6

I *should eat* yogurt for lunch.
I *will eat* some today.
I *might have eaten* two candy bars yesterday; I've forgotten.
I *may be eating* a gourmet dinner at Carol's tonight.

You'll notice that these sentences include another word in the verb string: *should, will, might,* or *may.* These are the **modal auxiliaries.** To account for these strings, we will add (M) to the formula:

T + (M) + (have + -en) + (be + -ing) + VERB

Like the other auxiliaries, the modal is shown in parentheses because it is optional, and when we use it, it always comes first in the string:

pres + will + eat = will eat
past + can + eat = could eat
past + can + have + -en + eat = could have eaten
past + can + have + -en + be + -ing + eat = could have been eating
pres + may + be + -ing + eat = may be eating

As these strings show, we can use a modal as the only auxiliary or in combination with *have* and/or *be.*

The modals differ from the auxiliaries *have* and *be,* both of which can be main verbs as well as auxiliary verbs: The modals never fill the main verb slot, nor do they have all five forms that verbs have. They have a maximum of two forms, that is, the base form and the *-ed* form:

can / could   will / would   shall / should   may / might

Although we call these forms *present* and *past,* they do not indicate present and past time; these are simply labels indicating **form.** For example, in the sentence "I may eat" (present), the act of eating is not going on; in "I might eat" (past) the act of eating is not over; in fact, in both cases the act of eating may never take place. We should note, too, a difference in the base form of verbs and of modals: The base form of the modal is not used as an infinitive, as the base form of a verb like *eat* is. We say "to eat," but we do not say "to shall."

In addition to these four modals, which include past forms, there are two that have only one form: *must* and *ought to*. One other modal-like auxiliary with two forms is *have to* / *had to*. It differs from the regular auxiliary *have* in that it fills the modal slot in the formula. We refer to it as *modal-like* because it does not pattern with *have* + *-en* and *be* + *-ing* as freely as the other modals do. Incidentally, its past form, *had to*, also supplies the past meaning of *must:*

> I *must go* today.
> I *had to go* yesterday.

With the addition of the modal slot to the verb expansion formula, you can probably see how it's possible to come up with fifty or more variations of every verb.

EXERCISE 4
> *Write a complete sentence for each of the verbs given.*

> 1. pres + shall + be + -ing + go
> 2. past + shall + have + -en + go
> 3. past + will + come
> 4. pres + may + have + -en + be + -ing + play
> 5. past + may + play
> 6. past + can + have + -en + drink

FOR CLASS DISCUSSION
Do any of the sentences you wrote for Exercise 4 include adverbials of time? Would you consider any of the adverbials required? Think also about the use of adverbials with the "perfect" tenses, for example, *have gone* and *had gone*. Formulate a rule.

2.7 *The Moods of the Verb*

The modal auxiliaries affect what is called the *mood* of the verb. They convey conditions of probability, possibility, obligation, and necessity: I *may* eat; I *should* eat; I *could* eat; I *must* eat. These are known as the **conditional mood**. We should also note that the modals

2.7 *will* and *shall* produce what we usually think of as "future tense": *will eat, shall eat.* We call a sentence without a modal auxiliary the **indicative mood**—a sentence stated as fact, not probability.

The modal auxiliaries enable us to express variations in the meaning of sentences:

> Would you lend me ten dollars?
> Will you lend me ten dollars?
> Could you lend me ten dollars?
> Can you lend me ten dollars?

These questions express subtle differences—in the degree of politeness, in the extent of the speaker's expectation of getting the money or hesitation in asking, and in the perception of the ability of the person addressed to lend the money. In spite of such subtleties, a native speaker of English has little trouble in choosing the precise modal to fit the social situation.

The following passage from "Bartleby the Scrivener" by Herman Melville illustrates a variety of the "conditional" meanings produced by the modal auxiliaries. The speaker has found himself in a perplexing situation as he tries to rid himself and his premises of Bartleby, his former employee:

> What shall I do? I now said to myself, buttoning up my coat to the last button. What shall I do? what ought I to do? what does conscience say I *should* do with this man, or rather ghost? Rid myself of him, I must; go, he shall. But how? You will not thrust him, the poor, pale, passive mortal,—you will not thrust such a helpless creature out of your door? you will not dishonour yourself by such cruelty? No, I will not, I cannot do that. Rather would I let him live and die here, and then mason up his remains in the wall. What then will you do? For all your coaxing, he will not budge. Bribes he leaves under your own paper-weight on your table; in short, it is quite plain that he prefers to cling to you.

The Subjunctive Mood

Before leaving the subject of the verb moods, we should mention another one you may have heard of: the **subjunctive.** The subjunctive is not a matter of adding modal auxiliaries, as the conditional mood is. Rather, it is a simple variation of the verb that we use in special circumstances. For example, after verbs that convey a strong suggestion or recommendation, we often use a *that* clause:

2.7

We suggested *that Mary go with us.*
We insisted *that Bill consult the doctor.*
The doctor recommended *that Bill stay in the hospital.*
I move *that the meeting be adjourned.*

Notice that the verbs in these *that* clauses use subjunctive, which is the base form of the verb—even for a third-person singular subject (which would normally take the -*s* form) and for the past tense. Other verbs that commonly take clauses in the subjunctive mood are *command, demand, ask, require, order,* and *propose.*

The subjunctive mood also occurs in *if* clauses that express a wish or a condition contrary to fact:

If I were you, I'd be careful.
If Joe weren't so lazy, he'd probably be a millionaire.
If my parents were rich, I wouldn't need a bank loan.

Don't worry about memorizing rules. Chances are that you use these forms in your speaking and writing already; your ear tells you that they're the correct forms. This description of the subjunctive is included mainly to explain the existence of these forms, in case you suddenly wonder how "Bill consult" and "I were" and "Joe weren't" can be grammatical when out of context they sound wrong.

We should also note that in everyday speech the nonsubjunctive is fairly common:

If Joe was here, he'd agree with me.
I recommended that he should help.

In writing, however, the subjunctive is the standard form in these sentences:

2.8

If Joe were here, he'd agree with me.
I recommended that he help.

FOR CLASS DISCUSSION

1. What other method or methods, besides the use of *shall* and *will*, do we have for conveying our thoughts about the future? Talk about your plans for tomorrow: How do you do it?
2. Notice the auxiliaries in the following sentences:

> Ted doesn't smoke very much, but he certainly does enjoy a good cigar.
> Why didn't Chuck come with you?
> Why do grades have to be so important?

Our verb-expansion rule doesn't include *do* (*does, did*) as an auxiliary. Why have we used it in these sentences?

Here are some sentences with tag questions, some of which include a form of *do*. Why don't the others?

> Mark has decided to try out for the band, hasn't he?
> He plays the trombone beautifully, doesn't he?
> Both he and his sister are talented, aren't they?
> You heard him play last night, didn't you?

2.8 Summary of Verb Forms

As was pointed out earlier in this chapter, if you are a native speaker of English your use of verbs in speech is all but automatic: You rarely hesitate about the form to use; you rarely deviate from the standard. The written language, however, requires thought. In writing, there will be many occasions when you will have to think twice about verb forms; consequently, the more you know about them in a conscious way, the more in control of your writing you will be.

Following is a summary of our most common verb forms and the ways in which we use them:

2.8

Base form and -s form (SIMPLE PRESENT)

I live in Omaha.

The news comes on at six.

The leaves on our maple tree turn absolutely golden in October.

Milton's poetry speaks to everyone.

} *Habitual or timeless present*

I understand your position.   *Present point in time*

Pres + *be* + *-ing* (PRESENT PROGRESSIVE)

I am living in Omaha.   *Present action of*

John is taking philosophy this term.   *limited duration*

Note that both of these present forms can indicate future time with the addition of an appropriate adverbial:

The bus leaves *at seven.*

We're having pizza *tonight.*

Past + V (SIMPLE PAST)

I moved to Omaha last March.

Diane passed her law board exam.   *Specific point in time* (PAST)

The computer swallowed all of my data.

Note that with an appropriate adverbial, this form can indicate a period of time in the past:

I studied Spanish *for three years* in high school

Past + *be* + *-ing* + V (PAST PROGRESSIVE)

A baby was crying during the entire ceremony this morning.

I was trying to sleep last night during the party, but it was no use.   *Past action of limited duration (often to show one particular action during a larger span of time)*

2.8

Pres + *have* + *-en* + V (PRESENT PERFECT)

The leaves have turned yellow
already.

I have finished my work.

I have memorized several of
Frost's poems.

*A completed action extend-
ing from a point in the past to
either the present or the near
present or occurring at an
unspecified past time.*

Past + *have* + *-en* + V (PAST PERFECT)

The hikers had used up all their
water, when finally they found
a hidden spring.

The students had finished only
the first page of the test by the
time the bell rang.

*Past action completed before
another action in the past.*

Pres + *have* + *en* + *be* + *-ing* + V (PRESENT PERFECT PROGRESSIVE)

The authorities have been looking for the arson suspect since
last Sunday.

*Past action continuing into the
present.*

Past + *have* + *-en* + *be* + *-ing* + V (PAST PERFECT PROGRESSIVE)

The authorities had been looking
for the suspect even before the
fire broke out.

*Continuing past action com-
pleted before another
mentioned action.*

VERB PRACTICE

You have probably noticed how important the adverbials are in
the accurate use of all of these verb tenses. For this exercise, think
carefully about the adverbials needed to finish the following sentences. Add a word, a phrase, or a clause that will make the sentence
meaningful.

1. Cheryl had drunk too much beer _____.

   Cheryl drinks too much beer _____.

   Cheryl was drinking too much beer _____.

   Cheryl is drinking too much beer _____.

2. Jack was feeling dizzy _____.

   Jack had felt dizzy _____.

   Jack feels dizzy _____.

3. The team was hoping to win the game _____.
   The team hoped to win the game _____.
   The team had hoped to win the game _____.
4. The defense budget was rising _____.
   The defense budget had risen _____.
   The defense budget rose _____.
   The defense budget has been rising _____.
   The defense budget had been rising _____.
5. John works at Ye Olde College Diner _____.
   John is working at Ye Olde College Diner _____.

2.9 *The Irregular Verbs*

The following list includes some of the common irregular verbs. Notice that some of them have more than one form of the past tense (the *-ed* form) or the past participle (the *-en* form), both of which are used in standard English. The list includes only the base, the *-ed*, and the *-en* forms, as the other two (the *-s* and *-ing* forms) never vary.

Base Form	-ed Form	-en Form
arise	arose	arisen
awake	awoke, awaked	awaked, awoke
bear	bore	(have) borne
		(was) born
beat	beat	beaten
befall	befell	befallen
begin	began	begun
behold	beheld	beheld
bend	bent	bent
bet	bet	bet
bid	bade, bid	bidden, bid
bind	bound	bound
bite	bit	bitten
bleed	bled	bled
blow	blew	blown
break	broke	broken
breed	bred	bred
bring	brought	brought
broadcast	broadcast, broadcasted	broadcast, broadcasted

2.9	Base Form	-ed Form	-en Form
	build	built	built
	burst	burst	burst
	buy	bought	bought
	cast	cast	cast
	catch	caught	caught
	choose	chose	chosen
	cling	clung	clung
	come	came	come
	cost	cost	cost
	creep	crept	crept
	cut	cut	cut
	deal	dealt	dealt
	dig	dug	dug
	dive	dove, dived	dived
	do	did	done
	draw	drew	drawn
	dream	dreamed, dreamt	dreamed, dreamt
	drink	drank	drunk
	drive	drove	driven
	eat	ate	eaten
	fall	fell	fallen
	feed	fed	fed
	feel	felt	felt
	fight	fought	fought
	find	found	found
	flee	fled	fled
	fling	flung	flung
	fly	flew	flown

(**Note:** The baseball term *to fly out* is regular: *He flied out to the centerfielder.*)

forget	forgot	forgotten
forgive	forgave	forgiven
forsake	forsook	forsaken
freeze	froze	frozen
get	got	got, gotten
give	gave	given
go	went	gone
grind	ground	ground
grow	grew	grown
hang	hung	hung

(**Note:** The verb *hang* meaning "execute" is regular: *They hanged him at dawn.*)

Base Form	-ed Form	-en Form
have	had	had
hear	heard	heard
hide	hid	hidden, hid
hit	hit	hit
hold	held	held
hurt	hurt	hurt
keep	kept	kept
kneel	knelt	knelt
know	knew	known
lay	laid	laid
lead	led	led
leave	left	left
lend	lent	lent
lie	lay	lain
light	lighted, lit	lighted, lit
lose	lost	lost
make	made	made
mean	meant	meant
meet	met	met
put	put	put
read	read	read

(**Note:** The spelling is the same, but the -*ed* and -*en* forms are pronounced like the color red.)

ride	rode	ridden
ring	rang	rung
rise	rose	risen
run	ran	run
say	said	said
see	saw	seen
seek	sought	sought
sell	sold	sold
send	sent	sent
set	set	set
shake	shook	shaken
shine	shone, shined	shone, shined
shoe	shod	shod
shoot	shot	shot
shrink	shrank, shrunk	shrunk, shrunken
sing	sang	sung
sink	sank	sunk, sunken (adjectival)
sit	sat	sat

2.9

Base Form	-ed Form	-en Form
slay	slew	slain
sleep	slept	slept
slide	slid	slid
sling	slung	slung
slink	slunk	slunk
speak	spoke	spoken
spend	spent	spent
spin	spun	spun
spit	spit, spat	spit, spat
spread	spread	spread
spring	sprang, sprung	sprung
stand	stood	stood
steal	stole	stolen
stick	stuck	stuck
sting	stung	stung
stink	stank	stunk
stride	strode	stridden
strike	struck	struck, stricken
string	strung	strung
strive	strove, strived	striven, strived
swear	swore	sworn
sweep	swept	swept
swim	swam	swum
swing	swung	swung
take	took	taken
teach	taught	taught
tear	tore	torn
tell	told	told
think	thought	thought
throw	threw	thrown
thrust	thrust	thrust
tread	trod	trod
wake	waked, woke	waked, woken
wear	wore	worn
weave	wove, weaved	woven, weaved
weep	wept	wept
win	won	won
wind	wound	wound
wring	wrung	wrung
write	wrote	written

3

The Passive Voice

In all of the sentences we have examined so far, the subject serves as agent or actor, the performer of the action that the verb describes. We call this an "active" relationship, and it is expressed in the **active voice.** In the transitive verb patterns (1, 2, and 3), the opposite relationship, the **passive voice,** is also possible. A passive sentence results when the direct object—or, in the case of Pattern 3, the indirect object—becomes the subject.

This Pattern 1 sentence illustrates the changing roles of the two NPs:

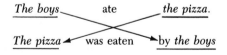

3.1 A *Three-Step Transformation*

The transformation from active to passive involves three steps:

1. The original direct object, NP_2, becomes the subject.
2. *Be* + *-en* is added to the active verb.
3. The original subject, NP_1, becomes the object of a preposition

3.1

(usually the preposition *by*). This third step is optional, in that the passive sentence is grammatical without the prepositional phrase.

Here are some further examples of the passive transformation:

The judge issued a search warrant. → A search warrant was issued by the judge.

Betsy Ross designed the first American flag. → The first American flag was designed by Betsy Ross.

The bank robber hid the money. → The money was hidden by the bank robber.

When we have both the active and the passive versions of a sentence to look at, the passive voice is easy to recognize. But how do we recognize the sentence as passive when we don't have both?

Joe was wounded in Vietnam.

Mario Cuomo was elected governor of New York in 1982.

To recognize these sentences as passive, we need to understand the relationship between the subject and the verb; that's where the term *passive* applies. Clearly, in the two passive sentences just cited, the subject is not the agent, that is, the "doer" of the action named by the verb; someone else did the deeds. It might be useful to think of the passive sentence as having a former life—an active version in which the current subject was the direct object:

(Somebody) wounded Joe in Vietnam.

(Somebody) elected Mario Cuomo governor of New York.

The role of "passive" receiver of the action still holds; when the passive receiver fills the subject slot, then we have a passive sentence.

The second step—the addition of *be* + *-en* to the verb—may not be obvious at first, especially when the sentence has a regular verb like *designed:*

Betsy Ross designed the first American flag. → The first American flag was designed by Betsy Ross.

The addition of *be* (in this case, *was*) is obvious, but the addition of *-en* is not. Here's where your understanding of the verb expansion rule from Chapter 2 comes into the picture.

First, let's analyze the components of the active verb:

past + design = designed

Now, to transform *designed* into the passive, we add *be* + *-en* in the slot before the main verb:

past + (be + -en) + design = was designed

In other words, in the active version of this sentence, *designed* is the *-ed* form, the past tense; in the passive version, *designed* is the *-en* form. (You'll recall that the *-en* and *-ed* forms of all regular verbs—and some irregular ones as well—are identical.)

In our sentence about the flag, *The first American flag was designed by Betsy Ross,* the clue that tells us that the verb is passive is the auxiliary *be* (*was*) without an *-ing* verb following. As you'll recall, the verb-expansion rule requires *-ing* following a form of *be,* so here it is clear that the *be* resulted not from the verb-expansion rule but from the passive transformation.

(Incidentally, the labels *past* and *passive* are not related: *Past* refers to tense; *passive* to voice. A passive verb can be either present or past.)

EXERCISE 1

Transform the following active sentences into the passive voice, retaining the same verb tense. (Don't forget step 1: The direct object becomes the subject of the passive.)

1. My roommate wrote the lead article in today's *Daily Collegian.*
2. Bach composed some of our most intricate fugues.
3. My brother-in-law builds the most expensive houses in town.
4. He built that expensive apartment complex on Allen Street.
5. The county commissioners try out a new tax-collection system every four years.

3.1 *Now transform these passive sentences into the active voice. You will have to supply a subject for the active if the agent is missing.*

    1. The football team was led onto the field by the cheerleading squad.
    2. This year's cheerleading squad was chosen by a committee last spring.
    3. Bill's apartment was burglarized last weekend.
    4. A shipment of fresh lobsters is expected any minute.
    5. The election was held on Tuesday during the regular meeting.

Other Passive Sentences

All of the transitive verb patterns can undergo the passive transformation. We've seen one example already of Pattern 2:

Active:

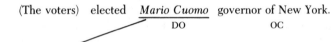

(The voters)   elected   *Mario Cuomo* governor of New York.
                       DO   OC

Passive:

Mario Cuomo   was elected   governor of New York.

Here is another:

Active:

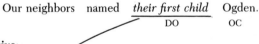

Our neighbors   named   *their first child*   Ogden.
                          DO   OC

Passive:

Their first child   was named   Ogden.

And here are two possibilities for Pattern 3 passive sentences, one using the indirect object and one the direct object as the subject:

Active:

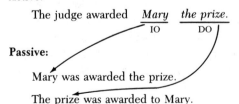

The judge awarded   *Mary*   *the prize.*
                        IO   DO

Passive:

Mary was awarded the prize.
The prize was awarded to Mary.

If this discussion of the passive voice sounds technical and complicated, don't worry! It's really not. The purpose of this detailed analysis is simply to help you understand how it works. You probably use the passive voice a great deal—more than you think you do. If you understand it, you have a better chance of using it effectively.

EXERCISE 2

Transform the following passive sentences into active sentences. Identify their sentence patterns.

1. FDR was first elected president in 1932.
2. The kidnapping victim was found in the woods unharmed.
3. My brother's tools are kept in immaculate order.
4. Nancy was finally given the recognition she deserves.
5. Women are erroneously called the weaker sex.

3.2 *Transformation of Expanded Verbs*

The passive verbs used in the examples so far have been two-word strings, passive transformations of the simple past or simple present-tense verbs:

T + **be** + -**en** + V.

Expanded verbs, verbs with auxiliaries, can also undergo the passive transformation. The steps are identical: We simply insert *be* + *-en* before the main verb:

T + (M) + (have + -en) + (be + -ing) + (**be** + -**en**) + VERB

Here are some examples:

The lab assistant *was helping* us.
(past + be + -ing + help)
(be + -en)
We *were being helped* by the lab assistant.

Max *has ruined* my roller skates.
(pres + have + -en + ruin)
$\widehat{(be + -en)}$
My roller skates *have been ruined* by Max.

You *should finish* your homework soon.
(past + shall + finish)
$\widehat{(be + -en)}$
Your homework *should be finished* soon.

Longer strings are possible, but they are rarely called for:

The neighbors *have been building* their house for five years. → The house *has been being built* for five years.

The ties between the transitive verb and the passive voice are so strong—there are so few exceptions—that we can almost define *transitive verb* in terms of this relationship. In other words, a transitive verb is a verb that can undergo the passive transformation. There are a few exceptions, including *have,* one of our most common verbs. In only a few colloquial expressions does *have* appear in the passive voice:

A good time was had by all.
I've been had.

Most *have* sentences cannot be transformed into the passive:

I had a cold. → *A cold was had by me!

Joe has a new car. → *A new car is had by Joe!

EXERCISE 3

Transform the voice of the following sentences, changing the active to the passive, the passive to the active.

1. We will probably elect a woman as mayor next year.
2. Gold had been found in Alaska long before the Gold Rush in California.
3. Help in the form of a fuel allowance is now being given to the poor by the federal government.

4. My son and his friends were mixing up a big batch of cookies this morning.
5. The gardeners next door are trying a new method of fertilizing this year.
6. Well-known and knowledgeable critics have called the play witty and warm.
7. According to the weather forecaster, a snowstorm has been expected for several days.
8. Six chapters should be studied before the next exam.

3.3 *Use of the Passive Voice*

The terms *active* and *passive* describe the relationship between the subject and the verb; they mean precisely what they say. In most active sentences, the subject—the actor or agent—is actively engaged; the subject is doing something, and the "something"—the action—is the verb:

The boys ate the pizza.
The judge awarded Mary the prize.

In the passive transformation the relationship between subject and verb is different: It is passive; the subject is doing nothing. As mentioned earlier, the relationship between the subject and the verb of the passive sentence remains what it was between the direct object and verb, or the indirect object and verb, of the active sentence: receiver of the action or, perhaps more accurate, the objective of the action:

The pizza was eaten by the boys.
Mary was awarded the prize.

Which version of the sentence is better, the active or the passive? Out of context, that question simply can't be answered. If the focus is on *the boys* and *the judge*, then the active is likely to be better. But what if you wish to focus on *pizza* and *Mary?* Should you use the passive voice? Not necessarily; sometimes there's an alternative that's better. For example, the passive sentence about Mary, *Mary was awarded the prize*, shows Mary as a passive recipient rather than

3.3

an active winner. By rewording the sentence, we can easily retain *Mary* as the subject without using the passive:

> Mary won the prize.
>   *or*
> Mary earned the prize.

We can also discuss the pizza in the active voice, although, admittedly, the sentence loses some information:

> The pizza disappeared.

In these examples, instead of sticking with the original, active sentences, with *the judge* and *the boys* as subjects, we found active verbs that we could substitute for the passive ones.

But certainly, the passive voice is sometimes the best choice. For example, the active subject, or agent, may have no bearing on the discussion:

> In 1905 the streets of Patterson, California, *were laid out* in the shape of a wheel.

> The Vikings have had a bad press. Their activities *are equated* with rape and pillage and their reputation for brutality is second only to that of the Huns and the Goths. Curiously, they also *have been invested* with a strange glamour which contradicts in many ways their fearsome image.
> —JAMES GRAHAM-CAMPBELL and DAFYDD KIDD, *The Vikings*

The author's purpose in the second passage is not to explain who equates the Vikings with rape and pillage or who invests them with glamour. The use of the passive puts these statements in the category of accepted beliefs.

Sometimes the agent is unknown, as in the first passive verb of the following passage:

> So far as we know, from Einstein's Special Theory of Relativity, the universe *is constructed* in such a way (at least around here) that no material object and no information *can be transmitted* faster than the velocity of light.
> —CARL SAGAN, *Broca's Brain*

In some cases the passive voice is simply more straightforward:

> Joe *was wounded* in Vietnam.

And sometimes, in order to add modifiers to the actor or the agent, we put it where we can do so more conveniently, after the verb:

> Early this morning my poodle was hit by a delivery truck traveling at high speed through the intersection of James Avenue and Water Street.

3.4 Misuse of the Passive Voice

Certainly the passive voice has a place in every kind of writing. It is especially common—and deliberate—in technical and scientific writing, in legal documents, and in lab reports, where the researcher is the agent, but to say so would be inappropriate:

Active:

> I increased the heat to 450° and allowed it to remain at that temperature.

Passive:

> The heat was increased to 450° and allowed to remain at that temperature.

The passive voice is a legitimate tool, but like any tool it must be right for the job. Too often the writer resorts to the passive voice in order to avoid *I* or *we* as the subject, either because the paper has too many of them already or because the teacher has ruled out the first-person point of view:

> The incessant sound of foghorns could be heard along the waterfront.

Here's an alternative sentence in which the verb describes sounds:

> The incessant sound of foghorns floated across the water.

3.4

Here's another version, this time using *sound* as the main verb:

The foghorn sounded along the waterfront.

Sometimes the writer simply doesn't realize that the passive voice may be the culprit producing the vagueness or wordiness in that first draft. For example, the writer of the following sentence ended a family Christmas story with no awareness of voice at all:

That visit from Santa was an occurrence that would never be forgotten by the family.

That kind of passive simply obscures the human element of the sentence. The active-voice revision produces a tight, straightforward sentence with a human subject:

The family would never forget that visit from Santa.

The writer could also have found an active sentence that retained *visit* as the subject if, for the sake of coherence, the paragraph had needed it:

That visit from Santa became part of our family legend.

In writing the first draft of your papers, you may want to get your thoughts down as fast as you can, without worrying much about the voice of the verbs. But in the various stages of revising and editing, you will want to think about such details. A clear understanding of active and passive voice will serve you well. (For further discussion of the passive voice in the revision stage, see pages 401–403.)

EXERCISE 4

Change the following sentences from passive to active, not as you did in Exercise 3, but by substituting a new verb that retains the essential meaning of the sentence; use the same subject.

Example:

The transitive verb patterns can be transformed into the passive voice. (PASSIVE)

Rewrite:
The transitive verb patterns can undergo the passive transformation. **3.4**
(ACTIVE)

1. The house was being built for five years.
2. Angry demonstrators could be seen crowding the front steps.
3. Rare postage stamps have been received from all over the world.
4. All of my computer cards were lost in the rush of registration.
5. Good family programs are rarely shown on the commercial networks.
6. Wood is now being used extensively for fuel in homes throughout the country.

FOR CLASS DISCUSSION
1. How would you classify the verb *settle*, as used in the following paragraph? Is it active or passive? Analyze the components of the verb strings.

> Settled down! Long after Rufus had fallen asleep, Jerry lay awake wondering what it would feel like to be settled down. His father was settled, his uncle was settled, Mr. Forson and Mr. Hyatt were settled, and Mr. Goodfellow looked like a settled man. Michael was settling, Phil would settle, Rufus was already more settled than most guys his age and probably would settle down completely in a few years. Only Jerry Engles did not seem to be settling. He didn't even know what it was like to want to be settled. Was he missing something?
>
> —THOMAS ROGERS, *At the Shores*

2. Identify the passive verbs in the following passage. Why do you think the author chose the passive instead of the active voice? Can you improve the passage by rewriting some or all of the sentences?

> Wild food is used at our house in a unique method of entertaining. Our "wild parties," which are dinners where the chief component of every dish is some foraged food, have achieved a local fame. Many different meals can be prepared almost wholly from wild food without serving anything that will be refused by the most finicky guest. Such dinners are remembered and talked about long after the most delicious of conventional dinners have been forgotten.
>
> —EUELL GIBBONS, *Stalking the Wild Asparagus*

4

Expanding the Noun Phrase: Adjectivals

A noun phrase occupies at least one slot in every sentence pattern: that of subject. In many of the patterns, noun phrases occupy one or more slots in the predicate as well: direct object, indirect object, subjective complement, and objective complement. And in every prepositional phrase a noun phrase serves as the object of the preposition. Most of the NPs used in the sample sentences have been simple two-word phrases: *the students, the fans, the players.* But in the sentences that we actually speak and write, the noun phrases are frequently expanded with modifiers—not only with adjectives (the basic noun modifier), but with other nouns and noun phrases and with prepositional phrases, verb phrases, and clauses:

the *lovely* roses *in Delpha's garden*
industrial robots *that assemble cars*
that *handsome* stranger *headed this way*

We refer to the function of all such modifiers in the noun phrase as **adjectival.**

We can think of the noun phrase as a series of slots (in much the same way as we looked at the expanded verb), with the **determiner** and the noun **headword** as the required slots and the modifiers before and after the headword as optional:

4.1

NP = <u>Determiner</u> (   ) (   ) NOUN (   ) (   ) (   )

Because of their frequency in the sentence and the variety of structures that we use to expand them, noun phrases provide a remarkable range of possibilities for putting ideas into words. In this chapter we will look at these possibilities, and we will come to appreciate the systematic nature of modification in the noun phrase.

4.1 *The Determiner*

The determiner class includes articles (*a, an, the*), possessive nouns (*John's, the dog's*), possessive pronouns (*my, his, our*), and demonstrative pronouns (*this, that, these, those*), as well as a variety of other common words. We think of the determiner as a "required" slot because most nouns are signaled by this structure class. (Proper nouns, however, and often abstract and plural nouns are not.)

Like the other structure classes, such as prepositions and conjunctions, determiners are learned early in the acquisition of speech and are used automatically; the native speaker rarely thinks about them. For the writer, however, a conscious understanding of the determiner's role becomes important. For example, as the first word of the noun phrase, and thus frequently the first word of the sentence and even of the paragraph, the determiner can provide a bridge, or transition, between ideas. The selection of that bridge can make subtle but important differences in emphasis:

> *This* attempt at reconciliation proved futile.
> *The* attempt at reconciliation . . .
> *Their* attempt . . .
> *Every such* attempt . . .
> *All of their* attempts . . .
> *Those* attempts . . .

In selecting determiners, then, writers have the opportunity not only to make such distinctions but also to help their readers move easily from one idea to the next in a meaningful way. (See also Chapter 7, pages 172–173.)

4.2 *The Headword*

Filling the headword slot in the noun phrase is, of course, the **noun**, the word signaled by the determiner. We usually think of a noun as the name of a person, place, thing, event, concept, or the like—a meaning-based definition that works fairly well. But we can also identify nouns by their form—both by their inflectional endings (the plural and the possessive) and by their derivational endings (such as *-tion, -ness, -ment,* and many more). (See also Chapter 7, pages 158–163.)

Recognition of the headword of the noun phrase can be an important help in preventing problems of subject–verb agreement. Consider the following noun phrase:

the stack of instruction forms

It would be natural to think of this noun phrase as plural and to avoid the *-s* form of the verb by writing

*The stack of instruction forms *were* misplaced.

But that sentence is ungrammatical. It is the headword of the noun phrase that determines the form of the verb, and in this NP the headword is singular: *stack.* In the next example, however, the headword is *instructions,* not *form,* so the choice of *confuses* is ungrammatical:

*The complicated *instructions* on the new income tax form really confuses me.

4.3 *The Prenoun Modifiers*

Adjectives and Nouns

These two classes generally fill the slots between the determiner and the headword. When the noun phrase includes both an adjective

4.3 and a noun as modifiers, they appear in that order; they cannot be reversed:

Determiner	Adjective	Noun	Headword
the	little		boy
the		neighbor	boy
the	little	neighbor	boy
a		marble	quarry
an	ancient	marble	bathtub
that	nervous	test	pilot
my	new	history	teacher

The adjective slot frequently includes more than one adjective, all of which modify the headword:

the little old man

the funny brown monkey

You'll notice that there are no commas in the preceding noun phrases, even though there are several modifiers in a row. But sometimes commas are called for. A good rule of thumb is to use a comma if it is possible to insert *and* between the modifiers. We would not talk about "a little and old man" nor "a funny and brown monkey." However, we would say "a strange and wonderful experience," so in using those two adjectives without *and*, we would use a comma:

a strange, wonderful experience

That comma represents juncture in speech—a pause and slight shift in pitch. Read the following pair aloud and listen to the difference in your voice:

On the table stood a little black suitcase.
On the table stood an ugly, misshapen suitcase.

In general, the system calls for a comma between two adjectives when they are of the same class, for instance, when they are both subjective qualities like "strange" and "wonderful" or "ugly" and "misshapen." In the earlier example, however, *funny brown monkey* the adjectives *funny* and *brown* are not alike: "funny" is a subjective, changing quality; "brown" is an objective, permanent quality.

4.3

Sometimes prenoun modifiers are themselves modified or qualified:

an extremely bright young lady

a really important career decision

In this situation we often have occasion to use a hyphen to make the relationship clear:

the *black-bordered* handkerchief
the *moss-covered* stones
a *French-speaking* community
a *bases-loaded* home run

Hyphens are especially common when the modifier in the adjective slot is a participle (the *-ing* or *-en* verb), as in the previous examples: *bordered, covered, speaking,* and *loaded* are verbs in form. And because participles are verbs, they are also commonly modified by adverbs:

a *well-*developed paragraph
the *fast-*moving train
the *low-*hanging clouds
this *highly* publicized event
a *carefully* conceived plan

The hyphen rule here is fairly straightforward: The *-ly* adverbs (such as *highly* and *carefully*) and *-ly* intensifiers (such as *really* and *extremely*) do not take hyphens; other adverbs in preparticiple position (such as *well* and *fast* and *low*) do take the hyphen.

Another occasion for hyphens in preheadword position occurs when we use a complete phrase in the adjective slot:

an *off-the-wall* idea
the *end-of-the-term* party
a *middle-of-the-road* policy
my *back-to-back* exams

4.4

When such a modifier fills the subjective complement slot in the sentence pattern, however, the hyphens are generally omitted:

His idea was really *off the wall.*
My exams during finals week are *back to back.*
The policy he subscribes to is strictly *middle of the road.*
The paragraph was *well developed.*

EXERCISE 1

Punctuate the prenoun modifiers in the following sentences with commas and hyphens, if needed. Remember the rule about commas: If you can add and, you probably need a comma.

1. I spoke to a witty delightful man in the cafeteria this afternoon.
2. There was a splendid old table for sale at the auction.
3. Several people were bidding on a well worn antique patchwork quilt.
4. We all tried to lift the big square heavy wooden box.
5. Her lovely gracious manner was apparent from the start.
6. The movie starred a huge gray elephant.
7. I found an expensive looking copper colored bracelet in the locker room.
8. Kristi wove a beautiful soft woolen blanket for her little niece.
9. I drank a large glass of delicious refreshing iced tea.
10. A commonly held notion among my cynical friends is that big business lobbyists run the country.

4.4 The Postnoun Modifiers

The postheadword position in the noun phrase may contain modifiers of many forms; when there is more than one, they appear in this order:

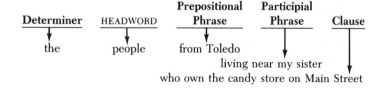

Determiner	HEADWORD	Prepositional Phrase	Participial Phrase	Clause
the	people	from Toledo		
			living near my sister	
				who own the candy store on Main Street

One other common postheadword modifier is the appositive, a noun phrase that renames the headword. The position of the appositive is somewhat flexible in relation to the other structures:

> my uncle, *a butcher at Phil's Market,* who makes his own salami
> the old gentleman who lives next door, *a World War I veteran*

In this section we will look at each of these structures following the headword, beginning with the most common modifier, the one that fills the first slot: the prepositional phrase.

The adjectival prepositional phrase, which modifies a noun, is identical in form to the adverbial prepositional phrase, which modifies a verb (described in Chapter 1). In its adjectival role the prepositional phrase identifies the noun headword in relation to time, place, direction, origin, and the like:

> The people *across the hall* rarely speak to me.
> The security guard *in our building* knows every tenant personally.
> I have always admired the lovely homes *on Sandy Ridge Road.*
> The meeting *during our lunch hour* was a waste *of time.*
> Jack is a man *of many talents.*

EXERCISE 2

Modify the nouns in the following sentences with prepositional phrases, using the prepositions suggested. Try to think of others that would be equally appropriate. (Refer to the list of prepositions on page 177 to jog your memory.)

1. The house ⎰ across _____
   ⎨ near _____ is different
   ⎱ on _____

   from all the others in the neighborhood.

2. The people ⎰ under _____
   ⎨ behind _____ shouted for help.
   ⎱ in _____

4.4

$$\text{3. The party}\begin{cases}\text{during}\underline{\hspace{2cm}}\\\text{after}\quad\underline{\hspace{2cm}}\\\text{at}\quad\underline{\hspace{2cm}}\end{cases}\text{turned into a riot.}$$

The Participial Phrase

Another postheadword modifier is the **participle, or participial phrase,** which consists of the *-ing* or *-en* form of the verb, together with any modifiers or complements that it may have:

The students *taking the law boards* look nervous.

In this sentence the verb phrase *taking the law boards* is clearly not the predicate; it is a modifier of *students*. The predicate is the linking verb pattern, *look nervous.*

(If the Pattern 6 main clause isn't readily apparent to you, there's another clue that tells you that *taking* cannot be the main verb: The *-ing* form of the verb always has a form of *be* as an auxiliary when it serves as the main verb. You might want to review the verb expansion rule in Chapter 2.)

The verb phrase *taking the law boards* is a modifier in the noun phrase *the students*. But because this modifying structure is a verb phrase in form, we can still think of it in terms of its sentence pattern. Underlying the participial phrase is a sentence—in this case a Pattern 1 sentence:

$$\begin{array}{ccc}NP_1 & V & NP_2\end{array}$$
The students   are taking   the law boards.

In other words, a participle is essentially one sentence embedded in another sentence, or, rather, in a noun phrase of another sentence.

Here's another important feature of participles that you may have noticed: The relationship of a noun headword to a participle modifier is *always* a subject–verb relationship: A participle modifies its own subject. This rule applies no matter what the position of the noun phrase in its sentence: subject, direct object, object of a preposition, or whatever:

I saw *a really beautiful girl studying in the library.*

In this sentence the noun phrase is the direct object; its headword, *girl*, is the subject of the participle *studying*.

4.4

> I talked to *the little kids playing soccer in the street.*

Here the noun phrase is the object of a preposition, *to;* its headword, *kids*, is the subject of the participle *playing*.

The importance of this rule will become apparent when we take up the problem of "dangling" modifiers on page 73.

Why do we use participles? Just like adjectives and prepositional phrases, participles add information about the noun headword; and because they are verb phrases in form, they add a whole verbal idea, just as the predicate does. Consider the following sentences:

> The man is sitting by the window.
> The man is talking to himself.

We can put these into a single sentence in a number of ways:

> The man is sitting by the window; he is talking to himself.
> The man is sitting by the window and talking to himself.

In neither of these compound structures is there a clear focus; the result is a kind of flatness or flabbiness. In most contexts a sentence that combines the two ideas in a focused way would probably be more effective. But the idea that should get the focus depends on the context:

> What is that noise I hear? The man *sitting by the window* is talking to himself.
> Where is the person doing all the mumbling? The man *talking to himself* is sitting by the window.

EXERCISE 3

Rewrite the following sentences by adding a participial modifier to each noun headword shown in italics.

1. *Experts* predict a record price for this year's corn *crop*.

4.4

2. The *miners* refused to ratify the labor *contract*.
3. The new *models* are expected to meet the government's fuel-efficiency *guidelines*.
4. The *officers* of the student government announced their resignation.
5. Several *students* volunteered to help clean up the campus after homecoming.
6. The *window* in the art museum commands a wonderful view of the *hills*.

Punctuation of Participial Phrases. The punctuation of a participial phrase depends on its purpose: Does it define the headword or simply comment on it? In other words, does the modifier provide information that is necessary for identifying the referent of the headword?

The merchants *holding the sidewalk sales* are hoping for good weather.

Which merchants are we talking about? We wouldn't know without the modifier. Which students look nervous?

The students taking the law boards look nervous.

Which man is talking?

The man sitting by the window is talking to himself.

In all of these sentences the purpose of the participial phrase is to make the referent of the noun clear, to define it. You'll notice that the modifier is *not* set off by commas; we call such a modifier **restrictive:** It restricts the meaning of the noun. In the sentences above we restrict the meaning of the words *merchants, students,* and *man* to a particular group or individual that the reader or listener can then identify.

But not all participial phrases are restrictive; sometimes we already know the identity of the noun being referred to. In such cases, the purpose of the modifier is different: It is simply to comment on or to add information about the noun, not to define it. Such modifiers are called **nonrestrictive.**

My mother, *sitting by the window,* is talking to herself.

In this sentence, the noun phrase *my mother* is already specific: It has only one possible referent. *Sitting by the window* simply adds a piece of information; its purpose is not the same as in the earlier sentence:

4.4

> The man *sitting by the window* is talking to himself.

To hear the difference between restrictive and nonrestrictive modifiers, you have only to listen to the sound of your voice when you speak these two sentences:

> The man sitting by the window is talking to himself.
> My mother, sitting by the window, is talking to herself.

The sentence stress is different. In the first one, the main stress—the loudest point of the sentence—is on *window;* the pitch of your voice rises until it gets to *window*, then falls, in one pattern. We call this pattern of pitch and stress an **intonation pattern.** In the sentence with commas, you'll notice not just one but three patterns, each with a point of stress, probably falling on *mother, window,* and *talking,* with almost equal degrees of loudness—perhaps a bit more on *talking.*
We can picture the intonation patterns something like this:

> The man sitting by the window is talking to himself.
> My mother, sitting by the window, is talking to herself.

Incidentally, if the sentence about the mother sounds strange when you say it, don't be surprised. We don't often use nonrestrictive participial phrases in our speech. In answer to the question "What's that noise I hear?" we'd be more likely to answer

> My mother is talking to herself; she's over there by the window.

You can use this difference in the intonation of the two kinds of modifiers to good advantage. Listen to your sentences after you've written them down; don't include any unwanted implications. For example, read this one without commas:

> My mother sitting by the window is talking to herself.

If you read that sentence with one intonation pattern, with the main stress on *window,* you are implying the existence of another mother, one who is not sitting by the window talking to herself. To write it that way may not mislead your readers, but the error will be obvious.

Here's another sentence to read aloud and listen to:

My sister living in Atlanta just called.

To say or to write that sentence as it is punctuated is to imply the existence of another sister, one who does not live in Atlanta. In other words, the modifier *living in Atlanta* is there to define the referent of the noun phrase *my sister.* If you don't have a second sister, then you have truly misled your readers.

Incidentally, the participle following a general noun such as *man* (as opposed to a specific noun like *mother)* is not always restrictive; if the reader already knows which man, the purpose of the modifier is different:

The park was empty except for a young couple near the fountain. The man, *holding an umbrella and a briefcase,* seemed nervous as he shifted his weight from one foot to the other.

The purpose of the participial phrase is not to identify, to define, which man. The reader knows that the man being referred to in the second sentence is the one already mentioned in the first; he's half of the couple. Read the passage without putting in the commas, and you'll be aware of an unwanted implication.

EXERCISE 4
Decide whether the participial phrases in the following sentences are restrictive (defining) or nonrestrictive (commenting) and punctuate them accordingly.

1.   A group of students held a protest rally in front of the administration building yesterday. The students hoping for a meeting with the provost were demonstrating against the tuition hike recently approved by the trustees. The increase expected to take effect in September will raise tuition almost 15 percent.

2. Many coal miners in West Virginia refused to approve two sections of the contract offered by management last week. They maintain that the two sections covering wages and safety represent no improvement over their present contract expiring on Friday at midnight.

4.4

3. The restaurant where I work was abuzz with excitement this morning. The cast and crew of a movie being made in the area came in unexpectedly for breakfast. Robert Redford dressed in black for his role as a gunfighter looked just like his picture. His co-star wearing a flouncy saloon-girl dress and lots of makeup was beautiful. I didn't notice what the director was wearing, but he was there, too.

The Movable Participle. We can think of the postheadword slot in the noun phrase as the "home base" of the participial phrase, as it is of the adjectival prepositional phrase. But unlike the prepositional phrase, the participial phrase can shift to the beginning of the sentence if it modifies the subject and if it is nonrestrictive:

Sitting by the window, my mother was talking to herself.

Carrying all their supplies, the Boy Scout troop trudged up the mountain in search of a campsite.

Laughing unroariously, the audience stood and applauded.

Notice that the participial phrase is set off by a comma; remember, it is nonrestrictive.

Sometimes, for purposes of emphasis or variety, we switch the nonrestrictive modifier to the end of the sentence, especially if the sentence is fairly short. Even there, however, the modifier is set off by a comma, and it still modifies the subject of the sentence:

The Boy Scout troop trudged up the mountain in search of a campsite, *carrying all of their supplies on their backs.*

The audience stood and applauded, *laughing uproariously.*

The rule about nonrestrictive participial phrases at the end of the sentence may seem quite simple—and it is—but it's also a surprising rule. The nonrestrictive participial phrase is different from other nonrestrictive modifiers in being limited to the subject. Even when

4.4

it's at the end of the sentence, it doesn't modify a noun in the predicate. For example, consider the following sentences:

Bill washed the car standing in the driveway.

Bill washed the car, standing in the driveway.

As the arrows indicate, in the first sentence the restrictive participial phrase modifies *car;* it's the car that's standing in the driveway. In the second, however, the phrase is nonrestrictive; it modifies *Bill.* Here's another illustration:

Bill talked to the mailman coming up the walk.
Bill talked to the mailman, coming up the walk.

Again, the subject of *coming* changes.

The rule is a surprising one because it doesn't apply to any other kind of noun modifier. If we were to turn those modifiers into clauses, for example, both would modify the object:

Bill washed the car *that* was standing in the driveway.

Bill washed the car, *which* was standing in the driveway.

Bill talked to the mailman *who* was coming up the walk.

Bill talked to the mailman, *who* was coming up the walk.

Understanding this tricky rule about participles will keep you from writing strange-sounding sentences like this one:

Bill washed his car, covered with dust from the trip home.

You can express that idea by using a different form for the modifier:

Bill washed his car, which was covered with dust from the trip home.
Bill washed his dust-covered car.

FOR CLASS DISCUSSION

4.4

Sometimes a verb phrase at the end of a sentence adds information that is more clearly adverbial than it is adjectival:

Pat spent the whole evening *cleaning house.*

Here the purpose of the verb phrase, rather than being simply to comment about Pat, is to tell "how" about the verb. In reading the sentence aloud, you will not hear the pause that signifies a comma. And to switch the verb phrase to the beginning of the sentence would make no sense.

Consider the following sentences. How should you punctuate them? The decision about whether to set off the final verb phrase is not always clear-cut. In making your decision, read the sentence aloud; then ask yourself how the verb phrase functions: Is it adverbial or is it adjectival? Then try to switch it to the beginning of the sentence.

1. Bill spent the night sleeping in the car.
2. Marcia came over to see me last night crying her eyes out.
3. My uncle made his fortune selling real estate.
4. My uncle worked hard all his life selling real estate and insurance.
5. The neighbors fled their burning house leaving all their valuables behind.
6. The neighbors miraculously escaped from their burning house saving only what they could carry in their hands.
7. Bill crossed the finish line smiling.
8. Bill finished the marathon placing sixteenth.
9. Bill finished the marathon in sixteenth place completely exhausted.
10. Bill finally crossed the finish line completely exhausted.

The Dangling Participle. The introductory participial phrase provides a good way to add variety to sentences by getting away from the standard subject opener. But it carries an important restriction: The participle can begin the sentence *only* if it modifies the subject—that is, when the subject of the participle is also the subject of the sentence and is in regular subject position. Otherwise the participle dangles. Remember, a participle modifies its own subject. Simply stated, a dangling participle is a verb in search of a subject:

> *Carrying all of our supplies for miles,* the campground was a welcome sight.
>
> *Having swung his five iron too far to the left,* Joe's ball landed precisely in the middle of a sand trap.

The campground, of course, did not do the carrying, nor did Joe's ball swing the five iron. You can fix such sentences (and avoid them in the first place) by making sure that the subject of the sentence is also the subject of the participle.

Another common source of the dangling participle—and other dangling modifiers as well—is the sentence with a "delayed subject," for example, a sentence beginning with *there* or *it:*

> *Having moved all the outdoor furniture into the garage, there was no room left for the car.
>
> *Knowing how much work I had to do yesterday, it was good of you to come and help.

In the second sentence, the subject of the participle, *you,* is there, but it appears in the predicate rather than in the usual subject position. Probably the most efficient way to revise such sentences is to expand the participial phrase into a complete clause. That expansion will add the missing subject:

> After *we moved* all the outdoor furniture into the garage, there was no room left for the car.
>
> It was good of you to come and help yesterday when *you learned* how much work I had to do.

EXERCISE 5

Rewrite the following sentences to eliminate the dangling participles.

1. Having endured rain all week, the miserable weather on Saturday didn't surprise us.
2. Having hiked five miles uphill, my backpack must have weighed a ton.

3. Hoping for the sixth win in a row, there was great excitement in the grandstand as the band played "The Star-Spangled Banner."

4. Guarding his bone as though it were his last meal, it was fascinating to watch the dog react to strangers.

5. Working ten hours a day, six days a week, Tom's first novel was completely finished in six months.

4.4

The Prenoun Participle. Before leaving the participle, we should note that when a participle is a verb alone—that is, a single word, with no complements or phrasal modifiers—it usually occupies the adjective slot in preheadword position:

Our *snoring* visitor kept the household awake.

The *barking* dog next door drives us crazy.

I should replace that *broken* hinge.

The old hound growled at every *passing* stranger.

As we saw in the earlier discussion of hyphens (page 63), an adverb sometimes modifies the participle:

a carefully conceived plan

a well-developed paragraph

The Relative Clause

Like the participial phrase, the **relative** (or **adjectival**) **clause** is also based on a sentence pattern; unlike the phrase, however, the clause is a sentence in form, complete with subject and predicate. The only difference between the relative clause and an independent sentence is the introductory word, the relative.

The relative may be a relative pronoun (such as *who, whose, whom, which, that, whoever,* or *whomever*) or a relative adverb (such as *where, when,* or *why*).

The relative pronoun (1) renames the headword, which is the antecedent of the pronoun and (2) plays the part of a noun in the relative clause:

The people *who live across the street* always share their surplus vegetables.

4.4

(The clause modifies *people;* the relative pronoun, *who,* renames *the people* and functions as the subject of the clause.)

In the next two sentences the relative pronouns are direct objects in their respective clauses:

> The cake, which Jenny baked from scratch, was delicious. (Jenny baked *which*)
>
> My roommate, whom I met just this week, already seems like an old friend. (I just met *whom*)

Note that we use the objective case form of the pronoun, *whom,* not the subjective form, *who.* The form is determined by the function of the relative in its clause.

In the next sentence the possessive relative pronoun, *whose,* acts as a determiner in the clause, the part that possessive pronouns usually play:

> The people whose car we bought gave us some good tips on fuel economy. (we bought *whose car*)

Incidentally, when the relative pronoun is an object in its clause, it can be deleted if the clause is restrictive—that is, if the clause is not set off by commas. In the earlier sentence with *whom,* the clause is nonrestrictive so the relative cannot be deleted. In the following example, however, the *whom* can be omitted and probably would be, especially in speech:

> King Edward VIII gave up the throne of England for the woman *(whom)* he loved.

The relative pronoun *that* always introduces restrictive clauses; it is never set off by commas:

> You choose a color *that you like.*
>
> A boy *that I knew in junior high* called me last week.

In both of the preceding sentences, *that* can be omitted. Some writers, in fact, would insist that the second sentence can *not* include *that,* that it must have *whom* instead because its referent is a person. The easiest and smoothest solution is to omit the relative:

A boy *I knew in junior high* called me last week.

4.4

In the case of a *nonrestrictive* clause, however, the relative pronoun is required:

Rob Miller, *whom I knew in junior high*, called me last week.

In speaking this sentence, we are more likely to say *who*, even though the objective case of the pronoun is called for; most listeners wouldn't notice the difference.

EXERCISE 6

Underline the adjectival clauses in the following sentences. Identify (1) the role of the relative in its clause and (2) the sentence pattern of the clause.

1. The man I love loves me.
2. I really like the posters that we put up in our room.
3. The people whose farm we rent like to gossip about the neighbors.
4. Vitamin C, which some people consider a defense against the common cold, is relatively inexpensive.
5. My grandfather once knew a man who bought a bicycle from the Wright brothers.
6. Our faithful dog, whom we all dearly loved, died last week at the age of seventeen.
7. Professor Watts, who is here for a conference, will be the guest lecturer in my economics class.
8. We're going to the concert that the string quartet is giving this afternoon.

Indefinite Relative Pronoun. The expanded, or indefinite, relative pronouns also introduce adjectival clauses:

I will give a prize to *whoever scores the most points.*

On the surface, this relative clause looks like a nominal (a structure that functions as a noun) rather than an adjectival, because it acts as the object of the preposition. We include it here because of its underlying meaning:

I will give a prize to (the person who) scores the most points.

The expanded relatives are called *indefinite* because they refer not to a specific noun, but to an understood, or general, referent. The above example again illustrates the concept of case: The case of the relative pronoun is determined by the function that it serves in its clause, not by the function of the clause. Here the clause follows the preposition, so you might be tempted to use the objective case (*whomever*); however, the relative pronoun is the subject of *scores* within its clause, so its form is subjective (*whoever*), not objective.

EXERCISE 7
Select the correct form of the relative pronoun in the following sentences:

1. Tell me the name of the man (who, whom) you are planning to marry.
2. The foreman promised bonuses to (whoever, whomever) the committee wanted to recommend.
3. Ruth is the candidate (who, whom) I expect will win the election.
4. I will ask (whomever, whoever) I want to the party.
5. (Whoever, Whomever) leaves last must turn out the lights.
6. Our senator, (who, whom) we all believe to be an honorable man, seems reluctant to talk about his campaign funds.

Relative Adverbs. All of the relative pronouns fill slots in their clauses that nouns normally fill, the usual job of pronouns. When a relative clause is introduced by one of the relative adverbs—*where, when,* or *why*—the relative fills an adverbial slot in its clause. The relative adverb *where* introduces clauses that modify nouns of place:

> Newsworthy events rarely happen in the small town *where I was born.*
> (I was born *where*)
> I'll never forget that history class *where we first met.* (we first met *where*)

When clauses modify nouns of time:

> We are all looking forward to Tuesday, *when the results of the audition will be posted.*

Why clauses modify the noun *reason:*

I understand perfectly the reason *why Barbara got that job.*

4.4

Where, when, and *why* clauses are often equally acceptable—and sometimes smoother—without the relative:

I understand perfectly the reason *Barbara got that job.*
We are all looking forward to the day *the results will be posted.*

Punctuation of Relative Clauses. The rules governing the punctuation of restrictive and nonrestrictive relative clauses are the same as those that apply to participial phrases. Is the referent of the noun that is modified clear to the reader? If there is only one possible referent (as in the case of "my mother"), the modifier cannot restrict the noun's meaning any further: The modifier is therefore nonrestrictive and should be set off by commas. It might be useful to think of the commas around nonrestrictive modifiers as parentheses, and to think of the modifiers as optional; if the modifier is optional, we can assume that it's not needed to make the referent of the noun clear.

If the referent of the noun is not clear to the reader—that is, if there is more than one possible referent or if the limits are not known—the purpose of the modifer is quite different: to restrict or define the meaning of the noun.

Notice the difference in the punctuation of the following pair of sentences:

The football players *who were wearing shiny orange helmets* stood out in the crowd.

The clause is restrictive: It defines which players stood out in the crowd. And, equally important, it implies the presence of players who were *not* wearing orange helmets and who did *not* stand out in the crowd.

The football players, *who were wearing shiny orange helmets,* stood out in the crowd.

Here the clause is nonrestrictive: It merely comments. We already know who stood out in the crowd: All of the football players did.

As with the participles, the context will make a difference in

4.4

the way you, the writer, punctuate relative clauses. What does the reader already know? For example, out of context the clause in the following sentence appears to be restrictive:

> The president *who was elected in 1932* faced problems that would have overwhelmed the average person.

Ordinarily we would say that the noun phrase *the president* has many possible referents, so the *who* clause is needed to make its referent clear; the clause defines and restricts the president to a particular person, the man elected in 1932. But what if the reader already knows the referent?

> Franklin Delano Roosevelt took office at a time when the outlook for the nation was bleak, indeed. The president, *who was elected in 1932,* faced problems that would have overwhelmed the average person.

In this context the clause is simply commenting; the referent of the noun phrase *the president* is already defined by the time the reader gets to it.

So in reaching a decision about commas, the writer must take into account (1) what the reader knows (Is the referent of the noun clear without this information?) and (2) what the reader will infer if the modifier is restrictive.

In the punctuation of relative clauses, the relative pronoun provides some clues:

1. The *that* clause is always restrictive; it is never set off by commas.
2. The *which* clause is generally nonrestrictive; it is set off by commas. (For many writers—in this book, for example—the rule is invariable: The *which* clause is always nonrestrictive.)
3. If the relative can be deleted, the clause is restrictive:

> The bus (that) I ride to work is always late.
> The woman (whom) I work with is always early.

The next two rules of thumb apply to both clauses and phrases:

4. After any proper noun, the modifier will be nonrestrictive:

Willamette University, which was established seven years before the Gold Rush of 1849, is within walking distance of Oregon's capitol building.

4.4

5. After any common noun that has only one possible referent, the modifier will be nonrestrictive:

My twin sister, who lives in Houston, is much more domestic than I am.

The highest mountain in the world, which resisted the efforts of climbers until 1953, looks truly forbidding from the air.

EXERCISE 8

Identify the postnoun modifiers in the following sentences as restrictive or nonrestrictive by adding commas if needed.

1. My parents who retired to Arizona in 1980 love the dry climate there.
2. The driver of the bus that I take to work knows all of her passengers by name.
3. My favorite teacher who always celebrates Fridays with cookies for the class will be leaving at the end of this semester.
4. After our first assignment in history class which everyone complained about I'm not looking forward to the second.
5. The little log house that sits so precariously on the bank downstream from the dam is occupied by our county's only known recluse whom I often see nearby with a fishing pole in his hand.
6. Robert Redford and his co-star wearing their costumes and makeup for the movie they're shooting just outside of town unexpectedly came into the restaurant where I work.

The Appositive

In form the **appositive** is itself a noun phrase with the same referent as the headword; it renames the headword:

my best friend, *Meda*

my neighbor lady, *a butcher at the A & P*

the security guard in our building, *an ex-Marine who once played professional football*

Mr. and Mrs. Ebbitt, *the people living across the hall*

As these examples demonstrate, the appositive can be expanded with modifiers just as any other noun phrase can be.

The appositive noun phrase has the same relationship to the headword it renames as the subjective complement has to the subject that it renames. In fact, we could turn these noun phrases into Pattern 5 sentences simply by adding a form of *be:*

My best friend *is* Meda.

My neighbor lady *is* a butcher at the A & P.

The security guard in our building *is* an ex-Marine who once played professional football.

Mr. and Mrs. Ebbitt *are* the people living across the hall.

This operation works the other way around as well. For the writer who overuses Pattern 5, who tends to fill the page with *be* as the main verb of sentences, the appositive may offer an alternative:

Pattern 5:

Apricots and raspberries are my favorite kinds of fruit. Unfortunately, the supermarket rarely has them.

Rewrite:

Unfortunately, the supermarket rarely has apricots and raspberries, *my favorite kinds of fruit.*

Pattern 5:

Gallo is the world's largest winery. It bottles 250,000 cases of wine a day.

Rewrite:

Gallo, *the world's largest winery,* bottles 250,000 cases of wine a day.

Because of the complementlike nature of appositives, it might be more accurate and appropriate to think of them as nominals—that is, to think of the appositive slot as an NP slot. But because appositives fit into the noun phrase, adding descriptive information to the headword, we include it here with the noun modifiers, the adjectivals.

The Movable Appositive. The appositive shares the movability feature of the participial phrase; it can introduce the sentence when it modifies the subject:

An ex-Marine who once played professional football, the security guard in our building makes us feel secure indeed.

The world's largest winery, Gallo bottles 250,000 cases of wine a day.

The explanatory appositive introduced by the expletive *or* does not share the movability feature of other appositives; it always follows the noun that it renames:

> The study of sentences, or *syntax,* helps us to appreciate the richness of our language.
>
> The African wildebeest, or *gnu,* resembles both an ox and a horse.

EXERCISE 9

Identify all of the noun phrases that are functioning as appositives. Remember, an appositive noun phrase has the same referent as the headword of the noun phrase that it renames.

1. My sister Susan's husband, Bill, watches television every night of the week except Wednesday, his bowling night.
2. The president's latest economic proposal, a crackpot plan from the word go, was rejected out of hand by Congress.
3. Nearly all the way across Kansas, we followed a pack of highway monsters, sixteen-wheelers carrying strange-looking machinery.
4. John Barth's first novel, *The Floating Opera,* is easy to read compared with his later works, some of which involve the reader in fantastic mental gymnastics.
5. Black lung, an incurable disease of the respiratory system, affects countless coal miners in Pennsylvania and West Virginia.
6. We keep hearing about the computer revolution, a change in our way of life that will affect every one of us within a few years.

The Punctuation of Appositives. Most appositives are nonrestrictive; those we have looked at so far are set off by commas. However, the issue of punctuation often does come up when the appositive is a proper noun:

> My daugher Kristi lives in San Jose.
>
> My husband, Jack, was born in Salem.

4.4

In the first sentence the restrictive (defining) appositive makes one statement and implies its opposite. Like the participles and the clauses, the appositive that is restrictive carries an implication: The reader can infer from the absence of commas the existence of another daughter whose name is *not* Kristi and who does *not* live in San Jose. If such is not the case, the reader has been misled; the appositive needs commas. The second sentence includes no such implications.

Reading the two sentences aloud can make the distinction clear: The first one has one main stress and one intonation contour; the second has three:

My daughter Kristi lives in San Jose.

My husband, Jack, was born in Salem.

We cannot read the second sentence with only one main stress:

My husband Jack was born in Salem.

—unless, of course, the writer of the sentence has another husband named Tom or Dick or Harry who wasn't born in Salem!

Like the other nonrestrictive modifiers, the appositive that merely comments is rarely used in speech. Depending on the knowledge of the listener, we would be more likely to say either

My husband was born in Salem.

or

Jack was born in Salem.

Remember, an understanding of this relationship between intonation and meaning can often come to the rescue of the writer who is unsure of punctuation.

THE COLON WITH APPOSITIVES. To understand appositives is to understand that tricky mark of punctuation, the colon. The structure that the colon signals is, in fact, an appositive, or—as is so often the case—a list of appositives.

Notice how the noun phrase following the colon renames a noun in the sentence:

I'll never forget the birthday present my dad bought me when I was twelve: *a new three-speed bicycle.*

Our visitor was a stranger with a long, jet black beard and unexpected light blue eyes: *a real mystery man.*

4.4

Both of the foregoing sentences could be written without the colon. In the first, a comma could simply replace it, because the appositive renames the direct object:

I'll never forget the birthday present my dad bought me when I was twelve, *a new three-speed bicycle.*

With the comma, there is less anticipation; the appositive gets less emphasis.

To write the second sentence without the colon, we would have to shift the appositive close to the noun it renames. Notice here that the appositive renames both the subject and the subjective complement, as they have a common referent:

Our visitor, *a real mystery man,* was a stranger with a long, jet black beard and unexpected light blue eyes.

or

Our visitor was a stranger, *a real mystery man,* with a long, jet black beard and unexpected light blue eyes.

Both of these are effective sentences. The original, the one with the colon, simply focuses its attention on the appositive.

Certainly one of the most common purposes of the colon is to signal a list—actually, a list of appositives:

Caves are the habitat of untold numbers of organisms that creep across the cave floor, skitter along the walls, and weave soundlessly through streams: *spiders, crickets, beetles, millipedes, mites, springtails, shrimps, amphipods, isopods, and dozens of others.*

—adapted from DONALD DALE JACKSON, "Close Encounters with Another World"

The colon conveys a clear message: "Here it comes, that list of organisms."

4.4

Sometimes the list following the colon includes internal punctuation other than commas:

> The study of our grammar system includes three areas: *phonology, the study of sound; morphology, the study of meaningful combinations of sounds; and syntax, the study of sentences.*

Here our list includes three nouns, each of which has a nonrestrictive postnoun modifier of its own. This is one of the two occasions in our writing system that call for the semicolon. (The other, the joining of clauses in compound sentences, is discussed on pages 133–136.) Without the semicolons, the list becomes difficult to read; even when the reader knows that only three areas are going to be mentioned, it still looks like a list of six:

> phonology, the study of sounds, morphology, the study of meaningful combinations of sounds, and syntax, the study of sentences.

Here's a variation in the form of the appositive. This one is a pair of verb phrases rather than noun phrases:

> The Senate minority leader recently explained his party's priorities for the coming session: *to curb spending* and *to bring the deficit down.*

Although these are not noun phrases, they are still appositives: clearly they name the priorities. Even prepositional phrases can follow the colon to complete the sentence:

> We went so many places on Saturday night that I can hardly remember them all: *to the movies, to the shopping mall, to the pizza parlor, to the party at Connie's,* and then *to the disco.*

These are adverbial-like prepositional phrases, but they also name the places, so in that sense they function as appositives.

DASHES WITH APPOSITIVES. In revising an earlier sentence with a colon, we shifted the appositive from the end of the sentence to the noun phrase it renamed:

> Our visitor was a stranger with a long, jet black beard and unexpected light blue eyes: *a real mystery man.*
>
> Our visitor, *a real mystery man,* was a stranger . . .

4.4

Such a revision is also possible when the appositive following the colon is a list:

> Three committees were set up to plan the convention: *program, finance,* and *local arrangements.*

However, to insert that appositive, with its internal commas, after the headword *committee* would cause the reader some confusion:

> Three committees, program, finance, and local arrangements, were set up to plan the convention.

Here's where we use a pair of dashes. Dashes make the relationship between the headword and the appositive absolutely clear:

> Three committees—program, finance, and local arrangements—were set up to plan the convention.

The difference between the two sentences—the one with dashes and the one with the colon—is a matter of focus. Although the appositive with dashes stands out clearly, the real focus of the sentence is in the predicate, in the statement about planning. The version with the colon does a much better job of focusing on the committees.

Notice, by the way, that the appositive list set off by dashes requires two dashes, not just one. We use one dash alone only at the end of the sentence, often as an alternative to the colon. It represents a somewhat less formal colon.

> I'm looking forward to the big event tomorrow—my first glider flight.

Incidentally, we also use a dash or a colon (but more commonly the dash) to signal what we call a *sentence appositive,* a noun phrase

4.4

that renames or, more accurately, capsulizes the idea in the sentence as a whole:

> The musical opened to rave reviews and standing-room-only crowds—*a smashing success.*
> A pair of cardinals has set up housekeeping in our pine tree—*an unexpected but welcome event.*

COMPOUND SENTENCES WITH COLONS. Another use of the colon, somewhat related to the appositive use, is in certain compound sentences. Sometimes the second clause is a statement that completes the idea—in a sense *renames* the idea—before the colon, so that it has a kind of appositive or complement function. (There are a number of such examples in this book; maybe you'll spot some now that you're starting to notice colons.)

Often the sentence following the colon is a question:

> One problem always comes up in any discussion of the economy: *How can we stop inflation?*
> The people living on pensions are especially concerned about inflation: *How can they make their 1960 dollars stretch to cover 1980 prices?*

Probably the most common use of the colon is with the direct quotation. The following examples are taken from a *Time* story about the funeral of Leonid Brezhnev (November 29, 1982):

> Said a Western diplomat: *"It seemed as much a military event as the Nov. 7 parade."*
> Concluded a Western diplomat in Moscow: *"The main impression Bush and Shultz had was of Andropov's great self-confidence and control."*
> Asked about the probable outcome, Huang replied: *"I am optimistic."*

When the second clause is not a question or a direct quotation, the decision about whether to use the colon is less clear-cut. The following examples are from the same issue of *Time:*

> Hong Kong's real estate market is sagging: *land and building prices have dropped by as much as 30 percent in less than three months.*
> Once hired, minority journalists say, they are caught in a double bind: *the same preference that helps them get in also leads white colleagues to doubt their competence.*

Minority reporters complain that for them there is often no middle ground: *if they are not extraordinary, they are considered inferior.*

4.4

The question of capitalization of the complete sentence following a colon is one of our punctuation conventions that remains on the fence. When the sentence is either a direct quotation or a question, the standard convention is to use a capital letter. (We would use a capital even for the direct quotation that is not a complete sentence.) The use of the capital letter for other sentences following the colon, as in the last three examples, is a matter of divided opinion. In this book, all complete sentences are capitalized; *Time's* editorial policy is obviously different.

PUNCTUATION ERRORS WITH THE COLON. The colon is a useful and necessary signal to the reader in the foregoing sentences. It clearly indicates the relationship of the following structure to what has just been said. In using colons, you must remember one important rule:

WHEN A COLON IS USED TO SIGNAL AN APPOSITIVE, A
GRAMMATICALLY COMPLETE SENTENCE ALWAYS
PRECEDES IT.

If you remember that rule, you will not be tempted to write sentences like the following:

*The three categories of residents in homes for the aged are: people who have no families, people who have never been married, and very old people who are widowed.

Look at the sentence pattern. The verb *be* tells you it is Pattern 5, a pattern that *requires* a subjective complement. As the sentence reads now, however, the list is *not* an appositive; it is a subjective complement, so you cannot include the colon. In other words, the colon wrongly separates the verb from the subjective complement.

Another sentence that violates this rule is the list that is preceded by *such as* and a colon:

*There are many different kinds of structures that can be used to modify nouns, such as: prepositional phrases, participial phrases, relative clauses, adjectives, and nouns.

4.4

Remember, the colon comes at the end of a *complete sentence;* here the *such as* phrase is left unfinished before the colon.

One of the most common ways to correct these incomplete sentences is to add *the following* just before the colon. *The following* is an elliptical noun phrase (an elliptical structure is one in which something has been left out but is clearly implied):

> The three categories of residents in homes for the aged are the following: . . .

Now the sentence pattern slots are filled; *the following (categories)* functions as the subjective complement:

> There are many different kinds of structures that can be used to modify nouns, such as the following: prepositional phrases . . .

The above revisions—with *the following* added—solve the problem of the incorrect colon, but they are certainly not the only solution, nor are they necessarily the best. A more concise, straightforward version of the first is simply the original sentence without the colon:

> The three categories of residents in homes for the aged are people who have no families, people who have never been married, and very old people who are widowed.

If you want to retain the anticipation that the colon adds to the sentence, since the categories are described in rather long phrases, simply rewrite the main sentence, using a verb other than *be:*

> Three categories of people live in homes for the aged: those who have no families, those who have never been married, and very old people who are widowed.

The other sentence, the one beginning with *There are*, can easily be rewritten to avoid *the following:*

> Many different kinds of structures can be used to modify nouns: prepositional phrases . . .

The first revision—the one that includes *such as the following* followed by the colon—simply doesn't need all three signals: *such as*, *the following*, and the colon. The colon alone says, "Here comes the list."

4.4

FOR CLASS DISCUSSION

Revise and/or combine each of the following sentences by providing an appositive or by changing its focus. Experiment with commas, colons, and dashes.

Example:

> My favorite activities are skiing, playing golf, and bowling; unfortunately, they cost more than my budget can stand.

Revision 1:

> The activities that I enjoy the most—skiing, playing golf, and bowling—all cost more than my budget can stand.

Revision 2:

> I simply can't afford the activities that I enjoy the most: skiing, playing golf, and bowling.

1. The cost of repairs to the nation's public transportation facilities is an expenditure that cannot be delayed much longer if the system is to survive. Roads, bridges, and railroads are all in need of repair.
2. Potassium is fairly rare in nature foods. Three main sources are bananas, mushrooms, and wine.
3. To many people, the mushroom, a lowly fungus with little food value, is a real gourmet's delight.
4. In early 1983 the Chinese banned the import of certain American goods, such as cotton, synthetic fibers, and soybeans. The restriction had an adverse effect on the economy, especially on the farmers.
5. A rare marine animal, the paper nautilus octopus, which normally lives in the coastal waters of Japan, has been found recently in the squid nets off Santa Catalina in California.
6. The doctor's diagnosis came as a complete shock. He said that Joe had lung cancer.
7. According to fashion experts, the crew cut will be back in style before long. That particular haircut was more or less the hallmark of the 1950s.

4.4

8. *Time*'s "Man of the Year" for 1982, the computer, was a controversial choice. Many people complained.

Multiple Modifiers

So far we have used examples of noun phrases with a single postheadword modifier, either a clause or a phrase. But we often have more than one such modifier, and when we do, the order in which they appear is well defined: prepositional phrase, participial phrase, and relative clause:

the security guard *in our building   who checks out the visitors*
the woman *from Buffalo   staying with the Renfords*
the DC-10 *on the far runway   getting ready for takeoff,   which was hijacked by a group of terrorists*

Misplaced Modifiers. A word of caution is in order. Multiple modifiers in a postheadword position can be the cause of confusion; sometimes they're ambiguous, or open to more than one possible meaning:

the driver of the bus standing on the corner

The embedded prepositional phrase *of the bus* automatically adds another noun headword, as every prepositional phrase includes an object. So the question arises: Which headword, *driver* or *bus*, is modified by the participial phrase, *standing on the corner?* The writer will have no trouble revising the sentence to solve the problem:

the driver of the bus who was standing on the corner
the driver of the bus parked at the corner

The trick is to recognize the ambiguity in the first place.

Another, similar, source of ambiguity is the string of prepositional phrases, a fairly common occurrence in English:

My sister manages the flower shop *in that new brick building near the park on Center Street.*

Here the question may arise: What's on Center Street, the building or the park?

Another problem with prepositional phrases occurs when a phrase could be either adjectival or adverbial:

4.4

They discussed their problems *with the teacher.*

As you'll recall from Chapter 1, the adverbial prepositional phrase often comes at the end of the sentence; because that's also the slot for the objects and subjective complements, and because we know that noun phrases often include postnoun prepositional phrases, the source of the problem is clear.

A similar problem arises with the embedded clause. Is the prepositional phrase part of the clause or not?

Tony buried the knife he found *in the cellar.*

In this example, the question is not whether the phrase is adjectival or adverbial; but which verb the phrase modifies, *buried* or *found.*

Luckily, context usually prevents such ambiguities from happening—but not always. And often the misplacement results not in ambiguity but in an ineffective sentence, one that requires a second look:

The doctor examined the patient lying in bed with a stethoscope.

A larger percentage of women voters went to the polls in 1980 than men.

Her glasses, perched on the end of her nose, trimmed with sequins and butterflies, made everyone turn and stare.

The modification system, with all of its embedded and shifting phrases and clauses, gives the language its great richness and versatility—as well as a bagful of tricks.

SENTENCE PRACTICE
Expand the noun phrases in the following sentences by adding the modifiers called for.

1. a. Add a *who* clause that tells what your relatives are usually like:

My relatives (or cousin, uncle, sister, etc.), who ＿＿＿＿＿＿
＿＿＿＿＿＿＿＿＿＿＿＿＿＿＿＿＿＿＿＿＿＿＿＿＿＿＿＿,
surprised everyone at the family reunion with their crazy antics.

4.4

b. Now revise the sentence by using an appositive instead of a *who* clause to express the same, or a similar, meaning:

My relatives _____

_____,

surprised everyone at the family reunion with their crazy antics.

2. a. Add a participial phrase that tells what the cyclists were doing:

From the window we watched the cyclists _____

_____.

b. Now add an appositive at the end of the sentence as a comment on the whole scene:

From the window we watched the cyclists _____

_____

(PARTICIPAL PHRASE)

— _____.

(APPOSITIVE)

3. a. Add a prenoun adjective, a prepositional phrase, and a clause that describes the winds:

The _____ winter winds _____

_____ came as a

complete surprise after the mild autumn days of November.

b. Now introduce the sentence with a participial phrase. (Remember, the subject of the participle will be the subject of the sentence, *winds*.)

_____, the _____ winter winds _____

_____ came as a complete

surprise after the mild autumn days of November.

4. a. Add a participial phrase and a clause to make clear which runner took the lead:

The runner _____   _____
pulled in front at the mile mark, and after that she never lost the lead.

b. Now shift your participial phrase to the opening position and insert two prenoun modifiers before the subject headword:

_____, the _____   _____

runner _____ pulled in front at the

(CLAUSE)

mile mark, and after that she never lost the lead.

5. a. Use an appositive and a participial phrase to describe the trucker:

At the far end of the counter sat a trucker, _____

_____ , _____ .

b. Now explain what sort of counter it is so that the reader will be better able to picture the event:

At the far end of the _____ _____ counter

_____ sat a trucker, _____ ,

_____ .

FOR CLASS DISCUSSION

The adjectivals that we have discussed in this chapter can be found in every kind of writing, from newspaper editorials to classic works of fiction; it would be difficult indeed to construct English sentences without them. Examine the use of noun modifiers in the following passages. You might also want to test your understanding of sentence patterns by figuring out the pattern of the underlying sentence and identifying the slots that these modified nouns fill.

1. The fact that many educational practices lack a scientific foundation is not solely the fault of educators. The very nature of their business, learning or teaching, is not really well understood even by those who have attempted to study it under refined laboratory conditions.
—B.R. BUGELSKI, *The Psychology of Learning Applied to Teaching*

2. Cody was fifty years old then, a product of the Nevada silver fields, of the Yukon, of every rush for metal since seventy-five. The transactions in Montana copper that made him many times a millionaire found him physically robust but on the verge of soft-mindedness, and, suspecting this, an infinite number of women tried to separate him from his money.
—F. SCOTT FITZGERALD, *The Great Gatsby*

3. Presently he got up and turned on the ceiling fan, to create some motion and sound in the room. It was a defective fan which clicked with each revolution on and on. He lay perfectly still beneath it, with his

4.4

clothes on, unconsciously breathing in a rhythm related to the beat of the fan.

—EUDORA WELTY, "The Hitch Hiker"

4. So, as a child, and even now that she was grown up, it helped her to think of her father's face—those pale surprised green eyes that could be simple or cunning, depending upon the light, and the lines working themselves in deeper every year around his mouth, and the hard angle of his jaw going back to the ear, burned by the sun and then tanned by it, turned into leather, then going pale again in the winter.

—JOYCE CAROL OATES, "By the River"

5. Dictators' pastimes are far more striking because they often contrast with the rulers' normal behavior. Nero, no fiddler incidentally, did play the lyre and sing to vast, appreciative audiences. Hitler was a painter who started out doing postcard-size works of art and, as his career improved, worked his way up to large watercolors of wartime destruction: rubble, crumbled walls, caved-in roofs. Eventually he created his own subjects, a rare chance for an artist. According to his lackey, the featherbrained Putzi Hanfstaengl, Hitler also adored whistling. His best numbers were Harvard fight songs, which Putzi, a Harvard alumnus, would thump on the piano whenever the Führer was in a frisky mood.

—ROGER ROSENBLATT, "Looking for Mr. Goodpov," *Time* (December 6, 1982)

6. He and Phil were jealous of their own secret places: a deep bed of sphagnum moss on which they had once rolled naked, a hollow oak in which they used to hide Sucret boxes filled with treasure. They had their own inaccessible blueberry patches and lookout spots to which they had given their own names: The White Throne, The Maze, The Hidden Valley. This was their world, and it was not a masculine world. Nothing was flat, nothing was straight, nothing was fenced. They roamed freely across the landscape of the Shores, a landscape which to Jerry's mind was like the great, sprawled body of a woman. Rounded drifts of white sand spilled forward from the burst bodice of a grass-covered hill. Fern-fringed, sun-warmed pockets of sand invited you to rest a while . . . and think of women.

—THOMAS ROGERS, *At the Shores*

7. There is a giant crop standing in rows on the windswept hills of Jess Ranch. It is not the wheat or barley one can see from the freeway, an hour's drive east of San Francisco, nor the native scrub oaks, thistles or ubiquitous golden grass. Rancher Joe Jess has 600 acres of rangeland dotted with tall white wind machines that tower over his Herefords and produce a new cash crop: electricity. The wind farm at Jess Ranch is part of a young energy endeavor beset with financial and technical difficulties. But, with any luck, the slightly rickety wind-power industry—complete with crazy contraptions, earnest inventors and lofty megawatt turbines—may soon take off.

—JANET L. HOPSON, "They're Harvesting a New Cash Crop in California Hills," *Smithsonian* (November 1982)

4.4

5

Nominals and Sentence Modifiers

5.1 Nominals

Much of the versatility of our language and the details we put into our writing result from the wide variety of modifiers that we include in noun phrases, as we discussed in Chapter 4. But we are equally versatile in our ability to use verb phrases and clauses, instead of noun phrases, to fill the NP slots in our sentence patterns. We refer to these noun substitutes as **nominals** (just as we use the term *adjectival* for structures that function as adjectives and *adverbial* for those that function as adverbs).

Gerunds

A common noun phrase substitute is the *-ing* verb; when the verb functions as a nominal, it is known as a **gerund.** In form, gerunds and participles (verbs used as adjectivals) are identical; only their functions distinguish them. Participles modify nouns; gerunds act as nouns:

Living off campus is very expensive.

In this sentence the entire verb phrase acts as the subject.

5.1

Because they are nounlike, we can think of gerunds as names. But rather than naming persons, places, or things, as nouns generally do, gerunds, because they are verbs in form, name actions or behaviors or states of mind or states of being. In the sentence given, for example, *living off campus* names an activity. Something is very expensive; the gerund phrase names that "something."

All of the sentence patterns can serve as the source of gerunds. And because they are verbs, the gerunds include all of the complements and modifiers that main verbs include; in our example, an adverbial prepositional phrase modifies the intransitive verb *living*, a Pattern 4 gerund.

A Pattern 5 gerund, like a Pattern 5 sentence, has a subjective complement following the verb *be:*

Pattern 5 Sentence	Pattern 5 Gerund
The teacher is angry.	*the teacher's being angry*

Note that we convert *is* into the *-ing* form and its subject into the possessive case:

The teacher's being angry surprised us.

This gerund names an activity or a state of mind; that state of mind is the "something" that surprised us.

The Subject of the Gerund. The subject of the gerund is not always stated, especially when the gerund names a general, rather than a particular, action or behavior:

Raising orchids requires patience.
Becoming a lawyer is not easy.

But as we saw in the earlier example, when the subject of the gerund is part of the gerund phrase, it is often in the **possessive** case:

The teacher's being angry surprised us.
I appreciated *Bill's giving me a lift*.

In these gerund phrases the subjects of the gerunds, *teacher* and *Bill*, have become determiners of sorts, playing the same role that possessive nouns and pronouns ordinarily play: *John's* hat, *his* hat, *the teacher's* state of mind, *the teacher's* being angry, *Bill's* giving me a lift.

Although the possessive case may sometimes sound excessively formal or even incorrect, we can see by substituting a pronoun that the possessive case is the proper choice. The other forms of the pronoun—subjective (*he, they*) and objective (*him, them*)—simply sound ungrammatical:

*He being angry surprised us.
*They being angry surprised us.
*Him being angry surprised us.
*Them being angry surprised us.
 Their being angry surprised us.
 His being angry surprised us.

When the subject of the gerund includes postheadword modifiers, we generally omit the possessive inflection. We would say

I appreciate *the man next door* giving me a lift.

rather than

I appreciate *the man next door's* giving me a lift.

Functions of the Gerund. In most of the examples we have seen, the gerunds occupy the subject slot of the sentence, but they commonly occupy other NP slots as well:

Direct Object:
   My brother enjoys *collecting stamps.*

Subjective Complement:
   His hobby is *collecting stamps.*

Object of Preposition:
   Mike and Jenny were in trouble for *handing in their papers late.*

Appositive:
   The favorite of all my hobbies, *collecting antique coins,* is also the most expensive.

5.1

Appositive:

That was a great idea, *cooking steaks on the grill.*

EXERCISE 1

Identify the sentence pattern of each gerund phrase and the part that the gerund phrase plays in the sentence.

1. After clearing the courtroom, the judge began admonishing the lawyers.
2. I got stopped for going through a red light.
3. I really dislike cleaning my room.
4. Studying math gives me a headache.
5. Staying in the hospital for a week nearly drove me crazy.
6. It's nice being here with you.
7. My roommate enjoys giving me a bad time.
8. His favorite trick is hiding my toothbrush.

The Dangling Gerund. Like the dangling participle (page 73) and the dangling infinitive (page 14), the dangling gerund occurs when its subject is neither stated nor clearly implied. This situation arises at times when the gerunds serves as the object in an opening or closing prepositional phrase:

> *After *cooking the snails in white wine,* none of the guests would eat them.
> *In *filling out the form,* an original and two copies are required.
> *The rust spots must be carefully sanded and primed before *giving the car its final coat of paint.*

We certainly have no problem understanding such sentences; the message comes through. In fact, *dangling* may be too strong a word, as these sentences don't have the obvious weakness of those with dangling participles. Of the three sentences preceding, the first is probably the least acceptable; here the activity named by the gerund is a specific, one-time event, and we expect the subject of the gerund to be the first available noun. So it appears that "none of the guests" did the cooking. One alternative is to expand the opening phrase into a clause, turning *cook* into the main verb of the clause:

> *After I cooked the snails in white wine,* none of the guests would eat them.

5.1

Another version leaves *cooking* as a gerund, but its subject is now clearly stated:

> *After I went to all the trouble of cooking the snails in white wine,* none of the guests would eat them.

But even when gerunds refer to general, rather than specific, activities, there tends to be fuzziness in such prepositional phrases, simply because we expect the subject of the sentence to serve as the subject of the gerund as well.

EXERCISE 2

Rewrite the other two sample sentences to correct the dangling gerunds.

In filling out the form, an original and two copies are required.
The rust spots must be carefully sanded and primed before giving the car its final coat of paint.

Now improve the following sentences by providing a clear subject for the gerund.

1. Before starting to bake a cake, the ingredients should be assembled.
2. Heavy meals should be avoided before swimming.
3. In making a career decision, my counselor was a big help.
4. After storing the outdoor furniture in the garage, there was no room left for the car.

Infinitives

Another fairly common nominal verb phrase is the infinitive, the base form of the verb with *to.* Like gerunds, infinitives in nominal positions name actions or behaviors or states of being; and like the gerunds, nominal infinitives can be derived from all the sentence patterns and can fill a variety of roles in the sentence:

Subject:

> *To fly a helicopter* is one of my ambitions.

5.1

Direct Object:

> Since ancient times, people have attempted *to fly.*

Subjective Complement:

> My goal is *to become an accountant.*

Appositive:

> My parents aren't very enthusiastic about my plans for term break, *to hitchhike to Fort Lauderdale.*

Appositive:

> It would be exciting *to go to New Orleans.*

In the last sentence the infinitive is the actual subject; the *it* construction allows us to delay the subject in order to give it greater emphasis. (See page 381 for other examples of the delayed subject.) Another version of the appositive infinitive is Hamlet's famous phrase, with the infinitive in apposition to *that:*

> *To be or not to be,* that is the question.

Clause Nominals

In the preceding sections, we have seen examples of verb phrases—gerunds and infinitives—filling NP slots. In this section, we will see that complete sentences—clauses—can also fill NP slots:

> I wonder *what our history midterm will cover.*
> I suspect *that it will be hard.*

In each of these examples, the clause fills the direct object slot in a Pattern 1 sentence:

> I wonder *something.*
> I suspect *something.*

The clause names the "something."

These two sentences also illustrate the two kinds of introductory words that signal nominal clauses (sometimes called *noun clauses*): interrogatives, such as *what*, and the expletive *that*. Notice that the interrogative *what* fills a grammatical role in the clause that it introduces—in this case, that of direct object:

5.1

> Our history midterm will cover *what.*

That feature of the interrogative is important to remember when the interrogative is *who,* because you will have to make a choice between variations in case, between *who* and *whom.* To do so, simply figure out what role the interrogative plays in its own clause.

> I wonder (*who* will be there).

In this sentence, the interrogative is the subject of the clause, so we use *who.* In the following example, however, the interrogative is the object:

> He wouldn't tell me (*whom* he had decided to take).

Whom functions as the object of the verb *take:* "He had decided to take *whom.*" In speech we would probably use *who* instead of *whom,* which has an overly formal sound. But in writing, edited standard English calls for *whom.*

Unlike the interrogative, the expletive *that* does not have a role in the clause that it introduces:

> I suspect *that it will be hard.*

It will be hard is a complete sentence. The expletive is an operator of sorts, an added element that enables us to manipulate a structure for reasons of emphasis and the like. The expletive *that* enables us to embed one sentence as a nominal in another sentence. In the example above, the nominal clause *it will be hard* becomes the direct object.

The expletive *that* can turn any declarative sentence into a nominal clause:

> Tim loves to play poker. → I know *that Tim loves to play poker.*
> He loses as often as he wins. → I suspect *that he loses as often as he wins.*

Note that when the *that* clause fills the direct object slot, as in the preceding examples, the sentence may be grammatical without the expletive:

> I know Tim loves to play poker.
> I suspect he loses as often as he wins.

Sometimes, however, the *that* prevents confusion:

> I believe her mother and others in the family disapprove of me.
> I've always understood the road to success is paved with hard work.

In these sentences, the reader needs the signal that a clause is coming; as they read now, we expect *mother and others* in the first sentence and *the road* in the second to be direct objects. *That* can also make a difference in the pace of the sentence and the point of main stress. (These features are discussed further in Chapter 18, "Revision and Style.")

When the clause is in the subject position, *that* is required:

> *That Tim can enjoy gambling* simply amazes me.

The expletive *that* also enables us to turn a direct quotation into an indirect one:

Direct:

> He said, "I will get to the gym soon."

Indirect:

> He said *that he would get to the gym soon.*

Note the change in the tense of the verb. It is common to change the present tense to the past when one is transforming a direct quotation into indirect discourse. If the verb in the direct quotation is already in the past tense, we would probably add *have* + *-en*, the usual verb form for indicating a past completed action or, in this case, a past completed statement:

Direct:

> He said, "I polished off the cake yesterday."

Indirect:

> He said *that he had polished off the cake yesterday.*

5.1

But we could also use the simple past in the indirect version:

> He said that he *polished* off the cake yesterday.

In these indirect quotations following the verb *say*, the expletive *that* could be omitted, but after verbs such as *reply, explain,* and *state*, the *that* is usually retained:

> He said *he had polished off the cake yesterday.*
> He explained *that he had polished it off.*

Punctuation of Nominal Clauses. In this chapter, we have seen some fairly long phrases and clauses filling NP slots. With one exception, the punctuation of these sentences remains exactly the same as the punctuation of the basic sentence: NO COMMAS BETWEEN THE SENTENCE PATTERN SLOTS. The exception occurs when the direct object is a direct quotation, as we have seen. The usual convention calls for a comma between a verb like *say* or *reply* and the quoted passage:

> He said, "I will get to the gym as soon as I can."

Sentences in which the nominal clauses are introduced by interrogatives often turn out to be fairly long; even so, there is no punctuation between the basic sentence slots.

A Tricky Punctuation Problem. One of the trickiest of our punctuation problems occurs with the nominal clause. Remember, we said that we could turn any sentence into a nominal clause just by putting the expletive *that* in front of it. The system applies even to long sentences with all kinds of modifiers. For example,

> I think *that one of the trickiest of our punctuation problems occurs with the nominal clause.*
> At the beginning of this section, I said *that I think that one of our trickiest punctuation problems occurs with the nominal clause.*

And so on.

5.1   Another point to bear in mind is this: There is never a comma between the expletive and the clause, as you can see in the above examples. But here's another comma rule, one you read about in Chapter 1 (and that we will take up later in this chapter):

> A SUBORDINATE CLAUSE IN OPENING POSITION
> IS ALWAYS SET OFF BY A COMMA.

For example,

> *When the curtain fell,* an eerie silence settled over the audience.

Now comes the tricky question: What happens when you combine these two rules? Let's try it with the sentence about the theater:

> Joe said that when the curtain fell, an eerie silence settled over the audience.

Notice what has happened. We've put a comma between *that* and the main clause of our direct object clause. You can tell just by looking at that sentence that something's wrong with the punctuation. The part after the comma seems tacked on somehow. What we've done is to violate the rule that says NO PUNCTUATION BETWEEN SENTENCE SLOTS. Our direct object has been separated here.

What's the solution? No comma.

> WHEN A DIRECT OBJECT IS A NOMINAL CLAUSE WITH AN
> INTRODUCTORY MODIFIER, THAT INTRODUCTORY MODIFIER
> IS NOT SET OFF BY A COMMA.

Here are some further examples of sentences with introductory clauses turned into direct objects:

> If I go, Joe will go too.

As direct object:

> I think that *if I go Joe will go too.*

> Because of the weather report, we are going to cancel the picnic.

As direct object:

> I heard that *because of the weather report we are going to cancel the picnic.*

Even though Sue was getting a C in history, she decided to drop the course.

5.1

As direct object:

I heard that *even though Sue was getting a C in history she decided to drop the course.*

If omitting the comma in the nominal clause bothers you—if the comma seems necessary—you can solve the problem by shifting the subordinate clause to the end of the nominal:

I think that Joe will go if I do.

I heard that we are going to cancel the picnic because of the weather report.

I heard that Sue decided to drop her history course, even though she was getting a C.

EXERCISE 3

Identify the sentence pattern of each of the following sentences. Then identify the form of the structure filling the main sentence slots. Do any of the sentences call for punctuation? If so, insert it.

1. I can't believe what the teacher expects us to do for an A.
2. Tell me whose car you borrowed for the trip to the game last night.
3. I just can't remember if I turned off the television set.
4. Whether I turned it off or not doesn't really matter.
5. The astronomer who visited our science class today assured us that the chances of a comet's striking the earth are very remote.
6. Professor Watts who visited our economics class said that even though we already spend a great many of our resources on social programs the young and the old need to be helped even more.
7. The idea that our powerful defense couldn't stop the Cornhuskers was unthinkable.
8. The reason for our defeat was that the Cornhuskers' backfield outsmarted us on every play.
9. At halftime the coaches talked to the linebackers about how they could stop those tailbacks.
10. The immigration authorities have reported that even though they patrol the border constantly thousands of Mexicans continue to come to the United States illegally.

11. I sometimes wonder how the people who cross the border illegally have the courage to do what they do.

12. I can't remember the name of the official who told us about the problems they have with the illegal aliens from Mexico.

5.2 Sentence Modifiers

Like the modifiers of nouns and verbs, modifiers of the sentence as a whole also come in the form of single words, phrases, and clauses. In general, **sentence modifiers** resemble adverbials: The information they contribute is, for the most part, adverbial information (time, place, manner, and the like), and most single-word sentence modifiers are adverbs in form. The choice of whether to call a certain phrase or clause a sentence modifier or a verb modifier is, in fact, sometimes hard to make; there are few definitive rules. Within a sentence the sentence modifier is usually set off by commas, but at the beginning or end of the sentence it may not be. As a result, often the only structures classified as sentence modifiers are those that are clearly parenthetical or independent in meaning or those in which an obvious contrast would exist as a result of the presence of the comma, as in the following pair of sentences that we saw earlier:

Clearly, he did not explain the situation.
He did not explain the situation *clearly.*

This contrast in meaning shows the difference between the two functions of *clearly:* It is a sentence modifier in the first example, but an adverbial in the second.

This kind of single-word sentence modifier is often set off by a comma. We can usually identify its relationship to the sentence as a whole, even without the obvious contrast in meaning that a word like *clearly* illustrates:

Increasingly, college students are taking practical courses that will prepare them for the job market.

Invariably, the sweater or pair of shoes I like best is the one with the highest price tag.

Luckily, the van didn't get a scratch when it hit the ditch.

But not all sentence modifiers are separated by commas:

5.2

> *Perhaps* the entire starting lineup ought to be replaced.

Here it is fairly clear that *perhaps* raises a question about the idea of the sentence as a whole. If it were moved to a position within the sentence, it would probably be set off by commas:

> The entire starting lineup, perhaps, ought to be replaced.

As a general rule, parenthetical expressions that are clearly parenthetical are set off by commas no matter where they appear:

> *As a matter of fact,* I forgot to eat lunch.
> *To tell the truth,* I have never read *Silas Marner*.
> The driver of the Corvette walked away from the accident, *much to our amazement*.
> The driver of the van, *on the other hand*, had to be rescued by the emergency squad.

Sentence modifiers—whether single words or parenthetical phrases—can be useful tools for writers to use. They are interrupters, slowing the sentence down; they change the stress pattern; they act as transition devices to prepare the reader for the next idea; and they add variety.

The Subordinate Clause

Subordinate clauses—clauses introduced by subordinating conjunctions, such as *because, since, if,* and *when*—are traditionally classified as adverbial clauses. Certainly the meaning they add to the sentence is the same kind of information that adverbs and other adverbial structures add (see pages 12–14). But the purpose of the subordinator is to relate the idea in its clause to the rest of the sentence, so subordinate clauses are often referred to as *sentence modifiers*. Whatever we call them, such clauses are structures that the writer ought to understand and use for adding information about time, place, cause, and possibility:

> The audience gasped *when the magician thrust his sword into the box.*
> I didn't expect to have a good time this week *because you went away.*
> *After the Brewers won the pennant,* the city of Milwaukee went wild.
> We hunted for the treasure precisely *where the map specified.*
> You ought to have something to eat *before you drink any more beer.*
> I went home to get ready for the party *before the guests arrived.*

Like other adverbials and sentence modifiers, clauses are often movable, so they are especially useful for the writer as transition devices and as a way of varying the stress, pace, and emphasis of the sentence.

The inexperienced writer must be especially careful to recognize when clauses are independent sentences and when they are not. The subordinate clause punctuated as a complete sentence is one of the most frequent kinds of sentence fragments. Remember, a subordinate clause is a complete sentence to which a signal has been added; the subordinator signals the reader that the sentence is connected to another sentence:

Complete Sentence	Subordinate Clause
He went away.	*after* he went away
The party was a success.	*even though* the party was a success
The Brewers won the pennant.	*when* the Brewers won the pennant

If you don't connect that subordinate clause to a sentence, you've given the wrong signal; the result is a sentence fragment.

Punctuation of Subordinate Clauses. In opening position, the subordinate clause is always set off by a comma; in closing position, punctuation is related to meaning. As a general rule, when the idea in the main clause is conditioned by or dependent on the idea in the subordinate clause, there is no comma. For example, the idea of the main clause—the opening clause—in the following sentence will be realized only if the idea in the subordinate clause is carried out; thus the main clause depends on the *if* clause:

5.2

> I'll go to Jan's party if you promise to be there.

But in the next sentence the subordinate clause does not affect the fulfillment of the main clause:

> I'm going to the party that Jan's giving on Saturday night, even though I know I'll be bored.

In general, *even though* and *although* are preceded by commas; *if* and *because* are not. Actually, the use of the comma with final subordinate clauses is probably one of the least standardized of our punctuation rules. The final criterion must be readability and clarity.

Elliptical Subordinate Clauses.   In many sentences, the subordinate clause is **elliptical**—that is, certain understood words are left out:

> While (we were) waiting for the guests to arrive, we ate all the peanuts.
> When (you are) in doubt about home-canned vegetables, be sure to bring them to a boil before you taste them.
> If (it is) possible, get here before five.

In these clauses, the missing words could be included; both versions are grammatical. But in the case of some subordinate clauses, only the elliptical version is grammatical:

> I'm a week older than Bob (is old).
> My sister isn't as tall as I (am tall).
> > *or*
> I'm a week older than Bob is (old).
> My sister isn't as tall as I am (tall).

In both of these examples we are comparing an attribute in the two clauses. But the ellipses in such comparisons can produce ambiguity when the main clause has more than one possible noun phrase for the subordinate clause to be compared with:

5.2

The Rangers beat the Dolphins worse than the Broncos.

Joe likes Mary better than Pat.

In these sentences we don't know if the comparison is between subjects or objects because we don't know what has been left out. We don't know whether

The Rangers beat the Dolphins worse than the Broncos (beat the Dolphins).

or

The Rangers beat the Dolphins worse than (the Rangers beat) the Broncos.

We don't know whether

Joe likes Mary better than (Joe likes) Pat.

or

Joe likes Mary better than Pat (likes Mary).

FOR CLASS DISCUSSION

1. Using your understanding of elliptical clauses, explain how it's possible for both of the following sentences to be grammatical:

   My little sister likes our cat better than me.

   My little sister likes our cat better than I.

2. The following sentences are both illogical and ungrammatical. What is the source of the problem?

   *The summer temperatures in the Santa Clara Valley are much higher than San Francisco.

   *The Pirates' stolen-base record is better than the Cardinals.

EXERCISE 4

Rewrite the following sentences, supplying the words missing in the elliptical clauses. Are the sentences clear?

1. I picked up a Midwestern accent while living in Omaha.

2. My accent is not as noticeable as Mary's.

3. Holmes hit Ali harder than Norton.
4. If necessary, strain the juice before adding the sugar.
5. While waiting at the train station in Lewistown, there was no place to sit.
6. If handed in late, your grade will be lowered 10 percent.

5.2

The Absolute Phrase

The **absolute phrase** (also known as the *nominative absolute*) is a structure independent of the main sentence; in form the absolute phrase is a noun phrase that includes a postnoun modifier. The modifier is commonly an -*en* or -*ing* participle or participial phrase, but it can also be a prepositional phrase, an adjective, or a noun phrase. The absolute phrase introduces an idea related to the sentence as a whole, not to any one of its parts:

Our car having developed engine trouble, we stopped for the night at a roadside rest area.

The weather being warm and clear, we decided to have a picnic.

Victory assured, the fans stood and cheered during the last five minutes of the game.

Absolute phrases are of two kinds—with different purposes and different effects. (Moreover, both are structures used principally in writing rather than in speech.) The preceding examples illustrate the first kind: the absolute that explains a cause or condition. In the first sentence, the absolute phrase could be rewritten as a *because* or *when* clause:

When our car developed engine trouble,
      or   }   we stopped for the night . . .
Because our car developed engine trouble,

The absolute construction allows the writer to include the information without the explicitness that the complete clause requires. In other words, the absolute phrase can be thought of as containing both the meanings in the two versions shown here rather than only one of them.

5.2

In the following sentence the idea in the *because* clause could be interpreted as the only reason for the picnic:

> *Because the weather was warm and clear*, we decided to have a picnic.

The absolute construction, on the other hand, leaves open the possibility of another reason for the picnic:

> *The weather being warm and clear*, we decided to have a picnic.

It also suggests simply an attendant condition rather than a cause.

In the second kind of absolute phrase, illustrated by the sentences following, a prepositional phrase (*above his head*), an adjective phrase (*alert to every passing footstep*), or a noun phrase (*a dripping mess*), as well as a participle (*trembling*), may serve as the postnoun modifier. This second kind of absolute adds a detail or a point of focus to the idea stated in the main clause:

> Julie tried to fit the key into the rusty lock, *her hands trembling.*
> The old hound stood guard faithfully, *his ears alert to every passing footstep.*
> *Hands above his head,* the suspect advanced cautiously toward the uniformed officers.
> *Her hair a dripping mess,* she dashed in out of the rain.

This technique of focusing on a detail allows the writer to move the reader in for a close-up view, just as a filmmaker uses the camera. The absolute phrase is especially effective in the writing of description. Notice how the authors of the following passages have used the main clause of the sentence as the wide lens and the absolute phrase as the close-up:

> Silently they ambled down Tenth Street until they reached a stone bench that jutted from the sidewalk near the curb. They stopped there and sat down, *their backs to the eyes of the two men in white smocks who were watching them.*
> —TONI MORRISON, *Song of Solomon*

> There was no bus in sight and Julian, *his hands still jammed in his pockets and his head thrust forward,* scowled down the empty street.
> —FLANNERY O'CONNOR, "Everything That Rises Must Converge"

The man stood laughing, *his weapons at his hips.*
—STEPHEN CRANE, "The Bride Comes to Yellow Sky"

He smiled a little to himself as he ran, holding the ball lightly in front of him with his two hands, *his knees pumping high, his hips twisting in the almost girlish run of a back in a broken field.*
—IRWIN SHAW, "The Eighty-Yard Run"

William Faulkner's style of writing depends heavily on the use of the absolute phrase. Probably no writer has used it more frequently or more effectively in setting scenes and describing characters. The following passages are from "Barn Burning":

Then his father was gone, *the stiff foot heavy and measured upon the boards, ceasing at last.*

From the woodpile through the rest of the afternoon the boy watched them, *the rug spread flat in the dust beside the bubbling wash-pot, the two sisters stooping over it with a profound and lethargic reluctance,* while the father stood over them in turn, implacable and grim, driving them though never raising his voice again.

This time the sorrel mare was in the lot before he heard it at all, *the rider collarless and even bareheaded, trembling, speaking in a shaking voice as the woman in the house had done, his father merely looking up once before stooping again to the hame he was buckling, so that the man on the mare spoke to his stooping back.*

Notice that both of the absolute constructions in the preceding passage include subordinate (in this case, adverbial) clauses, the first introduced by *as,* the second by *so that.*

EXERCISE 5

Underline any absolute phrases in the following sentences. Is the modifier of the headword an adjective, a prepositional phrase, a noun phrase, or a participle?

1. The cat lay by the fire, purring contentedly, her tail moving from side to side like a metronome.
2. Chuck and Margie kicked their way through the fallen leaves, their arms draped across each other's shoulders.
3. The rain having persisted for over an hour, the game was officially stopped in the sixth inning.

5.2

4. With the Grand Tetons looming majestically above, Jackson Hole, Wyoming, looks like a picture postcard.

5. Having slipped on the ice three times already, I decided to wear sensible boots for a change.

6. Then the boy was moving, his bunched shirt and the hard, bony hand between his shoulder-blades, his toes just touching the floor, across the room and into the other one, past the sister sitting with spread heavy thighs in the two chairs over the cold hearth, and to where his mother and aunt sat side by side on the bed, the aunt's arms about his mother's shoulders. (WILLIAM FAULKNER)

The Relative Clause

Most relative clauses are modifiers of nouns, as we saw in Chapter 4, and most of them are introduced by a relative pronoun that refers to that noun:

> Joe's car, *which he brought just last week*, looks like a gas guzzler to me.

In this sentence the antecedent of *which* is the noun *car;* the noun is modified by the clause.

But in some sentences *which* refers not to a particular noun but to a whole idea; it has what we call **broad reference.** In the following sentence, the antecedent of *which* is the idea of the entire main clause:

> Joe bought a gas guzzler, *which surprised me.*

All such broad-reference clauses are introduced by *which*, never by *who* or *that*, and all are nonrestrictive—that is, they are set off by commas:

> Tom cleaned up the garage without being asked, *which made me suspect that he wanted to borrow the car.*
>
> This summer's heat wave in the Midwest devastated the corn crop, *which probably means higher meat prices for next year.*

Many writers try to avoid the broad-reference relative clause, instead using *which* only in the adjectival clause to refer to a specific noun. In inexperienced hands the broad-reference *which* clause often has the vagueness associated with dangling modifiers:

5.2

I broke out in a rash, *which really bothered me.*

In this sentence the referent of *which* is unclear; *which* could refer to either the *rash* or the *breaking out.* There are a number of alternatives in which the meaning is clear:

Breaking out in a rash really bothered me.
The rash I got last week really bothered me.

Even though they are not particularly vague, the earlier examples, too, can be paraphrased in ways that avoid the broad-reference *which:*

When Tom cleaned up the garage without being asked, I suspected that he wanted to borrow the car.
Tom's cleaning up the garage without being asked made me suspect that he wanted to borrow the car.
This summer's heat wave in the Midwest, which devastated the corn crop, probably means higher meat prices for next year.

EXERCISE 6
Rewrite the following sentences to eliminate the broad-reference which.

1. I had to clean the basement this morning, which wasn't very much fun.
2. Wendell didn't want to stay for the second half of the game, which surprised me.
3. The president criticized the Congress rather severely in his press conference, which some observers considered quite inappropriate.
4. The first snowstorm of the season in Denver was both early and severe, which was not what the weather service had predicted.
5. We're having company for dinner three times this week, which probably means hotdogs for the rest of the month.
6. I have noticed that Uncle Al has started to talk to himself, which I suspect is a sign of old age.
7. The college library has finally converted the central card catalog to a computer system, which took over four years to complete.

5.2

SENTENCE PRACTICE

A. Turn each of the following sentences into a verb phrase; then use that verb phrase as a nominal in another sentence.

Example:

> Congress voted for a tax increase on gasoline during their lame-duck session.

Revision:

> To vote for a tax increase on gasoline during their lame-duck session seems to me an irresponsible action for Congress to take.
>
> *or*
>
> Their voting for a tax increase on gasoline during the lame-duck session was not a particularly responsible act on the part of Congress.

1. The police suspect arson in last week's barn fire on Buffalo Run Road.
2. The Pittsburgh Ballet Company will perform *The Nutcracker* during the Christmas holidays.
3. The European Space Agency will launch a satellite to study Halley's Comet in 1986.
4. My roommate is playing Snoopy in the campus production of *You're a Good Man, Charlie Brown.*
5. Bill called the pizza shop at midnight.
6. The committee members completely disregarded one another's suggestions.
7. The miners have refused to sign the contract that management offered.
8. Several dozen people in this country make and sell kaleidoscopes for a living.
9. We went through four cords of firewood last winter.
10. Everyone complains about the food in the dining hall.

B. Add an absolute phrase to each of the following sentences—a phrase that describes a detail of the whole.

Example:

> The campus looks just like a Christmas card.

Revision:

> The campus looks just like a Christmas card, every twig on every tree covered with snow.

1. The pizza looked like a work of art.
2. The maintenance crew worked at full speed to get ready for winter.
3. The committee members began to argue among themselves.
4. We spotted an abandoned shack in a small clearing.
5. The coal miners refused to ratify the new contract.
6. The road stretched before us.
7. The first flowers of spring always work wonders on my winter doldrums.
8. Crowds lined the street to see the Thanksgiving Day parade.
9. The rain beat against the windshield.
10. The TV weather forecaster gestured toward the map.

C. Now transform the sentences given in parts A and/or B above into subordinate clauses; you supply the main clause. (See page 179 for a list of possible subordinators.)

Example:

Bill called the pizza shop at midnight.

Revision:

When Bill called the pizza shop at midnight, I was sure they would say it was too late to deliver.

6

Coordination

The technique of **coordination,** of putting together compound structures in sentences, is old hat; you've been doing it for years. Coordination is a natural part of language, one that develops early in speech. If you pay attention to sentence structure the next time you're within hearing distance of a small child, you'll hear the **conjunction** *and* used frequently between parts of sentences and between the sentences themselves:

We built a snow fort and threw snowballs.
Robbie is mean, and I don't like him.

Compound structures also show up early and often in writing. Certainly in this book you can't read very far without hitting an *and* or a *but* or an *or.* Your own writing is probably filled with them, too.

So why do we need a chapter on coordination? Because it's so easy!

Any structure or technique that we use as often as we do coordination needs to be under control. Remember, a written sentence is there to be looked at and pondered about, to be read over and over again. We want to be sure not only that every one of those compounds is grammatically correct but that it's the right structure

6.1

for the job. And, equally important, we want to use the most efficient and accurate conjunction for that compound structure.

In this chapter we will look first at coordination of structures within the sentence and then at coordination of complete sentences, paying special attention to parallelism and to punctuation. The conjunctions are listed on page 179.

6.1 Coordination Within the Sentence

All of the sentence slots and the modifiers within the slots can be coordinated:

> John *and* Tim worked out on Saturday, *both* in the weight room *and* in the gym. (COMPOUND SUBJECT; COMPOUND ADVERBIAL PREPOSITIONAL PHRASE)
>
> Molly's dessert was simple *yet* elegant. (COMPOUND SUBJECTIVE COMPLEMENT)
>
> Molly served a simple *but* elegant dessert. (COMPOUND PRENOUN ADJECTIVE)
>
> He can *and* should finish the job before dinner. (COMPOUND AUXILIARY)
>
> He will *either* do the job right *or* do it again. (COMPOUND VERB PHRASE)
>
> Cathy said that she would get here sooner or later *and* that I shouldn't start the rehearsal without her. (COMPOUND NOMINAL CLAUSE AS DIRECT OBJECT)

As these examples show, *and* is not the only coordinating conjunction; the compound structure need not be a matter of simple addition. *Or* and *either–or* express an alternative; *but* and *yet* introduce a coordinating contrast. In the sentences about Molly's dessert, for example, you can see how concisely and effectively those contrasting conjunctions work within the sentence. Here's a less concise way of expressing those ideas:

> Molly's dessert was simple, but it was elegant.
> Molly's dessert wasn't very fancy, but it tasted terrific.

EXERCISE 1
Revise and tighten the following compound sentences by means of internal coordinate structures.

Example:

> The weather for our picnic yesterday was warm, but it rained most of the time.

6.1

Revision:

> The weather for our picnic yesterday was warm but wet.

1. My new jogging outfit is inexpensive, and it is extremely well made.
2. I may drive into the city tomorrow morning, or I may wait until evening.
3. Discuss the development of the railroads in the West during the nineteenth century and explain their importance to the westward movement.
4. The holiday parties are such fun, but afterward I am usually exhausted.
5. Compound sentences are often wordy, but not always; sometimes they are quite concise.
6. The trip to Fort Lauderdale during spring break was really fun; it was also expensive.
7. My history professor said that my term paper was a bit rambling; she also found it inaccurate.
8. My sister has become a real expert at programming the family's new home computer; her husband writes his own programs, too. They use their computer for their home business; they also use it for their appointments and even for their Christmas card list.

Punctuation of Coordinated Parts

Notice in the examples on page 124 that none of the compound words and phrases have commas with the conjunction. This is a well-established punctuation rule:

> BETWEEN THE PARTS OF TWO-PART COMPOUND STRUCTURES WITHIN THE SENTENCE, WE USE NO COMMA.

This rule applies even when the two elements are fairly long, as in a pair of nominal clauses. We do, however, use commas with a series of three or more elements:

> We gossiped, laughed, and sang together at the class reunion.

Those commas represent the pauses and slight changes of pitch that occur in the production of the series. You can hear the commas in

6.1

your voice when you compare the two—the series and the pair. Read the following sentences aloud:

> We gossiped, laughed, and sang together at the class reunion.
> We laughed and sang together at the class reunion.

You probably noticed a leveling of the pitch in reading the pair, a certain smoothness that the series did not have. In the series with conjunctions instead of commas, you'll notice that same leveling:

> We gossiped and laughed and sang together at the class reunion.

When conjunctions connect all of the elements, we use no commas.

In the series of three, some writers—and some publications as a matter of policy—use only one comma, leaving out the one immediately before *and:*

> We gossiped, laughed and sang together . . .

Perhaps they do so on the assumption that the conjunction substitutes for the comma. But it really does not. In fact, this punctuation misleads the reader in two ways: It implies a closer connection than actually exists between the last two elements in the series, and it ignores the pitch change, however slight, represented by the comma. The main purpose of punctuation, after all, is to represent graphically the meaningful signals—pitch, stress (loudness), and juncture (pauses)—that the written language otherwise lacks. That small pitch change represented by the comma can make a difference in emphasis and meaning.

EXERCISE 2

Punctuate the following sentences.

1. Pete sanded the car on Friday and painted it with undercoating on Saturday.
2. Even though the car's new paint job looks terrific now I suspect it will be covered with rust and scratches and dents before next winter.
3. I spent a fortune on new tires shock absorbers and brake linings for the car last week.

4. The car that my father drove back in the 1930s and 1940s a 1929 Whippet required very little maintenance and no major repairs during the ten or more years he drove it.

5. I have decided to park my car until gas prices go down and to ride my bicycle instead.

6. I don't suppose I'll ever be able to afford either the down payment or the interest or the insurance on a new Corvette the car of my dreams.

Parallel Structure

An important requirement in coordinate structures is that they be **parallel**. A structure is parallel when all of the coordinate parts are of the same grammatical form. The conjunctions must join comparable structures, such as pairs of noun phrases, verb phrases, or adjectives:

> *The little white-haired lady* and *her blond poodle* seemed to belong together. (NOUN PHRASE + NOUN PHRASE)
>
> The stew *smells delicious* and *tastes even better.* (VERB PHRASE + VERB PHRASE)
>
> The entire cast gave *powerful* and *exciting* performances. (ADJECTIVE + ADJECTIVE)

Unparallel structures occur most commonly with the correlative conjunctions: *both–and, either–or, neither–nor,* and *not only–but also.* For example, in the following sentences, the two coordinators introduce structures of different forms:

> *Either *they will fly straight home* or *stop overnight in Dubuque.* (SENTENCE + VERB PHRASE)
>
> *I'll either *take a bus* or *a taxi.* (VERB PHRASE + NOUN PHRASE)

Those sentences probably sound perfectly normal and grammatical to you. As a matter of fact, they're quite common in speech; chances are, no one would notice the unparallel structures. But writing is a different matter; written sentences deserve to be crafted carefully.

The problem in such sentences is easy to correct. It's just a matter of shifting one part of the correlative pair so that both introduce the same kind of construction:

> They will either *fly straight home* or *stop overnight in Dubuque.* (VERB PHRASE + VERB PHRASE)

6.1

I'll take either *a bus* or *a taxi*. (NOUN PHRASE + NOUN PHRASE)
Either *I'll take a bus* or *I'll take a taxi*. (SENTENCE + SENTENCE)

EXERCISE 3
Rewrite the following sentences, paying particular attention to the unparallel structures.

1. I can't decide which activity I prefer: to swim at the shore in July when the sand is warm or jogging along country roads in October when the autumn leaves are at their colorful best.
2. I almost never watch television. There is either nothing on that appeals to me or the picture disappears at a crucial moment.
3. I neither enjoy flying across the country nor particularly want to take the train.
4. The movie's starting time and whether we could afford the tickets were both more important to us than were the opinions of the reviewers.
5. According to the *Guinness Book of World Records*, each person in the United States posted an average of 413 letters in 1971 and a total of 85,187,000,000 letters and packages.
6. Either we Americans write a lot of letters or get a lot of junk mail.

Subject–Verb Agreement with Compound Subjects

Subject–verb agreement, which came up earlier in the discussion of verb forms, can also be a problem in sentences with compound subjects.

And. When nouns or noun phrases in the subject slot are joined by the coordinating conjunction *and* or the correlative *both–and*, the subject is plural:

My friends *and* relatives *are* coming to the wedding.
Both my friends *and* relatives *are* coming.

Or, Nor. The coordinating conjunction *or* and the correlatives *either–or* and *neither–nor* do not have the additive meaning of *and;* with *or* and *nor* the relationship is called disjunctive. In

compound subjects with these conjunctions, the verb will be determined by the closer member of the pair:

> Neither the speaker nor *the listeners were* intimidated by the
> protestors.
> Either the class officers or *the faculty advisor makes* the final decision.
> *Do the class officers* or the faculty advisor make the final decision?
> *Does the faculty advisor* or the class officers make the final decision?

If the correct sentence sounds incorrect or awkward because of the
verb form, you can simply reverse the compound pair:

> Either the faculty advisor or the *class officers make* the final decision.

When both members of the pair are alike, of course, there is no
question:

> Either *the president* or *the vice-president is* going to introduce the
> speaker.
> Neither the *union members* nor *the management representatives were*
> willing to compromise.

For most verb forms, you'll recall, there is no decision to be made
about subject–verb agreement; the issue arises only when the -*s*
form of the verb or auxiliary is involved:

> Either the class officers or *the faculty advisor will make* the final
> decision.
> Either the faculty advisor or *the class officers will make* the final
> decision.

6.2 *Coordination of Complete Sentences*

The concept of parallelism that applies to coordinate structures
within the sentence applies also to compound sentences. A compound sentence is effective only when the two clauses are, in fact,
coordinate: when they are equal in meaning or in the significance of

6.2

the information they convey. Here, for example, are some compound sentences—two complete sentences joined by *and:*

> We had a flat tire on the way to the picnic, and it really spoiled our day.
> We waited almost an hour for the train, and there was not even a place to sit.
> We went skiing on Saturday, and we had a wonderful time.
> The shelves were made of walnut, and they extended the length of the room.

Each of these sentences is grammatical, to be sure, but is the *and* really accurate? Are the ideas in the two coordinate structures equal in their importance to the sentence and its context? For example, does the coordinate structure in the first sentence reflect accurately the relationship of two experiences, the flat tire and the spoiled day? Would a cause–effect relationship be more accurate?

> The flat tire we had on the way to the picnic simply spoiled our day.
>
> *or*
>
> We had a miserable time at the picnic because of our flat tire.

Every sentence has a focus, a purpose. A compound sentence put together with *and* necessarily has two points of focus; the *and* says that they are equal. If that statement is inaccurate—if the two ideas are not equal—then *and* is the wrong connector; the sentence will lose all focus.

FOR CLASS DISCUSSION

1. Revise the other three sentences with *and* to give them a single point of focus:

   a. We waited almost an hour for the train, and there was not even a place to sit.

   b. We went skiing on Saturday, and we had a wonderful time.

   c. The shelves were made of walnut, and they extended the length of the room.

2. Consider the following sentence from a legal report on oil leases:

   > Many attorneys are unacquainted with oil and gas law, *and,* therefore, they are unable to offer advice concerning oil and gas leases to their clients.

Is *and* really accurate? How might you revise the sentence to focus on one idea instead of two?

6.2

The Coordinate Sentence with *But*

The two clauses joined by the coordinating conjunction *but* are also equal; they are equal in focus even though the second clause, the one signaled by *but*, introduces a contrast:

Jack went to the game, *but* Jill stayed home.
The turkey and dressing were delicious, *but* the rest of the dinner was disappointing.

Both of these sentences convey a clear contrast and an equal focus in their two clauses.

Here is another compound sentence with *but*; it is from an early draft of this book:

You're interested in the topic, but you just don't know much about it yet.

Is *but* accurate? Are the two ideas equal in focus? Is the second a genuine contrast to the first?

One way to answer those questions, to test the effectiveness of the compound with *but*, is to look at the first clause and try to predict the contrast:

You're interested in the topic, *but*—

But what?

You're interested in the topic, but *you don't want to write about it.*
or
You're interested in the topic, but *your teacher isn't.*

If you read the original sentence carefully, you'll discover that the first clause is clearly subordinate to the second; the sentence has only one main focus: the second clause. The revised sentence makes that relationship clear:

Even though you're interested in the topic, you just don't know much about it yet.

6.2

The second clause, the one introduced by *but*, was not predictable because it was not, in fact, a genuine contrast.

Remember, the compound sentence is appropriate only when the ideas in the two clauses are coordinate in meaning as well as in form, that is, when they are equals.

Punctuation of the Compound Sentence

We have two ways of punctuating the compound sentence: (1) using a comma along with the coordinating conjunction, as we have seen; and (2) using the semicolon, either with or without the conjunctive adverb.

The Comma-Plus-Conjunction. In the compound sentence with *and* or *but* or any other coordinating conjunction, we use a comma before the conjunction:

> I disapprove of his betting on the horses, *and* I told him so.
> He claims to have won fifty dollars, *but* I suspect he's exaggerating.

Notice that even when the conjunction is *but*, the comma comes before, not after, it. The slight pause you sometimes hear after *but* often fools the writer into putting a comma there. But that's wrong. *But* is one of the coordinating conjunctions; the comma comes before it.

The punctuation rule that applies to the compound sentence differs from the rule regarding internal coordinate structures. Between the sentences in a compound sentence we *do* use a comma with the conjunction; between the parts of a coordinate structure within the sentence we *do not.* When the clauses of a compound sentence are quite short and closely connected, however, writers sometimes omit the comma. The following sentence, for example, would probably be spoken without the pitch change that we associate with the comma:

> October came and the tourists left.

Incidentally, the coordinating conjunctions *and* and *or* can link a series of three or more sentences. When they do, the comma is used with each *and:*

Blanche filled the bags with hot roasted peanuts, *and* I stapled them shut, *and* Oggie packed them in the cartons.

The kids can wait for me at the pool, *or* they can go over to the shopping center and catch the bus, *or* they can even walk home.

6.2

In these two sentences, the first conjunction can be replaced by a comma:

Blanche filled the bags with hot roasted peanuts, I stapled them shut, *and* Oggie packed them in the cartons.

The Semicolon. Some people manage to go through life without ever using a semicolon—even people who do a lot of writing. If you are one of that group, you can be sure of one thing: Your writing is not as effective as it could and should be. But take heart! The semicolon is easy to use.

Think of the semicolon as the equivalent of the comma-plus-conjunction that connects compound sentences. You could even put that relationship into a formula:

$$(, + and) = (;)$$

That's one use of the semicolon. Here are some examples:

Pete packed the hot roasted peanuts into bags; I stapled them shut.

There was silence; I stood awkwardly, then moved to the door. There was still silence; white faces were looking strangely at me.
—RICHARD WRIGHT

She [Marilyn Monroe] seemed to have become a camp siren out of confusion and ineptitude; her comedy was self-satire, and apologetic—conscious parody that had begun unconsciously. She was not the first sex goddess with a trace of somnambulism; Garbo was often a little out-of-it, Dietrich was numb most of the time, and Hedy Lamarr was fairly zonked. But they were exotic and had accents, so maybe audiences didn't wonder why they were in a daze; Monroe's slow reaction time made her seem daffy, and she tricked it up into a comedy style.
—PAULINE KAEL

In such compound sentences the semicolon sends a message to the reader: "Notice the connection," it says. To understand the importance of the semicolon, imagine these compound sentences written separately—with periods instead of the semicolons. The connection between ideas would be much weaker.

The Semicolon with a Conjunctive Adverb. Another common use of the semicolon is in the compound sentence that includes a **conjunctive adverb,** such as *however, therefore,* or *moreover,* in the second clause:

> We worked hard for the Consumer Party candidates, ringing doorbells and stuffing envelopes; *however,* we knew they didn't stand a chance.
>
> We knew our candidates didn't have a hope of winning; *nevertheless,* for weeks on end we faithfully rang doorbells and stuffed envelopes.

As their name suggests, the conjunctive adverbs (or *adverbial conjunctions,* as they're sometimes called) do their joining job with an adverbial emphasis. And they also differ from other conjunctions in that, like so many of the adverbials, they tend to be movable; they need not introduce the clause:

> We worked hard for our candidates; we knew they didn't stand a chance, *however.*
>
> My tax accountant is not cheap; the amount of money she saves me, *however,* is far greater than her fee.

Note, too, that the conjunctive adverb is set off by a comma or commas.

Of all the adverbial conjunctions, only *yet* and *so* can be used with a comma instead of a semicolon between clauses:

> Several formations of birds were flying northward, *so* I guessed that spring was on the way.
>
> Several formations of birds were flying northward, *yet* I suspected that winter was far from over.

In both of these sentences, a semicolon could replace the comma, depending on the writer's emphasis. The semicolon would put extra emphasis on the second clause. *So* and *yet* straddle the border between the coordinating conjunctions and the conjunctive adverbs; they are often listed as both. In meaning, *so* is similar to *therefore,* and *yet* is similar to *however;* but unlike these conjunctive adverbs, *so* and *yet* always introduce the clause—they are not movable—so in this respect they are perhaps closer to the conjunctions. Sometimes we use both the conjunction and the adverbial: *and so; but yet.* (Incidentally, *yet* is also used to coordinate structures within the sentence: "a simple *yet* elegant dessert." The conjunction *so* is used only between sentences.)

6.2

The Semicolon with a Conjunction. The two uses of the semicolon we have just described—by itself and with a conjunctive adverb—are probably the most common; but there are also times when you will want to use a coordinating conjunction along with the semicolon, as in this sentence you are reading. As you can see, in the second clause the conjunction *but* signals a contrast. In fact, *but* is much like *however*, except that it is less formal. This use of the semicolon, then, includes the connection along with the conjunctive meaning of the coordinating conjunction—in this case the contrastive meaning—without the formality of the conjunctive adverb. Here are some other examples of the conjunction with the semicolon:

> The film, toward the end especially, mystified most audiences; *and* Arthur Clarke, who collaborated with the director Stanley Kubrick both on the screenplay and as scientific adviser, wrote the novel *2001* apparently to clear up the ideas behind the mystification.
>
> . . . .
>
> The film does not handle these ideas; *and* indeed it cannot, for movies cannot think without losing all their power of immediacy.
>
> —WILLIAM BARRETT

> They [Hemingway heroes] drink early and late; they consume enough beer, wine, anis, grappa, and Fundador to put them all into alcoholic wards, if they were ordinary mortals; *but* drinking seems to have the effect on them of a magic potion.
>
> —MALCOLM COWLEY

> For naturally the mock-attack [of tickling] will make the baby laugh only if it knows that it is a mock-attack; *and* with strangers one never knows. Even with its own mother there is an ever-so-slight feeling of uncertainty and apprehension, the expression of which alternates with laughter in the baby's behaviour; *and* it is precisely this element of apprehension between two tickles which is relieved in the laughter accompanying the squirm.
>
> —ARTHUR KOESTLER

6.2

Add punctuation to the following sentences—if they need it.

1. I took piano lessons for several years as a child but I never did like to practice.

2. When I started college I surprised both my mother and my former piano teacher by signing up for lessons moreover I practice every spare minute I can find.

3. I've discovered that although my hands are small I can stretch an octave I couldn't do that when I was twelve.

4. My fingers are terribly uncoordinated however every week the exercises and scales get easier to play.

5. I was really embarrassed the first few times I practiced on the old upright in our dorm's lounge but now I don't mind the weird looks I get from people.

6. Some of my friends even hum along or tap their feet to help me keep time.

7. I have met three residents on my floor who are really good pianists they've been very helpful to me when I've asked them for advice.

8. When I'm in my room studying I often play my collection of Glenn Gould records for inspiration.

9. I'm so glad that Bach and Haydn and Schumann composed music simple enough for beginners.

10. I'm sure that when I go home for term break my parents will be amazed at my progress when they hear me play some of my lessons from *The Little Bach Book.*

SENTENCE PRACTICE

Combine each group of ideas into a single sentence using any of the connection devices that you have studied, such as coordinating conjunctions, conjunctive adverbs, or subordinating conjunctions.

First think about which idea—or, in the compound sentence, ideas—should get top billing as the main clause; then experiment with various methods of connecting the other ideas in subordinate ways: as sentence modifiers, adjectivals, or adverbials.

1. The Leaning Tower of Pisa is 179 feet high.
   It leans 17 feet off the perpendicular.

The Italian Parliament recently authorized $12 million to keep the 809-year-old marble monument from falling.

2. Marathon County, Wisconsin, produces about 90 percent of the nation's ginseng.
Local farmers earn about $25 million a year from the crop.
The ginseng root is popular in China.
It is ground into tea or soup.
It has been credited with relieving tension, indigestion, high blood pressure, and arthritis, and with adding years to human life.
Ginseng is probably best known as an aphrodisiac.

3. Fingerprints have been used for criminal identification since 1891.
A police officer in Argentina introduced the method.
The FBI has the prints of over six million people on file.

4. The koala is the prototype of the cuddly teddy bear.
The koala is not a bear at all.
Its coat is not cuddly.
The koala is a marsupial.
Like its cousin the kangaroo, the female koala has a pouch.

5. The federal witness-protection service began in 1968.
It is under the aegis of the U.S. Marshal Service.
Four thousand people have been relocated under the program.
They have been given new identities.
The people are in extreme danger because they have testified against criminals.

6. The west coast of Norway has spectacular scenery.
Its fjords are unlike anything else on earth.
The fjords are narrow fingers of sea reaching up to eighty miles inland.
Mountain walls rise straight up out of the water thousands of feet.

7. In 1982 the New York State Legislature raised the drinking age from eighteen to nineteen.
Eighteen-year-olds from neighboring states will no longer be able to drive across the border to buy alcohol.
There will probably be fewer drinking problems among high school students.

8. Punctuation is important for the writer to understand.
Punctuation can change the meaning of a sentence.
Some aspects of punctuation are somewhat arbitrary.
The decision to set off opening and closing adverbials with commas is often arbitrary.

6.2

9. The weather in December is usually very winterlike.
   Last year Christmas Day was warm.
   The temperature hit the seventies.

10. There is a worldwide resurgence of interest in goats.
    Many people are still prejudiced against these useful and admirable beasts.
    Goats are raised for milk, for meat, for clothes (kidskin), and for their hair (mohair and cashmere).

Glossary of Grammatical Terms

(For further explanation of the terms listed here, check the index for page references.)

Absolute phrase.   A noun phrase that includes a postnoun modifier (commonly a participial phrase) related to the sentence as a whole. One kind of absolute explains a cause or condition (*"The weather being warm,* we decided to have a picnic"); the other adds a detail or a point of focus to the idea in the main clause ("He spoke quietly to the class, *his voice trembling"*).

Active voice.   A feature of transitive verb sentences in which the subject is the agent and the direct object is the goal or objective of the action. *Voice* refers to the relationship of the subject to the verb. (See also *Passive voice.*)

Adjectival.   Any structure, no matter what its form, that functions as a modifier of a noun—that is, that functions as an adjective normally functions.

Adjectival clause.   See *Relative clause.*

Adjective.   One of the four form classes, whose members act as modifiers of nouns; most adjectives can be inflected for comparative and superlative degree (*big, bigger, biggest*); they can be qualified or intensified (*rather big, very big*); they have characteristic derivational endings such as *-ous* (*courteous*), *-ful* (*beautiful*), and *-ary* (*complementary*).

Adverb. One of the four form classes, whose members act as modifiers of verbs, contributing information of time, place, reason, manner, and the like. Like adjectives, certain adverbs can be qualified (*very quickly, rather fast*); some can be inflected for comparative and superlative degree (*more quickly, fastest*); they have characteristic derivational endings such as *-ly* (*quickly*), *-wise* (*lengthwise*), *-like* (*crablike*).

Adverbial. Any structure, no matter what its form, that functions as a modifier of a verb—that is, that functions as an adverb normally functions.

Affix. A morpheme, or meaningful unit, that is added to the beginning (prefix) or ending (suffix) of a word to change either its meaning or its grammatical role or its form class: (prefix) *un*likely; (suffix) unlike*ly*, mean*ing*.

Agent. The initiator of the action in the sentence, the "doer" of the action. Usually the agent is the subject in an active sentence: "*John* groomed the dog"; "*The committee* elected Tim chairman."

Agreement. (1) Subject–verb. A singular subject in the third person takes the *-s* form of the verb: "*The dog barks* all night"; "*He bothers* the neighbors." A plural subject takes the base form: "*The dogs bark; they bother* the neighbors." (2) Pronoun–antecedent. The number of the pronoun (whether singular or plural) agrees with the number of its antecedent. "*The boys* did *their* chores; *each* boy did *his* best."

Appositive. A structure, usually a noun phrase, that renames another structure. An appositive can be thought of as either adjectival ("My neighbor, *a butcher at Weis Market*, recently lost his job") or nominal ("It is nice *that you could come*").

Auxiliary. One of the structure-class words, a marker of verbs. Auxiliaries include forms of *have* and *be*, as well as the modals, such as *will, shall,* and *must.* (See Chapter 2.)

Base. The morpheme that gives a word its primary lexical meaning: *help*ing, *reflect*.

Base form of the verb.   The uninflected form of the verb. In all verbs except *be*, the base form is the present tense: *go, help*. The base form also serves as the infinitive, usually preceded by *to*, called the sign of the infinitive. The base form of *be* is the infinitive, *be*.

Broad-reference clause.   An adjectival clause introduced by *which* that instead of modifying a noun modifies a complete sentence: "Judd told jokes all evening, *which drove us crazy*." The term *broad reference* also refers to pronouns such as *that*: "Judd told jokes again last night; *that* really drives me crazy." Often such sentences can be improved if the pronoun is turned into a determiner: "*That silly behavior of his* drives me crazy."

Case.   A feature of nouns and certain pronouns that denotes their relationship to other words in a sentence. Pronouns have three case distinctions: subjective (e.g., *I, they, who*); possessive (e.g., *my, their, whose*); and objective (e.g., *me, them, whom*). Nouns have only one case inflection: the possessive. The case of nouns when they are subjects and objects is sometimes referred to as *common case* because the two roles do not have distinctive forms.

Comparative degree.   See *Degree.*

Complement.   A slot in the predicate of the sentence that "completes" the verb. The term includes the subjective complement, the direct object, the indirect object, and the objective complement.

Compound.   See *Coordination.*

Conditional mood.   The attitude of probability designated by the modal auxiliaries *could, may, might, would*, and *should.*

Conjunction.   One of the structure classes, which includes connectors that coordinate ideas (e.g., *and, or*); subordinate ideas (e.g., *if, because, when*); and connect them with an adverbial emphasis (e.g., *however, therefore*).

Conjunctive adverb.   A conjunction that connects two sentences with an adverbial emphasis, such as *however, therefore, moreover, yet*, and *nevertheless.*

Coordination.   A way of expanding sentences in which two or more structures of the same form function as a unit. All of the sentence slots and modifiers in the slots, as well as the sentence itself, can be coordinated. Compound (coordinate) subject: *"Bill and Mary* went fishing." Compound verb: "They *laughed and sang.*" Compound adjectives: "Molly prepared a *simple but elegant* dessert."

Declarative.   A sentence in the form of a statement (as opposed to a command, a question, or an exclamation).

Degree.   The variations in adjectives that indicate the simple quality of a noun ("Bill is a *big* boy"); its comparison to another, the comparative degree ("Bill is *bigger* than Tom"); or to two or more, the superlative degree ("Bill is the *biggest* person in the whole class"). Certain adverbs also have degree variations, usually designated by *more* and *most.*

Derivational affixes.   Morphemes (combinations of sounds with meaning) that are added to the form classes, either to change the class of the word (*friend→ friendly; act→ action*) or to change its meaning (*legal→ illegal; boy→ boyhood*).

Determiner.   One of the structure-class words, a marker of nouns. Determiners include articles (*a, an,* and *the*); possessive nouns and pronouns (e.g., *Chuck's, his, my*); demonstrative pronouns (*this, that, these,* and *those*); quantifiers (e.g., *many, some*); specifiers (e.g., *each, every*); and numbers.

Direct object.   A nominal slot in the sentence pattern following a transitive verb. The direct object names the objective or goal or the receiver of the verb's action: "We ate *the peanuts*"; "The boy hit *the ball*"; "I enjoy *playing chess.*"

Elliptical clause.   A clause in which a part has been left out but is "understood": "Chester is older than I *(am old)*"; "Bev can jog farther than Otis *(can jog)*"; "When *(you are)* planning your essay, be sure to consider the audience."

Exclamatory.   A sentence that is an exclamation. It includes a shift in the word order of a basic sentence that focuses on a complement: *"What a beautiful day we're having!"* It is often punctuated with an exclamation point.

Expletive.   Often called an *empty word,* a structure word that enables the writer to delay the subject or to shift the stress: "A fly is in my soup. → *There's* a fly in my soup." The expletive *that* introduces a nominal clause: "I know *that he loves me.*" The expletive *or* introduces an explanatory appositive: "The African wildebeest, *or* gnu, resembles both an ox and a horse." The expletive plays a structural rather than a lexical role.

Form-class words. The large, open classes of words that provide the lexical context of the language: nouns, verbs, adjectives, and adverbs. Each has characteristic derivational and inflectional morphemes that distinguish its forms. (See also *Structure-class words.*)

Gerund. A verb functioning as a nominal: "I enjoy *jogging*"; "*Playing tennis* is good exercise."

Headword. The word that fills the noun slot in the noun phrase: "the little *boy* across the street."

Imperative. The sentence—and also the verb—in the form of a command. The imperative sentence includes the base form of the verb with an "understood" subject (*you*): "*Eat* your spinach"; "*Finish* your report as soon as possible."

Indicative mood. The expression of an idea as fact (as opposed to probability). Verb phrases without modal auxiliaries and those with *will* and *shall* are considered the indicative mood: "We *will go* soon"; "We *are going* tomorrow"; "When *are* you *going?*" See also *Subjunctive mood* and *Conditional mood.*

Indirect object. The nominal slot following the verb in a Pattern 3 sentence. In a sentence with a verb like *give*, the indirect object is the recipient; the direct object is the thing given: "We gave *our friends* a ride home."

Infinitive. The base form of the verb (the present tense), usually expressed with *to*, which is called the *sign of the infinitive.* The infinitive can function adverbially ("I stayed up all night *to study for the exam*"); adjectivally ("That is no way *to study*"); or nominally ("*To stay up all night* is foolish").

Inflectional suffixes. Morphemes (combinations of sounds, or single sounds, with meaning) that are added to the form classes (nouns, verbs, adjectives, and adverbs) to change their grammatical role in some way. Nouns have two inflectional suffixes (plural and possessive); verbs have four (*-s*, *-ing*, *-ed*, and *-en*); adjectives and some adverbs have two (*-er* and *-est*).

Interjection. A word considered independent of the main sentence, often punctuated with an exclamation point: "*Ouch!* My shoe pinches"; "*Oh!* Is that what you meant?"

Interrogative. A sentence that is a question in form: "Are you leaving now?" "When are you leaving?" The term *interrogative* is also used to describe pronouns and adverbs that introduce questions or nominal clauses: "*Where* are you going?" "I wonder *where* he is going."

Intonation pattern. The rhythmic pattern of a spoken sentence, determined by its stress and pitch and pauses.

Intransitive verb. The verbs of Pattern 4 sentences that require no complement to be complete. Some intransitive verbs require adverbials ("We *live in the country*"), but most are grammatical with nothing in the predicate except the verb: "The baby *is sleeping*"; "The children *rested.*"

Irregular verb. Any verb in which the *-ed* and *-en* forms are not that of the regular verb; in other words, a verb in which the *-ed* and *-en* forms are not simply the addition of *-d*, *-ed*, or *-t*. Compare the regular verb *walk* (*walked, walked*) with the irregular verb *eat* (*ate, eaten*). The irregular verbs are listed in section 2.9.

Linking verb. The verbs of Patterns 5 and 6, which require a subjective complement to be complete. *Be* is the most common of our linking verbs ("I *am* happy"; "He *is* my brother"). Other common linking verbs are verbs expressing the senses (*feel, smell, taste, sound*): "I *feel* good"; "It *tastes* funny."

Manner adverb. An adverb that answers the question of "why" or "in what manner" about the verb. Most manner adverbs are derived from adjectives with the addition of *-ly: quickly, exceptionally, merrily.*

Modal auxiliary. Auxiliaries that occupy the first slot in the verb string and may affect what is known as the *mood* of the verb, conveying probability, possibility, obligation, and the like. Four modal auxiliaries have both a base and a past form: *may/might, can/could, will/would,* and *shall/should. Must* and *ought to* have only one form. The modals *shall* and *will* are used to produce what we traditionally call the future tense: *will eat, shall eat.*

Mood. A quality of the verb denoting fact (indicative), conditions contrary to fact (subjunctive), and probabilities or possibilities (conditional).

Morpheme. A sound or combination of sounds with meaning.

Morphology. The study of morphemes.

Nominal. Any structure that functions as a noun phrase normally functions. The subject slot in the sentence, for example, is a nominal slot. Other nominal slots are the direct object, the indirect object, the subjective and objective complements, and the object of the preposition.

Nominative absolute. See *Absolute phrase.*

Nonrestrictive modifier. A modifier in the noun phrase that comments about the noun rather than defines it. Nonrestrictive modifiers following the noun are set off by commas.

Noun. One of the four form classes, whose members fill the head-word slot in the noun phrase; most nouns can be inflected for plural and possessive (*boy, boys, boy's boys'*). Nouns have characteristic derivational endings, such as *-ment* (*contentment*), *-ness* (*happiness*), and *-ion* (*action, compensation*).

Noun phrase. The noun headword with all of its attendant pre- and postnoun modifiers. See also *Nominal.*

Number. A feature of nouns and pronouns, referring to singular and plural.

Objective complement. The nominal or adjectival slot following the direct object in Pattern 2 sentences. The objective complement has two functions: (1) It completes the idea of the verb; and (2) it modifies (if an adjective) or renames (if a nominal) the direct object: "I found the play *exciting*"; "We consider Pete *a good friend.*"

Parallel structure. A coordinate structure in which all of the coordinate parts are of the same grammatical form: "The stew *smells delicious* and *tastes even better*" (parallel verb phrases); "The entire cast gave *powerful* and *exciting* performances" (parallel adjectives); "I'll take either *a bus* or *a taxi*" (parallel noun phrases).

Participial phrase. A verb phrase functioning as an adjectival: "The baby *sleeping in the crib* looks peaceful"; "The children, *excited by all the activity,* couldn't sleep." (See also *Participle.*)

Participle.   The *-ing* (present participle) and *-en* (past participle) forms of the verb: *eating, eaten.* It is traditional also to use the term *participle* to refer to these forms in their adjectival function: "the *swinging* door"; "the *broken* vase."

Passive voice.   A feature of transitive sentences in which the direct object (the objective or goal) is shifted to the subject position. The term *passive* refers to the relationship between the subject and the verb. To form the passive voice, we add *be* + *-en* to the active verb: "*The kids ate the cake.* → *The cake was eaten by the kids.*" (See also *Active voice.*)

Past tense.   The *-ed* form of the verb, usually denoting a specific past action: "I *raked* the yard yesterday."

Person.   A feature of personal pronouns that distinguishes the speaker (first person), the person or thing spoken to (second person), and the person or thing spoken of (third person).

Positive degree.   The uninflected form of an adjective or adverb that denotes a quality (*big*) without reference to another (*bigger*) or others (*biggest*). (See also *Degree.*)

Possessive case.   The inflected form of nouns (*John's, the dog's*) and pronouns (*my, his, your, her, their; its*) that denotes ownership ("*John's* book"); a measure ("*a day's* wages"; "*a dollar's* worth"); origin ("*his* suggestion"); and the like.

Predicate.   One of the two principal parts of the sentence, the comment made about the subject. The predicate includes the verb, together with its complements and modifiers.

Prefix.   An affix added to the beginning of a word to change its meaning: *un*likely, *il*legal, *pre*scribe, *re*new. One prefix, *en-*, can change the class of the word: *enable, endear, encourage, enthrone.*

Preposition.   A structure-class word found in pre-position to—that is, preceding—a noun phrase. Prepositions can be classed according to their form as simple (e.g., *above, at, in, of, off, on, through*) or phrasal (e.g., *according to, instead of*).

Prepositional phrase.   The combination of a preposition and a noun phrase; the noun phrase is known as the object of the preposition: *in the attic, over the hill, throughout the year, because of the weather.* Prepositional phrases function as adjectivals, adverbials, and, only rarely, nominals.

Present tense.   The base form and the *-s* form of the verb, used without auxiliaries: *help, helps.* The present tense denotes a present point in time ("I *understand* your position"), a habitual action ("I *jog* five miles a day"), or the "timeless" present ("Shakespeare *helps* us understand ourselves").

Pronoun.   A word that substitutes for a noun—or, more accurately, for a nominal—in the sentence.

Pronoun–antecedent agreement.   See *Agreement.*

Qualifier.   A structure-class word that qualifies or intensifies an adjective or adverb: "We worked *rather* slowly."; "We worked *very* hard."

Referent.   The thing (or person, event, concept, action, and so on)—in other words, the reality—that a word stands for.

Regular verb.   A verb in which the *-ed* form (the past tense) and the *-en* form (the past participle) are formed by adding *-ed* (or, in some cases, *-d* or *-t*). The two forms of regular verbs are always identical: "Yesterday I *walked* home"; "I *have walked* home every day this week."

Relative clause.   A clause introduced by either a relative pronoun (*who, which, that*) or a relative adverb (*where, when, why*) that modifies a noun: "The man *who lives next door* is ninety-five years old"; "The town *where I was born* just celebrated its centennial." The labels *relative clause* and *adjectival clause* are interchangeable.

Restrictive modifier.   A modifier in the noun phrase whose function is to restrict the meaning of the noun. A modifier is restrictive when it is needed to identify the referent of the headword. The restrictive modifier is not set off by commas.

Sentence modifier.   A word or phrase or clause that modifies the sentence as a whole. It generally comes at the beginning or the end of the sentence and is set off by commas.

Structure-class words.   The small, closed classes of words that explain the grammatical or structural relationships of the form classes: determiners, auxiliaries, qualifiers, prepositions, conjunctions, interrogatives, and expletives. (See also *Form-class words*.)

Subject. The opening slot in the sentence patterns, filled by a noun phrase or other nominal, that functions as the topic of the sentence: "*The evening* is lovely"; "*My friends* left early"; "*What you don't know* can't hurt you."

Subjective complement. The nominal or adjectival slot in Patterns 5 and 6 that completes the linking verbs: "The soup tastes *delicious*"; "John is *a teacher*." A Pattern 2 sentence in the passive voice also includes a subjective complement: "Ronald Reagan was elected *president*."

Subject–verb agreement. See *Agreement*.

Subjunctive mood. An expression of the verb in which the base form, rather than the inflected form, is used (1) in certain *that* clauses conveying strong suggestions or resolutions or commands ("We suggested that Mary *go* with us"; "I move that the meeting *be* adjourned"; "I demand that you *let* us in"), and (2) in expressions of wishes or conditions contrary to fact ("If I *were* you, I'd be careful"; "I wish it *were* summer"). The subjunctive of the verb *be* is expressed by *were*, or *be*, even for subjects that normally take *was*.

Subordinate clause. A dependent clause introduced by a subordinating conjunction, such as *if*, *since*, *because*, and *although*.

Subordinator. A subordinating conjunction that turns a complete sentence into a subordinate clause.

Suffix. An affix added to the end of a form-class word to change its class (*act → action; commend → commendable*) with derivational suffixes or to change its grammatical function (*boy → boys; walk → walking*) with inflectional suffixes. (See also *Derivational affixes* and *Inflectional suffixes*.)

Superlative degree. See *Degree*.

Tense. A feature of verbs expressing time. Tense is designated either by an inflectional change (*walked*), by an auxiliary (*will walk*), or both (*am walking, have walked*).

There **transformation.** A variation of a basic sentence in which the expletive *there* is added and the subject is shifted to a position following *be:* "*A fly is in my soup.* → *There is a fly in my soup.*"

Transitive verb.   The verbs of Patterns 1, 2, and 3, which require at least one complement, the direct object, to be complete. With only a few exceptions, transitive verbs are those that can be transformed into the passive voice.

Verb.   One of the four form classes, traditionally thought of as the action word in the sentence. A better way to recognize the verb, however, is by its form: Every verb, without exception, has an *-s* and an *-ing* form; every verb also has an *-ed* and an *-en* form, although in the case of some irregular verbs these forms are not readily apparent. Many verbs also have characteristic derivational forms, such as *-ify* (*typify*), *-ize* (*criticize*), and *-ate* (*activate*).

Verb-expansion rule.   The formula that describes our system for expanding the verb with auxiliaries to express variations in meaning: T + (M) + (*have* + *-en*) + (*be* + *-ing*) + V.

Verb phrase.   The main verb with all of its complements and modifiers, constituting the predicate of the sentence.

Part II

Words

Words, according to Aldous Huxley, "form the thread on which we string our experiences." In Part I we examined the patterns that our strings of experience fall into. In this section we shall look at the words themselves, the individual parts of the patterns.

This method of going from the larger unit to the smaller may seem illogical to you, but it's really not. Now that you have thought about sentence patterns and noun phrases and verb phrases, as well as various structures for expanding them, you have a context for thinking about the words themselves, a framework of sorts for helping you to organize them into logical categories.

We will begin, in Chapter 7, with the categories of words known as the parts of speech, after first looking briefly at morphemes, the units that make up words. Chapter 8 discusses the meaning of words and their effective use. Chapter 9 offers both hope and help for the poor speller. And, finally, Chapter 10 takes up some common questions of usage. At the end of this section is a glossary of usage, an explanation of terms that are often confusing for writers.

7

The Parts of Speech

If you heard a man say, "Boy wants drink water," your first response would probably be to label the speaker as foreign. Your second would be to share your water supply, because in spite of the ungrammatical sentence you would have understood the message. Under the same circumstances, a native speaker would have said, "My boy wants a drink of water," or "This boy wants to drink that water," or "The boy wants a drink of your water." The message would be more explicit, but the result would be the same: You'd share your water. The extra words wouldn't change the effect of the message, but they would provide a certain kind of meaning, a precision that the nonnative speaker's sentence lacked. Clearly, then, different kinds of words function in different ways to contribute different kinds of meaning.

In this chapter we will consider such differences in meaning and function, as well as differences in form. These are the differences that determine the classification of words into categories known as the *parts of speech.*

First, consider the differences between the words that the nonnative speaker used and those he left out. The ones he included gave the sentence the lexical meaning necessary to get the message across: "Boy wants drink water." What he omitted were certain grammatical signals. We don't know, for example, if *drink* is a noun or a verb; nor do we know the relationship of the speaker or the listener to the nouns *boy* and *water*. Nevertheless, the circumstances of the conversation (its setting or context) made the message clear.

This distinction between lexical and grammatical meaning determines our first division of the parts of speech: **form-class** words and **structure-class** words. In general, the form-class words provide the primary lexical content; the structure classes explain the grammatical or structural relationships. We can think of the form-class words as the bricks of the language and of the structure words as the mortar that binds them together.

Form Classes	Structure Classes
Noun	Determiner
Verb	Auxiliary
Adjective	Qualifier
Adverb	Preposition
	Conjunction
	Interrogative
	Expletive

When we look at the classes separately, we see that in general the form-class words are those that can undergo changes in form—those that are, in fact, distinguishable by their form—whereas the structure classes are not. But, as with almost every "rule" of the language, we will encounter exceptions. For example, auxiliaries are among the structure classes although some of them, because they are verbs, show form variations; some of the qualifiers are also distinguishable by their form. On the other hand, there are many words in the form classes that have no distinctions in form and do not undergo change—nouns like *chaos*, adjectives like *main*, and adverbs like *there*.

There is also one important class that doesn't appear on either of the preceding lists: the **pronoun.** Most pronouns have variations in form, and because they substitute for nouns and noun phrases, they are like the form-class words; but they also belong with the structure classes, because the possessive and demonstrative pronouns constitute important subclasses of the determiners (*my* house, *that* boat). Also, like the structure classes, pronouns are a small, closed class, admitting no new members. But such exceptions detract very little from the overall scheme of form and structure classes, which we will see reflects our intuitive understanding of words.

Before looking at the classes individually, we need to take up the basic unit of word formation, the **morpheme;** an understanding of the morpheme is central to the conscious understanding of words. Then we will take up the form classes, the structure classes, and the pronouns.

7.1 *Morphemes*

Syntax refers to the arrangement of sentence elements into meaningful patterns. When we study sentence patterns and their transformations and expansions, we are studying syntax. But the structural linguist begins the study of grammar not with syntax but with the study of individual sounds. At the next level comes **morphology,** the study of morphemes, combinations of sounds with meaning that make up words. So in this chapter, before taking up the word classes—the parts of speech—we will look briefly at morphemes, the units of meaning in words.

The definition of *morpheme,* "a combination of speech sounds that has meaning," may sound to you like the definition of *word.* That's not surprising because many morphemes are, in fact, complete words; *head* and *act* and *kind* and *walk* (as well as *and*) are words consisting of a single morpheme, a single meaningful combination of sounds. But others, such as *heads* and *actively* and *unkindly* and *walking,* consist of two or more morphemes, each of which has meaning itself. The success you had years ago in learning to read and spell depended in part on your awareness of the parts of words. For instance, in spelling a word like *actively,* you probably break it into its three morphemes automatically: Its **base,** or stem, is the verb *act;* the **suffix** -*ive* turns it into an adjective; and the suffix -*ly* turns the adjective into an adverb. Each of these three morphemes, the base and the two suffixes, has meaning itself; and each appears in other environments (other words) with the same meaning. These are the features that identify morphemes.

The individual morphemes in a word are not always quite as obvious as they are in words like *actively.* In the word *reflections,* for example, we can recognize the verb *reflect,* the *ion* that turns it into a noun, and the *s* that makes it plural: *reflect* + *ion* + *s.* But how about the word *reflect?* Is that a single morpheme or is it two? Are *re* and *flect* separate morphemes? Do they both have meaning? Do they appear in other environments with the same meaning? Certainly there are many words that begin with the prefix *re-*, for example, *reverse, rebound,* and *refer.* In all of these, *re* means "back," so *re* passes the morpheme test. How about *flect?* There's *inflect* and *deflect.* The dictionary reveals that all three words with *flect* are based on the Latin verb *flectere,* meaning "to bend." So in the word *reflections* we can identify four morphemes: *re + flect + ion + s.*

Incidentally, it's not unusual to need the dictionary to understand the morpheme structure of a word. The meanings of words often change, and their origins become obscure. Take the word *obscure,* for example. How many morphemes does it have, one or two? What does *scure* mean? Does it appear in other words with the same meaning? And is *ob* the same morpheme that we find in *observe?* What does it mean? And how about *observe?* Is that the verb *serve?* Such meanderings into the dictionary in search of clues about morphemes can heighten our awareness of words and our appreciation of language. And certainly an awareness of morphemes can enhance the understanding of language essential to both reader and writer. When we study etymology or historical linguistics, we begin to understand the intricacies of morphemes, their changes, and their variations. But in our limited examination of morphemes here, we will look mainly at those that signal the form classes, that contribute to our understanding of the parts of speech.

All words, as we have seen, are combinations of morphemes or, in the case of a word like *act* (as well as the eight words preceding it in this sentence), single morphemes. All morphemes are either **bases** (*act*), which we define as the morpheme that gives the word its primary lexical meaning, or **affixes** (for example, *-ive* and *un-*; and all affixes are either **prefixes,** those that come at the beginning of the word (*re-*), or suffixes, those that come at the end (*-ion*):

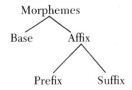

EXERCISE 1

> The following three sets of words illustrate some of the relationships of morphemes. In each set find the common base. What does the base mean? Draw vertical lines in the words to show the separate morphemes.

7.1

nova	auditor	durable
novitiate	audience	endure
innovate	inaudible	duration
novice	auditorium	during
novelist	audio	endurance

Derivational and Inflectional Affixes

There is one more feature of morphemes that we want to recognize: the classification of affixes as either **derivational** or **inflectional**. In the word *reflections*, the suffix *-ion* turns the verb *reflect* into the noun *reflection;* we call this a derivational suffix because we derive a noun from a verb. The *-s* does not change the class of the word, but it changes the meaning from singular to plural; we call this an inflectional suffix. All of the prefixes and suffixes change the word in one way or another. Prefixes, which are all derivational, usually change the meaning of the word rather than the class: *in*decent, *ab*normal, *pro*noun, *con*form, *re*flect. Derivational suffixes usually change the class: reflec*tion* (verb into noun), legal*ly* (adjective into adverb), legal*ize* (adjective into verb). But sometimes the derivational suffix simply alters the meaning while the class remains the same, as, for example, in turning a concrete noun into an abstract noun: *boyhood*. The inflectional suffixes, on the other hand, never change the class.

Of all the suffixes, only eight are inflectional:

1. *-s* (PLURAL) ⎱ **Noun inflections**
2. *-s* (POSSESSIVE) ⎰

3. *-s* (PRESENT TENSE) ⎫
4. *-ed* (PAST TENSE) ⎬ **Verb inflections**
5. *-en* (PAST PARTICIPLE) ⎪
6. *-ing* (PRESENT PARTICIPLE) ⎭

7. *-er* (COMPARATIVE) ⎱ **Adjective and adverb inflections**
8. *-est* (SUPERLATIVE) ⎰

7.2

Although we have several hundred suffixes, distinguishing between those that are derivational and those that are inflectional is easy. All the suffixes other than these eight, as well as all the prefixes, are derivational.

7.2 The Form Classes

The contrast in the sentences of the native and nonnative speakers at the beginning of this chapter illustrates the difference in the kind of meaning that form-class words and structure-class words contribute to the sentence. The nonnative speaker communicated with nouns and verbs, the form-class words that provide the lexical content of the language: "Boy wants drink water." The native speaker's version of that sentence includes such word classes as determiners and prepositions, the structure words that signal grammatical meaning: "*My* boy wants *a* drink *of your* water." One difference between the two kinds of words, then, is the distinction between lexical and grammatical meaning.

The characteristic of form, introduced in the discussion of morphemes, is another difference between them. In general, words of the four form classes are distinguishable by their inflectional suffixes and by certain characteristic derivational suffixes and prefixes. In this section we will look at these features of nouns, verbs, adjectives, and adverbs.

Nouns

We traditionally define *noun* on the basis of meaning, as "the name of a person, place, thing, idea, event, or the like," and that definition works fairly well. After all, we've been learning names since we spoke our first words: *Mama, Daddy, cookie, baby.* The word *noun*, in fact, comes from *nomen*, the Latin word for "name."

But meaning is only one clue in distinguishing nouns from other parts of speech. We also recognize nouns by the words that signal them. When we see a determiner—a word like *the, my,* or *an*—we know what part of speech will follow, although not necessarily as the next word: *the* books, *my* sister, *an* honest opinion. Determiners are simply not used without nouns. Our third criterion, form, is somewhat more objective than the others; we can often differentiate the form classes from each other without reference to either meaning or context, simply on the basis of their derivational and inflectional suffixes.

7.2

Noun Derivational Suffixes. Each of the four form classes has its own inventory of derivational suffixes. The *-ion*, for example, converts the verb *reflect* into a noun, so we call it—and its variations *-tion*, *-sion*, *-cion*, and *-ation*—a noun-forming suffix. A quick check of the dictionary reveals that all of the *-ion* words listed on the first few pages are also nouns formed from verbs:

abbreviation	abstraction	accusation
abolition	acclamation	acquisition
abomination	accommodation	action
abortion	accreditation	activation
abrasion	accumulation	adaptation

Two examples of *-ion* words that function as both nouns and verbs are *partition* and *mention;* you may be able to think of others. But chances are that you will find few, if any, *-ion* words that are not nouns; *-ion* is a reliable signal. Many other derivational suffixes do the same job, that of converting verbs into nouns:

accomplish	+	-ment→	accomplishment
accept	+	-ance →	acceptance
arrive	+	-al →	arrival
assist	+	-ant →	assistant
deliver	+	-y →	delivery
depart	+	-ure →	departure
teach	+	-er →	teacher

We also derive nouns from adjectives with such suffixes as *-ness* (*happiness, gentleness*); *-ity* (*purity, humidity*); and *-ery* (*bravery*).

EXERCISE 2
  Transform the following words into nouns by adding a derivational suffix. Are there any that have more than one noun form?

  1. please + _____ = _____
  2. wise + _____ = _____

7.2

3. ideal + _____ = _____
4. heal + _____ = _____
5. derive+ _____ = _____
6. inflect + _____ = _____
7. form + _____ = _____
8. revive + _____ = _____
9. seize + _____ = _____
10. retire + _____ = _____

Noun Inflectional Suffixes. The other aspect of form that differentiates the four form classes both from the structure classes and from each other is the set of inflectional morphemes that each form class has. Our nouns have two grammatical inflections, one indicating number (*plural*) and one indicating case (*possessive*):

Singular	Plural	Singular Possessive	Plural Possessive
cat	cats	cat's	cats'
dog	dogs	dog's	dogs'
horse	horses	horse's	horses'
mouse	mice	mouse's	mice's

In Chapter 9 we take up some of the spelling problems that occur with these inflections.

Other Noun Classes

NONCOUNTABLE NOUNS. The foregoing set of inflectional forms describes many—perhaps even most—nouns, but certainly not all of them. Many nouns are noncountable, so they have no plural form; and many nouns are simply not used in the possessive case.

The noncountable nouns can be classified according to meaning, as either concrete or abstract:

Concrete	Abstract
luggage	happiness
furniture	peace
homework	contentment
cinnamon	trouble
water	appreciation

Frequently these noncountable nouns are used without determiners:

7.2

> I have *trouble* finding time for *homework*.

Whether or not to use a determiner is often a problem for nonnative speakers; anyone who says

> *I have *a trouble* finding time for *the homeworks*.

is obviously not a native speaker of English. But the native speaker uses determiners automatically when the occasion calls for them:

> *The trouble* I have with *my homework* never goes away.

PLURAL-ONLY FORMS. Some nouns, even when singular in meaning, are plural in form. One such group refers to things that are in two parts—that are bifurcated, or branching: *scissors, shears, clippers, pliers, pants, trousers, slacks, shorts, glasses, spectacles*. As subjects of sentences, these nouns present no problems with subject-verb agreement: They take the same verb form as other plural subjects do. Interestingly, even though a pair of shorts is a single garment and a pair of pliers is a single tool, we use the plural pronoun in reference to them:

> I bought a new pair of shorts today; *they're* navy blue.
> I've lost my pliers; have you seen *them*?

A different situation arises with certain plural-in-form nouns that are sometimes singular in meaning. Nouns such as *physics, mathematics,* and *linguistics,* when referring to an academic discipline or course, are treated as singular:

> Physics *is* my favorite subject.
> Linguistics *is* the scientific study of language.

But sometimes such nouns as *mathematics* and *statistics* are used with plural meanings:

> The mathematics involved in the experiment *are* very theoretical.

7.2

The statistics on poverty levels in this country *are* quite depressing.

These uses also call for the plural pronoun.

COLLECTIVE NOUNS. Nouns such as *family, choir, team, majority, minority*—any noun that names a group of individual members—can be treated as either singular or plural, depending on context and meaning:

> The *family have* all gone their separate ways.
> The whole *family is* celebrating Christmas at home this year.
> The *majority* of our city council members *are* Republicans.
> The *majority* always *rules.*

Other singular-in-form nouns also have a plural meaning in certain contexts; among them are *remainder, rest,* and *number.* Their number depends on their modifiers:

> The *remainder* **of the job applicants** *are* waiting to fill out forms.
> The *rest* **of the books** *are* being donated to the library.
> A *number* **of customers** have *come early.*

This system also applies to certain indefinite pronouns, such as *some, all,* and *enough:*

> *Some* **of the books** *were* missing.
> *All* **of the cookies** *were* eaten.

Notice what happens to the verb in such sentences when the modifier of the subject headword is singular:

> The *rest* **of the map** *was* found.
> *Some* **of the water** *is* polluted.
> *All* **of the cake** *was* eaten.
> The *remainder* **of this chapter** *is* especially important.

The pronoun to use in reference to these noun phrases will depend on the meaning, and it will usually be obvious:

They (some of the *books*) were missing.
It (some of the *water*) is polluted.

One special problem occurs with the word *none*, which has its origin in the phrase *not one*. Because of that original meaning, many writers insist that *none* always be singular, as *not one* clearly is. However, a more accurate way to assess its meaning is to recognize *none* as the negative, or opposite, of *all* and to treat it in the same way, with its number (whether singular or plural) determined by the number of the modifier:

None **of the guests** *want* to leave.
None **of the cookies** *were* left.
None **of the cake** was *left*.

FOR CLASS DISCUSSION

Identify the nouns in the following passage. Which of them have inflectional and/or derivational morphemes that helped you identify their class? Do any of the nouns have no clues of form? If so, how did you recognize them as nouns?

We hold these truths to be self-evident, that all men are created equal, that they are endowed by their creator with certain unalienable rights, that among these are life, liberty, and the pursuit of happiness.

Verbs

The traditional definition of *verb*, like that of *noun*, is based on meaning: "a word denoting action, being, or state of being." When we look for the verb in a sentence, we look for the word that tells what is happening, and most of the time this method works. But a much more reliable criterion for identifying a verb is that of form. Some verbs have derivational endings that signal that they are verbs; and all verbs, without exception, fit into the verb-expansion rule, the system of adding auxiliaries and inflections described in Chapter 2.

Verb Derivational Affixes. Many of the root words, or bases, that take noun-forming suffixes are verbs to begin with; for example, most

of our nouns with *-ion* are formed from verbs. The opposite operation—deriving verbs from other form classes—is less common. We
are more likely to use a noun as a verb as it is, without changing its
form at all: We *chair* meetings and *table* motions; the carpenter *roofs*
the house; the cook *dishes* up the food; the painter *coats* the wall with
paint; the gardener *seeds* the lawn and *weeds* the garden; the
winemaker *bottles* the wine.

But there are a few verb-forming affixes that combine with
certain nouns and adjectives:

type	+	-ify	→	typify
dark	+	-en	→	darken
active	+	-ate	→	activate
legal	+	-ize	→	legalize

In addition to these suffixes, one prefix, *en-*, can turn nouns and
adjectives into verbs and alter the meaning of other verbs: *enable,
enact, enchant, encounter, encourage, encrust, endear, enforce,
enlighten, enthrone.* But compared with the large number of derivational morphemes that signal nouns, the inventory of verb-forming
affixes is fairly small.

Verb Inflectional Suffixes. The verb-expansion rule describes the
system of adding auxiliaries and inflectional suffixes to all verbs,
without exception. So, as a clue in identifying the part of speech we
call the *verb*, the inflectional system is completely reliable. All verbs,
without exception—even those with irregular *-en* and *-ed* forms—
have both *-s* and *-ing* forms. This is one of the few rules in English
without an exception, and it means we can identify a word as a verb
simply by noting its *-s* and *-ing* forms. Every verb has the other three
forms as well—the base, the *-ed*, and the *-en*—but they may not be as
recognizable: Verbs like *hit* and *put*, for instance, show no changes in
form from the base (*hit, put*) to the *-ed* form (*hit, put*) to the *-en* form
(*hit, put*). Yet the *-s* and the *-ing* forms are exactly like those of every
other verb: *hits, puts, hitting, putting.* The verb inflectional system is
so regular, in fact, that we can define *verb* on that basis alone: A word
belonging to a set that doesn't include an *-s* or an *-ing* form is simply
not a verb.

FOR CLASS DISCUSSION

   Try using the following words (which we generally think of as nouns) as verbs by adding the four inflections that verbs have (-*s*, -*ed*, -*en*, and -*ing*): *tree, water, rock, air,* and *fire.* Look around the room for other nouns—names of objects or parts of the room—and try using them as verbs, for example, *pencil, paper, wall, board,* and *chalk.*

Adjectives

   In terms of form, adjectives are not as easily identifiable in isolation as are nouns and verbs. Often we need either meaning or context for clues. In Chapter 1 we made use of a fairly reliable "adjective test" frame, a way to use the context of a sentence to discover if a word is an adjective:

   The _____ NOUN is very _____.

Only an adjective will fit into both slots. But in some cases the form of the word also provides clues. A number of derivational suffixes signal adjectives.

Adjective Derivational Suffixes. The most reliable derivational suffix identifying a word as an adjective is -*ous*. We know that *gorgeous, porous, courageous,* and *contagious* are adjectives simply on the basis of form. Here are some other adjective-forming suffixes:

-*y*	merry, funny
-*ful*	beautiful, wonderful
-*ic*	terrific, ascetic
-*ate*	fortunate, temperate
-*ish*	childish, reddish
-*ary*	fragmentary, complimentary
-*ive*	punitive, active
-*able*	variable, amenable

As clues to adjectives, these suffixes are not as reliable as -*ous* because they show up occasionally in other form classes, too: hand*ful* (noun), pan*ic* (noun, verb), pun*ish* (verb). But it is safe to say that most words with these endings are adjectives.

7.2 *Adjective Inflectional Suffixes.* The inflectional suffixes that pattern with adjectives are *-er* (the sign of the **comparative degree**) and *-est* (the **superlative**):

Positive:	young	smart
Comparative:	younger	smarter
Superlative:	youngest	smartest

The *-er* form is used in the comparison of two nouns—that's why this form is called the *comparative degree:*

> Mary is *younger* than Phyllis.
> Phyllis is the *smarter* of the two.

The comparative degree with *than* can also be followed by a complete sentence rather than a noun phrase:

> Mary is smarter *than I suspected.*

We use the *-est* form, the superlative degree, when singling out one of more than two nouns:

> Tom was *the oldest* person in the room.
> Of the three candidates, Sarah is *the smartest.*

A small group of words that take these inflections can serve as either adjectives or adverbs, so the inflectional test is not completely reliable in identifying a word as an adjective:

early	fast	late	high
earlier	faster	later	higher
earliest	fastest	latest	highest
hard	long	low	deep
harder	longer	lower	deeper
hardest	longest	lowest	deepest

Another word that we could add to this list is *near* (*nearer, nearest*), which can serve not only as an adjective or an adverb, but also as a preposition ("Our seats were near the fifty-yard line"); *near* is the only preposition that takes inflections. In short, the possibility of making a word comparative or superlative is not exclusive to adjectives.

For many adjectives the comparative and superlative degrees are not formed with *-er* and *-est* but with *more* and *most*, which we can think of as alternate forms of the morphemes *-er* and *-est*. In fact, adjectives of more than one syllable generally pattern with *more* and *most*, with certain exceptions: two-syllable adjectives ending in *-y* or *-ly* (*prettiest, friendlier, lovelier*); some ending in *-le* (*nobler, noblest*); *-ow* (*narrower, narrowest*); and *-er* (*tenderest*).

But *more* and *most* are not exclusive to adjectives either. The *-ly* adverbs, those derived from adjectives, also have comparative and superlative versions: *more* quickly, *most* frequently. And there are some adjectives, such as *former, main,* and *principal,* that have no comparative and superlative forms.

In spite of all of these limitations, we have no difficulty distinguishing adjectives in sentences. First of all, we know the positions they fill in the sentence patterns: as subjective and objective complements and in noun phrases as prenoun modifiers. And although nouns can also fill all of these slots, the differences in the forms of nouns and adjectives make it easy to distinguish between them.

On the subject of the comparative and superlative degree, we should also note that adjectives can be compared in a negative sense with *as, less,* and *least:*

This picnic is not *as exciting as* I thought it would be.

This picnic is *less exciting than* I thought it would be.

This is *the least exciting* picnic I've ever attended.

(A different version of the first sentence would be "The picnic is about as exciting as I expected" or, simply, "The picnic is as exciting as I expected," both of which may convey a somewhat negative meaning.)

We should also note some exceptions to the regular comparative and superlative forms:

good	bad	far	far
better	worse	farther	further
best	worst	farthest	furthest

7.2

EXERCISE 3

Fill in the blanks with the comparative and superlative degrees of the adjectives listed. Some may require more *and* most.

Positive	Comparative	Superlative
friendly	_____	_____
helpful	_____	_____
staunch	_____	_____
wise	_____	_____
awful	_____	_____
rich	_____	_____
mellow	_____	_____
expensive	_____	_____
valid	_____	_____
pure	_____	_____
able	_____	_____
cheap	_____	_____

Subclasses of Adjectives. The adjective test frame ("The _____ NOUN is very _____"), which is useful in identifying adjectives, is also useful in helping distinguish subclasses of adjectives: those that are limited to the prenoun slot and those that are limited to the complement slots.

There are actually three slots that adjectives fill in the sentence patterns: They are used as subjective and objective complements (where they are called *predicative adjectives*) and as modifiers in the noun phrase (where they are called *attributive adjectives*). Most adjectives can fill all three slots; the test frame uses two of them.

But a small number are limited. We say *the main reason* but not *The reason is main.* On the other hand, we say *The house was ablaze* but not *the ablaze house.*

There are a few others, such as *fond, ready, ill,* and *well,* that rarely appear in attributive position in reference to animate nouns. We may refer to a "ready wit" but rarely to a "ready person." We may talk about an "ill omen" but rarely an "ill person"; we are more likely to say a "sick person."

Incidentally, not all predicative adjectives take *very,* the sample **qualifier** in the test frame. We probably wouldn't say "very afraid" or "very awake"; we would be more likely to say "very much afraid" or "very much awake." But these so-called A-adjectives do combine with other qualifiers: *quite* afraid, *extremely* afraid, *completely* awake, *wide* awake.

Another subclassification of adjectives relates to their ability to combine with qualifiers. Certain adjectives denote meanings that are absolute in nature, for example, *unique, round, square, perfect, single,* and *double.* These can fill both the attributive and the predicative slots, but they generally cannot be qualified or compared:

> The plan is unique.
> *The plan is very unique.
> The plan is very unusual.
> *My plan is more unique than yours.
> My plan is more unorthodox than yours.

Unique means "one of a kind"; there are no degrees of uniqueness, just as there are no degrees of roundness: Something is either round or it's not. Because of this absolute meaning, many writers avoid such phrases as "more perfect" or "very round."

Adverbs

Of all the form classes, adverbs are the hardest to pin down in terms of both form and position. Many of them have no distinguishing affixes, and except with certain verbs, such as *live, put, set,* and *lay,* they fill no required slots in the sentence patterns. The fact that adverbs are often movable is perhaps their most distinguishing characteristic.

Adverb Derivational Suffixes. One common indicator of form that we do have is the derivational suffix -*ly,* which we use to derive adverbs of **manner** from adjectives—adverbs that tell *how* or *in what way* about the verb:

> He walked *slowly.*
> She answered *correctly.*

But it is not a completely reliable adverb signal, as -*ly* also appears on nouns (*folly, bully*) and on adjectives (*friendly, homely, godly, lovely, ugly*). But we are safe in saying that most -*ly* words are adverbs, simply because there are so many adjectives that we can turn into adverbs with this addition.

Besides -*ly*, three other derivational suffixes produce adverbs: -*ward*, -*like*, and -*wise*. Words ending in -*ward* signal direction: *homeward, forward, backward, upward, downward;* -*like* words indicate manner: *birdlike, wavelike;* -*wise* words include both old usages, such as *otherwise, lengthwise,* and *crosswise,* and new ones that are regarded by some writers as unnecessary jargon, such as *budgetwise, weatherwise, moneywise,* and *profitwise.*

Adverb Inflectional Suffixes. The comparative and superlative inflections, -*er* and -*est* (or their alternate forms *more* and *most*), combine with adverbs as well as with adjectives, although in a much more limited way. In the discussion of adjectives, we listed a few words that serve as both adjectives and adverbs: *early, late, hard, fast, long, high, low, deep,* and *near.* These are simply adverbs made from adjectives without the addition of -*ly;* they are sometimes referred to as *flat adverbs.* Except for a few others like *soon* and *often,* they are the only adverbs that take -*er* and -*est;* most of the -*ly* adverbs take *more* and, occasionally, *most* in forming the comparative and superlative degrees.

A great many adverbs have neither derivational nor inflectional affixes that distinguish them as adverbs. Instead, we recognize them by the information they provide, by their position in the sentence, and often by their movability:

> **Time:** now, today, nowadays, yesterday, then, already
>
> **Duration:** always, still
>
> **Frequency:** often, seldom, never, sometimes, always
>
> **Place:** there, here, everywhere, somewhere, upstairs
>
> **Direction:** away, thence
>
> **Concession:** still, yet

There are also a number of words without form distinctions that can serve as either prepositions or adverbs: *above, around, behind, below, down, in, inside, out, outside, up.*

FOR CLASS DISCUSSION

Demonstrate the class of the following words by adding the inflectional endings that will combine with them:

7.2

launch	deep	nice
staunch	keep	rice
paunch	jeep	splice

EXERCISE 4

Fill in the blanks with variations of the words shown on the chart, changing or adding derivational morphemes to change the word class.

	Noun	**Verb**	**Adjective**	**Adverb**
1.	grief			
2.		vary		
3.				ably
4.		defend		
5.	economy			
6.			pleasant	
7.	type			
8.		prohibit		
9.				long
10.			valid	
11.		appreciate		
12.	beauty			
13.		accept		
14.			pure	
15.		continue		
16.			customary	

7.3 *The Structure Classes*

In contrast to the large, open form classes, the *structure classes* are small; they comprise only a few hundred words in all. And these classes are closed. Although new words regularly enter the language as nouns and verbs as the need arises for new vocabulary, determiners, prepositions, auxiliaries, and the like remain constant from one generation to the next. As native speakers, we pay little attention to the structure words, and until we hear a nonnative speaker struggling with them, we probably don't appreciate the importance of the grammatical sense that they contribute.

Part of that grammatical sense comes from the stress–unstress pattern of speech, the rhythm of the language. Most structure words are unstressed: They have the lowest volume, providing valleys between the peaks of loudness that fall on the stressed syllables of the form-class words. One reason we must listen so carefully in order to understand the inexperiencned foreign speaker—and often the experienced one as well—is the breakdown of that signaling system. When structure words are given equal stress, their role as signaler tends to be lost.

The first three structure classes we will look at are those that signal specific form classes: determiners, the signalers of nouns; auxiliaries, the signalers of verbs; and qualifiers, the signalers of adjectives and adverbs. Then we will look at prepositions and conjunctions, both of which have connective roles; interrogatives, the signalers of questions; and expletives, which serve as structural operators of various kinds.

Determiners

This chapter opened with a sentence lacking all of the structure words: "Boy wants drink water." Most noticeably missing are the determiners, the signalers of nouns. Determiners signal nouns in a variety of ways: They may define the relationship of the noun to the speaker or the listener (or the reader); they may identify the noun as specific or general; they may quantify it specifically or refer to quantity in general. Following are the most common classes of determiners:

7.3

Articles	Possessive Nouns	Demonstrative Pronouns	Numbers
the	John's	this	one
a	my son's	that	two
an	etc.	these	etc.
		those	

Possessive Pronouns		Quantifiers		Specifiers
my	its	all	few	each
your	our	some	fewer	every
his	their	many	more	either
her	whose	much	most	neither
		any	less	
		enough		

EXERCISE 5
Identify the determiners in the following sentences.

1. My sister doesn't have enough money for her ticket.
2. John's roommate went home for the weekend.
3. Every course I'm taking this term has a midterm exam.
4. Bill spent more money on the week's groceries than he expected to.
5. I spend less time studying now than I did last term.
6. I haven't seen either movie, so I have no preference.

Auxiliaries

Here are the auxiliaries, which you studied in Chapter 2:

have	be	can	do
has	is	could	does
had	are	will	did
having	am	would	
	was	shall	
	were	should	
	been	may	
	being	might	
		must	
		ought to	

Like the determiners and the other structure classes, the auxiliary class is limited in membership and closed to new members. Including all the forms of *have* and *be*, the modals, and the forms of *do*, the list of regular auxiliaries numbers around two dozen. The verbs *have to*, *get*, and *keep* also sometimes function as modal-like auxiliaries:

> He *has to* go.
> She *got* going.
> She *got* to go.
> They *kept* going.

Two other verbs, *dare* and *need*, sometimes function as modals in negative sentences and in questions:

> She *need* not go.
> I don't *dare* go.
> *Dare* we try?
> *Need* you go?

The auxiliaries differ from the other classes of structure words somewhat in both form and function. With only two exceptions, *must* and *ought to*, the auxiliaries have inflectional variations that signal changes in meaning. Because *have* and *be*, our most frequently used auxiliaries, fill the verb slot themselves, they of course have all of the usual verb inflections. *Be* has even more than usual, with its eight forms. Even the stand-in auxiliary *do* and the other marginal modals undergo inflectional variations in their auxiliaries. So, in terms of their form, auxiliaries are very much like the form-class words.

In function the auxiliaries are perhaps more intimately connected to verbs than are determiners to nouns, because they alter the verb's meaning in important ways and often determine the form that it takes. Forms of *have* require the *-en* form of the main verb and forms of *be* the *-ing* form—or, in the case of the passive transformation (see Chapter 3), the *-en* form.

EXERCISE 6

   Underline the auxiliaries in the following sentences. Circle the main verb.

1. I have been having problems with my car.
2. Many women don't dare walk alone in this neighborhood after dark.
3. I should never eat tomatoes.
4. My sister has always been called Raggie.
5. Sally will be helping us with the party.
6. Margie has to leave early.
7. The kids are really frustrating me today.
8. The teens can be frustrating years for some adolescents.
9. Bill didn't get his car registered before the deadline.
10. Mine has been registered for months.

Qualifiers

As the following lists demonstrate, there are many words that can serve as qualifiers or intensifiers to alter the meaning of adjectives and adverbs. (In the adjective test frame, the word *very* is used to represent all the possible qualifiers.)

In the traditional classification of parts of speech, these modifiers of adjectives and adverbs are classed with the adverbs. However, we are limiting our use of the label *adverb* to modifiers of verbs, that is, to those words that add to the verb information of time, place, frequency, cause, manner, and the like. We separate the two classes, adverbs and qualifiers, because, except for a few words like *really* that serve both functions ("I really tried," "I tried really hard"), they tend to be mutually exclusive classes. In American English we rarely use *very* or *quite* or *extremely* to modify verbs; they generally qualify or intensify only adjectives and adverbs:

   We walked *very* slowly.
   *We walked *very*.
   He tried *quite* hard.
   *He *quite* tried.

7.3

The following list of qualifiers can be used with the positive form of most adjectives, such as *good* and *soft*, and with adverbs of manner, such as *rapidly:*

very	really	fairly
quite	pretty	mighty
rather	awfully	too

A second group of qualifiers can be used with the comparative degree of adjectives, such as *better* and *nicer,* and with comparative adverbs, such as *sooner, later, nearer,* and *farther:*

still	even	much	no

And there are a number of others that have a limited distribution:

right now	*just about* there
wide awake	*almost* there
just so	

Many others are used in colloquial expressions:

right nice	*darn* right	*real* pretty

And some of the adverbs of manner, the *-ly* adverbs, are themselves used as qualifiers with certain adjectives:

dangerously close
particularly harmful
absolutely true

Prepositions

The preposition (meaning "placed before") is a structure word found in pre-position to—preceding—a noun phrase. Prepositions are among our most common words in English; in fact, of our twenty most frequently used words, eight are prepositions: *of, to, in, for, with, on, at,* and *by.*[1] Prepositions can be classified according to form as **simple** (one-word) or **phrasal** (multiple-word).

Simple Prepositions. The following list includes the most common simple prepositions:

about	beneath	in	through
above	beside	into	throughout
across	between	near	till
after	beyond	of	to
against	but (except)	off	toward
along	by	on	under
among	concerning	onto	underneath
around	down	out	until
at	during	over	up
before	except	past	with
behind	for	regarding	within
below	from	since	without

Note that we label these words as *prepositions* only when they are followed by a noun phrase—that is, only when they are part of prepositional phrases. In the following sentence, for example, *up* functions as an adverb, not a preposition:

The price of heating oil went *up* again.

Words like *up* also function as part of two-word, or phrasal, verbs, such as *hold up:*

A masked gunman *held up* the liquor store.

But in the following sentence, *up* is a preposition, part of a prepositional phrase:

We hiked *up the steep trail.*

---

[1] This frequency count, based on a collection of 1,014,232 words, is published in Henry Kučera and W. Nelson Francis, *Computational Analysis of Present-Day English* (Providence, R.I.: Brown University Press, 1967).

7.3 ***Phrasal Preposition.*** Some phrasal prepositions are simply two prepositions combined to produce a third meaning:

> along with   but for
> up to   out of

Many of the phrasal prepositions are combinations of other parts of speech with prepositions:

according to	in place of
because of	in spite of
in accordance with	instead of
in connection with	in regard to
in front of	on account of
in lieu of	on top of

The above lists include the most common, although certainly not all, of the prepositions. We use prepositions automatically, as we do the other structure words, in spite of the sometimes subtle differences in meaning that they can express: *below* the stairs, *beneath* the stairs, *under* the stairs, *underneath* the stairs; *in* the room, *inside* the room, *within* the room. As native speakers we understand these distinctions, and, except for a few idioms that sometimes cause problems of usage, we rarely hesitate in selecting the right preposition for the occasion.

Conjunctions

We use conjunctions to connect words and phrases and clauses within the sentence and to connect the sentences themselves. Within the sentence our most common connectors are the simple coordinating conjunctions and the correlative conjunctions. For joining sentences we use, in addition, the subordinating conjunctions, also called *subordinators,* and the conjunctive adverbs. Relative pronouns also function as connectors, joining relative, or adjectival, clauses to nouns; relative adverbs introduce both adjectival and adverbial clauses. These categories of conjunctions are also discussed in the pages noted.

Coordinating Conjunctions (pages 124–132)

7.3

and, or, but, yet, for

Correlative Conjunctions (pages 127–129)

both–and, either–or, neither–nor, not only–but also

Conjunctive Adverbs (pages 134–135)

Result: therefore, so, consequently, as a result
Concession: however, nevertheless, yet, at any rate
Apposition: namely, for example, that is
Addition: moreover, furthermore, also, in addition
Time: meanwhile, in the meantime
Contrast: instead, on the contrary, on the other hand

(Note that the above list includes certain simple adverbs, such as *also* and *instead,* and adverbial prepositional phrases, such as *in the meantime* and *on the contrary,* that often function as sentence connectors.)

Subordinating Conjunctions (pages 111–113)

Simple: after, although, because, before, if, since, when, while
Phrasal: as if, as long as, as soon as, even though, in order that, provided that

Relatives (pages 75–81)

who, whose, whom, which, that, where, when, why, whoever

Interrogatives

As their name implies, the **interrogatives**—*who, whose, whom, which, what, how, why, when,* and *where*—introduce questions:

What are you doing here?
How did you get here?

7.3

The function of such questions, of course, is to elicit particular information.

The interrogatives also introduce clauses that fill NP slots in the sentence patterns. Such clauses are sometimes referred to as indirect questions:

> Tell me *why he came.*
> I wonder *who came with him.*
> *Whose car he drove* is a mystery to me.

These clauses, which act as noun phrase substitutes, are discussed in Chapter 5. (We should note that the interrogatives are the same words that in other contexts are classified as relative pronouns or relative adverbs.)

Expletives

Rather than providing grammatical or structural meaning as the other structure words do, the expletives—sometimes defined as "empty words"—generally act simply as operators that allow us to manipulate sentences in a variety of ways.

THERE. The *there* transformation, as we saw in Chapter 1, enables us to delay the subject in certain kinds of sentences, thus putting it in the position of main stress, which generally falls in the predicate half of the sentence:

> An airplane is landing ⟶ There's an áirplane landing
> on the fréeway   on the freeway.

IT. In the following sentences, the expletive *it* acts much as *there* does, in that it delays the actual subject:

> *It's* nice *to be here with you.* (To be here with you is nice.)
> *It's* nice *seeing you again.* (Seeing you again is nice.)
> *It* was really beautiful, *that display of blooms at the orchid show.* (That display of blooms at the orchid show was really beautiful.)

THAT. One of our most common expletives, *that*, introduces a nominal clause (see pages 104–109):

I hope *that our exam is easy.*

OR. The expletive *or* introduces an explanatory appositive:

The study of sentences, *or syntax,* helps us to appreciate how much we know when we know language.

This *or* should not be confused with the conjunction *or.*

EXERCISE 7
Identify the part of speech of each italicized word.

1. I found some rare stamps *and* postmarks *on an* old envelope.
2. *Four* friends of mine *from* the dorm waited in line *for* sixteen hours, *for* they were determined to get tickets *for* the World Series.
3. *As* the experts predicted, the Republicans chose *an* ultraconservative *at* the convention.
4. We should *be* arriving *by* six, *but* don't wait for us.
5. Our group *of* tourists will take *off* at dawn *if* the weather permits.
6. We *are* now studying the structure *of* sentences, *or* syntax, in *our* English class.
7. We *will* warm up *with* a game of one-on-one *while* we wait for the rest of the players.
8. We had *too* many problems with our *two* new puppies, so we gave them both *to* the neighbors.

7.4 Pronouns

Because pronouns straddle the line between the form classes and the structure classes, we will regard them as separate from both groups. Like the form-class words, many pronouns have inflectional endings, so they do have form distinctions similar to those of nouns, and because they substitute for nouns and noun phrases, we could argue that they belong with the form classes. On the other hand, the

7.4

possessive and demonstrative pronouns act as determiners; and like the structure classes, pronouns constitute a small, closed class, admitting no new members. So we will simply consider the pronouns by themselves.

As their name suggests, pronouns are words that stand for nouns. Perhaps a more accurate label would be *pronominal*, as they actually stand for any construction that functions as a nominal in the sentence. We refer to the noun or nominal that the pronoun stands for as its antecedent.

Most pronouns replace an entire noun phrase:

> *The pistachio nut ice cream at Meyer's Dairy* is delicious.
> ↓
> *It* is delicious.

Sometimes the pronoun includes a modifier that is, itself, pronoun-like:

> Actually, I like *all their flavors*.
> ↓
> Actually, I like *them all*.

Pronouns also substitute for other nominals, such as verb phrases and clauses:

> The judge warned my brother *to stay out of trouble*.
> ↓
> He told me *that*, too.
> *Where you spend your time* is none of my business.
> ↓
> { *That* } is none of my business.
> { *It* }

All pronouns are not alike. The label *pronoun* actually covers a wide variety of words, many of which function in quite different ways. What follows is a brief description of the main classes of pronouns.

Personal Pronouns

The personal pronouns are the ones we usually think of when the word *pronoun* comes to mind. We generally label them on the basis of person and number:

Person	Number	
	Singular	*Plural*
1st	I	we
2nd	you	you
3rd	$\left\{\begin{array}{l} \text{he} \\ \text{she} \\ \text{it} \end{array}\right.$	they

For example, we refer to *I* as the "first-person singular" pronoun and to *they* as the "third-person plural." In addition, the third-person singular pronouns include the feature of gender: masculine (*he*), feminine (*she*), and neuter (*it*).

Incidentally, the source of a great deal of the sexism in our language is the lack of a singular personal pronoun in the third person that includes both genders. Our plural pronoun (*they*) includes both. But when we need a pronoun to refer to a person who could be either male or female, such as "a student" or "the writer," the long-standing tradition has been to use the masculine (*he/his/him*). Attempts to promote *s/he* in recent years have been unsuccessful. The most likely solution, a usage that is becoming quite common, is the adoption of *they* for both singular and plural, which is fairly standard in speech in reference to such pronouns as *someone* and *everyone*:

> Someone broke into our car last night; *they* stole our camera and luggage.
>
> Everyone dashed out immediately when the teacher said *they* could leave.

(This issue is discussed further on pages 245–246.)

The forms of the personal pronouns given in the preceding set are in the subjective case; this is the form used when the pronoun serves as the subject or the subjective complement. The personal pronouns also inflect for the possessive case, as nouns do, and for the objective case, an inflection that nouns do not have. The possessive-case forms of pronouns function as determiners, as we saw in Chapter 4. The objective case is used for pronouns in all of the other NP slots: direct object, indirect object, objective complement, and object of the preposition.

7.4

Subjective:

| I | we | you | he | she | it | they |

Possessive:

| my | our | your | his | her | its | their |
| (mine) | (ours) | (yours) | (his) | (hers) | | (theirs) |

Objective:

| me | us | you | him | her | it | them |

The alternative forms of the possessive case, shown here in parentheses, are used when the headword of the noun phrase is deleted. They function as nominals:

> This is *my book*. This is *mine*.
> This is *her book*. This is *hers*.

The same system applies to possessive nouns. They sometimes function as nominals:

> This is *John's book*. This is *John's*.
> *Mary's book* is missing. *Mary's* is missing.

Pronoun Errors. Most of the pronoun errors that writers make occur with the subjective and objective cases:

> *Me and my brother are good friends.
> *There's no rivalry between my brother and *I*.

All of the object slots in the sentences—direct, indirect, objective complement, and object of the preposition—take the objective form of the pronoun. The subject slot, of course, takes the subjective case. So in the two foregoing sentences, the pronouns need to be switched, as follows:

> *I* and my brother (or, more commonly, My brother and *I*) are good friends.
> There's no rivalry between my brother and *me*.

EXERCISE 8

7.4

Substitute personal pronouns for the italicized nouns and noun phrases
in the following sentences.

1. *John and Betty* have bought a new house.
2. *Bev and I* will be going to the game with *Otis*.
3. *Betsy* bought *that beautiful car of hers* in Chicago.
4. Both of *her cars* are gas guzzlers.
5. There have always been uneasy feelings between *the neighbors and my husband*.
6. I want *Tony* to approve of *the project*.
7. The kids gave *their father and me* a bad time.
8. *My brother, who works for the U.S. Navy in California*, spends his weekends in Las Vegas.

Reflexive Pronouns

Reflexive pronouns are those formed by adding -*self* or -*selves* to a form of the personal pronoun:

Person	Number	
	Singular	*Plural*
1st	myself	ourselves
2nd	yourself	yourselves
3rd	himself herself itself	themselves

The reflexive pronoun is used as an object when its antecedent is the subject of the sentence:

John cut *himself.*

I glanced at *myself* in the mirror.

I cooked dinner for Tim and *myself.*

Raggie cooked dinner for Phil and *herself.*

7.4

The reflexive pronoun *myself* is also fairly common in certain spoken sentences where the standard version would call for the objective case, *me:*

> Joe cooked dinner for Mary and *myself.*

In standard written English the object of the preposition *for* would be *Mary and me* because the antecedent of *myself* does not appear in the sentence.

> Joe cooked dinner for *Mary and me.*

Both versions are unambiguous; both forms of the first-person pronoun, *me* and *myself,* can refer only to the speaker. However, with third-person pronouns different forms produce different meanings:

> Joe cooked dinner for Mary and *himself* (Joe).
> Joe cooked dinner for Mary and *him* (someone else).

EXERCISE 9
Fill the blanks with the appropriate reflexive pronouns.

1. Mary gave _____ a black eye when she fell.
2. Joe and Henry cooked _____ a steak.
3. The ceramic figurine sat by _____ on the shelf.
4. We sat by _____ in the front row.
5. Kris cooked a delicious Mexican feast for Ross and _____ .
6. Wearing our new designer jeans, Karen and I admired _____ in the mirror.

Intensive Pronouns

Also known as the *emphatic reflexive pronouns,* the intensive pronouns have the same form as the reflexives. The intensive pronoun serves as an appositive to emphasize a noun, but it need not directly follow the noun:

> I *myself* prefer white wine.

I prefer white wine *myself*.

Myself, I prefer white wine.

Reciprocal Pronouns

Each other and *one another* are known as the *reciprocal pronouns*. They serve either as determiners (in the possessive case) or as objects, referring to previously named nouns: *Each other* refers to two nouns; *one another* generally refers to three or more:

John and Claudia help *each other*.

They even do *each other's* chores.

All the students in my study group help *one another* with their homework.

Demonstrative Pronouns

The demonstrative pronouns, one of the subclasses of determiners, include the features of "number" and "proximity."

Proximity	**Number**	
	Singular	*Plural*
Near	this	these
Distant	that	those

That documentary we saw last night really made me think, but *this* one is simply stupid.

Those trees on the ridge were almost destroyed by the gypsy moths, but *these* seem perfectly healthy.

Like other determiner classes, the demonstrative pronoun can be a substitute for a nominal as well as a signal for one:

These old shoes and hats will be perfect for the costumes.

These   will be perfect for the costumes.

To be effective as a nominal, the demonstrative pronoun must replace or stand for a clearly stated antecedent. In the following

74

example, *that* does not refer to "solar energy"; it has no clear antecedent:

> Our contractor is obviously skeptical about solar energy. *That* really surprises me.

Such sentences are not uncommon in speech, nor are they ungrammatical. But when a *this* or a *that* has no specific antecedent, the writer can ususally improve the sentence by providing a noun headword for the demonstrative pronoun—by turning the pronoun into a determiner:

> Our contractor is obviously skeptical about solar energy. *That attitude* really surprises me.

A combination of the two sentences would also be an improvement over the vague use of *that:*

> Our contractor's skepticism about solar energy really surprises me.

Indefinite Pronouns

The miscellaneous category of the indefinite pronouns includes a number of words listed earlier as determiners:

Quantifiers: all, some, many, much, any, enough

Specifiers: each, every, either, neither

One is also commonly used as a pronoun (as are the other cardinal numbers—*two, three,* and so on), along with its negative, *none.* As a pronoun, *one* often replaces only the headword, rather than the entire noun phrase:

> The blue *shoes* that I bought yesterday will be perfect for the trip.
> The blue *ones* that I bought yesterday will be perfect for the trip.

The personal pronoun, on the other hand, would replace the entire noun phrase:

> *They* will be perfect for the trip.

Some of the indefinite pronouns can be expanded with *-body,* *-thing,* and *-one:*

some	body thing one	every	body thing one	any	body thing one	no	body thing one (two words)

These pronouns can take modifiers in the form of clauses, verb phrases, and prepositional phrases:

Anyone who wants extra credit in psych class can volunteer for tonight's experiment.

Everyone reporting late for practice will take fifteen laps.

Nothing on the front page interests me anymore.

And unlike most nouns, they can be modified by adjectives in postheadword position:

I don't want *anything sweet.*

I think that *something strange* is going on here.

Such indefinite pronouns as *each, someone,* and *anyone* are clearly singular; others, such as *everyone* and *everybody,* are clearly plural in meaning, although singular in form. We can think of these as having collective reference, just as nouns like *crowd* and *team* sometimes have. The pronoun that refers to them should be plural:

The teacher told *everyone* to sit down, and *they* did.

This issue is discussed in more detail in pages 245–246.

Relative Pronouns

The relative pronouns *who, which,* and *that* introduce clauses (adjectival clauses) that modify the nouns that are the antecedents of these pronouns. *Who* inflects for both possessive (*whose*) and objective (*whom*) cases. Also among the relative pronouns are the expanded or indefinite relatives, those that include *-ever: whoever, whosever, whomever, whichever,* and *whatever.* See the discussion of adjectival clauses on pages 75–81.

7.4 Interrogative Pronouns

The list of interrogative pronouns is similar to that of the relatives: *who* (*whose, whom*), *which*, and *what*. See page 179.

EXERCISE 10

Identify all of the pronouns in the following sentences. Identify the subclass to which each pronoun belongs.

1. When Bob ordered a pizza with everything, I ordered one, too.
2. Karen and Kristi shopped for new shoes but couldn't find any they liked.
3. Someone was standing in the shadows, but we couldn't see who it was.
4. All that I had for lunch was an apple.
5. Jim and Ralph didn't eat much either, but they both ate more than I.
6. I will go along with whatever you decide.
7. One hour of studying was enough for me.
8. Quarreling among themselves, the committee members completely disregarded one another's suggestions.
9. Tell me what you want.
10. The employment office will find a job for whoever wants one.

8

Using Words Effectively

8.1 The Meaning of Words

In one sense the heading you just read—"The Meaning of Words"—is meaningless. The theory of general semantics, which deals with the study of meaning, holds that words themselves have no meaning. The meaning of words is in the people who use them, not in the words themselves.

To understand what the semanticists mean, try to imagine yourself as part of a nonliterate society. Not only are there no books or newspapers or billboards or junk mail in your world, there is not even a writing system: no alphabet, no way of recording experiences or feelings or ideas. Further—and this may tax your imagination the most of all—there is no dictionary.

Such a nonliterate world is like the world of a young child just learning language. The child at first hears and internalizes and uses language completely outside the world of writing. The language of the family unit may even include words that are uniquely its own—words that have never been written down. The word for water may be *wawa;* the word *horse,* a hard one for children to pronounce, may become *wasie;* a particular toy may have its own invented name, such as *blim.* The meanings of the words *wawa* and *wasie* and *blim* reside only in the users. A conversation about the wawa and the wasie and the blim will have no meaning for the outsider who hears it. The family unit, then, is a kind of speech community in which agreed-on combinations of sounds have meaning for its members. That, of course, is what language is: meanings shared by the speakers. The child learning to talk about the environment comes to internalize meanings. The family cat—a yellow, striped alley cat named Tigger—is, for the child, the embodiment of the word *cat*, just as the individual parents are the embodiment of the words *mama* and *daddy*. The dictionary may define *cat* and *mama* and *daddy* in a general way—and it does—but it cannot and does not record the meanings of the words as they have been internalized by the child. The dictionary can record only generalities; it cannot record the meanings that individuals have for words.

In thinking about the heading "The Meaning of Words," then, we will acknowledge two referents for the word *meaning*. It refers primarily to an individual's responses to words based on that person's own experiences; it also refers to the shared, generalized meanings of the larger speech community, as recorded in the dictionary. These two ways of looking at meaning are related to, although not synonymous with, the connotation and denotation of words.

8.2 *Denotation and Connotation*

We generally think of the denotative meaning, or denotation, of a word as its dictionary definition, and of the connotative meaning, or connotation, as an individual's feelings about or emotional response to the word. As those definitions suggest, the denotation of the word tends to be the same for everyone and the connotation different.

An obvious illustration is the word *grandmother*, defined by the dictionary as "the mother of one's father or mother." But along with that objective definition, each of us responds to the word in an individual way. Our response to *grandmother*—our internalized meaning—comes from many quarters: from our own grandmothers, from Little Red Riding Hood's grandmother, from Norman Rockwell paintings of grandmothers, and from various women with grandchildren whom we have known. Our response to the word is likely to be bound up with feelings about all of those grandmothers. On meeting her friend Billy's grandmother for the first time, a little girl com-

8.2

mented, "You don't look like Billy's grandmother." The little girl's internalized meaning of *grandmother* simply did not fit the slender, sun-tanned woman wearing a tennis dress.

But it is not only the connotation of words that includes subjective judgments; denotative meanings do so as well. The dictionary definition—the shared definition—often includes features that go beyond objective qualities. For example, consider the words we have in English to denote "the absence of flesh," as the dictionary puts it: *thin, skinny, slender, slim, lean, spare, lanky, scrawny,* and *gaunt,* among others. The dictionary differentiates among these according to the feelings or responses that the words stimulate:

- *Lean* implies a healthy, natural absence of fat.
- *Spare* suggests a sinewy frame without superfluous flesh.
- *Lanky* implies an awkward tallness and leanness, and often loose-jointedness.
- *Skinny* and *scrawny* imply extreme thinness that is unattractive and indicative of a lack of vigor.
- *Gaunt* implies a bony thinness such as that caused by a wasting away of the flesh from hunger or suffering.
- *Slender* and *slim* suggest a physical spareness that is more-or-less pleasing in proportion.

We think of these differences as connotative, but they are actually denotative differences. They are shared definitions, recorded in the dictionary.

It is our personal, internalized definitions or responses to words that constitute their connotations. The word *lanky* may bring to mind the 6'8" center on the basketball team or the thirteen-year-old boy next door who grew six inches during the summer. If we consider them nice people, then *lanky* will probably evoke a positive response. The word *gaunt,* on the other hand, may bring to mind pictures of starving children in Southeast Asia or the emaciated title character in Melville's story "Bartleby the Scrivener," who wasted away and died. The word *gaunt* is upsetting. The dictionary and the thesaurus can suggest generalizations with their definitions and synonyms; they cannot record the particulars. Our connotations for the words are the particulars.

What are the consequences of denotation and connotation for the writer? Our purpose in any writing task is to call up a response in the

8.3

reader: We will accomplish that purpose to the extent that the reader's response is the one we intended. If we could understand and predict all the meanings that the reader has for the words we write, then perhaps we could predict the response. But of course we can't do that; often we don't even know our own responses to words before they impinge on our nervous system.

Then what can we do as writers? First, we can be word-conscious, recognizing the powers of suggestion that words have for people. We can pay attention to the distinctions among words, to the nuances of meaning in our shared definitions. We didn't describe Billy's grandmother as "skinny" because of the connotation of that word. For most people, the words "skinny, sun-tanned grand-mother" would suggest an old woman with white hair and tan, perhaps leathery, wrinkled skin; she certainly wouldn't be wearing a tennis dress. We wanted the reader to see Billy's grandmother as an attractive woman, one who would look good in a tennis dress, the response that *slender* evokes.

Words do indeed have powers of suggestion. Consider another pair of similar-sounding words: *mystic* and *mysterious*. In writing about her work in a hospital, a student described a room that was out of bounds, one that only a chosen few had access to. She was curious about the closed door. She wrote that there was something "mystic" about it. Did she really mean "mystic"? The dictionary defines *mystic* as "belonging to esoteric rites or doctrines; of obscure or occult character or meaning." Our shared meanings for *mystic* are associated with the supernatural. That wasn't her intention at all. She meant, simply, *mysterious*, a word with quite different powers of suggestion.

Obviously the writer has no control over the reader's personal definitions, or connotations, of words. But personal definitions develop in part from the shared meanings of the community, those denotative meanings recorded in the dictioary.That is, the dictionary's sources for definitions are our sources, too—the language in use all around us.

8.3 Categories of Meaning

All of us carry around in our heads a dictionary of sorts, or lexicon—an inventory of the words that belong to us. Every word in the lexicon is cloaked in layers of meaning, some that are connotative and others that are denotative. A noun, for example, occupies a place in our lexicon according to certain built-in denotative features that limit its use in various ways. We can picture these features in a hierarchy, each level of which has consequences for our use of the noun itself as well as for the determiner and the other words we use with it:

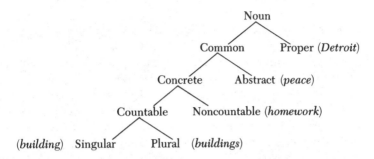

The categories are, in fact, restrictions built into the word that determine which branch it belongs in; each noun carries with it only those features in the higher intersections (or nodes) that it is connected with: *Homework* is a noncountable, concrete, common noun; *building* is a singular, countable, concrete, common noun. Determiners also include built-in features or restrictions that are related to those of nouns. The determiner *a* (or *an*) includes the features "singular" and "countable," so we are restricted from using it with *homework*. It signals only those nouns that fit in the lowest, left-hand branch, like *building*.

The countable–noncountable feature applies also to certain adjectival modifiers, such as *less, fewer, amount of,* and *number of.* The commercials that advertise a certain brand of soft drink as having "less calories" than another have failed to make the countable–noncountble distinction: *Calories* is a countable noun (the fact that it's plural tells us that). We generally use *less* with noncountables. That soft drink may have *fewer* calories; it does not have *less.* We would also talk about the "number of calories" not the "amount of calories." Such noncountables as *water* and *sugar* and *love* and *homework* pattern with "amount of"; *calories* does not.

All nouns have features other than those shown in the foregoing hierarachy. Here, for example, are some further characteristics of countable nouns:

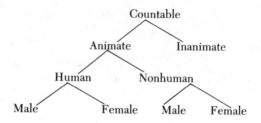

All of the lowest branches can be further divided into "singular" and "plural" and into "child" and "adult." The word *girl*, for example, would include the features "singular, child, female, human, animate, countable."

Our definitions of the words in our lexicon also include features that differentiate the words within a particular semantic field. We can picture these features as a hierarchy, too, much like the taxonomy that scientists use in classifying plants and animals. Each level—phylum, class, order, family, genus, and species—includes features that differentiate it from the other levels. The farther down the hierarchy, the smaller the details that distinguish the classes.

Here, for example, is a classification of the semantic features of the "building" words in our lexicon:

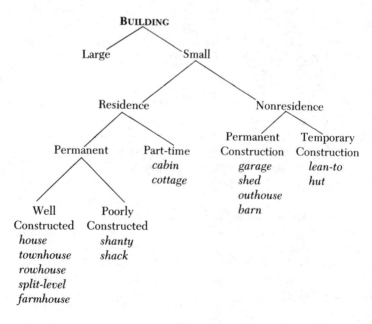

Again, what are the consequences for the writer? If this semantic scheme is accurate, the word *shanty*, which includes all of the features of the nodes above it, can be defined as a small residential building of poor construction that is used as a permanent residence. That's its denotation. For many people the word *shanty* brings to mind—connotes—the pictures we have seen of makeshift living conditions in slums, of the "shantytowns" and "Hoovervilles" that are, unfortunately, often permanent quarters for the poor. The instructor who reminds you to use concrete words is saying, in effect, "Go farther down the hierarchy." That's where the words become specific and loaded with meaning.

8.3

Incidentally, the context in which these words appear can certainly alter their place in the hierarchy. Obviously someone could live permanently in a cabin or a garage or a lean-to or a hut; and, of course, there are shanties that are temporary, not permanent, dwellings. As a writer you must be sensitive to the generally accepted meaning that readers are likely to bring to the word and then make clear your specialized use of it.

FOR CLASS DISCUSSION

1. Finish the other side of the "building" hierarchy with words that denote large buildings. Here are some to start you off: *high-rise, tenement, skyscraper, office complex, convention center, church, capitol, mansion, arena.* What subclasses do you have for such buildings in your lexicon?

2. Take a general verb like *move* and think of all the subclasses of verbs that we use to express movement. Put them into a hierarchy, beginning perhaps with *slow* and *fast.* Here are some words to start you off: *run, race, jump, saunter, shuffle, hop, leap.* You might also consider branches that refer to direction or to style of movement. Now try a hierarchy for a mental activity like *think.*

3. Words are powerful. As a writer you can use to advantage the power of suggestion that words hold in calling up images in the mind of the reader. But to use words effectively, you have to understand the responses that they are likely to evoke. Consider the following sets of related words. What is the difference in your response to each? In what setting would you use or avoid them?

house / home   a good time / a blast
hearth / fireplace   lad / boy

8.3

infant / baby	genius / egghead
slumber / sleep / snooze	famous / notorious
pleasure / fun	foolhardy / daring / rash / bold
dinner / supper	cabin / cottage
companion / friend / buddy	woman / lady
colleague / co-worker	change / degenerate
dine / eat	skillful / cunning
picky / careful	stingy / thrifty / tight
frock / dress	cocky / confident

4. In *Language in Thought and Action* S.I. Hayakawa says that a language is "not just the sounds and the spellings, but more importantly the whole repertory of semantic reactions which the sounds and spellings produce in those who speak and understand the language." Think about how that "repertory of semantic reactions" would differ with each word in the sets listed in question 3. What differing responses are the words likely to evoke? You might think of them on such scales as these:

```
positive  ................................... negative
modern..................................... old-fashioned
formal ..................................... informal
intimate.................................... distant
purr ....................................... growl
```

5. Betrand Russell is credited with the following "conjugation of an irregular verb":

> I am firm.
> You are obstinate.
> He is pigheaded.

Using some of the groups of words in question 3, and adding to them as necessary, try your own conjugations. Example: "I am slender; you are thin; he is scrawny."

6. No one understands the power of words (and pictures, too, of course) better than the advertising industry. The writers of advertising copy of both print ads and television commercials understand fully the power that words have to stimulate images in the mind of the reader or listener. Consider the following captions from cigarette ads, all from a single issue of *Time;* all of the ads picture healthy-looking, active people enjoying themselves— jogging or skiing or exploring exotic places:

Pleasure is where you find it. Discovery Viceroy satisfaction. Lucky Strikes again. The moment is right for it. Vantage pleasure when you want good taste and low tar, too. Kent when you know what counts. The pleasure is back. Barclay.

8.4

What immediate response is the writer expecting? (The eventual response, of course, is the purchase of the particular brand.) Notice also the brand names, especially Viceroy, Vantage, Kent, and Barclay? What responses does the cigarette manufacturer expect from the name?

7. Check recent magazines for car advertisements. What do the words say about the response that the writer expects from the reader? What are some of the connotations of the words that the ads attribute to cars?

8. Stereotypes are word associations. The stereotypical grandmother is the gray-haired plump lady in the Norman Rockwell pictures—the "grandmotherly type." What are some other types that you associate with particular words? Describe the following people; then compare your descriptions with those of your classmates. Include the person's clothes, facial expressions, hobbies, and reading preferences.

   a. The driver of a red pickup truck.

   b. The driver of a red Corvette.

   c. The driver of a Buick station wagon.

   d. A farmer.

   e. A chess player.

   f. A librarian.

8.4 Levels of Diction

Another basis on which we categorize the words in our lexicon has to do with their appropriateness. At what level of diction—that is, in what kinds of writing situations—is a particular word or phrase appropriate? The situations for language (which, after all, is a form of social behavior) resemble other forms of social behavior, such as dress codes. Certain occasions call for special clothes: For weddings we dress up; for picnics we don't; blue jeans are inappropriate for formal

8.4

banquets; bathing suits are inappropriate almost everywhere in public except at beaches and swimming pools.

Words, too, have their place. Although most words are fairly neutral and are thus appropriate to most situations, others are somewhat limited in their use. For example, a person may be cocky in some ways and genteel in others, but it's unlikely that the two adjectives would appear in the same description. *Cocky* and *genteel* represent different levels of diction. For the same reason, the verbs *fetch* and *reiterate* are unlikely to appear in the same passage, as are *cops* and *police officers*.

The level of diction is the degree of formality or informality of a particular writing situation. (The term *writing situation*, as you will discover in Chapter 11, refers to the interplay of topic, purpose, and audience.) Here, for example, is a most unlikely note for you to write to your roommate—or even to your teacher or your boss:

> Please excuse my absence from our scheduled engagement.

Such formality smacks of pretentiousness. You'd be much more likely to write, simply,

> Sorry I missed our meeting. See you later.

Most of the prose that you read and write falls somewhere between the highly formal and the highly informal—between the language of presidential inaugural addresses and the language of informal notes. The diction of most essays that you read in general-interest magazines and newspapers, as well as the diction appropriate for your own essays and exams, is what we call a *general* or *middle level* of diction.

The range between formal and informal diction is fairly wide, but even so you should have no trouble figuring out which words and phrases are appropriate to the writing situation. In speech you have been making such decisions for a long time. You have understood the "relativity" of diction since you started moving away from the confines of your family—probably from the time you started school. From an early age you perceived that the language of the classroom was not the language of the playground, that the language you used with your best friend was not the language you used with your best friend's mother. All of us have different levels of language that we use for different speaking situations. The written language has that same diversity: The language of the informal note would be highly inappropriate in a letter of condolence; the language of a humorous essay on working conditions in the dining hall would be out of place in a serious essay on the working conditions in coal mines. Most diction problems arise from the tendency to use "big words" where ordinary everyday words are called for. The result is pompous, pretentious diction that obscures the writer's personal voice. In Chapter 18, 'Revision and Style,' we ask the question, "Can you hear your own voice coming through in your writing?" If you are using words that you would never say, then probably your personal voice is absent. Here is a sample of impersonal diction from that discussion, a "personal statement" written by an applicant for law school in answer to the question, "Why do you want to study law?"

> It has long been a tenet of my value system that as a capable individual I have a social and moral duty to contribute to the improvement of the society in which I live. It seems that the way to make a valuable contribution is by choosing a means that will best allow me to utilize my abilities and facilitate my interests.

The writer of that statement had never in her life begun a sentence "It has long been a tenet of my value system." In fact, no one talks like that. Pompous diction can only obscure the personal voice, the most important single quality for a piece of writing to have.

Pompous diction perhaps results from misunderstanding the notion that writing is different from speech. It's true, of course, that they are different in certain ways. But most of the differences lie in the structure of sentences. For example, certain modifiers, such as absolute phrases and nonrestrictive clauses, are rarely used in speech. As for diction, the main differences between speech and writing tend to be at the lower end of the formal–informal scale; that is, in writing at the middle level of diction, as we do for essays, we simply don't use some of the informal expressions of speech ("I *sort of* like my history class"); we don't use as many elliptical constructions, those in which words have been left out ("See you later"; "Coming with us?"); and we avoid slang, except when writing dialogue.

We eliminate or change those informalities when we write. But most of our spoken words and expressions are equally at home in our writing. To write "My companions accompanied me to the cinema" instead of "My friends went to the movies with me" is simply pompous.

8.5

Does using a personal voice mean that in writing we should use only those words we also use in speech? Certainly not. We all have a reading vocabulary that includes words we rarely speak or hear others speak. When our topic calls for *hiatus* or *recalcitrant* or *abate* or *detritus* or *deem* or *judicious,* then certainly we should use them. It's when a word is not called for, when it calls attention to itself, that we should leave it out.

FOR CLASS DISCUSSION

Pinpoint the words or phrases in the following passages that are generally not a part of the level of diction appropriate to essay writing. Revise them.

1. George may be kind of nice, but Marianne is certainly not very enthused about her date with him.

2. The movie we had in health class was the dumbest propaganda about drugs I've ever seen, mainly on account of the overacting and exaggeration.

3. I teed off at the fourth hole, oblivious to the myriad of golfers waiting in line as well as to the menacing pond located to the left of the green, which shatters the majesty and serenity of the hole.

4. Red has more than a few talents, including piano playing and a knack for frequently finding and relating humorous anecdotes. He derives great pleasure from being the center of attention at any social function.

5. It kind of bothers me that our history teacher smokes in the classroom. A bunch of us are going to sign a petition asking him to cut it out.

6. I used to be nuts about licorice jelly beans, but now I just can't hardly stand them. They turn my stomach.

7. The view from Pike's Peak was spectacular, as we had been told, although whether it was worth the tribulation it afforded us is debatable.

8.5 *The Writer's Attitude*

The inaccurate use of words brings up another aspect of meaning, another kind of power of suggestion that words have: the message that the reader gets about the writer. Words expose the writer.

The writer who used *mystic* instead of *mysterious* in describing the hospital room may have been expressing an attitude far different from the one intended. The word may suggest for the reader a highly developed imagination or an overly emotional attitude toward the situation. The reader might also assume that the writer really meant *mysterious*, not *mystic*. In that case, the writer may come across as ignorant or careless.

Attitude is the point of view or bias that you, the writer, bring to the writing situation. The words you use are clues to that attitude, whether intentional or unintentional. For example, consider the description of a fashion show that includes the following sentence:

The gaunt-looking fashion models paraded down the runway.

or

The scrawny models paraded down the runway.

Most of us have mental pictures of fashion models, pictures of tall, slender women. When we read that the models are "scrawny" or "gaunt," our mental picture of the models probably doesn't change much, if at all; what changes is our image of the writer. Such words expose the writer's attitude or bias toward the topic.

The careful reader looks for clues to the writer's attitude. In the description of the fashion show, they are easy to find. The careful writer includes them, but all too often the inexperienced writer, with a word chosen carelessly, may convey an unintended message.

8.6 *Figurative Language*

Nothing is more important for the writer than the accurate and precise use of words. But the writers we remember the best are those who use language not only precisely but also creatively, who use words that help the readers respond in new ways. Some writers do so using what we call *figurative language*.

We use language figuratively when we deliberately bypass the hierarchies of meaning. For example, the writer who allows the wind to complain or the houses to stand at attention has moved the words *wind* and *houses* from the inanimate to the animate or human branch of the hierarchy. We call this shift *personification*.

The writer who calls the White House "a cabin in the bureaucratic woods" is imposing all of the characteristics from the *cabin* branch of the *building* hierarchy on *White House*. This we call *metaphor*. And when John Updike, in *Rabbit is Rich*, says that a salesman's smile is "like a switchblade without the click," he is using a simile, a comparison that uses *like*.

Although we tend to think of figurative language in connection with poetry and fiction, personification and metaphors and similes are common in everyday kinds of writing as well. In fact, they are common in everyday speech. For example, we use the language of cooking and eating in all sorts of situations:

> We digest information, swallow our pride, feast our eyes, simmer down, chew on half-baked ideas, hope for our share of the pie, want to have our cake and eat it, too, and admire a meat-and-potatoes kind of guy.

Using the vocabulary of sports,

> we strike out or we make a hit; we lose yardage when our ideas appear to be way out in left field; we gain points when our ideas are on target.

The figurative language of cars and body parts and weather is also part of our everyday speech:

> We put the brakes on spending.
> We move to the head of the class.
> Our thinking gets cloudy at times.

Figurative language can give us insights into issues and people. It can help us see the picture that the writer sees. Here is John Updike's prose again (from *Rabbit is Rich*), this time describing Rabbit's view of his new daughter-in-law's mother when he sees her for the first time:

> His head is pounding. This mother bothers him, her smile has been on her face so long it's as dry as a pressed flower, she doesn't seem to belong to his generation at all, she's like an old newspaper somebody has used as a drawer liner and then in cleaning house you lift out and try to read; Pru's looks must have come from the father's side.

(Notice, incidentally, the punctuation of the two Updike sentences.

How does it differ from conventional punctuation? Why did he choose to deviate from the standard?)

8.6

Figurative language should be used not so much sparingly as carefully. The metaphor or comparison should be accurate and useful; and it should be consistent. If you compare an old man to a weathered ship, you don't show him walking with shuffling steps; ships don't shuffle. They may sway from side to side; they may move slowly; but they don't shuffle. When the metaphor is out of control, it loses all of its impact.

Here, for example, is the first paragraph of an article on education from the government publication *Humanities*. Its title is "American Education: Has the Pendulum Swung Once Too Often?"

> Since the middle 1940s, American schools have been at the center of a tug of war between competing educational philosophies. With striking regularity, educational policy has swung from domination by "progressives" to domination by "traditionalists" in roughly ten-year periods.

The title prepares the reader for a metaphor, but not for the tug-of-war metaphor. Regularity that is "striking" suggests a clock; the verb *swung* suggests the pendulum that we were expecting to read about but didn't.

The effective metaphor often suggests much more than a simple comparison. In using the word *fallout* in the following passage from "Television Advertising: The Splitting Image," Marya Mannes shocks the readers into thinking beyond simple effects that commercials might have:

> It can be argued that commercials are taken too seriously, that their function is merely to amuse, engage, and sell, and that they do this brilliantly. If that were all to this wheedling of millions, well and good. But it is not. There are two more fallouts from this chronic sales explosion that cannot be measured but that at least can be expected. One has to do with the continual celebration of youth at the expense of maturity. . . .

Clearly, fallout is a serious matter.

News columnists use metaphor frequently. Here is the opening

8.6

of a column by James Reston, published in *The New York Times* on February 15, 1981, shortly after Ronald Reagan took office:

> When Ronald Reagan moved into the White House, there was a tendency here to regard his promises to cut the budget, cut taxes and be tough on the Soviets as so many New Year's Resolutions soon to be destroyed by the brutal facts and politics of the day.
>
> His assumption was that the country had been on a binge, that he was going to dry it out, get it back on the wagon and maybe even back to the church.

Two writers used personification in postelection stories after the citizens of Houston elected a woman as mayor in 1981:

> Only yesterday, it seems, this city was a brash adolescent in jeans and cowboy hat, careening down the highway of urban growth and development in a pickup truck. But adolescents grow up, and Houston today seems more like an adult, with a more complex personality that displays new facets, shadings and sensitivities.
>
> —WILLIAM K. STEVENS, *The New York Times* (November 29, 1981)

> To folks in Dallas, Houston is a loud, boorish, blue-collar place, overwhelmed by nouveau riche high rollers and overrun with Cadillacs and pickup trucks. To folks in Houston, Dallas is a dull, snobbish, white-collar town, dominated by banking and defense interests, and overrun with Rolls-Royces and Mercedes.
>
> —KURT ANDERSON, *Time* (November 30, 1981)

FOR CLASS DISCUSSION

1. The purpose of metaphor is to help the reader understand the writer's idea more clearly or in a new way. Assess the effectiveness of the following:

> Sen. Howard Baker scored a few points with me recently. A story in the Los Angeles Times informed me that Baker, who loves poetry, had taken up the practice of reading poems to the Senate.
>
> Alas, he lost those points a couple of paragraphs into the article. It seems that he has a "poem picker." According to the story, one of Baker's speechwriters is, like Baker, a "poetry buff." This young man, a veritable poetry pimp, supplies his parliamentary patron with verse for any

occasion—Auden on autumn, Whittier on work, Dickinson on dedication. Baker provides the topic, his procurer provides the poem.

Baker loves poetry, you see, but not enough to keep it around the house

—BRUCE BAWER, *Newsweek* (November 8, 1982)

2. Following are two quotations that use the metaphor of construction and architecture. The first is from Chapter 7 of this book, describing the parts of speech. The second is from a newspaper interview with writer John Irving.

In general, the form classes provide the primary lexical content; the structure classes explain the grammatical or structural relationships. We can think of the form-class words as the bricks of the language and of the structure words as the mortar that binds them together.

A novel is a piece of architecture. It's not random wallowings or confessional diaries. It's a building—it has to have walls and floors and the bathrooms have to work. It goes together by inches and by days.

Do you find these metaphors useful in helping you understand the parts of speech and the form and writing of a novel? Can you think of other artifacts like the novel or other abstractions that would be made more understandable by means of analogies to construction or architecture? Think about such ideas as peace, love, marriage, friendship, poetry, and painting.

3. In the following excerpt from a *Time* article on the subject of slang, Lance Morrow used personification:

But slang cannot live forever on the past, no matter how magnificent it may have been. Slang needs to be new. Its life is brief, intense and slightly disreputable, like adolescence. Soon it either settles down and goes into the family business of the language (like *taxi* and *cello* and *hi*) or, more likely, slips off into oblivion, dead as Oscan and Manx. The evening news should probably broadcast brief obituaries of slang words that have passed on. The practice would prevent people from embarrassing themselves by saying things like *swell* or *super*. "*Groovy*, descendant of *cool* and *hip*, vanished from the language today."

—*Time* (November 8, 1982)

Can you think of other aspects of everyday life that would be appropriate metaphors for the coming and going of slang that Morrow described? One possibility would be stray cats; another

8.7

would be the flowers in the garden, some of which are annuals and others perennials. Write a paragraph similar to the one above, using a different metaphor.

8.7 Euphemism

Most people don't believe in magic words. Most of us don't believe in the kind of witchcraft that endows words with the magical powers to cast spells. Yet we do recognize the power of words. "Open sesame!" may not open a door, but those words do open up in each reader a meaning—perhaps a picture of Ali Baba and the forty thieves or a memory associated with that story or a person with a handlebar mustache we once knew who resembles our image of Ali Baba. The euphemisms in our language acknowledge that power.

Euphemism means, in the Greek original, "words of good omen." We use euphemisms to alter the meaning and associations that people have for concepts. For example, the connotations of words like *die* and *death* are likely to be painful ones, especially for people who have witnessed death at close hand. For that reason we substitute terms like *pass away. Pass away* means, in its denotation, "die"; but the connotative meaning that many people have probably associates *pass away* with a peaceful death, a painless dying in one's sleep. If that association makes the concept of death easier to accept, then the euphemism indeed becomes a word of good omen.

But too often the purpose of a euphemism is simply to obscure reality. When Congress labels a tax increase *revenue enhancement,* their motives are clear. They want to be reelected, and legislators who raise taxes don't always get reelected. The realities of war are always obscured by euphemisms too: Dead soldiers become *casualties;* killing an enemy soldier becomes *protective reaction;* a bomb becomes an *air-to-surface weapon;* guns of all kinds become *antipersonnel devices;* and war itself becomes a *peace-keeping action.*

But there are also euphemisms, like *pass away*, that make life easier. To call old people *senior citizens* or *elders* gives them a dignity that *old people* does not connote. If calling a garbageman a *sanitary worker* or a janitor a *custodian* gives the worker a better feeling about the job, then the euphemism serves a good purpose.

Many of our euphemisms have their origins in the prudishness of Victorian society, where anything connected with the human body—

let alone its functions—was considered a taboo subject. Even the word *leg* was out of bounds, so *limb* became a body part. And words like *drumstick* and *white meat* kept the taboo words *leg* and *breast* from being bandied about at dinnertime. Such language restrictions may seem silly to us because we live in a time when topless bathing suits and nude beaches are part of the culture. But notice that even we say *nude*. Why not *naked?*

What are the consequences for the writer? The writer must always consider the effect of the words on the reader, both the shared meanings that a word has and the individual meanings that it is likely to have. For example, should you describe a person as having "tinted hair" or "dyed hair"? *Hair coloring* and *hair tint* are euphemisms for *hair dye*. But they also have different connotations for the reader, just as *nude* and *naked* do. On the other hand, to call underwear *unmentionables* and to say a pregnant woman is *in the family way* will strike most readers as just plain silly. Such terms say more about the writer than about the topic.

FOR CLASS DISCUSSION

1. Robert E. Morsberger called euphemisms "the fig leaves of language." Can you think of another, equally appropriate metaphor that applies?
2. What is the effect on you as a reader when a car is described not as *used* but as *preowned?*
3. Examine magazine ads for the use and effect of euphemisms.
4. What is the difference between a "thief" and a "rip-off artist"? Can you think of other euphemisms for people who commit crimes?
5. In toothpaste commercials we often hear about the cleaning problems of "dentures," never "false teeth." Think of euphemisms we have for other "false" parts that people have.
6. How many euphemisms can you think of for *drunk?* What connotations do they have?

8.8 *Predictability and Redundancy*

In many ways English is a highly predictable language. This predictability is the basis of a popular television game-show in which the contestants win prizes for filling in blanks with words that

8.8

match the words of the celebrity panelists. For example, they must guess what word is next:

Wet _____

House _____

Rock _____

The contestants and the panelists have no clues of context; they simply choose the word that they think the others will also choose:

wet blanket or *wet paint* or *wet suit*
house mother or *housewife* or *house plant*
rock and roll or *Rock Hudson* or *rock garden*

To test this predictability for yourself, guess the next word that will follow in each of these partial sentences; then check your answers with your classmates.

1. It's dark in here; will you please turn _____.

2. Don't give me a bad _____.

3. The dog barked and the duck _____.

4. We all went inside when it started _____.

5. The door was hermetically _____.

6. I'd like to change your grade, _____.

7. As long _____.

8. Chances _____.

Another term for predictability is *redundancy*. English is a highly redundant language. Many of the words we use add no new information; that is, the reader or listener already knows what's coming, as the previous eight sentences demonstrate. We have certain idioms and stock phrases that are highly predictable. And certain structure words, such as prepositions and determiners, are often given so little stress that we don't even hear them, but we still understand what's being said. We know they're there. For example, if in the blanks of the following sentence you hear only "uh" or some other sound,

I'm going _____ _____ bank _____ afternoon,

or if a truck goes by and you can't hear those unstressed syllables at all, you will still get the message. In a sense, then, those words are redundant because they add no information to the message. Certain features of syntax are also redundant:

8.8

I bought several books Saturday.

The word *several* tells us that *book* is plural, so from the standpoint of new information, the plural *s* is redundant. And, in fact, in that sentence, where the following word begins with *s*, the plural inflection is probably not even pronounced. The past-tense inflection is also highly redundant; if this were not so, then irregular verbs such as *hit* and *put* would be confusing, as the present and past forms are identical. But they're not confusing. We understand this sentence as past tense:

I put new siding on the house,

just as this one is:

I painted the house.

You've probably heard about redundancy before; you may have been told to avoid it. "Unnecessary repetition" is the definition that usually applies to *redundancy* in writing. Certainly that is one definition of the word. Redundancy becomes unnecessary repetition when it gets in the way of the reader's expectation. That kind of redundancy is really the opposite of the examples we've just seen. The redundancies built into the language—our expectations—act as guideposts to understanding. They contribute to the cohesiveness of language. They move us along. In short, they are positive redundancies.

Unnecessary repetition, on the other hand, is a negative kind of redundancy that thwarts our expectations. For example, read the following sentence. Then ask yourself what is coming next:

Hank and Charlie turned off their flashlights and crept down the cellar stairs, breathing not a sound as they strained to see what lay in the blackness below.

Now, what do you expect to read next? You don't know the details of what's coming, but you probably do have certain expectations. You expect to learn what Hank and Charlie saw in the blackness or what they couldn't see or maybe what they heard. Now read the sentence again; this time a second one has been added:

> Hank and Charlie turned off their flashlights and crept down the cellar stairs, breathing not a sound as they strained to see what lay in the blackness below. *They were very quiet.*

How disappointing! That's not what we were expecting. Of course they were quiet; we already knew that. They "crept" down the stairs "breathing not a sound," didn't they? To say that they were quiet is an example of unnecessary repetition—redundancy of the wrong kind. Why? Because it frustrates our expectations. The writer has set us up for one thing and then pulled the rug out from beneath us.

Another kind of unnecessary repetition, or redundancy, is the cliché, the trite expression that adds no new information. To say that an object is "as white as snow" or "as black as coal" or "as cold as ice" or "as cool as a cucumber" is to say absolutely nothing about the object beyond saying that it is white or black or cold or cool. The *as* phrase adds no new information—not about the object, at least. It does perhaps say something about the writer—something negative.

It is in your descriptive passages that you'll be tempted to use clichés. Resist the temptation. Use fresh comparisons and original figurative language that actually add to the information.

FOR CLASS DISCUSSION

1. Demonstrate the redundancy of the following clichés by filling in the blanks. Remember that if you can finish the phrase so can your reader; resist the temptation to use such phrases.

   the apple of my _____

   avoid like the _____

   face the _____

   a _____ old age

   the lap of _____

   hit below the _____

   light as a _____

sell like hot _____

sharp as a _____

worth its weight in _____

swear like a _____

straight from the _____

clean as a _____

quiet as a _____

pretty as a _____

2. Try your hand at turning the above clichés into fresh ideas by substituting an unexpected word for the expected one: a *rotten* old age; straight from the *shoulder holster;* quiet as a *sealskin coat.*

3. Restaurant menus are rich repositories of clichés and redundancies: garden peas, ruby-ripe tomatoes, farm-fresh eggs. See how many you can find. Invent your own description of the dining-hall menu for the cliché-minded diner.

9

Spelling

Here you are, in college, still thinking about spelling! You've been thinking about it since kindergarten—maybe even before. You probably can't remember when you first learned to spell your name, it was so long ago. But you probably can remember all those spelling lists you had to study and those spelling tests that came along every week in elementary school. You may even remember some of the rules: "*i* before *e* except after *c* . . ."; "change the *y* to an *i* and add *es*."

Years of lists and tests and rules—and still you may not be such a great speller. But then—

- "Spelling doesn't matter. There are lots of successful people who can't spell. It's the thought that counts."
- "I've always been a poor speller, just like my dad. It runs in the family."
- "The way words are spelled in English is absurd; there are more exceptions than there are rules."
- "I won't have to spell when I leave school; I'll have my secretary do it for me."
- "Good spellers are born, not made."

It's easy to take refuge in myths. And that's exactly what those statements are: myths. The first one on the list is probably the most

215

pervasive—and the most harmful. The fact is that spelling does matter. The outward sign of a literate, educated person is the ability to speak and write standard English. To the casual observer, as well as to the potential employer, the most obvious deviation from the written standard is the misspelled word. People outside school who see your writing—whether in a personal letter, an employment application, or a casual note—will rarely notice a dangling modifier or a poorly developed paragraph; but they will notice a misspelled word. And—rightly or wrongly—you will be judged by your spelling.

It's always comforting to the poor speller to be able to cite cases of brilliant world leaders and famous writers who were, or were reported to be, poor spellers. F. Scott Fitzgerald is often cited as an example of one whose writing ability was not impeded by his lack of spelling ability. But if it's true that his spelling was atrocious, then as a successful writer he was an exception. Poor spellers are, in fact, quite likely to be inhibited as writers. They hesitate to use new or uncommon words, even though such words would convey the precise meaning. And although it may be true that spelling ability and intelligence are not highly correlated, research has shown that people who feel inhibited by their own spelling errors are less likely to explore language in ways that lead to vocabulary growth. Competent and confident spellers, on the other hand, experiment in their writing; they are more likely to turn their "passive" vocabulary (the words they understand but do not themselves use) to active use, even when they're not quite sure of the correct spelling.

"But good spellers are born, not made," you may insist. "And anyway, here I am in college, all grown up. You can't teach an old dog new tricks." Such myths are common—but they are myths nevertheless. For over eighty years psychologists and educators have studied the teaching and learning of spelling. And although most of the work has dealt with spelling in the elementary grades, much of what the research shows can be useful for all of us.[1] Here are some of the findings:

1. Good spellers feel motivated to spell accurately. A corollary of this statement is that poor spellers who are determined to improve, who have come to the point of caring about their spelling ability, have

---

[1] Spelling research is discussed in Richard E. Hodges, *Learning to Spell* (Urbana, Ill.: National Council of Teachers of English, 1981).

taken an important first step. Researchers have also discovered a negative self-image to be common among poor spellers. People who label themselves poor spellers (or who have been thus labeled by someone else) seem to perpetuate that negative self-image almost consciously. So it is important to recognize and to understand in a conscious and positive way that poor spelling ability is not a permanent condition.

2. Good spellers have a high degree of visual acuity and a longer visual memory than poor spellers. Further, good spellers see words as combinations of morphemes—that is, meaningful units—not simply as strings of individual letters. Fortunately for the poor speller who wants to improve, these skills can be enhanced through practice.

3. The English spelling system is not as arbitrary as we sometimes think. Researchers have found that from 70 to 90 percent of the words that children use in their writing are spelled according to the sounds. This finding suggests that for most words there are indeed rules that apply. Thus, poor spellers can improve by paying attention to the system and learning how it works. Poor spellers can also profit from discovering if their own particular errors are systematic in any way—attributable, for example, to problems with final consonants or the silent *e* or to mispronunciations or some other common source of error.

FOR CLASS DISCUSSION

Probably the biggest mistake that self-labeled poor spellers make is in not realizing how much they actually do know about spelling. Study the following words. Five of the ten include spelling errors. All of them are uncommon words that you may not have seen before, but even so, you can probably pick out the five that are spelled correctly.

1. bevatroj	6. epizooty
2. novercal	7. pekkoe
3. inrefragable	8. mesophilic
4. leporine	9. detersiv
5. levvirate	10. cosmoline

On the basis of the errors you found, explain the "spelling rules" that they have broken.

9.1 *Spelling Rules*

The lesson to be learned from the foregoing exercise is that there are different kinds of spelling rules, some of which we don't even have to think about; we know them intuitively. Certain combinations of letters simply don't appear in English; certain letters don't appear in certain positions; certain letters, such as *x* and *v*, are never doubled. The word *Exxon* may look familiar to us now, but back in the 1960s, when that big red-and-white sign first appeared on gasoline stations, it looked strange indeed. The company was roundly criticized for taking such liberties with our spelling system.

These rules that we know intuitively never get written down in spelling books. The rules that do get written down are those that help us to make choices, especially when adding suffixes to words. But there are also a great many words that seem to follow no rules at all. Why, for example, do *through, stew, boo, to,* and *clue* all have different letters to represent the same vowel sound? How about *tomb* and *room*? *Home, comb,* and *foam*? Such examples of discrepancies between sounds and spelling abound.

For decades, reformers, despairing about such anomalies, have tried to change the spelling system—to no avail. The printed word is hard to change. In fact, a great many of our spelling discrepancies have come about precisely because the printed word did not change when the pronunciation did.

Probably the best known of the reformers was George Bernard Shaw, who until his death in 1950 spent a great deal of time and money advocating such spellings as *thru* and *nite*. Shaw once ridiculed our spelling system by pointing out that *fish* ought to be spelled "ghoti." To understand his reasoning you can find the sounds you need to spell *fish* in these three words: *laugh, women,* and *mention*.

Not only are spelling reforms given little chance of success, they are rarely even taken seriously. Here is a tongue-in-cheek report from the Smithsonian Institution reprinted in *Time* (May 6, 1957):

A Drim Kum Tru

If he had not tried to rush it, George Bernard Shaw might have succeeded in giving the English-speaking peoples a phonetic alphabet. Says the Smithsonian Torch, a slim house organ put out by the Smithso-

nian Institution for the museum set: "We are in complete accord with
Bernard Shaw's campaign for a simplified alphabet. But instead of
immediate drastic legislation, we advocate a modified plan.

9.1

"In 1957, for example, we would urge the substituting of 'S' for soft
'C'. Sertainly students in all sities of the land would be reseptive to this.

"In 1958, the hard 'C' would be replased by 'K' sinse both letters are
pronounsed identikally. Not only would this klarify the konfusion in the
minds of spellers, but typewriters and linotypes kould all be built with
one less letter and all the manpower and materials previously devoted to
making the 'C's' kould be used to raise the national standard of living.

"In the subsequent blaze of publisity it would be announsed that
the troublesome 'PH' would henseforth be written 'F'. This would make
words like 'fonograf' 20 persent shorter in print.

"By 1959, publik interest in a fonetik alfabet kan be expekted to
have reatshed a point where more radikal prosedures are indikated. We
would urge at that time the elimination of al double leters whitsh have
always ben a nuisanse and desided deterent to akurate speling.

"We would al agre that the horible mes of silent 'E's' in our
language is disgrasful. Therefor, in 1961, we kould drop thes and
kontinu to read and writ merily along as though we wer in an atomik ag of
edukation. Sins by this tim it would be four years sins anywun had used
the leter 'C,' we would then sugest substituting 'C' for 'TH'.

"Kontinuing cis proses year after year, we would eventuali have a
reali sensibl writen languag. By 1975, wi ventyur tu sa cer wod bi no mor
uv ces teribli trublsum difikultis. Even Mr. Shaw, wi beliv, wud bi hapi
in ce noleg cat his drims finali kam tru."

A more recent call for spelling reform comes from Isaac Asimov,
who believes that the home computer industry may hold the solution
to the problem; he believes that computer companies could make
changes in the system actually work. Writing in *Popular Computing*
("A Question of Spelling," July 1982), Asimov suggested that an
"Academy of Spelling Reform" agree on the spelling changes to be
made and that computer manufacturers then use the new spelling in
their software for word-processing units.

Meanwhile, there are rules that can be helpful. Following are ten
of them. Don't try to memorize the list; chances are you're applying
most of the rules already. But do keep a record of the words you

misspell and the ones you have to look up. Write them down and think about them; try to discover patterns in your errors; then work on the rules that apply. You may find, as you begin to notice words, and as you pay closer attention to the rules and their exceptions, that your visual acuity and visual memory for words are growing. With such growth, your spelling ability is bound to improve.

Rule 1: *ie/ei*

The rule is *i* before *e* except (1) after *c* (*receive, deceit*) or (2) when it sounds like long *a*, as in *neighbor* and *weigh* (also in *vein* and *eight*).

Although this common rhyme is useful, it doesn't cover all the complexities of *ie* and *ei*. There are a number of common words besides the "after *c*" and "sounds like *a*" exceptions in which the *e* comes first:

either	sheik	forfeit
neither	heir	height
leisure	seize	foreign

Rule 2: Doubling Consonants

When adding a suffix beginning with a vowel (*-ed, -ing,* and the like), double the final consonant of the word:

1. If it is a one-syllable word ending in a single consonant preceded by a single vowel:

bet	betting
rub	rubbing

2. If it is a multisyllable word ending with a single-vowel–single-consonant combination with the main stress (accent) on the last syllable:

begin	beginning
regret	regretted
infer	inferring
label	labeled

FOR CLASS DISCUSSION

9.1

1. We do not double the consonant in the syllable preceding the suffix of the following words. Why not?

traveling[2]	inference	cheated
rendered	pampered	soaring
repeating	helped	

2. Write the past tense form (the *-ed* form) of the following verbs:

plot	collide	redeem	plant
tease	rim	type	defer
tap	place	remember	tape
plan	file	repel	pass
fill	bias	lace	exclaim
gossip	develop		

3. How do you account for the spelling of the words *picnicking* and *panicked*? (You may find a clue in the discussion of the silent *e*, which follows.)

Rule 3: The Silent *e*

The silent *e*, as you probably know, refers to the final *e* that is not pronounced: *bite, use, love*. The silent *e* rule applies when a suffix that is added to such a word begins with a vowel:

Drop the *e* when you add a suffix beginning with a vowel:

bite	biting
use	usable
love	lovable

The exceptions to the silent *e* rule occur when dropping the *e* would result in confusion or a mispronunciation. For example, without the *e*, we would be tempted to pronounce *changeable* with a "hard *g*" rather than the "soft *g*"—or *j*—sound. And in *noticeable*, without the *e* we would be tempted to pronounce the *c* as a *k* instead of an *s*.

---

[2] One of the differences between American and British spelling occurs with this rule. Some words with an unstressed second syllable do have the doubled final consonant in British English: *labelled, travelled*. We should also note that some words are spelled both ways in American English: *programed, programmed*.

9.1

Add the suffix *-able* to the following words:

| like | peace | manage | desire | value |

Add *-ous* to the following words:

| outrage | fame | courage | monotone | space |

Explain your decisions.

The *-ing* form of the following verbs is also an exception to the silent *e* rule. Why?

| singe | dye | hoe | lie | die |

Rule 4: *-ize/-ise*

In general, verbs ending in *-ize* (in contrast to those ending in *-ise*) can become nouns with the addition of *-ation:*

generalize	generalization
civilize[3]	civilization
authorize[3]	authorization

Verbs that end in *-ise* cannot be made into nouns (with one exception):

| surprise | advertise | despise | exercise |

The exception is *improvise*, which does have a noun form: *improvisation.*

The spelling confusion arises with this second group because the *-ise* ending sounds exactly like the *-ize* of the first group. Note also that many of our *-ise* words are both nouns and verbs without any change in form, whereas most *-ize* words are verbs only.

---

[3] Again we should point out another difference between British and American spelling. The British spell some of our *-ize* words with *-ise:* civilise/civilisation; authorise/authorisation.

We also have two -*yze* words:

analyze   paralyze

Rule 5: -*eed*/-*ede*

The problem of the "seed" words can be solved by the learning of only four words:
Three multisyllable words in English end in -*eed:*

1. exceed   2. proceed   3. succeed

Only one word ends in -*sede:*

4. supersede

All the rest are -*ede:*

accede   concede   intercede
precede   recede   secede

The trickiest words to remember in this group are probably these:

precede
proceed

And although the base of *proceed* remains the same for the -*ing* and -*s* forms, as you would expect, it changes when the suffix -*ure* is added to form a noun: *procedure.*

Rule 6: Regular Noun Plurals

For the majority of nouns, the plural is formed with the simple addition of -*s:*

boy → boys   cat → cats

9.1

Exceptions to this rule are as follows:

1. When the noun ends with *y* preceded by a consonant, we change the *y* to an *i* and add *-es:*

baby → babies	party → parties
reply → replies	fly → flies

Note that in the following nouns the preceding rule does not apply:

delay → delays	decoy → decoys
play → plays	ploy → ploys

In these words the *y* is preceded by a vowel, not a consonant.

2. When we pronounce the plural of nouns ending with a sibilant sound (an *s*-like sound), we add a complete syllable, not just an *-s;* so in writing the plural we add *-es:*

latch → latches	sash → sashes
buzz → buzzes	kiss → kisses

We should note that the two preceding rules also apply in the formation of the *-s* form of verbs:

replies	delays	kisses
catches	plays	buzzes

(These are among many of the words in English that are both nouns and verbs.)

FOR CLASS DISCUSSION

Explain why the following words, which end in a sibilant sound, take only an *-s* (not an *-es*) to form the plural. How does the *-s* manage to add an entire syllable?

place	judge	breeze	splice

Rule 7: Irregular Noun Plurals

Even though we have many nouns that form their plurals in irregular ways, they are almost always spelled as they sound. If you're a native speaker of English, spelling these plurals should not be a problem—if you know how to pronounce them (and chances are, you do).

A. *f/ves.* There is no real system underlying this change from *f* in the singular to *ves* in the plural. Some words change; some do not; and some are correct both ways. In all cases, however, they are spelled as they are pronounced. If you're unsure of the correct form, the dictionary will tell you. If the *v* form is not listed as the plural or as a separate entry, stick to *fs.*

Most nouns ending in *f* or *fe* change to *v* in the plural:

wife → wives	half → halves	calf → calves
leaf → leaves	knife → knives	wolf → wolves

There are a number of nouns that retain the *f* in the plural:

chief → chiefs	roof → roofs	belief → beliefs
serf → serfs	proof → proofs	

Here are three that can go either way:

hoof → { hooves / hoofs }   wharf → { wharves / wharf }   dwarf → { dwarves / dwarfs }

The spelling of the verb form of some of these nouns is also somewhat arbitrary, but, as with the noun plurals, the spelling matches the sound:

to calve	to dwarf
to halve	to knife

B. *o → oes or o → os.* Most words ending in *o* form the plural by adding -*s*, but there are enough exceptions—words that take -*es*—to make this a troublesome spelling problem. Here are some common -*es* words:

echoes	heroes	tomatoes
embargoes	potatoes	vetoes

9.1

Moreover, a few can be spelled either way in the plural:

mottos/mottoes   buffalos/buffaloes   mementos/mementoes

C. Other Irregular Plurals. Some irregular plurals are old forms of English that have resisted becoming regularized:

foot → feet   man → men
tooth → teeth   child → children

A number of animal and fish names are irregular in that there is no change in the plural:

sheep   deer   bass   salmon   trout

A large number of borrowed words have retained their foreign plural inflections:

larva → larvae   criterion → criteria
analysis → analyses   datum → data

Some of these borrowings are now in the process of acquiring regular plurals. *Appendixes, indexes,* and *formulas* are even more common than *appendices, indices* and *formulae; stadiums* has all but replaced *stadia. Memorandum* is giving way to the shortened *memo,* along with its regular plural *memos;* and the added complication of gender in *alumnus–alumni* (masculine) and *alumna–alumnae* (feminine) no doubt encourages the use of the simpler, gender-free—and informal—*alum* and *alums.* The borrowed words ending in *s*— *analysis–analyses, nucleus–nuclei, hypothesis–hypotheses, stimulus–stimuli*—are less likely to lose their foreign inflections because the substitution of *-es* for the plural would be cumbersome.

   Please note that the plurals of proper nouns are always regular. The plural inflection is *-s* or *-es,* even though another rule applies when the same words are used as common nouns:

Mr. and Mrs. Penny are the *Pennys* (not the *Pennies*).
John and Mary Self are the *Selfs* (not the *Selves*).
The children of the Wolf family are the *Wolfs* (not the *Wolves*).

Mr. and Mrs. Deer are the *Deers* (not the *Deer*).
East and West Germany are the two *Germanys* (not *Germanies*).

Rule 8: The Possessive Case

For most nouns the singular possessive is formed with the addition of the apostrophe and *s* (*'s*) and the plural with only the apostrophe (*'*), because the plural form already has an *s*:

Singular	Singular Possessive	Plural	Plural Possessive
cat	cat's	cats	cats'
horse	horse's	horses	horses'

You'll notice that in speech we cannot distinguish among the inflected forms: *Cat's* and *cats* and *cats'* are all pronounced exactly the same way.

Spelling the plural and the possessive of words ending in *s* or *z* is sometimes confusing; they not only sound strange, they tend to look strange when they're written:

Mr. and Mrs. Jones are the *Joneses*. (PLURAL)
Their cat is the *Joneses'* cat. (PLURAL POSSESSIVE)

To turn *Joneses*, the plural of *Jones*, into the possessive case, we add only the apostrophe because we add no new sound, the usual procedure for possessive plurals: *cats'*, *horses'*, *leaders'*, *Joneses'*. The possessive singular of nouns ending in *s* or double *s* can also look strange:

The cats of Ross and Kris are *Ross's* and *Kris's* cats.
The nephew of the boss is the *boss's* nephew.

Here we add the extra syllable when we pronounce the possessive of these words, so we add *'s* when we spell them, the usual procedure for the singular possessive.

We should note that some writers prefer to add only the possessive mark, the apostrophe, even though they add a syllable in speech: *Ross'* and *Kris'* and *boss'*. Both spellings are acceptable.

9.1 When the singular has more than one syllable and more than one sibilant sound in the final syllable, we generally do not add a sound, so we do not add an *s* when we write the possessive:

> The followers of Jesus are *Jesus'* followers.
> The laws of Texas are *Texas'* laws.

A good rule of thumb is this: If the pronunciation does not change when you make a noun possessive, then do not add the *s* inflection when you spell it; add only the apostrophe.

Note that the irregular plurals that are not formed with the addition of *s* or *es* take the apostrophe and *s* (*'s*) to form the possessive, just as singular nouns do:

men → men's	people → people's
women → women's	alumni → alumni's
children → children's	larvae → larvae's

Possessive Case of Pronouns. The personal pronouns have distinctive forms for the possessive case, so they do not need apostrophes. This rule applies even when the word ends in *s*, such as *its* and *hers* and *theirs*. The following are all possessive forms—no apostrophes needed:

my/mine	your/yours	his	her/hers	its
our/ours	their/theirs			

Note that all of the possessive pronouns, except *his* and *its*, have separate forms for the possessive determiner and the possessive nominal:

That is *my book.*	That is *mine.*
That is *her book.*	That is *hers.*
That is *their new car.*	That is *theirs.*
That is *his car.*	That is *his.* (no change)

The possessive pronoun that causes the biggest problem is *its.* Remember, *its* is possessive without an apostrophe. With an apostrophe, *it's* means *it is.*

The cat hurt *its paw.*
but
It's a nice day. = *It is* a nice day.

9.1

The above rule applies without exception to the possessive pronouns. However, some pronouns in the other classes do take the apostrophe with *s* (*'s*) in the possessive case:

Pollution is *everybody's* problem.
Julie and Jenny often do *each other's* chores.

One other pronoun has a special form for the possessive case: *whose,* the possessive of *who:*

I wonder *whose* car Tim is planning to borrow.
The man *whose* car Tim borrowed didn't even charge him for the gas.

Don't confuse *whose* (the possessive case) with *who's* (the contraction for *who is* or *who has*):

Who's in here? (*Who is* in here?)
Who's got my hat? (*Who has* got my hat?)

PRACTICE WITH POSSESSIVES
Transform the of *possessive phrase into the inflected noun.*

1. The son of Mr. Price is Mr. _____ son.
2. The daughter of Ms. Hedges is Ms. _____ daughter.
3. The Rolls belonging to James is _____ Rolls.
4. The Governor of Massachusetts is _____ Governor.
5. The blanket belonging to Linus is _____ blanket.
6. The garden of the neighbor is the _____ garden.
7. The garden of the neighbors is the _____ garden.
8. The curls on the head and tail of Miss Piggy are _____ curls.
9. The club the women belong to is the _____ club.
10. The wisdom of Confucius is _____ wisdom.

Rules 9 and 10: Pay Attention!

9.1

The next two rules are really suggestions for enhancing your visual acuity, a trait that is characteristic of good spellers. Notice that both of these rules direct attention to the middle of words, where most spelling errors occur.

Rule 9: Be Observant. A. Look for units within words. Take the word *observant,* for example:

1. It begins with *ob,* as many words do (*object, obscure, obnoxious*),
2. followed by the word *serve,* to which the silent *e* rule has been applied for adding
3. the suffix *-ant.*

Note that the units are sometimes complete words, sometimes suffixes and prefixes:

undoubtedly	loneliness
conscience	livelihood
realistic	prejudice
delightful	reimbursement

Spelling mistakes commonly occur when the same letter appears at the end of one unit and at the beginning of the next:

mis spell	mean ness
final ly	dis service
un natural	real ly

B. Sometimes the units are complete words put together to form compound words. Again, spelling problems may arise when a letter appears at the end of one word and at the beginning of the next, as in the first five words in the following list:

roommate	bookkeeper	commonplace
earring	daydream	helpless
underrate	knitwear	underestimate
overreaction	handmade	plaything
	throughway	
	(sometimes thruway)	

Remember also that the silent *e* may appear in the middle of a compound word:

9.1

useful	pacesetter	household
limestone	troublesome	forecast

    C. Observe the difference in meaning with prefixes that are homonyms, that is, that sound alike:

1. *fore-* (meaning "before" or "in front")

forecast	forehead	foresee
forego	foreman	forestall
forehand	forerunner	forewarn

    for- (other meanings, such as "separate—away, apart, or off")

forget	forgo	forswear
forgive	forsake	

Also notice that some words with *for* are actually words with *form*, for example, *formal, formula, formation, formality,* and *informal.*

2. *anti-* (meaning "against")

antiseptic	antithesis	antibody
antipathy	antitrust	antifreeze

    ante- (meaning "before")

antecedent	antedate	antebellum

3. *inter-* (meaning "between")

interact	intercontinental	intervene

    intra- (meaning "within")

intramural	intravenous

4. *-ion* (usually an action or condition, and often a part of the longer *-ation, -tion,* or *-sion*)

action	composition	precipitation
condition	decision	pronunciation
recommendation	revision	

-*ian* (meaning "belonging to a group" or "one who")

barbarian	historian	optician
clinician	librarian	politician
collegian	magician	reptilian
dietician	musician	technician
electrician		

Note also that -*ian* words refer to people or animals; -*ion* words do not.

Rule 10: Think About Pronunciation: Listen. It's true, of course, that there are many words in English that are not spelled as they are pronounced; but there are also a great many common words that are often misspelled because they are mispronounced. All of the words in the following list are *misspelled* to reflect those common mispronunciations. Correct them! Look up the correct pronunciation in the dictionary if you're not sure:

*pronounciation	*mischievious	*canidate
*atheletic	*similiar	*quanity
*rememberance	*grievious	*libary
*suprise	*excape	*mathmatics
*disasterous	*enterance	*maintainance

Unfortunately, some of the foregoing errors result from recognizing the little words within the big words, such as *remember, disaster, enter,* and *maintain.* Being observant is not always helpful!

9.2 Spelling Tricks

Sometimes, when all the rules fail, there are mnemonic devices (memory aids) that can come to the rescue. For your own particular problem words, try to find a sentence or a saying that helps you to avoid the mistakes. The following are useful tricks:

There is no *a* in my whole *existence*.

Ind*e*p*e*nd*e*nt means fr*e*e.

You write a lett*er* on station*er*y. (When the word means "immovable," it is spelled with *ar: stationary*.)

Be a fri*end* to the *end*.

Your school princi*pal* is your *pal*.

Surv*eil*lance may mean looking through a *veil*.

Remember the *story* in hi*story*.

Scientists do their *labor* in a *labor*atory.

There's one *e* in the *end* of cal*end*ar.

The *there* of location includes *here*.

The *their* of possession includes *I*.

The *v* di*v*ides two *i*'s.

You can always *tell* an in*tell*igent student.

All right is like *all wrong*. (two words)

All railroad tracks are par*all*el.

There's always *a rat* in sep*arat*e.

9.3 Frequently Misspelled Words

You might find it useful to review the following words, which are commonly misspelled. It will be even more helpful to you to keep your own personal list of problem words and to review the spelling rules that apply to them.

absence	amateur	balance
accept	among	bargain
accessible	analysis	basically
accidentally	analyze	beautiful
accommodate	anticipate	beginning
accompanied	anxiety	believe
accumulate	apologize	beneficial
achievement	apparent	biased
acknowledgment	appearance	Britain
acquaintance	appreciate	broccoli
acquire	arctic	bureaucratic
across	argument	business
address	article	
admission	artistically	calendar
adolescence	athlete	candidate
advantageous	athletic	careful
against	attendance	carrying
aggravate	awkward	category

9.3

ceiling
challenge
changeable
character
chief
choose
chose
clothes
coarse
column
committee
competition
concede
conceivable
condemned
conscience
conscientious
conscious
continuous
controlled
courtesy
curiosity
curriculum

dealt
debatable
deceive
definite
description
develop
dining room
disappoint
discern
divine
duly

echoes
eighth
ellipse
embarrass
environment
exaggerate
existence

except
experience
explanation
extremely

familiar
family
fascinate
favorite
February
fiend
finally
financial
foreign
foreseeable
forty
foreward
friend
fulfill

government
grammar
grandeur
grievance
guarantee
guidance

happily
harass
heard
height
here
hindrance
hoping
humorous
hundred
hurriedly
hypocrisy
hypocrite

ignorant
illogical
imagine

immediately
incidentally
indispensable
insistent
irrelevant
irreplaceable
irresistible

judgment
judicial

knowledge
knowledgeable

laboratory
liable
library
lieutenant
loneliness
loose
lose
lying

maintenance
manageable
medicine
miniature
miscellaneous
mischievous
misspelled
morals
muscle

naturally
necessary
niece
nineteen
noticeable
noticing
nuclear

occasion
occur

occurred
occurring
occurrence
omission
oneself
one's self
opponent
opposite
ordinarily
originally

parallel
particularly
perceive
perseverance
persistence
physician
picnicked
playwright
preference
prejudice
privilege
probably
proceed
procedure
protein
psychology
purpose

quantity
questionnaire
quiet
quite

recede
receipt

receive
recommend
reference
reservoir
resistance
restaurant
rhythm
ridiculous
roommate

sacrifice
sacrilegious
safety
sandwich
schedule
sentence
separate
sergeant
similar
sincerely
sophomore
strength
supersede
suppose
surprise

technique
temperament
temperature
tender
than
their
thinness
thorough

though
through
tomorrow
tragedy
truly
twelfth
typical
Tuesday

unanimous
unconscious
undoubtedly
unforeseen
unnecessary
until
usable
using

vacuum
valuable
various
vegetable
vengeance
villain
visible

weather
Wednesday
weird
whether
wholly
wintry
women
writing

9.3

10

What Is "Good English"?

"Good English" has many voices. In Pittsburgh you might hear someone say, "The car needs washed." In a black neighborhood a speaker may tell you, "Joe not here; he be working." And in communities throughout the South you can hear, "We might could go." All of these speakers are using "good English." Theirs may not be the "good English" that you speak or that you're used to hearing; it's not the "good English" of presidential candidates campaigning on college campuses or the "good English" of network broadcasters reading the nightly news; nor do these quotations reflect standard written English, the "good English" of most books and magazines and term papers. But in using the standard spoken dialect of their particular communities, those speakers are using "good English."

"Good English" is relative. The language that is appropriate in one region may be highly inappropriate in another. And "good English" is relative to the situation as well. The language that broadcasters use on the air is not the same as the language they use at the breakfast table. And in a southern community, "We might be able to go" would probably replace "We might could go" at a business conference. Different situations call for different language.

Every speaker learns this principle of human behavior at an early age. Children understand that the language they use with their playmates is different from the language they use with adults. The

237

negative "huh-uh" on the playground becomes "No, thank you" when the teacher is asking the question. And the vocabulary that a child uses at home with the family is different from the vocabulary for school. Most of the time we understand what is appropriate in a given situation, and we have no trouble shifting from one level of formality to another.

In the written language, too, what is appropriate in one situation may be inappropriate in another. The message scrawled on the kitchen bulletin board and the informal note to a friend are both noticeably different from the language of the job application letter. As with speech, the purpose and the audience make all the difference. Most of the writing you do in college—the papers for your composition class as well as lab reports and essay exams—are closer to the formality of the job application than to the informality of the hasty note. This style of writing is known as *standard written English*.

The grammar system described in Part I of this book is grounded in speech. We have defined grammar as the set of internal rules that native speakers somehow follow in speaking and in listening. The rules we have looked at are those that produce the sentences of the majority dialect—what we call *standard English*. This is the dialect on which standard written English is based.

The three speakers quoted at the opening of this chapter were using speech patterns that, although standard and therefore "good English" in their own speech communities, are nonetheless not the standard of the majority of Americans. The verbs in "He be working" and "We might could go" cannot be generated from the verb-expansion rule described in Chapter 2. This is not to say that these verb strings are unsystematic; on the contrary, they are generated by highly systematic rules that belong to the grammar of a great many native speakers of English in this country. But these particular verb strings—no matter how systematic, no matter how appropriate at a particular time or place—do not conform to standard written English and are generally not appropriate (and are therefore not used) in formal speech or in formal writing. Even though they are part of the local dialect, they are generally not used in local newspapers, where standard written English predominates.

So not only do we have differences in speech—differences between speakers of various dialects and, for individual speakers, variations dependent on the occasion—we also have differences between speech and writing. For the speaker of a nonmajority dialect, there are many more speech/writing differences than there are for the speaker of the majority dialect. As we noted, even the verb-expansion rule may be different. But speakers of the majority dialect, too, have adjustments to make and rules to learn about the conventions of standard written English.

In the preceding chapters we have commented on punctuation and other conventions of writing. We have also looked at some of the differences between speech and writing, noting in particular the structures rarely used in speech, such as absolute phrases and nonrestrictive clauses, and some of the differences in diction. But the most important consideration is effectiveness. How can the writer achieve the precision of style, tone, clarity, and diction that makes a piece of writing effective? Certainly, an understanding of grammar can help the writer achieve that goal. A conscious knowledge of the grammar system can illuminate the wide range of choices that the language provides for putting words and sentences and paragraphs together.

An understanding of the grammar can also help the writer answer questions about usage and standards of correctness. Some of the old do's and don't's—those persistent issues of "grammar etiquette" we still hear about—can be especially troublesome for the student writer. In the pages that follow we will take up some of the questions about "good English" that writers ask:

- Is it good English to end a sentence with a preposition?
- Is it good English to split an infinitive?
- In good English do pronouns like *everyone* and *everybody* always have singular referents?
- Is it good English to use *he* in reference to a person of unknown gender, or is that usage sexist?

10.1 Is It Good English to End a Sentence With a Preposition?

In his short story "An Outpost of Progress," Joseph Conrad (who, incidentally, was not a native speaker of English) went out of his way to avoid using *to* at the end of a sentence:

Besides, the rice rations served out by the Company did not agree with

10.1

them, being a food unknown to their land, and to which they could not get used.

To avoid writing "which they couldn't get used to," Conrad produced what can only be labeled as an ungrammatical sentence—"ungrammatical" insofar as a native speaker would never say "to which they could not get used." It's even hard to pronounce.

Most books of grammar and usage no longer include this absurd warning against ending sentences with prepositions. As a result, people may conclude that the rule has changed through the years, that standards have deteriorated, or that teachers and textbook writers are getting more liberal. Those conclusions would be wrong. Nothing has changed.

The so-called rule never existed.

Grammarians in the eighteenth and nineteenth centuries who made pronouncements about prepositions at the end of the sentence were attempting to make English conform to the system of Latin. They decided that what was correct in Latin ought to be the rule in English as well. Unfortunately, they disregarded reality:

> Did you turn the light out?
> Laziness is something I won't put up with.
> It's something I'm simply not used to.

These sentences may look as if they end with prepositions, but in fact the *out* and *with* and *to* that end them are not prepositions at all. They are simply part of the phrasal verbs *turn out, put up with,* and *be used to.* When sentences with such phrasal verbs undergo transformations that turn them into questions or clauses, or that alter word order in some other way, the verb, or part of it, often ends up as the last element in the sentence.

There is nothing ungrammatical about such phrasal verbs. If we can say

> That's something I won't tolerate.

then we can also say

> That's something I won't put up with.

The first may be more appropriate in some situations; it may even be clearer; it is undoubtedly more formal. It is *not* more grammatical. Moreover, in a Pattern 4 sentence, the verb can easily be the last word in the sentence, even without a transformation, because an intransitive verb takes no complement:

10.1

> It's time to *turn in.*
> Last night at the party, Mark and Karen *made up.*

Phrasal verbs are not the only source of the phenomenon. Many times such words at sentence end are, indeed, prepositions—part of prepositional phrases in which the noun phrase has been shifted:

> Chocolate is a flavor I'm especially fond *of.*
> What kind of music are you interested *in?*
> Nothing else happened that I'm aware *of.*

These sentences include adjectives that commonly pattern with phrases or clauses as complements: *fond, interested, aware.* In these particular transformations the object of the preposition has shifted, while the preposition has remained with the adjective at the end of the sentence.

For a teacher to suggest that such sentences are ungrammatical because they end with prepositions is absurd. Perhaps the writer could improve on "Chocolate is a flavor I'm especially fond of" by being more concise:

> I like chocolate.
> I'm especially fond of chocolate.
> Chocolate is my favorite flavor.

The teacher might want to suggest that "Chocolate is a flavor" is unnecessarily redundant. The alternatives are shorter and tighter; they may be more effective. But they are *not* more grammatical.

The "what for" question also produces an end preposition:

> *What* did you say that *for?*

10.2

This, of course, is another way of asking

> *Why* did you say that?

What for may be less formal than *why*, but it is certainly not less grammatical.

The "who" question is a somewhat stickier problem because it often introduces another "grammatical error":

> *Who* are you going *with*?

This common structure illustrates a genuine difference between speaking and writing. Anyone who would correct the speaker, insisting on

> *Whom* are you going *with*?
> *or*
> *With whom* are you going?

does not understand communication. Neither of these "corrected" versions represents the language as it is spoken by most people.

The form that the question should take in standard *written* English is another matter. Rather than use *who*, most writers would either use *whom* or reword the sentence to avoid the problem altogether. But in conversation, "Who are you going with?"—in spite of its end preposition and its subjective *who*—is "good English."

10.2 Is It Good English to Split an Infinitive?

We could say that technically it is impossible to "split an infinitive," because the infinitive is the uninflected form of the verb: *be, go, see, hear, consider.* The notion of the split infinitive assumes that the *to* is a part of it. In Old English, the infinitive was inflected with *-an* or *-n*. When that ending was dropped, the preposition *to* became the signal; it is now called the *sign of the infinitive*, but the infinitive is the verb itself. Actually, there are a number of constructions in which the *to* is not used with the infinitive. With certain verbs that take infinitives as complements, for example, the *to* is either missing or optional:

10.2

> I expect Joe *to mow* the lawn.
> I helped Joe *mow* the lawn.
> The coach let the players *choose* their own captain.
> I don't want *to drive* to the city alone.
> I don't dare *(to) drive* to the city alone.

And there are a few other constructions, such as those using *rather–than, but,* and *except,* that occur with the bare infinitive:

> I would rather *go* with you than *stay* here alone.
> Mike did nothing today but *complain.*
> I did everything you asked me to except *mow* the lawn.

However, most occurrences of the infinitive do require *to:*

> Jogging is a good way *to keep fit.*
> I decided *to lose five pounds before the holidays.*
> I went home *to get ready for the party.*

These infinitive constructions consist of entire verb phrases, not simply the base form of the verb. Such infinitives are actually the predicate half of sentences, complete with complements and modifiers:

> to keep fit (Pattern 6)
> to lose five pounds before the holidays (Pattern 1)
> to get ready for the party (Pattern 6)

What, then, is a "split infinitive"? The "split" occurs when an adverbial—usually a single adverb—comes between the *to* and the verb. Is that "good English" or not?

As you know, adverbials can occupy a number of slots in the sentence patterns, including the slot before the verb:

> I *finally* understand algorithms.
> Rick *simply* stopped attending class.
> Our neighbors *never* watch television on Sunday.

10.2   Any predicate phrase can be turned into an infinitive phrase for use as a nominal or an adjectival or an adverbial in a sentence. When that predicate phrase includes an adverbial in the preverb slot, then so does the infinitive phrase. It's that simple:

> It's such a relief *to finally understand* algorithms.
>
> *To simply stop* attending class as he did was a real mistake on Rick's part.
>
> *To never watch* television on Sunday is to miss the week's best programs.

Most infinitives do not have preverb modifiers simply because most sentences do not. Adverbials are more likely to fill other slots, at the beginning or the end of the sentence. But certain adverbs often do fill the preverb slot; it makes no sense to say that they cannot do so in infinitive phrases. The preceding "split infinitive" examples would sound unnatural if the adverb were shifted from its preverb position. And, what is more important, the adverb–verb relationship would lose its emphasis.

The warnings against splitting the infinitive are aimed not at logical adverbials, such as those in the examples above, but at awkward and ineffective constructions, and also, perhaps, at the overuse of *really*, which finds its way so frequently into the sentences of student writers. *Really* is the culprit in a great many split infinitives:

> We promise *to really try* hard.
>
> This weekend we're going *to really hit* the books.

Other adverbials, too, are generally more effective outside the infinitive:

> It was unusual of the dog *to all of a sudden snap* at the children like that.
>
> We want *to certainly help* if we can.
>
> The police expect *to quickly apprehend* the culprit.

Most adverbials, like these, belong outside the infinitive. But "good English" includes split infinitives, too. It always has.

10.3 In Good English Do Pronouns Like Everyone *and* Everybody *Always Have Singular Referents?*

The pronouns *everyone* and *everybody* are, in form, singular; as subjects, they take the *-s* form of the verb or auxiliary in the present tense:

Everyone *is* leaving the room at once.

An illustration of the scene described by this sentence would show more than one person—more than two or three, probably—leaving the room, even though the form of *everyone* is singular. In spite of this anomaly, the issue of subject–verb agreement is not a problem.

But often such a sentence calls for a possessive pronoun; the long-standing tradition has been to use the masculine pronoun when the gender is not known:

Everyone picked up *his* books and left the room.

But an alternate, nonsexist form has become fairly standard in recent years:

Everyone picked up *his or her* books and left the room.

But even more common is the plural, in spite of the singular form of *everyone.* The plural, in fact, makes much more sense; in terms of meaning, it is the only logical choice, because *everyone* refers to more than one person:

Everyone picked up *their* books and left the room.

It is interesting to discover that the problem arises only with the possessive pronoun. In the subjective case, the only pronoun choice is *they:*

The teacher asked everyone to leave, and *they* did.

10.4

Certainly *he* would make no sense at all, nor would *he and she:*

> *The teacher asked everyone to leave, and *he* did.
> *The teacher asked everyone to leave, and *he and she* did.

The objective case, too, requires the plural:

> Everyone cheered when I told *them* to leave.

In fact, if *him* were used in this sentence, the meaning would change.

There is simply no logic in insisting on the singular for the possessive case when both logic and good grammar call for the plural in every other situation.

It's true that in form *everyone* is singular; this is also true of collective nouns, such as *crowd* or *group*. But these nouns call for plural pronouns when the members of the collection are seen as individuals:

> The group picked up *their* books.
> The crowd began to raise *their* voices.

It is in this collective-noun sense that *everyone* is plural in spite of its form. To label as ungrammatical "Everyone picked up their books and left" makes no sense at all.

But tradition dies hard. To avoid both the "ungrammatical" *their* and the sexism of *his* and the awkwardness of *his or her*, the writer can simply find a substitute for *everyone* in this situation:

> *All the students* picked up *their* books and left.

More difficult than the problem of *everyone–their*, where the underlying referent of *everyone* is actually plural, is the problem of *one* or *someone* or *a person*, where the meaning is actually singular and the gender is unknown.

10.4 Is It Good English To Use He in Reference to a Person of Unknown Gender or Is That Usage Sexist?

An invitation to membership recently sent by the Smithsonian Institution included a "registered number" for the addressee only, along with the following statement:

10.4

> This registered number is not transferable. If *a friend* wishes to become a member, please ask *them* to write for information.

The gender of *a friend* is unknown, but its referent is clearly singular, so in terms of agreement *them* appears ungrammatical. To avoid *him*, with its masculine designation—and apparently to avoid the awkwardness of *him or her*—the Smithsonian chose to use *them* in its indefinite and singular sense.

A few years ago neither the Smithsonian's writer nor anyone else would have hesitated to use *him:*

> If a friend wishes to become a member, please ask *him* to write for information.

Long-established usage in English calls for the masculine pronoun to refer to either sex in this structure, just as the word *man* has long been used in reference to both sexes in such words as *mankind* and such statements as "Man is the thinking animal." This custom was even institutionalized by an Act of Parliament in 1850 with "An Act for shortening the language used in acts of Parliament," which announced

> ... that in all acts words importing the masculine gender shall be deemed and taken to include females, and the singular to include the plural, and the plural the singular, unless the contrary as to gender and number is expressly provided.[1]

But times and attitudes change. We have come to recognize the power of language in shaping attitudes. So an important step in reshaping society's view of women is to eliminate the automatic use of *he* and *his* and *him* when the person referred to could just as easily be female, as in the following:

> Someone should lend *his* coat to the accident victim.
>
> Ask a friend to get *his* own number.

---

[1] Quoted in Robert C. Pooley, *The Teaching of English Usage* (Urbana, Ill.: The National Council of Teachers of English, 1974): 86.

10.4

What can the writer do? The pronoun system simply does not provide a singular version of *they/their/them* in reference to people. For inanimate nouns and for animals we use *it;* sometimes we even use *it* for very small babies of unknown gender:

Isn't *it* cute?
When is *it* due?

In reference to grown-up people we seem to have two choices: Like the Smithsonian, we can be language liberals and use *they,* or we can be awkward and use *he or she (his or her),* or, as some writers do, *s/he* (which has no possessive or objective case so far):

Someone should lend *their* coat to the victim.
Someone should lend *his or her* coat to the victim.

Eventually, perhaps, the plural pronoun may be common for both singular and plural; in the second person (*you/your/you*), we make no distinction between singular and plural, so it's not unreasonable to do the same in the third person. But such changes come about very slowly.

Meanwhile, what shall the writer do who wants to be not only logical and conservative but nonsexist as well? A number of current publications have adopted a policy of nonsexism in their pages, and more and more books (including this one) are doing so as well, so it obviously can be done.

One alternative that often works when the writer is referring to students or teachers or people in general is to use the plural. The Smithsonian could easily have avoided the issue:

If you have *friends* who wish to become members, please ask *them* to write for information.

The plural will not solve the problem in the sentence about the coat: "Someone should lend *their* coat." But sometimes in such cases another determiner can be substituted for the possessive pronoun:

Someone should lend *a* coat to the victim.

The authors of the following passages could easily have found ways to avoid the masculine pronoun:

10.4

Of all the developments in the history of ~~man~~ *the human race*, surely the most remarkable was language, for with it ~~he was~~ *our ancestors were* able to pass on ~~his~~ *their* cultural heritage to succeeding generations who then did not have to rediscover how to make a fire, where to hunt, or how to build another wheel.

—CHARLES B. MARTIN AND CURT M. RULON

For thousands of years philosophers have been pondering the meaning of "meaning." Yet, everyone who knows a language can understand what is said ~~to him~~ and can produce strings of words which convey meaning.

—VICTORIA FROMKIN AND ROBERT RODMAN

It has been said that whenever ~~a person~~ *people* speak~~s~~, ~~he is~~ *they are* either mimicking or analogizing.

—CHARLES F. HOCKETT

It is a rare sentence, indeed, that cannot be stated in an alternative way. English is enormously versatile; we almost always have a choice.

FOR CLASS DISCUSSION

The following passages represent a range of written English spanning 120 years. Revise them to reflect today's concerns about sexism in language. Eliminate the generic use of the masculine gender, if possible. The first selection was published in 1857 in *The Atlantic Monthly:*

1. This business of conversation is a very serious matter. There are men that it weakens one to talk with an hour more than a day's fasting would do. There are men of *esprit* who are excessively exhausting to some people. They are the talkers that have what may be called *jerky* minds. Their thoughts do not run in the natural order of sequence. They say bright things on all possible subjects, but their zigzags rack you to death. After a jolting half-hour with one of these jerky companions,

10.4

talking with a dull friend affords great relief. It's like taking the cat in your lap after holding a squirrel.

—OLIVER WENDELL HOLMES, "The Autocrat of the Breakfast-Table," *119 Years of the Atlantic*

2. Of all born creatures, man is the only one that cannot live by bread alone. He lives as much by symbols as by sense report, in a realm compounded of tangible things and virtual images, of actual events and ominous portents, always between fact and fiction. For he sees not only actualities but meanings. He has, indeed, all the impulses and interests of animal nature; he eats, sleeps, mates, seeks comfort and safety, flees pain, falls sick and dies, just as cats and bears and fishes and butterflies do. But he has something more in his repertoire, too—he has laws and religions, theories and dogmas, because he lives not only through sense but through symbols. That is the special asset of his mind, which makes him the master of earth and all its progeny.

—SUSANNE K. LANGER, "The Prince of Creation," *Fortune* (January 1944)

3. To the average American, the energy problem is mainly his monthly fuel bill and the cost of filling up his gas tank. He may also remember that in 1979, and way back in 1974, he had to wait in long lines at gasoline stations. For all of this, he blames the "Arabs" or the oil companies or the government, or perhaps all three. Much of the information that he gets from the media, as well as his own past experience, tells him that energy prices will continue to go up sharply and that gas lines are going to come back whenever a conflict flares up in the Middle East.

—FRED SINGER, "Hope for the Energy Shortage," *Newsweek* (May 18, 1981)

Glossary of Usage

Accept / except.   *Except* is sometimes a verb (meaning "exclude") but it is more often a preposition with a meaning like "but"; *accept* is the verb meaning "receive with consent":

>   He should *accept* help if he needs it. (verb)
>   I like all vegetables *except* squash. (preposition)

Understanding the meanings of *acceptable* and *exception* may help you to remember *accept* and *except*.

Affect / effect.   Both can be either a noun or a verb, but the common noun of the two is *effect*. (*Affect* is rare as a noun.)

>   The overall *effect* of the movie was funny. (noun)

The common verb of the two is *affect*:

>   The movie *affected* us all. (verb)

The verb *effect* means "to cause" or "to bring about"; it often has a noun like *change* as its direct object:

>   The new treatment *effected* a change in the patient's condition.

Aggravate / irritate.   The use of *aggravate* to mean "irritate" is a
fairly recent usage:

> Her behavior really *aggravates* me.

Many people avoid that usage, reserving *aggravate* to mean "to make
worse":

> The new treatment simply *aggravated* her condition; she got worse
> instead of better.

All right / *alright.   The asterisk, you will recall, indicates an ungrammatical (in this case misspelled) form. This mistake is understandable, because the language includes *already* and *altogether* in a
single-word form (as well as *all ready* and *all together*). But here's the
difference: Those two single word forms are adverbs:

> His appearance has *altogether* changed. (To what extent?)
> They have *already* come. (When?)

There is no adverbial form of *all right:*

> *They *alright* came.

In the two-word forms, *all* is a pronoun; *right, together,* and *ready*
are adjectives; together the two words constitute a noun phrase, here
functioning as a subjective complement:

> They are *all right.*
> They are *all ready.*
> They are *all together.*

Almost / most.   The substitution of *most* for the adverb *almost* is a
dialectal variation not used in standard written English:

> *I am *most* finished with my homework.
> I am *almost* finished with my homework.

Most is an indefinite pronoun, often used as a determiner:

Most spectators left before the final whistle.

Another dialectal variation uses *most* as a qualifier of *all:*

*Most all of the spectators left before the final whistle.

*Alot. This misspelling of the noun phrase "a lot" fails to recognize *a* as a determiner and *lot* as a noun.

Among / between. The traditional rule specifying *between* to show a relationship between two and *among* for three or more is nearly always accurate. However, in some situations we do use *between* with numbers larger than two, here denoting discussions between individuals in the larger group:

Discussions were held *between* all the Common Market representatives.

But we can say with accuracy that *among* is never used correctly for only two, as in:

**My husband and I discussed a problem *among* ourselves.

Amount of / number of. These adjectival phrases signal nouns; *amount of* goes with noncountables (the *amount of* food; the *amount of* money) and *number of* goes with countables (the *number of* accidents; the *number of* dollars). The same distinction determines the use of *fewer* (countable) and *less* (noncountable): *fewer* dollars, *less* money. See page 258.

Anymore. A regional variation of *nowadays* or *lately;* not used in standard written English:

Anymore we don't get good TV reception.

Anyways. A colloquial form of *anyway;* not used in standard written English.

Awhile / a while.   The one-word version is an adverb in form, which we use to modify a verb:

> We waited *awhile* for the bus.

The two-word version is a noun phrase, which we use in a nominal slot in the sentence—as the object of a preposition or as a completer of the verb:

> We waited for *a while*.
> It took *a while* to finish.

The noun *while* often has a pre- or postmodifier:

> It took *a short while* to finish.
> He came *a while ago*.

Beside / besides.   These two prepositions may have different meanings or the same one. *Beside* usually means "next to":

> Sit *beside* me.

Besides usually means "in addition to":

> *Besides* turkey, we're going to have baked ham.

But both are sometimes used to mean "except":

> No one *beside(s)* the secretary was needed to witness the transaction.

(The word *except* is actually more common in sentences like the foregoing example.)
Besides, meaning "in addition," can also be used adverbially without a following noun phrase:

> I've had a lot of dishwashing experience, so they hired me; *besides*, no one else wanted the job.

Between / among.   See *Among / between*.

Bust / burst. The verb meaning "break open" is *burst*, not *bust:* "He *busted* the balloon" is nonstandard. *Bust*, however, is commonly used as a passive verb in connection with drug arrests:

> He was (or got) *busted* for possession.

Bust is also used in specialized contexts as a noun:

> The economy went through a boom and a *bust.*
> The agents confiscated tons of marijuana in the drug *bust.*

*Center around. To use *around* with the verb *center* is a contradiction of sorts. The writer who uses this phrase probably means to express either "revolve around":

> The plot *revolves around* a series of mistaken identities.

or "focus on":

> The plot *focuses on* the relationship between two sisters.

Cite / site / sight. Although these homonyms have distinctive meanings, they are often mistakenly interchanged. *Cite*, a verb, means "to mention" or "to make reference to":

> He *cited* a passage from Hamlet to make his point.

Site, a noun, means "location":

> This is the *site* of the new shopping mall.

Sight, both a noun and a verb, refers to seeing:

> He *sighted* the deer in the rifle scope. (verb)
> The evening sky was a beautiful *sight.* (noun)

Contractions. Contractions are a part of both the spoken and the written language. Certain constructions actually require contractions:

Shouldn't the students who live on campus have parking privileges?
Hasn't the architect done a marvelous job?

To speak these negative questions without contractions would be unidiomatic in present-day English. It's possible, of course, to say

Should the students who live on campus *not* have parking privileges?
Has the architect *not* done a marvelous job?

But the context for the noncontracted form is different, as are the speaker's emphasis and message.

So in discussing the use of contractions, we must recognize three different levels: (1) those like the above examples that are required in both speech and writing; (2) those that, although not required, inhabit the natural idiom of all native speakers and are generally used in all but the most formal writing; and (3) those that are strictly colloquial—that is, not used in writing.

Examples of the third group are run-together phrases, such as *they've, John'll, must've, couldn't've,* and *they'd.* These contractions might appear in dialogue, but there's really no question about their inappropriateness for other written contexts.

It is the second group that causes problems for writers: Is it appropriate to use such contractions as *it's, isn't, they're, can't, don't,* and *couldn't?* The question can be answered only in reference to a particular writing situation and context, but for all except the most formal circumstances contractions are certainly part of the writer's personal voice. Textbooks such as this one, as well as essays in prestigious journals, newspapers, magazines, and popular books include contractions.

Contractions can make a difference in meaning. Compare the following:

He doesn't own a car.
He does not own a car.

In the contracted sentence the stress is on *own;* in the noncontracted form it is more likely to be on *not.* The contraction gives the writer control.

The number and kind of contractions certainly affect the writer's tone; there is undoubtedly a positive correlation between the degree of informality and the use of contractions. The writer should bear that relationship in mind in making choices. But, certainly, to avoid all contractions merely for the sake of avoiding them is contrary not only to the rules of idiomatic English but to common sense.

Could of. This spelling error is based on pronunciation. In contractions the auxiliary *have* is pronounced like *of: could've, should've, would've.*

Different from / different than. Standard usage calls for the preposition *from* following the adjective *different:*

> My new diet is *different from* all the others I've tried.

We use *than* with the comparative form of adjectives:

> The new diet is *easier* to follow *than* the old one.

However, for the sake of economy we often do use *than* when a clause follows the word *different:*

> It was different *than I expected it to be.*

Effect / affect. See *Affect / effect.*

Except / accept. See *Accept / except.*

Farther / further. The distinction between these two comparative forms of the adjective *far* is quite blurred in reference to physical distance, although *farther* is more widely used:

> We went *further* than we had planned.
> We went *farther* than we had planned.

With abstractions, however, *further* is the standard form:

> We'll look *further* into the matter.
> We'll discuss it *further* tomorrow.

Fewer / less. We use the adjective *fewer* with countable nouns and *less* with noncountables:

> Apples have *fewer* calories than avocados.
> People with hypertension should eat *less* salt than other people.

An exception to this usage occurs in comparisons involving numbers where *than* is not separated by a noun; in this instance we tend to use *less than* even with countables:

> We have *less than* two weeks to get ready for opening night.
> We have *less than* ten dollars to last until payday.

Flaunt / flout. These unrelated words are often mistakenly interchanged:

> We *flout* the law when we don't obey the rules.
> (*flout:* to scorn)
> We *flaunt* our furs and diamonds when we show off.
> (*flaunt:* to show off)

Further / farther. See *Farther / further.*

Had better. This is an informal, colloquial version of the modal auxiliary *should:*

> You *had better* wear your boots today.

In writing this, be sure to include *had,* even in the contracted form:

> You'*d* better be going.

The colloquial expression without *had*—"You better go"—is not used in standard written English.

Imply / infer. The message (whether spoken or written) *implies;* the audience (whether hearer or reader) *infers:*

> The president *implied* in his speech that the huge budget deficits were not his fault.

We *inferred* from his speech that someone else was to blame for the huge budget deficits.

(**Note:** The president made the *implication;* we drew the *inference.*)

Its / it's.   The possessive personal pronouns have no apostrophes (see page 228). The apostrophe + *s* added to *it* is the contraction that means "it is" or "it has":

> The dog wagged *its* tail. (possessive pronoun)
> *It's* a nice day. (contraction of "it is")
> *It's* been nice all week. (contraction of "it has")

Kind of / sort of / type of.   These expanded determiners often contribute only fuzziness to a noun phrase. Guard against them.

> This *type of*
> This *kind of*   } movie simply doesn't appeal to me.
> That *sort of*

A more concise statement:

> Such movies simply don't appeal to me.
>
> *or*
>
> Violent movies like this one simply don't appeal to me.

Lay.   The present (base) form of the transitive verb:

> *Lay* your coat on the chair.

Also, the past (the *-ed*) form of the intransitive verb *lie:*

> Yesterday we *lay* on the beach all afternoon.

Leave / let.   In most dialects of English *leave* means "allow to remain":

> *Leave* the door open.

Let means "permit":

> The teacher *let* me take a makeup test.

In a nonstandard dialectal variation, the meanings are reversed:

> **Let* the door open.
> **Leave* me go with you.

These are not used in standard written English.

Less / fewer.   See *Fewer / less.*

Let / leave.   See *Leave / let.*

Lie.   This is an intransitive verb:

> I'm going *to lie* down.

The use of *lay* in that sentence, although fairly common, is nonstandard. The past of *lie* is *lay*, a form easily confused with the transitive verb *lay:*

> Yesterday I *lay* on the beach all afternoon.

Maybe / may be.   The single-word form is an adverb meaning "perhaps." The two-word version is the modal auxiliary used with the verb *be*. If you can substitute *might be*, you'll know that the two-word version is correct:

> We *may* (*might*) be going soon.
> *Maybe* (*perhaps*) we'll have a good time.

Maybe is best reserved for speech and informal writing.

*Might of.   This is a spelling error based on pronunciation. See *Could of.*

Most / almost.   See *Almost / most.*

*Must of.   This is a spelling error based on pronunciation. See *Could of.*

Plus. This preposition, a mathematical term, is often misused as a coordinating conjunction. See page 414.

Principal / principle. The *al* version is generally an adjective, meaning "main":

> The *principal* reason for the delay was the weather.

It is also the noun designating the main administrator in a school ("The *principal* is your pal"). The *le* version is always a noun, referring to a belief or a fundamental truth:

> The governor is a man who cares about *principles*.

*Reason is because. *Because* introduces an adverbial clause. In the following sentence, however, we need a nominal clause to fill the subjective complement slot:

> *The reason for the delay was *because the car wouldn't start*.

The *because* clause, however, can be used to modify the verb or the whole sentence:

> We were late *because the car wouldn't start*.

Set. This is the present tense (base form), past tense (*-ed*), and past participle (*-en*) of the transitive verb *set*. Following are both active and passive sentences using *set:*

> We *set* the table early. (*-ed* form)
> The table *was set* early. (*-en* form)

Sight. See *Cite / sight / site.*

Sit. This is the present tense (base form) of the intransitive verb *sit:*

> The cats *sit* on the windowsill all day long.

Site. See *Cite / sight / site.*

Sort of. See *Kind of.*

Their / there / they're. If you think about context, you should have no trouble with these three sound-alikes. *Their,* the possessive case of *they,* is always used as a determiner:

> *Their* shoes were wet and muddy. (See page 173.)

There can be an expletive (see page 180) or an adverb of place:

> *There* was a strange car sitting *there* in the driveway.
> (EXPLETIVE)   (ADVERB)

They're is always a contraction of "they are":

> *They're* discussing a rematch.

To / too / two. The preposition *to* denotes direction; *to* is also the sign of the infinitive:

> We want *to* go *to* town.

The qualifier *too* modifies adjectives and adverbs; it intensifies their meaning (see page 176):

> The steak was *too* rare for me.
> He walked *too* fast for me.

The adverb *too* means "also":

> I like rare steak *too.*

Two is the number:

> We bought *two* tickets to the play.

Try and. The verb *try* is one that takes other verbs as objects. Most of the time that object is an infinitive in form:

> I tried *to help* the accident victim.
> I'm going to try *to help* the accident victim.

In most contexts *and* would simply be inaccurate in place of *to:*

*I'm going to try *and* help the victim.

Who's / whose.   *Who's* is the contracted form of "who is" or "who has":

Who's been eating my porridge? (*who has*)
Who's going with me? (*who is*)

Whose, the possessive relative or interrogative pronoun, is almost always a determiner:

Whose house is this?
The people *whose* house we rent now live in Florida.

(See also pages 76 and 173.)

You're / your.   *You're* is the contracted form of "you are":

You're doing well this term.

Your, the possessive pronoun, is always a determiner:

Your test has been postponed.

(See also pages 60 and 173.)

Part III

The Whole Theme

So far our subject matter has been limited to sentences and the words that comprise them—the subject matter of grammar. In Part III, "The Whole Theme," we turn to rhetoric.

What moves the people to write? What are the conditions under which people produce an actual piece of writing? In Chapter 11 we examine those conditions, the three sides of the "rhetorical triangle"—topic, audience, and purpose—which you can compare to the three necessary preconditions for a fire. The fuel is not the only thing you need to produce a flame, nor is the topic all you need for writing. Something has to spark your interest, to get you going, to give you purpose. And the fire needs oxygen to get started and to stay alive, just as the audience informs and directs the writer.

In most of the writing we do outside of school, the three parts of the writing situation described in Chapter 11 are already given. For example, the boss may ask for a report on a particular job we've been doing or an assessment of our last year's accomplishments or our plans for next year. In such rhetorical situations, the topic and the audience and the *purpose are clear. Likewise, when we are moved to write a letter to the editor in response to a news report or an editorial, the three components of the writing situation are all in place. However, we are still left with two decisions: What shall we say about the topic? And how shall we say it? In Chapters 12 through 15 we shall answer the second of those two questions.*

The four traditional categories of rhetoric provide an outline for our answer to the "how" question. The four categories, or modes of discourse, are essentially patterns for organizing ideas:

Description *presents the essence of something, or someone, in words; it draws a picture for the reader. Such presentations are a part of all writing; narration, exposition, and argumentation can all include description.*

Narration *tells when and how something happened; it moves the reader through time. Narration is often an important part of exposition and argumentation.*

Exposition *explains and informs; it exposes the reader to ideas. It uses description and narration to do so; and exposition itself is the mainstay of argumentation.*

Argumentation *tells why something is good or bad, why something happened, or why something should or should not happen.*

It might be useful to picture the four modes of discourse as concentric circles. Description is in the center, a part of all the modes; argumentation, the outer circle, includes all of the others:

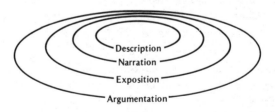

11

The Writing Situation: Topic, Audience, and Purpose

Like most people, you probably write for many reasons. At times your purpose may be simply to express your feelings, to get something out of your system, as when you record your thoughts in a diary or when a special experience moves you to compose a poem. More often your purpose involves another person, as in letters to your family or friends, when you describe what college is like or explain why you haven't written sooner or try to persuade a friend to visit campus next weekend. In the writing you do for college courses—the essay exams and lab reports and term papers—several purposes are usually working together. The obvious one is to provide the information asked for in the experiment or exam question, but underlying that purpose is another: to project an image of yourself, to persuade your teacher that you deserve the C or B or A you're hoping for.

In many writing situations, such layers of purpose are present. Even in your letters home you probably have more than one purpose: You want to let your mother know what college life is like, but you also want to help her feel less lonely in your absence and to assure her that you are indeed capable of being on your own; you may even want to demonstrate your writing ability. And toward the end of the month, when you write a letter appealing for funds, you probably have more than that single persuasive purpose in mind: You also want

267

to show your parents that although you are broke you are not irresponsible or extravagant.

The writing you do in your English composition class has a purpose, too; in fact, it has more than one. One purpose for writing an essay may seem more obvious than others: to fulfill an assignment. That, of course, is the triggering purpose, the one that gets you under way. But the ease with which you carry it out will depend on how clearly you can create a specific purpose for your paper, and that purpose is bound up with your audience.

Who is your audience? Is it your teacher? In the case of the lab report or the essay exam, it is; or it may be an assistant who does the grading for the teacher, or perhaps both of them. In any case, in such actual writing situations you have the reader–audience clearly in mind as you write the report or answer the question. In such situations you write for a particular audience to accomplish a particular purpose; and you accommodate your writing to that audience. But when you write a composition for English class, the reader and the audience are not necessarily the same. The reader is your teacher (and possibly your classmates), but the audience can be someone else. In one sense, of course, the composition class itself is a "real" writing situation, and to that extent your teacher is audience as well as reader. But the composition assignment may also be a simulation of a writing situation in which you practice the craft of writing. To make that practice as meaningful as possible, you must specify a writing situation beyond the classroom; you must find a topic that you can shape for a particular audience with a specific purpose in mind.

Even if you choose to write on that old standard topic that Lucy and Charlie Brown are assigned in the Peanuts comic strip every September—"What I Did on My Summer Vacation"—your essay will be shaped by the audience and your specific purpose. You may have spent an exciting summer filled with new adventures, but you can't write an effective essay about it until you establish a reason for doing so, a particular point you want to make clear to someone—that is, until you have defined the writing situation. And the more clearly you can define it, the easier the writing task will be.

Certainly, when you engage in casual conversation about your summer vacation, the speaking situation makes a big difference in what you say. For example, if you and your friends are discussing pets or experiences involving animals, you might draw on your summer adventure and say, "Some dog owners we met on our trip out West were really a strange breed," and then go on to recount the oddities of their behavior in a humorous or even sarcastic way:

> There was this one couple we met in a campground near Denver. They had this portable oxygen tank out on the picnic table, so we thought maybe one of them had emphysema or something. Well, it turns out, they had an old poodle who couldn't stand the altitude. My dad asked them why they brought the dog along. Why not leave him in a kennel or something? This lady really tore into him: "You didn't lock up that boy of yours, I notice." It was really weird. And the next morning when they drove out, I couldn't believe my eyes. The dog was in the front seat between them. You won't believe this: He was actually sitting in a little kid's car seat, and he had that oxygen gizmo in his mouth. Really weird.

In a different speaking situation—for example, when talking to your employer, who happens to be a dog lover—you might draw on the same experience, but you'd probably report it quite differently.

> We met some people this summer who treated their dog just like a member of the family. It had trouble breathing in the high altitude, but these people didn't want to leave him in a kennel while they took their vacation. You'll never guess what they did. They brought along a portable oxygen supply. Isn't that something?

In the writing situation the influence of audience and purpose works in the same way. The purpose and audience will provide the guidelines or principles for selecting and organizing the details of your essay.

11.1 Defining the Writing Situation

At the outset of every writing situation there are three questions to answer:

- What am I writing about?
- Who wants to know?
- Why am I writing about it?

If you can't come up with answers to these questions, you haven't thought enough about the writing situation; you're not ready to start

11.2

writing. And you can't answer only one of the questions or two: You need answers to all three.

These questions include the three essential components of every writing situation: topic (*What?*), audience (*Who?*), and purpose (*Why?*).

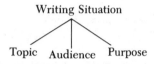

Writing Situation

Topic   Audience   Purpose

As we noted in the introduction, you can compare the elements essential to a writing situation to the necessary preconditions for a fire. A fire won't start without three essential components: a source of heat, combustible material, and oxygen. When the three get together, be prepared for flames. But if one component is missing, nothing will happen.

The fire starts at the site of the combustible material; we will start there, too, with the topic.

11.2 *Finding a Topic*

"I can't think of anything to write about. Maybe if I had done something exciting this summer, I could think of something, but all I did was stay home and work at a service station. There's not much to say about changing oil and pumping gas."

How do you find a topic when your teacher assigns an essay to be handed in next week? Where do you begin? Sometimes the assignment will include a general purpose, such as persuasion, or even a principle of organization, such as comparison and contrast, that will help you to narrow the field. Even then, however, you must find a specific topic. Let's assume that you have a list of general subject areas to choose from, such as the list on page 277. Probably your first inclination will be to pick the area you know the most about; that's a logical choice. But you might also consider an unfamiliar subject. Part of the pleasure of writing, like the pleasure of reading, is in expanding your world, in adding to your expertise and forming new opinions. In any case, let's assume that you've chosen (or the teacher has assigned) the general topic of "Energy." Now what? Where do you begin?

First, you must move from the broad topic of energy to a particular aspect of it. It's possible that you already have a specific interest in the area, but if not, you'll have to work at finding one. One technique for exploring the topic is to think of words that combine with the topic word—in this case, *energy*—to form noun phrases:

11.2

energy crisis	energy outlook
energy consumption	energy demand
energy policy	energy sources
energy shortage	energy cost

Other nouns and noun phrases will describe kinds of energy:

nuclear energy	solar energy
coal energy	wind energy
oil energy	waterpower
natural gas	wood

Although these words do limit the subject somewhat, as topics for short essays (one to two thousand words) all of them are still much too broad.

You can narrow them further by asking yourself the six questions that journalists ask: Who? What? When? Where? Why? How?

Take the broad topic of nuclear energy, for example. How does *who* apply? First, consider the people involved in nuclear energy—its production and its regulation. Who are they? Well, there's the Nuclear Regulatory Commission. What sort of influence do they have? And who, exactly, are they? Are they experts—scientists and engineers? Or are they politicians? Do they make the decisions about building power plants? Who puts up the money for such plants? Utility companies? The government? And who's responsible for accidents, like the one at Three Mile Island? And who else is involved besides the utility companies? People living in the area of power plants certainly are. And there are organized protestors all over the country. They involve themselves.

The *who* questions alone have led to many ideas about the topic of nuclear energy. The others will do the same. *What* is nuclear energy? *When* were nuclear power plants first built in this country? *Where* do they operate? Were there protestors at the time? *Why* is nuclear energy necessary? *How* can it be made safer? Or can it?

Another technique that leads you into and around a subject, producing questions similar to those of the journalist, is to consider the subject in terms of the parts and the whole.

First, what are *the parts* of nuclear energy? That question may lead to technical aspects, such as the difference between fusion and fission. Depending on your own background, you may or may not be interested in such details. It could also lead to the social aspects of a nuclear power plant: How does it affect the local economy? Has the prospect of a nuclear power plant caused a rift between the pro and con factions in the community? Are there evacuation plans in case of an accident?

Second, consider our nuclear industry as part of a larger entity. What is *the whole*? This question could direct your thoughts beyond our own country: What is the status of nuclear energy on a worldwide scale? How do other countries handle the decisions concerning power plants? Does nuclear energy have a place in the developing countries?

Still another technique for generating possible topics is to think of nuclear energy along a *time line:* past/present/future. When was nuclear power first developed for peacetime uses? What is its present status? How many nuclear power plants are now operating or under construction? Will the Tennessee Valley Authority plants ever be finished, or have they been abandoned for good? Will there be enough energy for the twenty-first century if we don't build more nuclear plants now? Will the protestors step up their efforts to delay construction?

The more questions you ask, the longer the list of possible topics grows; in fact, instead of getting easier, the task of deciding on a topic may seem to be getting harder. But remember that the reason for your exploring the subject in this way is to trigger a response in yourself, to hit on a topic that piques your interest. You can't write a paper that will be of interest to others if you're not interested in the idea yourself. And remember, too, that the list of questions and possible topics we've come up with so far is the result of exploring only one noun phrase: "nuclear energy." Of course, there will be some overlapping of ideas as you explore other noun phrases, such as "energy consumption," "energy policy," and "energy crisis"; but the chances are certainly good that somewhere in the broad subject of energy you'll find a topic that interests you.

11.3 Establishing Purpose and Audience

Let's assume that your curiosity has been aroused by the idea of civil disobedience, by the protest groups that go into action every time a nuclear power plant is proposed. You've decided on that as a topic. Now, what are you going to say about it?

Hold on! First things first! You're not ready to write. You're still in what we call the *prewriting stage.*

Before you can decide what you're going to write, you must identify the other two components of the writing situation: audience and purpose. After that you have some work to do: thinking about the topic and doing some research if necessary. But the first step is to fill in the blanks below.

Writing Situation

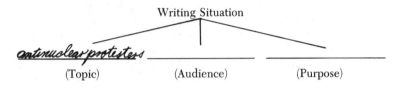

(Topic)   (Audience)   (Purpose)

And just how do you decide what goes in the other two blanks? First, ask yourself the next two questions on the list:

- Who wants to know about my topic?
- Why am I writing about antinuclear protestors?

Don't try to answer the questions independently. They go together, just like the oxygen and the heat source that start the bonfire burning.

Begin your exploration for answers with yourself. What do you already know about protest groups? What's your own attitude toward them? Why would you want to know more about them? Why would anybody?

"Let's see. I guess I haven't paid very much attention to the protestors and what they're saying, but I probably should have. I've seen them on TV often enough. The groups are always very diverse, now that I think about it: old and young, senior citizens and mothers with small babies, college kids, blue-collar workers, doctors. That's different from most protest groups. Now, why would I want to write about them, and what would I write? What should I know? Well, I wonder if they've had any real effect? Did their protest at Seabrook make a difference? That started a long time ago; I wonder if it's still going on. Does citizen protest ever make a difference? Sure, it does. Even a single person like Ralph Nader can make a difference in an industry. It would be interesting to know if protestors had brought about any changes in the way the nuclear industry works—in the safety of the plants or in the way the wastes are disposed of or in the prevention of accidents. I wonder if much has changed since Three Mile Island. I suspect there are a lot of people—politicians, too—who want us to stop spending money on nuclear power altogether and put our money into solar power and other energy sources.

"Now, who would want to know about protestors and their influence—if they've had any. My classmates? Well, college students always seem to be looking for a cause, and, after all, civil disobedience is an important part of our country's history. And of course we're concerned about the future and the energy of the future. In fact, I suspect a lot of us will have jobs that are connected with energy. And that energy may very well be nuclear. So we certainly have a stake. I'm not a scientist, so I'm not sure I can really evaluate the arguments about safety. But I can probably find out how widespread the antinuclear feeling is and how effective the protestors have been."

At this point you can tentatively identify all three components of your writing situation:

- *Topic:* The effects of protestors on the nuclear power industry.
- *Purpose:* To understand the issues involved in the antinuclear movement and the positive and/or negative consequences of the protestors.
- *Audience:* My classmates—in fact, anyone who is concerned about future energy supplies and the quality of life.

11.4 Writing the Thesis Statement

The next step in the planning stage is to formulate a thesis statement, a statement of the main point of your essay. Think of the thesis statement as your plan. That plan is as important to you as are the blueprints to the builder, the game plan to the coach, the road map to the traveler, or the formula to the scientist.

What exactly is a thesis statement? How do you come up with it? In a nutshell, the thesis statement is a sentence that pulls together your topic, your audience, and your purpose. You come up with it by thinking a lot. If your topic is "protestors against nuclear power," thinking may not be enough; you may have to do some research in the library before you can put your thesis into words. Although you're interested in the topic, you may not know much about it. So read about it and think about it and talk to people who know something about the topic. On the other hand, if you've chosen a personal experience for your topic—bicycling, for example, or working in the dining hall—then you may already know what point you want to make:

> An extended bicycle trip requires careful preparation.
> Dining hall employees deserve better working conditions.

To make sure that you have the writing situation well in hand, write out your thesis statement by filling in these blanks:

In this paper I plan to _____

SHOW/EXPLAIN/PERSUADE, ETC.

_____   _____;

AUDIENCE   TOPIC

I am writing this because _____

PURPOSE

For example:

> In this paper I plan to explain to my classmates that standing up for your beliefs, as the antinuclear protestors have done, can make a difference in the development of nuclear power; I am writing this because a great many students these days seem to be apathetic about public issues.

> In this paper I plan to show the Outing Club that a bicycle trip requires careful preparation; I am writing this because it is important to be prepared for the unexpected as well as for the day-to-day rigors of such a trip.

> In this paper I plan to convince the administration that the student employees in the dining halls deserve better working conditions; I am writing this because only the administration can do something about the problems—and the problems do exist.

11.5

Remember, this statement is for you, the writer; its purpose is to commit you to a goal and to keep you on track. Your reader will probably never see it—at least, not in so many words.

11.5 A *Summary of the Writing Situation: Six Steps*

Here is a step-by-step summary of the procedure for turning a broad subject like energy (or education or furniture) into a clear plan. In following this procedure, *take your time.* Don't go through all the steps in one sitting. Go through Step 1; then carry around in your head some of the topics that interest you. Next, apply Step 2 to those topics, and so on.

Step 1: Generate a list of noun phrases by (a) using the name of your topic as either the headword of a noun phrase or its modifier:

energy crisis	careers in education	furniture design
energy policy	education costs	furniture making
energy sources	education research	furniture sales

and (b) listing kinds (of energy, education, furniture):

water power	private education	antique furniture
oil	tutoring	unfinished furniture
atomic energy	rehabilitation education	office furniture

Step 2: Now ask the six questions that journalists ask about any or all of your noun phrases: Who? What? When? Where? Why? How?

Step 3: Generate further ideas by looking at your narrowed subject from these points of view: (a) as a whole with parts and as a part of the whole; (b) along a time line, past/present/future.

Step 4: Choose a topic.

Step 5: Now carry on a conversation with yourself (or someone else) in which you identify the writing situation by answering the following questions:

- Who wants to know this?
- Why am I writing about this?

Step 6: Continue talking until you can fill in the following blanks:

_____   _____   _____

     Topic   *Audience*   *Purpose*

Step 7: Write out a tentative thesis statement, as follows:

In this paper I plan to _____

                    SHOW/EXPLAIN/PERSUADE, ETC.

_____   _____;

   AUDIENCE   TOPIC

I am writing this because _____.

                            PURPOSE

FOR CLASS DISCUSSION

1. Carry on a conversation or a class discussion that will help you fill in the blanks for the following, or other, energy subtopics:

Topic	Audience	Purpose
a. Woodburning stoves	_____	_____
b. Imported cars	_____	_____
c. Solar energy	_____	_____

2. Generate as many subtopics as you can think of in one or more of the broad subject areas listed by following Step 1 in the summary:

agriculture	feminism	oceanography
animals	fiction	photography
art	fishing	politics
astronomy	forestry	professional sports
athletics	gambling	railroads
aviation	gardening	religion
banking	geography	science fiction
children	gold	sculpture
conservation	interest rates	space exploration
crime	journalism	steel
divorce	lotteries	stocks and bonds
drugs	medical ethics	television
economics	movies	travel
engineering	music	volcanoes
fashion	nutrition	war

12

The Modes
of Composition:
Description

We use and hear description every day in speaking situations:

My new cowboy boots are made of lizard skin.
What a beautiful day. Isn't the breeze refreshing?
I need the book with the blue and tan cover.
I'll have a cheeseburger with lettuce and pickles.
The midterm exam will cover Chapters 1 through 6; it will consist of fifty multiple-choice items, which will constitute half of the total score, and two essay questions, each worth 25 percent.

Sometimes a conversation will include an extended description. For example, a friend in your hometown may ask about your college campus, "What's it like?"

"Well, first of all, the place is huge. It covers blocks and blocks—actually acres and acres. The dorm complex where I live has about ten buildings housing four thousand students. My room is on the seventh floor, so I have a great view of the campus and the stadium. You should see the place on a football Saturday. There's a regular sea of people and cars in the parking lots around the dorms. But then every day is crowded with people. We stand in line for just about everything—the dining hall and the post office and the campus bus. This afternoon I'll be standing in line—well, sitting actually—in the hall outside my English professor's door waiting to talk about my final term paper. Yesterday the entire hall was covered with backpacks and kids in down jackets. Sit-ins like this are common the last two weeks of every term. "

In telling or writing such a description, you are drawing a picture for your listener or reader; you are helping your audience to see what you see. The more specific and concrete and detailed your description is, the more accurate the picture your audience will see. But description is generally not an end in itself; it is a means to an end. The purpose of your campus description is to inform or explain, to answer the question "What's it like?" You could even have a purpose beyond simple information; your actual goal may be to persuade your friend to transfer to your school or to come for a visit. In that case, you would select your descriptive details carefully, emphasizing the good features of the campus and downplaying the disappointments.

In the following description from *To Kill a Mockingbird*, notice how Harper Lee chose details that evoke the discomfort of rain and heat:

> Maycomb was an old town, but it was a tired old town when I first knew it. In rainy weather the streets turned to red slop; grass grew on the sidewalks, the courthouse sagged in the square. Somehow, it was hotter then: a black dog suffered on a summer's day; bony mules hitched to Hoover carts flicked flies in the sweltering shade of live oaks on the square. Men's stiff collars wilted by nine in the morning. Ladies bathed before noon, after their three-o'clock naps, and by nightfall were like soft teacakes with frostings of sweat and sweet talcum.

12.1 The Descriptive Essay: The Writing Situation

Chapter 11 suggests three questions to help identify the writing situation:

- What shall I write about?
- Who wants to know?
- Why should I write it?

The same questions apply when the assignment is a descriptive essay.

Even for the seemingly simple task of describing your dorm room or your apartment, you need to identify your purpose and audience, that is, to answer all three questions. Without a specific purpose and audience in mind, the description will have no focus, no main idea. And there's another, practical, reason for going through the preliminary steps of defining the writing situation: The essay will be much easier to write. For example, you could describe your apartment for a friend who will be moving into a similar one soon and is wondering how much decorating needs to be done, how much room there will be for the stereo, and how much closet space there is. With your purpose and audience clearly in mind, you'll know which details to include and which to leave out.

12.3

12.2 Arrangement

Another decision to make in writing description concerns the arrangement or order of details. One common order is *spatial*, the description that moves from left to right, from top to bottom, or from front to back. In describing your room, you could begin at the door, then move either around or across the room, depending, of course, on your purpose; in describing your neighborhood, you could go from one end of the block to the other.

Sometimes *functional* order is more appropriate, that is, grouping features of the room or the neighborhood or the campus on the basis of their use. For example, in a description of the student union you might describe its facilities for eating, lounging, recreation, business affairs, and so on.

In some descriptions, *dominant* order, based on value or importance, might be the logical arrangement. In a museum the exhibit rooms are more important than the gift shop or the lobby; in the library the books are the most important feature; in your room maybe your stereo equipment or your plant collection is more important to you than even your bed. Such descriptions are generally most effective if you mention the most important feature last.

12.3 Point of View

Still another consideration in writing description is *point of view*, the writer's relationship to the audience and the topic. In describing

12.4

your room for your mother, you would probably use the first person (*I*, *me*, *my*): "My closet is actually spacious." Or you might use a combination that includes *you:* "I suspect you wouldn't recognize this room as mine: The bed is made, the desk is organized, and the closet door actually closes."

But whether or not you use *I*, you must also consider your position in relation to what you're describing. Are you going to put yourself in the picture? If so, where are you? ("Sitting at my desk, I can see the stadium through my curtain of hanging plants.") Is your description of the neighborhood a bird's-eye view from the end of the street, or are you in your house looking out? Is it your personal view, using *I*, or a third-person point of view? ("The tall frame houses stand close together, shoulder to shoulder, on both sides of the block, like two ranks of old soldiers facing each other.") You will probably want to experiment with various points of view before you decide which is the most effective in your writing situation.

12.4 Word Choice

The purpose of descriptive writing, as of all writing, is to call up a response in the reader. The purpose of describing a place or a person or an event is to enable the reader to see that person or place or event as clearly as the writer does. To accomplish this purpose, the writer must understand the meaning that a word is likely to have for the reader.

Meaning, remember, resides in the minds of people. Take the word *hearth*, for example, a word rich in metaphorical meaning. The internalized definition of *hearth*, for most people, suggests a haven, safety, the warmth of family life, and peace. To choose the word *hearth* in describing a room suggests far more than the physical brick or stone around the fireplace. Writers of advertising copy choose words carefully. When real estate ads for houses include "brick hearth" or "fireplace with stone hearth," they do so for good reason.

So it's important to think about those internalized, connotative meanings that people have for certain words. It's also important to think about denotation as specifically and accurately as possible. The more specific the detail in your description, the more likely your reader will be to respond in the way you intend. That detail, incidentally, comes not only from adjectives or other modifiers in the sentence. (*Hearth*, after all, is a noun.) Nouns and verbs lay the groundwork. In Chapter 8 we looked at words in a hierarchy of meaning. The farther down the hierarchy—the farther down to earth—the more specific the referent: *Split-level* is more specific than *house*, which is more specific than *building*. *Saunter* is more specific than *walk*; it is even more specific than *walk slowly* or *walk leisurely*.

We've all heard that a picture is worth a thousand words; what's also true is that a single, well-chosen word is often worth a paragraph. Read again the details in the previously quoted description of the town of Maycomb:

> In rainy weather the streets turned to red slop; grass grew on the sidewalk, the courthouse sagged in the square.

The word *slop* is loaded with connotative meanings. The reader doesn't picture ordinary muddy streets. "Red slop" is sticky and disgusting; and it is everywhere. The streets "turned to" red slop; they weren't simply covered with it. The courthouse seemed to sink into the stuff. And listen to the figurative language—the simile—that the author used in describing the effect of heat on the ladies of Maycomb: "soft teacakes with frosting of sweat and sweet talcum." Her words stimulate the reader's senses.

Here is a description from a student's essay about her job in a veterinary hospital; notice her choice of words:

> The only disgusting part of the job was helping the vets euthanize dogs. A greyhound track nearby provided most of the victims. Greyhounds who couldn't run fast enough were soon strewn about the floor, often seven or eight at a time, eyes glazed and mouths frozen open, to be stuffed into Hefty trash bags and left for the garbage man.
> —KERRY RANKIN

The picture of dead dogs stuffed into Hefty trash bags is a vivid one, easy for a reader to visualize. The concrete detail of "Hefty" makes it ring true, truer than either "plastic bags" or "trash bags" alone would.

FOR CLASS DISCUSSION

1. Here are two passages from John Updike's novel *Rabbit is Rich*. In both of them Harry (Rabbit) Angstrom views his world using

12.4

concrete details and figurative language. Identify the specific words and figures of speech that help you picture the scene.

> The day is still golden outside, old gold now in Harry's lengthening life. He has seen summer come and go until its fading is one in his heart with its coming, though he cannot yet name the weeds that flower each in its turn through the season, or the insects that also in ordained sequence appear, eat, and perish. He knows that in June school ends and the playgrounds open, and the grass needs cutting again and again if one is a man, and if one is a child games can be played outdoors while the supper dishes tinkle in the mellow parental kitchens, and the moon is discovered looking over your shoulder out of a sky still blue, and a silver blob of milkweed spittle has appeared mysteriously on your knee.
>
> The fuzzy gray sofa and the chair that matches and the Barcalounger and the TV set (an Admiral) and Ma Springer's pompous lamps of painted porcelain and tarnished brass and the old framed watercolors sunk to the tint of dust from never being looked at, the table runners Ma once crocheted and her collection of brittle bright knickknacks stored on the treble corner shelves nicked and sanded to suggest antique wood but stemming from an era of basement carpentry in Fred Springer's long married life: . . .

2. Here's another descriptive paragraph that includes nouns and verbs rich in meaning. What is the author's attitude toward the river?

> As it leaves the Rockies and moves downward over the high plains towards the Missouri, the Platte River is a curious stream. In the spring floods, on occasion, it can be a mile-wide roaring torrent of destruction, gulping farms and bridges. Normally, however, it is a rambling, dispersed series of streamlets flowing erratically over great sand and gravel fans that are, in part, the remnants of a mightier Ice Age stream bed. Quicksand and shifting islands haunt its waters. Over it the prairie suns beat mercilessly throughout the summer. The Platte, "a mile wide and an inch deep," is a refuge for any heat-weary pilgrim along its shores. This is particularly true on the high plains before its long march by the cities begins.
>
> —LOREN EISELEY, *The Immense Journey*

WRITING EXERCISES

1. The principal of your old high school has asked you to contribute to a description of your college for a brochure to be distributed to

the senior class. Here are the instructions:

12.4

The students have access to information on the curriculum and on housing and food services; they've also read the student handbook. What we'd like from you for the brochure is a personal view, a description that will take the place of a campus visit.

Write a 300- to 500-word description of your college, following the principal's instructions.

2. Two of your friends have accepted summer jobs in your hometown (or your section of the city) working for the parks and recreation department in its summer playground program. They were there for the job interview in the middle of winter, and it seemed to them a rather gloomy place, so now they're a bit apprehensive about spending three months there. Write a description of your hometown (or neighborhood) in summer that will help them feel better about their decision to take the job.

3. When you write a letter to your parents (or to a friend) or when you read one from them, you can picture them in a setting. You see them in your mind's eye sitting at the kitchen table or watching television in the living room or working in the yard. But if your friend or your parents have never been to your dorm room or apartment, they have no setting in which to picture you when they write you a letter or read one from you. Write a description of your room that will provide a setting in which they can think about you.

4. An exchange student from England (or another country) will be living with you and your family for the school year. The visitor has asked you questions about your family. Write a description of your father or mother (or perhaps a brother or sister) that presents the essence of that person. Keep in mind the kinds of details of habit and personality and physical characteristics that it will be helpful for the visitor—a temporary member of the family—to know.

13

The Modes
of Composition:
Narration

In the introduction to Part III the four modes of discourse
are pictured as concentric circles, with narration encircling description and being encircled by exposition and argumentation. The
following account of a train derailment illustrates how the modes
work together:

> "I was standing right across the road there by my car getting ready
> to change a flat when I heard the train coming. Just as the engine
> reached the crossing, there was a terrible noise. It sounded like a crack
> of thunder. Then there was a loud grinding sound. And the noise didn't
> stop either, the way it would in a car wreck; it kept going on, thundering
> and crashing. All of a sudden the coal cars started to jackknife, falling off
> the tracks like toys, with coal pouring out all over the ground. Coal dust
> and dirt were flying everywhere. Then, in a minute or two, everything
> was still; the only thing moving was the coal, sliding out of the cars in
> piles. I just stood there and watched. It was like something you'd see in
> the movies."

The general purpose of the story is exposition: to explain what
happened, to inform. (This story was actually told to a television news
reporter at the scene of an accident.) The argumentation circle does
not apply in this case, but certainly the inner circle of description

13.1

does. The witness used words of the senses to describe the sounds of sights, to help the listener picture the event as it happened.

All of us tell stories; narration is part of our everyday conversation. But, like description, narration is not generally an end in itself; it is a means to an end. We narrate happenings in order to inform or instruct or to make a point, just as Jesus did with parables and Aesop with fables. The comic tells stories to entertain; the parent tells stories as part of the bedtime ritual to comfort the child. We use the narrative mode when we answer such questions as "What did you do last night?" or "How was your weekend?" or "What happened in the last inning?"

13.1 *The Components of Narration*

The account of the train derailment, which covers only a few minutes of elapsed time, illustrates the main components of the narrative form. The narrator begins by *setting the scene*. In this case, because both the speaker and the listener are at the actual scene of the event, the description of the setting is brief:

"I was standing right across the road there by my car . . ."

A written account of the accident would include details that specifically identify "across the road there."

Another feature of the narrative that requires special attention is the *movement through time*. The time spanned by the narrative may be years or decades, or it may be brief—only minutes or seconds. The time of the event may or may not be specified at the beginning, depending on its importance to the story, but the passing of time will certainly be indicated by adverbs and adverbial phrases and clauses:

"Just as the engine reached the crossing . . ."
"All of a sudden . . ."
"Then, in a minute or two . . ."

You'll notice that these adverbials are all sentence openers, as they so often are in a narrative. These time indicators provide the connection of one idea with the next.

Another important ingredient is the *conclusion,* a way of bringing the narrative to an end. When the storyteller says, "And they lived happily ever after," we know that nothing else will follow. The witness to the accident summarized his reaction, and we expect nothing more:

> "It was like something you'd see in the movies."

Often you can find a conclusion in the purpose, your reason for telling the story:

> That decision changed my life, but I've never regretted making it. You can be sure I never took that shortcut again.

More often than not the story's end has a finality in itself, so that no further concluding statement is necessary. The important consideration is that the reader know that the story is over.

13.2 The Narrative Essay: The Writing Situation

The narrative essay will succeed if you, the writer, have a specific purpose for narrating the experience—that is, when you are responding to a specific writing situation. Unless you have a reason for telling the story, you simply won't know how to tell it. If you write about your summer bicycle trip, for example, the details you emphasize will depend on your purpose and your audience. Do you want to show a potential traveler how important it is to be prepared for the unexpected? Do you want to explain to a cyclist how risky it is to ride on main highways or on narrow country roads? Do you want to dramatize the boredom of bicycling? Its excitement? There are countless ways to relate an experience, depending on the situation Why are you writing this story? Who wants to read it? Just as you select the details of a description on the basis of purpose and audience, you do the same in writing a narrative essay.

The first decision to make in writing the narrative, then, is to identify the writing situation: the topic, the audience, and the purpose. The next step is to establish two points: the point of view and the beginning point.

13.3 *Point of View*

First Person

In writing about an experience that happened to you, you will probably use the first person point of view:

> When the hypnotist asked for a volunteer from the audience, I raised my hand without thinking, and before I knew what was happening, I was standing on the stage in front of the entire student body. What a mistake that was!

As the story unfolds, we expect to continue learning about the feelings and thoughts of the narrator—the "I" of the story. We don't expect to learn firsthand what the hypnotist thinks or feels; those ideas will be filtered through the mind of the narrator:

> When Professor Gaylord extended his hand in greeting, I detected a strange look of satisfaction on his dark features. Maybe he knew an easy mark when he saw one.

Third Person

In writing someone else's story, you will probably use the third person; in other words, you will keep yourself out of it by not using *I*, the first-person pronoun. The following story is told from the point of view of someone other than the narrator—in this case, from the point of view of Doris, the glider pilot. But notice that even in the third person (*she* and *her* rather than *I* and *my*), the reader learns Doris's thoughts and feelings firsthand.

> Expertly catching the updrafts of wind, Doris piloted her sleek glider along the Appalachian ridges hour after hour. Before dawn the weather had looked threatening, but by the time the Piper Cub had towed her up and cut her loose, the sky had begun to clear. Now, after eight hours of concentration, with the sun moving down toward the horizon, Doris was almost sure of breaking her own long-distance soaring record.

Novels are often written from the point of view of a single character. In *At the Shores* the reader sees every scene through the eyes of Jerry Engels, the narrator. But notice that the story is told in the third person, not the first:

13.4

> He swam in the lake, sailed on it, and ran along its shore as if he loved the lake more than he loved Rosalind. And perhaps he did. One could love a lake. Certainly he loved that lake, Lake Michigan, that inland ocean of fresh water. "Michigan" *meant* fresh water, and there it lay, stretched out to the northern horizon, the faintest pale blue on summer mornings as he sat with his arms around his knees beside the pine tree on top of the ridge, waiting for Phil to join him for their morning swim. Phil would come down the path from his house, a beach towel over one shoulder, and then they would go down the dune together, sometimes without even saying "Good morning." Why should they? It was obviously a good morning, with the sun just up and the lake awaiting them. Pale blue in the calm mornings, cloud darkened in the afternoons, wind roughened and white-capped during storms, the lake was always awaiting him. He could not remember a summer day when he had not wanted to be in the lake.
>
> —Thomas Rogers

In some novels different chapters are narrated from different points of view, so that the reader gets "inside" of more than one character. Another technique is that of the omniscient, or all-knowing, narrator, one who knows everything about everyone, including their thoughts and motives, and who reveals to the reader as much as the reader needs to know.

The narrative essay that you write for the composition class will probably be not a work of fiction but a firsthand account of an actual experience, told with a specific audience and purpose in mind. Even so, you as the writer will have to decide on your relationship both to the audience and to the other people in the story in establishing your point of view. And it's important that your point of view be consistent throughout the narrative.

13.4 The Beginning Point

Besides point of view, another point to consider in writing a narrative is the beginning point: Where should you begin the story? A good rule of thumb is to begin as close to the ending as possible. For example, in writing about your experience as the hypnotist's assistant, there's probably no point in beginning the story before the actual experience:

> When I found out that a world-famous hypnotist was coming to campus, I decided that I'd get tickets even if it meant ruining my budget and standing in line all night. So I started to cut back on spending and saved the eight dollars I needed. I've always been fascinated by hypnotism; and I've always believed I could never by hypnotized myself. Little did I know when I bought the tickets that I'd be putting that belief to the test.

The ticket-buying information isn't necessary; it simply delays the action. Your beliefs about hypnotism, on the other hand, probably are important for the reader to know. If so, they can easily be included in the earlier version:

> When the hypnotist asked for a volunteer from the audience, I raised my hand. I've always been fascinated by hypnotism, but I've always believed I was immune to the power of suggestion. So there I was, standing on the stage in front of the entire student body, determined to keep my wits about me.

Suppose you're telling about a trip to the shore or the mountains. Where should you begin? That question can be answered only in terms of purpose. For example, if your purpose is to show how boring your day at the ocean was, you might want to include details of the boring two-hour drive to get there:

> Mother always began the "Did you remember" questions when we started loading the car. "Did you remember to pack the suntan lotion?" "Yes, Mother." "You know you'll get burned. You always do." The questions always continued for at least fifteen miles, but sometimes they lasted for the entire trip: "Did anyone remember the can opener?" "Yes, Mother." "Did you remember to feed the cat, Julie?"
> The drone of questions, the dreary landscape of southern New Jersey, mile after mile. Even the blue sky seemed dull that morning.

On the other hand, if your purpose is to relate the excitement of the day at the shore or an unexpected, perhaps frightening, event that happened there, then the details of the preparations and the drive would probably detract from your story. Instead, start as close to the climax as possible:

> Dad had begun to load the picnic basket, a signal that we'd be leaving soon, when Mother suddenly asked, "Where's Jenny?" I was lying on my beach towel, chin on hands, letting my suit dry out after a swim. I glanced around. Jenny was bound to be somewhere nearby. The place was crowded with people of all sizes and shapes, and there were lots of kids, so it was hard to spot a particular five-year-old.
> About that time all of us got up and started searching the crowd. Then Mother called, "Jenny! Jenny! Where are you?" Her voiced seemed to go nowhere, the sounds of the surf and the people drowning it out.

Even though you have begun this story near its climax at the end of the day, you can still bring in details of the earlier events. You can set the scene by using the technique of flashback:

> The day had been almost perfect until then—not too hot, a gentle breeze off the ocean. Julie and I had spent most of the morning with Jenny, first looking for shells under the pier, then later building a sand fortress. I even took her into the water with me, way out past the breakers. For a little kid, Jenny could certainly hold her own. I knew she was a strong swimmer in the pool, but I was surprised she had no fear at all of the surf; she almost bounced on top of the water.
> But now she was nowhere to be seen. "Hey, Julie," I suggested. "Why don't you look down by the pier. She might have gone back for more shells. I'm going down past the lifeguard's chair."

In using flashbacks, you must be especially careful to keep the reader informed when you shift from present to past time,

The day *had been* almost perfect *up until* then . . .

and then back again:

But now she was nowhere to be seen . . .

13.5 The Use of Quotations

One feature of narrative writing that will add life to your story is the use of direct quotations. The characters in good novels and short

13.5

stories, which are extended narratives, become real people when we hear them speak; we judge the characters in fiction on the basis of their words, just as we do people in real life. The quotations you include in a short narrative paper need not be extended conversations; often just a word or phrase quoted directly can make the difference between dull and lively prose:

> "Ladies and Gentlemen," Professor Gaylord announced, gesturing toward me with his black silk cape. "May I present my assistant."

Compare the direct quote with the report having no quotation:

> Then Professor Gaylord gestured toward me, waving his black silk cape, and introduced me to the audience as his assistant.

The use of direct quotations can also give the story an immediacy, an "I-was-there" quality, that the indirect, or reported, quotation does not have. Here's a different version of the first "trip to the beach" narrative, this time with indirect quotations:

> Mother always began the "Did you remember" questions when we started loading the car. She would ask if I had remembered to pack the suntan lotion. I would tell her I had. Invariably she would warn me about getting sunburned. The questions usually continued for at least fifteen miles. She would wonder aloud if anyone had remembered to pack the can opener or to feed the cat.

In this case the indirect quotations produce a flatness that may, in fact, enhance the feeling of boredom. But generally that flatness detracts from the narrative in that it filters direct speech through the narrator instead of letting the reader hear it firsthand. That directness adds to the tension and the drama. Compare the following version of the episode about Jenny with the earlier one:

> Dad had begun to load the picnic basket, a signal that we'd be leaving soon, when Mother suddenly asked where Jenny was. . . .
> About that time all of us got up and started searching the crowd. Mother called her name, but her voice seemed to go nowhere, the sounds of the surf and the people drowning it out.

The use of direct quotations can be effective even when no actual conversation takes place. Compare the following narratives:

> I was breezing along a smooth stretch of highway, a corridor of tall pines and firs so common in central Oregon, when I picked up speed on a downhill grade. All of a sudden I felt the bike start to vibrate. "Damn! Another flat." I braked carefully, doing my best to stay in control.

> I was breezing along a smooth stretch of highway, a corridor of tall pines and firs so common in central Oregon, when I picked up speed on a downhill grade. All of a sudden I felt the bike start to vibrate. I swore under my breath. I knew a flat tire well enough, so I braked carefully, doing my best to stay in control.

The quoted thoughts in the first version reflect the tension that a flat tire would actually produce. They also eliminate the need for the two additional uses of *I* that the second version includes; the overuse of *I* tends to be a problem for writers of first-person narratives.

13.6 Summary

Topics for narrative essays can be found in everyday happenings, not only in dramatic, headline-making events. As with any essay, the important consideration is purpose. Think of purpose as the point you want to prove with your story. Even an undramatic event like a shopping trip can prove a point:

Shopping with credit cards is too easy.

or

Shopping for groceries on an empty stomach is always dangerous to my budget.

or

Christmas shopping brings out the Scrooge in me.

And remember, in planning your narrative, to make careful decisions about point of view, the beginning point, the movement through time, the conclusion, descriptive details, and the use of quotations.

13.6

1. Write about an experience that revealed something to you about yourself or another person—for example, when you learned that

   • teachers are people too,
   • parents can make mistakes,
   • a brother or sister (or parent) can also be a friend,
   • neighbors don't always understand the meaning of "neighborly,"
   • it pays to mind your own business,
   • you are braver (or stronger) than you suspected.

   Your purpose can be to enable someone—a new friend perhaps—to know you better.

2. Narrate a personal experience that illustrates an aphorism or a proverb, such as one of the following:

   The road to hell is paved with good intentions.
   We have met the enemy and they are us.
   All that glitters is not gold.
   He who laughs last laughs best.
   A fool and his money are soon parted.

   This essay can be for a general audience, such as your class—anyone who can profit from your experience.

3. Write about a time when you experienced an emotion, such as fear, prejudice, loneliness, or the awareness of death. Here again, your purpose can be simply to enable someone to know you better. Or perhaps you wish to assure an unhappy friend that having such feelings is a normal part of life.

14

The Modes of Composition: Exposition

The term *exposition* refers to writing meant to inform or explain—to "expose." Unlike *narration*, a term that suggests a particular form, an expository essay can take many forms, including that of narration. The diagram of concentric circles in the introduction to Part III shows both description and narration enclosed within the exposition circle.

The expository patterns we will examine in this chapter constitute methods or techniques for dealing with topics. They are discovery procedures you can use to trigger ideas on a particular topic. In writing about the internal combustion engine, for example, given one audience and purpose you might explain how it works, step-by-step, in a process paper. For another you might analyze the engine, explaining its parts and how they work together, in a division or analysis paper. For another audience and purpose you might compare piston and rotary engines in a comparison/contrast paper.

On the other hand, the assignments for your composition course may be organized according to the modes of discourse. Instead of a topic, your assignment may be the mode itself: "Write a comparison/contrast essay" or "Write a definition essay." Your job, then, is to discover the writing situation—topic, purpose, and audience—that will best be served by that expository pattern.

The explanations in this chapter should help you in both situations. And the suggestions for writing papers may also trigger further ideas for successful topics and strategies.

14.1 Process

The process paper takes the form of narrative in that it involves movement through time; it is an explanation based on steps taken in chronological order. We use this form of exposition to explain how to do something or how to get somewhere rather than simply to relate an experience. We become the audience for this form of exposition when we read the packet of material from the registrar entitled "Registration Procedure" or when we find, after buying a table or a chair or an outdoor grill, that the box is labeled "Assembly Required."

As with any writing task, in the process paper it is important to be clear about the writing situation: the audience and the purpose. The situation will also include the writer's attitude toward the process:

"This is easy; anyone can do it."

or

"I know this looks complicated, but it's really not, and you'll be glad you took the time."

or

"This is complicated, so you'll have to pay attention; don't miss a single step."

or

"This is sheer drudgery, I know, but since you have to do it, you may as well do it right the first time."

The successful topic for a process paper is one that requires more than a simple list of instructions. It is a "how to" paper in which the writer gets involved with the reader in ways that the writer of printed recipes or assembly instructions does not. Further, it is a "how to" that can be explained by words; some instructions require actual "hands-on" demonstration and are best avoided as topics for essays. You don't learn to ski or to swim by reading instructions; and the best way to learn the forehand volley is to see it demonstrated and then to practice, preferably with a tennis coach standing by. Written instruction can, of course, help the skier or the swimmer or the tennis player to improve, so such topics can be successful when the essay is addressed to the experienced audience.

Besides the "how to" paper, which gives the reader instructions for accomplishing a particular goal, the process paper may have a purpose that is simply informative: to explain how something happens ("How Oil from the Desert Heats the Homes of Saint Paul") or happened ("An Environmental Success Story: The Clean-up of the Willamette River"). Such topics are clearly narratives, in that they tell about events through time, but they are narratives that emphasize a process: the steps by which something happened or happens. We also see this kind of essay in reports of a scientific or historical nature, such as this explanation of evolution (italics added to show the use of time indicators):

> Consider how a variety of one species might be converted into a new species. *To begin with*, some barrier may arise between one part of a species and another. Such barriers may be geographic—part of a population may cross a land bridge, for example, which might later become submerged under the sea. *Following reproductive isolation*, genetic changes may *then* occur that will yield an increasing number of differences between the isolated groups. Some of the newly acquired differences may be attributed to new and accidental genetic events that will be of selective advantage in the new environment. Other differences may result from previously existing characteristics that suddenly become much more or less favorable in a new environment and that are thus treated differently by the winnowing effects of natural selection. *Finally*, a point is reached at which divergence is so great that the two populations no longer can interbreed, which means speciation has occurred.
>
> —*Biology: An Appreciation of Life*

WRITING EXERCISES

1. Explain how a friend with very little time (a day, perhaps) and almost no money can have a good time in New York City (or Kansas City or Memphis or Denver or your hometown). Plan an excursion, taking into account the individual's personal interests, such as architecture, sports, horticulture, music, and so on.

2. Explain how to make homemade ice cream (or pita bread or potato chips). Ask yourself why anyone would want to bother, as the store-bought variety is readily available and tasty.

3. Explain how a news story gets from the reporter's notes to the front page of the campus newspaper. Your audience is someone who thinks it must be a terribly complicated process.

4. Explain what happens when a person places a "buy" or a "sell" order with a stock broker. Your audience is someone who understands nothing about all those shouting people at the stock exchange.

5. Explain how to start a typing service or a lawn-care service or some other money-making project. Your audience is someone who needs to earn some money but who is looking for a conventional part-time job in a fast-food restaurant.

6. Explain how to hold a successful auction or garage sale. Your audience is someone who doesn't realize that there are many details to think about in planning such an event.

7. Explain how to get an animal ready for showing at a livestock exhibit or at a dog show. Most people probably don't realize that there's more to showing an animal than simply leading it into the ring.

8. Explain how a dog (and its owner) are trained at obedience school. Your purpose could be to show how much patience and hard work such training takes.

9. Explain to someone you know how to get started with a hobby, or an activity that you enjoy. Be sure to help the novice avoid the pitfalls you might have encountered. Here are some possibilities:

stamp collecting	kite making
bookbinding	organic gardening
physical fitness	photography
herb growing	candle making
Chinese cooking	beer making
tie dyeing	jelly making

14.2 Division (or Analysis)

We use *division*, sometimes called *analysis*, in an expository essay when we explain an event or a place or an entity by analyzing its parts. Analysis also describes a way of thinking; for example, we automatically consider the separate parts when we think about Christmas (gifts, music, decorations, parties, food) or school (classes, teachers, social functions, friends, messy lockers) or the after-school job washing dishes (piles of dirty silverware, the temperamental machine, greasy pots, stacks of clean plates to carry, co-workers) or Disneyland (Main Street, the Magic Kingdom, Tomorrowland, the parking lot).

But in writing an essay about such events or places, we don't randomly list the parts as they come to mind; we first think through a principle of organization that will best suit the topic and purpose. For example, in describing the student union for the freshman handbook, we would probably divide or analyze it on the basis of its functions, emphasizing how many different needs it serves: recreation, eating, meeting, conducting business affairs, lounging, and so on. But for the campus visitor who's afraid of getting lost in such a big place, we would probably divide it spatially—east wing to west wing or basement to first floor to second—in order to show how easy it is to get to where you want to go.

We will sometimes use this kind of analysis to show that the subject is either (1) less complicated or (2) more complicated than it may seem at first glance. We make the point, then, by emphasizing either (1) the simplicity or (2) the complexity of the parts and the way they work together.

The following description of the nervous system illustrates the use of division in expository writing. It first divides the nerve cell into its parts, then describes the parts of the whole system, or network, explaining the function of each part and how the parts work together:

Although the activity of human nerve cells produces a great variety of effects, the cells are similar in structure. A nerve cell has three components: the cell body; a number of fibers, called dendrites, which can pick up electrical impulses from neighboring cells; and a single fiber, or axon, which can pass on impulses to other cells. With a few exceptions, nerve cells are elaborate chemical devices designed to conduct impulses in one direction only: from the tips of the dendrites into the cell body, and then from the cell body out along the axon, which usually terminates among a dendrite cluster of other cells.

The nerve cells of the human body are gathered into three great structures that comprise the nervous system. First and foremost is the brain, a mass of tissue inside the skull that consists of about 10 billion interconnected nerve cells. Stemming from the brain is the spinal cord, a sheath of nervous tissue enclosed in membranes, extending two thirds of the way down the backbone. The central core of this sheath is H-shaped and is made up of nerve cells; the surrounding matter is for the

14.2

most part long cables of fibers, for the axons of spinal nerve cells may extend two or three feet.

The brain and the cord are the two structures that make up the central nervous system.

The third structure of the nervous system as a whole is a network of nerves reaching throughout the body called the peripheral system. The main trunk lines consist of cell fibers emerging from the brain and the cord, bundled together into large cranial and spinal nerves. Each bundle is a cable composed of many thousands of fibers. These nerves divide and subdivide again and again so that, finally, single minute fibers reach into every area of the body. The peripheral system and the spinal cord together provide physical routes of communication, most of which can be seen with the naked eye, between every part of the body and the brain.

—JOHN ROWAN WILSON, *The Mind*

WRITING EXERCISES

1. Take a current issue that concerns your campus or town (e.g., parking regulations, public transportation, the alcohol policy, the curfew). Write a report for the campus newspaper in which you analyze its parts, emphasizing either its complexity or its simplicity to help the readers understand the issue better.

2. Explain how complicated a seemingly simple object really is by examining its parts: a baseball glove, skis, a wood-burning stove, a cowboy boot, a running shoe, a bicycle, a violin. Your audience is someone who doesn't understand why the object costs so much.

3. Show how simple a seemingly complicated object is by examining its parts: a bicycle, a computer, a television set, a radio, a stereo, a piano. Your audience is someone who is depressed by the complications of technology.

4. Examine the parts of an institution to show how it functions: local government, your school's administration, the library, a race track, the stock exchange, the state lottery, the criminal justice system in your county, the police department. Your purpose is to produce a description for the campus career center, showing potential employees the possibilities for employment.

5. Explain a job you have held on the basis of its separate parts or routines. Your principle of organization will be something other than chronological: major duties followed by minor duties, for

example. Your purpose is to explain to a skeptical friend either (a) that a seemingly boring job is really quite challenging or (b) that a job one would think challenging is, in fact, pretty boring.

14.3

14.3 Comparison/Contrast

Many of our decisions are the result of the comparing and the contrasting that we engage in every day. Comparing (seeing similarities) and contrasting (seeing differences) are among the primary tools of analysis that we use in making small decisions about what to have for dinner or which movie to see, as well as important ones about which college to attend or which job to take. When we are confronted with alternatives that seem almost alike at the outset, we look for the features that will help us to differentiate them and to see the contrasts. We use comparison when we recognize similarities in two seemingly different things (soap operas are like gothic novels) or when we examine the unfamiliar in terms of the familiar (the body's circulatory system functions as a city's transportation network does).

In writing the comparison/contrast essay, you should first outline the important points of similarity or difference that you plan to analyze and then decide which scheme of organization will best accomplish your purpose: a point-by-point analysis or a whole-subject analysis. This first step, you'll notice, makes use of division. For example, in an essay showing the difference between downhill and cross-country skiing, you would begin by outlining the components of both sports, by analyzing the parts. Here are five points of comparison you might consider:

A. the equipment needed
B. the cost
C. the terrain
D. the skills required
E. safety

Depending on your purpose and audience, you would then decide on your overall plan of organization. For example, if you want to tell your friends who are thinking about investing in downhill equipment about the joys of cross-country skiing, you might emphasize the terrain and the economics. Your scheme of organization

14.3

might be as follows, a whole-subject analysis:

> I. Downhill
>   A. Cost
>   B. Terrain
> II. Cross-country
>   A. Cost
>   B. Terrain

In the whole-subject scheme of analysis you cover all the points on downhill skiing followed by all the points of cross-country, and because your purpose is to emphasize the joys of cross-country, you would deal with it last; the last point will be remembered most clearly.

Perhaps your purpose is to show nonskiers that cross-country skiing is a good compromise if they're wary of ski lifts and steep slopes. In this case you'll probably emphasize different points, not only the terrain itself but also the safety factors and the skills involved. You might do so using a point-by-point scheme:

> I. Terrain
>   A. Downhill
>   B. Cross-country
> II. Skills Involved
>   A. Downhill
>   B. Cross-country
> III. Safety
>   A. Downhill
>   B. Cross-country

If the purpose of the essay is to show the advantages and the disadvantages of both downhill and cross-country skiing, you could follow either plan: a point-by-point discussion or a single analysis of each. And you would probably want to cover all five points of comparison.

Sometimes the purpose of a comparison/contrast essay is to show changes over a period of time: the early work of an artist compared with the later work; a city block fifty years ago and today. And we've all heard the comparison/contrast speeches from our parents that begin, "When I was young . . ." In essays showing the before and after of a person or a place or an activity, probably the whole-subject (rather than the point-by-point) scheme will be the most effective organization, as for example in comparing the early and late work of an artist. The purpose of the essay and the number of points of comparison will, of course, be the determining factors.

14.3

As in every writing task, you must identify the purpose and the audience in planning the comparison/contrast essay. Let's say you're planning to compare your hometown as it is today and as it was twenty years ago. First you must answer the two questions that define the writing situation:

- Why write about it?
- Who wants to know?

Depending on your purpose, you may want to discuss both similarities and differences. In what ways has the town changed? In what ways has it stayed the same? Has it changed haphazardly, or have zoning laws and planning commissions set the rules? Has the town gained a solid economic base with new industry? Has overregulation or a high tax rate or lack of a labor pool kept needed industry away? Have high real estate prices kept low-income people from finding decent housing? Are the changes good or bad?

You will want to ask and answer such questions in order to identify a purpose, an audience, and your own attitude toward the topic; then you can decide on the particular points of similarity and difference that you wish to emphasize and can determine which scheme of organization will be the most effective for your essay.

WRITING EXERCISES

1. Compare/contrast old and current western movies (or movie heroes or themes) to show how attitudes (toward Indians or toward the environment, for example) have changed or perhaps to show the difference in the degree to which the characters' lives are depicted realistically. Your audience is a movie fan who thinks that movies haven't really changed much.
2. Compare/contrast dorm life and Greek life for someone who is considering pledging a fraternity or sorority. Your friend is also committed to scholarship. Make your own attitude clear.

14.3

3. Compare/contrast the expectations of young women in the year your mother graduated from high school and in the year you did. Your audience is your mother (or someone of her generation, man or woman), who doesn't see any difference.

4. Show how attitudes toward women have changed by contrasting the way women are pictured in ads in magazines now with the way they were pictured thirty years ago. Your audience could be either a feminist who believes that little has changed or someone who believes that women have never been unfairly treated.

5. Compare the human brain and the computer for someone who thinks that computers are smarter than humans.

6. Show how the life of a dairy farmer (or a producer of cattle, poultry, corn) has changed in the past decade or two. Your audience is a city slicker whose only ideas of farming come from "Hee Haw" or "Little House on the Prairie."

7. The school district is considering the adoption of a twelve-month school plan. All students would get to choose their own vacation schedules: any three months, one month at a time, as long as there are at least two months between each vacation period. Teachers' vacations would be somewhat more flexible, with the possibility of two months at a time. Compare/contrast this system with the current nine-month school year for readers of the local paper. The idea is new to the community, a small town in northern Indiana, where the residents are accustomed to hot summers and snowy winters. Your purpose is strictly informative; you are not advocating one system or the other.

8. Your best friend has just learned that his or her family is moving from your small town of twenty thousand to a big city of a million people (or vice versa, from the city to the small town). Compare/contrast life in the two environments in order to reassure your friend that the world has not come to an end.

9. The following passage compares human growth to the growth of a lobster:

> We are not unlike a particular hardy crustacean. The lobster grows by developing and shedding a series of hard, protective shells. Each time it expands from within, the confining shell must be sloughed off. It is left exposed and vulnerable until, in time, a new covering grows to replace the old.
>
> With each passage from one stage of human growth to the next we, too, must shed a protective structure. We are left exposed and vulner-

able—but also yeasty and embryonic again, capable of stretching in ways we hadn't known before. These sheddings may take several years or more. Coming out of each passage, though, we enter a longer and more stable period in which we can expect relative tranquility and a sense of equilibrium regained.

—GAIL SHEEHY, *Passages*

Write an essay in which you show how an aspect of people—either people in general or someone in particular—resembles an animal or a bird or an insect. Your audience could be a small child or, perhaps, a fellow philosopher.

14.4 *Classification*

You engaged in classification the day you moved into your dorm room or apartment when you put your belongings into the closets and drawers and cupboards. You classified your blouses or shirts into those that wrinkle when folded and those that don't: One group went on hangers and the other into the drawer. The books on your bookshelves, the dishes in the kitchen cupboards, the tools and assorted paraphernalia in the garage or workshop—all have undergone the process of classification.

Scientists have a word for this activity of putting individuals into groups: *taxonomy,* the science of classification. You studied the taxonomy of plants and animals when you learned such terms as *phylum, class, order, family, genus,* and *species.* Each of these is a division in which particular characteristics define the members of the group.

As nonscientists we engage in classification whenever we take an array of items or ideas or people and put them into groups. The way we classify them depends on our purpose. In considering foods, for example, we may be counting calories (Class 1—eat all you want; Class 2—count carefully; Class 3—avoid completely); counting pennies (bargain, expensive but necessary, splurge item); or counting nutrients (good for you, so-so, strictly junk food). When we put the groceries away, we classify them on the basis of keeping ability: perishable (into the refrigerator or freezer) and nonperishable (into the cupboard). People with allergies classify foods on still another basis: safe, to be approached with caution, and to be avoided completely.

14.4

Classification can be thought of as the opposite of division: Classification begins with an array of individuals and puts them into groups on the basis of shared characteristics or similarities—from the parts to the whole; division begins with the whole and looks for the differences that determine the parts.

The classification essay uses the categories to explain a concept. For example, one way to show the diversity in the women's movement would be to classify all of the women's groups according to their purposes: political groups, support groups, professional associations, and so on. You can classify all of the services on your campus or in your community for a variety of purposes: according to the kinds of volunteers they need, perhaps, or the clientele they serve. What kinds of home businesses are being conducted in your community? A classification could serve a useful purpose for people who are trying to think of new ways of earning extra money or who want to go into business for themselves. Or you could explain what a particular job or profession entails by classifying the many facets of that job. What does it mean to be a stock broker or an estate planner or a personnel director? What does it mean to be in real estate or public relations?

The classification essay also enables the reader to see people or things in a new, often humorous or satirical, way. You might, for example, offer the reader a fresh look at tailgaters, classifying them on the basis of their menus (from the beer-and-potato-chip crowd to the champagne-and-caviar group), or you might classify sunbathers on the basis of their lotions, dieters on the basis of their conversations about dieting, or pet owners on the hairiness of their pets.

To write a successful classification essay, you need to keep in mind several guidelines, or steps, to follow:

1. Study the items to be classified in order to establish a principle for putting the individual members into groups.
2. Make sure that your classes are both mutually exclusive and exhaustive.
3. Don't classify something that's already been classified. (There's no reason to classify the courses available according to the departments that offer them; that's already been done thoroughly, in the college catalog.)
4. Make clear your reason for the classification. Humor, of course, can be a reason in itself.

5. Avoid stereotyping and incomplete classification of the group. Be sure that the categories are real, not imposed.

14.4

WRITING EXERCISES

1. Study your classmates in a fairly large class during a lecture. Write a humorous essay in which you classify them according to a particular principle: body or eye movement, perhaps, or posture, or note-taking behavior.
2. There are many other possibilities for humorous classifications of people. Study your fellow diners at breakfast or lunch; joggers; students in the computer center; spectators at a concert or a game; grocery shoppers in the checkout lines; customers where you work; teachers you have known.
3. Classify the groceries in your supermarket (or in just one aisle of the market) in order to do one of the following:
   a. Explain to your friends who are bored with their own cooking that they needn't be world travelers to enjoy a diversity of cuisine.
   b. Show the budget-conscious that in general we are extravagant shoppers, wasting a large part of our grocery money on food that provides little nutrition.
   c. Show how the technology of packaging and preserving has changed our eating habits.
4. Here's another grocery store task: Write down all of the kinds of groceries that you (or your family) *never* buy; classify them to discover something about yourself.
5. Classify the extracurricular activities at your school, emphasizing the diversity of interests and people they serve. Your audience is a student who constantly complains that there's nothing to do but study.
6. In the following quotation, Francis Bacon classified books into three categories:

   Some books are to be tasted, others to be swallowed, and some few to be chewed and digested.

   Write a classification essay in which you put your own personal collection of books into his three categories, explaining why they belong in a particular class. Do you find that you need other categories? Add them if necessary. Your purpose is to help a special friend to know you better.

14.5 Definition

The modes of exposition that we have looked at so far—process, division, comparison/contrast, and classification—are more than patterns of writing; they are modes of thinking as well. Nonliterate societies and preschool children engage in these kinds of exposition. Definition is another such method of exposition, one we use whenever the question "What is it?" comes up. And our answers to such questions, our definitions, make use of all the other modes.

To answer the question "What is it?" a scientific definition first establishes the class (genus) to which the member belongs, then shows the differences that set it apart from other members of the class. A dictionary definition records the current usage of a word with explanations, examples, and synonyms, along with its origin. Historical dictionaries, such as the thirteen-volume *Oxford English Dictionary,* give not only the origin of a word and its earliest recorded uses, but the changes in form and meaning that it has undergone through the years.

Writers often have occasion to include definitions, sometimes to explain an unfamiliar term and sometimes to stipulate the meaning of the term in a particular context. So, to a certain extent, definition is a part of all the modes of exposition, and certainly of persuasion as well.

But definition may also be the general purpose of the essay. An item in an exam, for instance, may call for an extended definition: Define *supply-side economics;* define the *ashcan school* of painting; define *expansionism* as used in the 1930s. In answering such questions, you would probably use both the scientific and the dictionary methods, explaining what the concept means, perhaps even what it ought to mean, and how it differs from similar concepts. For example, you might give the original, classical, meaning of *supply-side economics,* using actual illustrations of how the concept has worked in the economy, both past and present. You might also explain how different economists or economic philosophies judge it, giving the pros and cons.

The following description of a katydid is a good example of an extended definition. It begins by putting the katydid into the grasshopper class and then describing a feature that differentiates it from other members of the class; then it adds details of other distinguishing characteristics. The essay first appeared in *The New York Times* as one of Borland's regular nature columns.

> The katydid is a green grasshopper with a built-in fiddle that can play only one monotonous three-note tune. But nature so managed matters that the katydid has a reputation as a prophet, a reputation actually about as dubious as that of the woodchuck or the woolly bear caterpillar. In fact, whoever wrote the lyrics for the katydid's tune missed a bet by not using the words, "Frost is near," or "Six more weeks." Obviously, the prophet's mantle fell late on the katydid's green wings.
>
> As an insect, the katydid has few distinctions. It hatches from an egg that looks something like a miniature lentil. It has no wings to begin with, hence no "voice" since it creates its characteristic sound as a cricket does, by rubbing its wings together. It eats leaves but it's not the voracious type and does no lasting damage to the trees it patronizes. By August it reaches the winged stage and begins to make itself heard. The male does. The female is a silent partner. If she disputes her mate, human ears never hear her. Her ears, by the way, are near her knees, which may make the sound feel like sciatica.
>
> Sometimes it frosts six weeks after the first katydid is heard, but more often it doesn't in this area. Our katydids miss the mark by two weeks, at least. But there is no doubt that when the katydid begins to scratch the night the bloom is fading from the rose of Summer. Their clocks may be fast, but they are personally shaping the season, filing the echoing edges of the night, scraping them, rasping them, fitting August to September to Autumn.
>
> —HAL BORLAND, *Sundial for the Seasons*

In an essay defining *vulgar*, the author included a description of his uncle in order to illustrate what vulgar is *not*. Note especially how he differentiates "vulgar" from "gross" and "uncouth."

> But to see Uncle Jake in action you had to see him at table. He drank whiskey with his meal, the bottle before him on the table along with another of seltzer water, both of which he supplied himself. He ate and drank like a character out of Rabelais. My mother served him his soup course, not in a regular bowl, but in a vessel more on the order of a tureen. He would eat hot soup and drink whiskey and sweat—my Uncle

14.5

Jake did not, decidedly, do anything so delicate as perspire—and sometimes it seemed that the sweat rolled from his face right into his soup dish, so that, toward the end, he may well have been engaged in an act of liquid auto-cannibalism, consuming his own body fluids with a whiskey chaser.

He was crude, certainly, my Uncle Jake; he was coarse, of course; gross, it goes without saying; uncouth, beyond question. But was he vulgar? I don't think he was. For one thing, he was good-hearted, and it somehow seems wrong to call anyone vulgar who is good-hearted. But more to the point, I don't think that if you had accused him of being vulgar, he would have known what the devil you were talking about. To be vulgar requires at least a modicum of pretension, and this Uncle Jake sorely lacked. "Wulgar," he might have responded to the accusation that he was vulgar, "so vat's dis wulgar?"

—ARISTIDES, "What Is Vulgar?" *American Scholar* (Winter 1981/82)

WRITING EXERCISES

1. Write a narrative in which you make an abstract concept concrete, as in the story of Uncle Jake. Here are some possibilities: nonconformity, responsibility, revenge, injustice, viciousness, stupidity, expediency, procrastination.

2. The following noun phrases mean different things to different people; and such terms can often be defined in terms of people: *the Old West, the early bird, a tower of strength, a southern belle, a fanatic, a liberated woman, a genius, a pressure situation.* Define one of these terms, or a similar one, by describing a person, either from real life or from literature.

3. The news media often defend their publication of a story on the grounds of the "public's right to know." What does that phrase mean? Write an essay to explain its meaning to (a) an avid reader of the news tabloids that specialize in sensationalism and gossip, or (b) a reader of the *Washington Post* or *The New York Times* who thinks of such sensationalism as shoddy journalism.

15

The Modes
of Composition:
Argumentation

Argumentation is all around us. On a summer afternoon a friend persuades us to go swimming: "Come on. You'll enjoy yourself. Besides, it's too hot to work." We argue in favor of a particular movie: "It's good—a lot like the early James Bond pictures." A woman persuades her husband to rake the leaves: "The doctor says you need the exercise." Or to fix the roof: "The leaks are ruining the insulation." A parent persuades a child to eat spinach: "It's good for you." Or broccoli: "It's nothing like spinach."

Such snippets of conversation are so commonplace, you may not think of them as arguments at all. Certainly they're not the verbal knock-down-drag-out variety we usually think of as arguments. But we can classify them as arguments because their subject matter is arguable: They are statements that can be supported by evidence. And underlying them are questions, the answers to which are matters of probability, not fact:

Is the new spy movie a good one?
Would raking the leaves be good for my health?

In contrast, consider the following questions:

Who holds the world's ski-jumping record?
When did C.S. Lewis write *The Screwtape Letters*?

The answers to these questions are not arguable. Although you may not know them, someone does. Right or wrong, your answers are verifiable; these are matters of fact.

But the questions concerning the movie's quality and the effects of leaf raking on the health are not questions of fact; neither are they simply opinions, matters of personal taste. You may be tempted to dismiss someone's point of view about a movie as "mere opinion," and, in fact, sometimes it may be. For example, if someone says, "It's a terrible movie because I can't stand spy pictures," then there's no arguing; there's no evidence that can counter personal taste. But the usual movie review, the kind of thoughtful judgment we get from professional reviewers, is much more than personal taste. Movie reviewers back up their judgments with evidence: specific details about directing and casting and acting and editing and camera angles and special effects. To refute their judgment, you have to find fault with their evidence or come up with evidence of your own.

15.1 *Topics for Argument*

Argumentation and argumentative writing, then, concern matters on which people hold differing views, with reasons for holding them. Our lives are filled with such arguable matters, from questions and problems of a personal nature ("Should I let Joe borrow the car tonight?" "Is civil engineering the right major for me?") to complex global issues: ("Should the U.S. declare a freeze on nuclear weapons?" "Restrictive tariffs do more harm than good." "How can we best promote international cooperation to save the whales?")

The topics for argumentative essays are just such arguable questions:

Questions of value and/or ethics:
• Is it good or bad?
• Is it right or wrong?

Questions of definition and explanation:
• What is it?
• What is it like or unlike?
• What caused it?
• What will happen next?

Questions of policy:
•What should we do about it?
• Who should be held responsible?

An effective topic for the argumentative essay need not be a major controversial issue, such as nuclear weapons or tariff policies or saving the whales. Any issue on which opinions differ is a potential topic, from the merits of a movie to a plan of action for solving a local problem. Editorial pages and letters to editors abound with controversial issues. Specialized publications dealing with such subjects as art, child care, consumer protection, the drug industry, energy, entertainment, health care, the juvenile justice system, pornography, and religion reveal in their letters columns and editorial pages numerous controversial issues that you may not have thought about. Letters to the editor in weekly newsmagazines and daily papers— even your campus paper—are usually written to present a different side of a particular story or to take exception to a reporter's point of view. Controversies crop up every day on subjects both large and small, both personal and public. The argumentative essay gives you a chance to study a controversial issue and to take a stand.

15.2 The Argumentation Orbit

You'll recall the diagram of concentric circles on page 266, showing argumentation as the outer orbit; this placement illustrates the notion that in argument we make use of description and narration and exposition to accomplish our persuasive purposes.

In one sense the term *argument* names a purpose, whereas the other three modes—description, narration, and exposition— designate methods of achieving that purpose. In that sense we might think of all writing as essentially persuasive. We analyze and define and compare and classify in order to find answers to those arguable questions we listed earlier:

• Is it good or bad?
• Is it right or wrong?
• What is it?
• What's it like?

15.3

Certainly some of the topics we considered in the earlier chapters could easily have a persuasive purpose:

> Stacie describes the campus in glowing terms so her friend will visit next weekend.
>
> Mary compares downhill with cross-country skiing to persuade someone to give cross-country a try.
>
> Jamie analyzes the job market to convince his parents that he ought to switch to engineering.
>
> Teresa defines *vulgar* in terms of Uncle Jake to convince a friend that such a derogatory term doesn't apply to her uncle.

How, then, does the argumentative essay differ from the other modes of composition?

One difference between argument and the other modes is the extent to which the audience affects the content and the organization of the argumentative essay. As you know, a sense of audience is important in all writing. But in argumentation the audience has more influence; it is somewhat less passive. The audience becomes involved in your writing of argument, like a nagging voice constantly reminding you: "Prove it." "What about the other point of view?" As the writer, you must listen to that voice and accommodate the audience throughout the essay, in all of its parts.

15.3 The Parts of the Argumentative Essay

The number *three* seems to have special significance in the structuring of essays. It first cropped up in our discussion of the components of the writing situation: topic, purpose, and audience. In Chapter 16 we will use it again in describing the identifiable parts of every essay: beginning, middle, and end—or introduction, body, and conclusion. And now, in the discussion of the argumentative essay, another trio appears. The essay's middle part, the body, generally has three subsections: the *background*, the *evidence*, and the *refutation*. As we examine those parts, we will see the importance of the audience on the focus and content of each.

The discussion of introductions and conclusions in Chapter 16 applies to all essays, including argumentation. Here we will take up only the three components of the middle.

Background

15.3

The knowledge of the audience obviously determines how much background information is needed. For example, a newspaper editorial writer, in bringing a new issue before the public, may have to explain the background in great detail. When the issue is complex, this section could easily be a long one. In other circumstances, however, with a more informed audience, the background information may simply be a few words included in the introduction. For the essays you write, the amount will vary.

Let's say you're proposing that the local planning commission build bicycle paths in your area. Before writing the essay, you will make assumptions about the commission's current knowledge of the topic. If you are bringing up for the first time the problems that bicyclists encounter, you will probably have to spend time explaining the problem, even documenting that a problem exists. The knowledge of the audience determines the extent of your explanation. In writing about a campus issue—a problem regarding parking or dining-hall regulations or registration—you can assume that your fellow students understand the problem. But if your real audience is the administration, you may have to explain the background of the problem in detail, in ways they may not have thought about before.

Evidence

The evidence will probably make up the largest part of the essay, but, again, its extent will be determined by the current beliefs and knowledge of the audience and by the writer's purpose. Sometimes a single piece of evidence is enough to convince an audience. The data regarding heavy traffic in front of the school may be all the evidence the city council needs to approve of a traffic light. In other circumstances, you may need a variety of data or several examples to prove a point. In the next section we will look closely at ways of finding and using evidence.

Refutation

Here the term *refutation* means simply the awareness of another point of view. You must be prepared for counterevidence that the audience is likely to have heard or to believe; you must anticipate objections. For example, in writing an essay on the importance of developing nuclear power, you can't overlook legitimate fears about safety that your audience may have:

> Safety is an important issue in any discussion of nuclear power. Accidents like the one at Three Mile Island are of great concern to the nuclear power industry. But, interestingly, that accident, along with other smaller problems that have come up in recent years, has had an overall positive outcome. The nuclear power industry has learned a great deal from past mistakes. Further, new technology has made a recurrence of the TMI accident extremely remote. The small risk is more than offset by the enormous advantages of nuclear power to the nation's economy.

Acknowledging the audience's fears as legitimate in this way also enhances your credibility.

Except for the introduction and the conclusion, the order of the parts in the argumentative essay is not fixed, nor is it important that the background, the evidence, and the refutation occupy clearly separate sections. You might, for example, include the background or the refutation in the introduction. What is important is that you consider all the parts and that you take the audience into account as you make your decisions.

15.4 The Appeals of Argument

The word *appeals* here refers to evidence; it goes back to the days of classical Greek oratory, two thousand years ago. In this section, where we look at ways of discovering evidence for arguments, you'll see that the number *three* comes up once more. In discussing the rhetorical situation of argument, Aristotle identified three kinds of strategies, or appeals, that will persuade an audience: *ethical appeals, emotional appeals,* and *logical appeals.*

Ethical Appeals

We are making use of the ethical appeal whenever we follow the dictum "Consider the source." The extent to which an audience will judge arguments as sound or will accept them as valid depends in large measure on their perception of the person making the argument.

Ethical appeals apply in all of our dealings with others. If the dentist recommends a filling or a root canal, we will probably agree to have it done. We're convinced not by the X-ray evidence, which we don't understand, nor, often, even by pain, which we may not be feeling at the moment, but by our perception of the dentist's knowlege and integrity and character—and the dental school diploma on the wall. But if our first response to the dentist's suggestion is to wonder, "What's in it for you? A big fee?", then the ethical appeal is obviously not enough to convince us; we'll need other kinds of evidence. In fact, we probably ought to find a new dentist.

15.4

Ethical proof is not necessarily a matter of expert opinion; it simply involves the character of the speaker or writer: It involves credibility. Politicians spend great sums of money on public relations—on promoting their positive ethical appeal, their credibility. If our reaction is "He's a good man" or "I trust her," then we are more likely to be persuaded, no matter what the issue. If we perceive our dentist as trustworthy, we are likely to accept advice, even on subjects besides our teeth:

"What made you buy a Mazda?"
"Well, Dr. White says it's a great car."

The producers and casting directors of television commercials understand the ethical appeal. Celebrities who sell dog food and stomach tablets are the good guys of western movies and courtroom dramas, not the villains. And the unknown actors and actresses of commercials look like uncles or grandmothers or neighborly just plain folks—absolutely trustworthy, of course, when it comes to advice about paper towels and coffee and floor wax.

How does the ethical appeal apply when you write an essay? Your credibility—your positive ethical proof—will come through when your arguments are well reasoned. When you use evidence responsibly, avoiding fallacious arguments and questionable conclusions, you will be perceived as a thoughtful person who has considered all sides of the issue fairly. Your tone and diction, if they are appropriate to the occasion, will also help to establish that credibility.

Sometimes your ethical appeal is affected by the personal stake or interest you have in the topic. For instance, if you or a friend or a family member has been injured in an auto accident, you have good reason to argue for mandatory air bags or some other safety device on new cars. Such a personal interest does not make you an authority on the subject; it simply shows that you have a reason for caring about the topic and have the good interests of other passengers at heart. There are also going to be topics on which you do have expertise that will help to establish your authority and credibility. If you are an experienced cyclist arguing for spending money on bike trails, you can bring in your own experiences to show the need. But a word of warning is also in order: You must always be careful that your audience does not regard your position simply as one of self-interest.

Emotional Appeals

Homo sapiens, we know, is the rational animal. And one of our cherished prejudices about ourselves is that we are logical, that we base our decisions on sound reasoning. But of course we have emotions, too: pride, fear, anger, hope, joy, sorrow. And these emotions play a part in our decision making—whether we like it or not.

People in the business of persuasion certainly know that. Advertisers understand the pride we take in driving an expensive-looking car or having the greenest lawn in the neighborhood; they understand our fear of wrinkled skin and insomnia, our satisfaction in getting socks white and collars ring-free. Politicians understand the power of emotional appeals when they call on our sense of both patriotism and fear to support draft legislation and military spending, when they appeal to our generosity and fair-mindedness and even our pity to support federal spending for social programs. And certainly pride is at issue in our dealings with other countries whenever we talk about the image of the United States.

How do emotional appeals enter into the writing process? Throughout the last several chapters we have stressed the importance of the audience in defining the writing situation, especially in persuasive writing. To make readers accept your point of view, you must first try to understand theirs. Where do your readers now stand on the issue? Why?

Take the proposed bike trail, for example. Are the objections to it based solely on cost? Or do the opponents worry about all of those strangers on bikes in the area? If so, you must help them see that their fears are groundless. And you can appeal to their sense of fair play ("Surely bicyclists ought to have the same rights as motorists"), of patriotism ("We must conserve energy for the good of the economy"), and pride ("Ours will be a model for other communities to follow").

For most people and on most issues, emotional appeals are not enough. But understanding the emotions involved in an issue—those that may be affecting the audience at the outset as well as those that may help sway them—is essential in understanding the rhetorical situation.

Logical Appeals

When someone says "Prove it," we take that to mean, "Give me logical reasons for your point of view." Such reasons constitute Aristotle's third kind of evidence: logical appeals.

There are several ways of looking at an issue to find logical proof—to find the evidence of argument. They are known as the sources of argument: definition, cause and effect, and likenesses and differences (the three internal sources) and outside authority (the external source).

Definition. One of the most common forms of logical proof—and one of the most persuasive in arguing certain issues—is definition, or simply the nature of the thing. Often, in legal proceedings, definition itself is the issue. For example, someone slips on your sidewalk, breaks a leg, and sues you on the grounds of negligence. How does the law define negligence? Does your failure to keep the sidewalk in good repair constitute negligence? The courts are regularly being called on to decide if particular behavior or a particular situation constitutes child abuse or fraud or breach of contract or inciting to riot or libel. These cases are essentially definition cases.

Many social issues are argued on the grounds of definition, or the nature of the thing. In recent years the courts have even been challenged to define human life in cases involving the terminally ill. Does the act of breathing alone mean that a person is alive, or must there also be a certain level of brain-wave activity? Opponents of capital punishment use definition when they argue that the death penalty constitutes "cruel and unusual punishment," which is forbidden by the U.S. Constitution. Advocates on both sides of the gun control issue argue on the basis of definition: What is meant by "the right to bear arms"?

We argue from definition, then, when we establish a thing or an

15.4 event or a situation as a member of a larger class and then draw inferences based on that membership.

FOR CLASS DISCUSSION
1. Find a definition argument that you could use in support of the following propositions:

The sale of marijuana should be allowed for medical purposes.

Military spending must be increased.

Too much of our state's budget goes to welfare programs.

Parents have the right to forcibly "deprogram" their grown children who have joined religious cults.

Student loans should be increased.

Big-time football has no place in an academic institution.

College football needs a playoff like the one college basketball has.

Newspapers should not publish the names of juvenile offenders.

Communities have the right to regulate and/or tax video-game establishments.

2. Now use definition to argue against each of these propositions.

Cause and Effect. For some issues, the most convincing logical arguments are those of cause and effect, or consequences. Most legislative and governmental policies, for example, are debated on such grounds. Will the proposed tax increase really slow down inflation? Will the proposed tariff actually decrease imports and thus increase the consumption of domestic goods? Will an all-volunteer army ensure adequate military preparedness? Such complex issues are open to debate simply because there are so many variables in establishing both the causes and the probable outcomes. The winning side is the one that can make its arguments appear the most valid, its consequences the most likely.

FOR CLASS DISCUSSION
1. Consider a campus issue, such as the visiting policy in the women's dormitory. As it now stands, visiting is restricted to certain hours, with men allowed in the public lounge area only. The students want the restrictions abolished: twenty-four hour visitation for both sexes in private rooms as well as in the lounges.

One way to argue the issue is to examine the causes of the present policy: When were those rules established and why? Have they stayed the same even while society's attitudes (including those of most parents) have been changing? Has the university policy of *in loco parentis* ("in the place of the parents") become outdated?

15.4

a. In addition to the causal arguments in favor of changing the dormitory's visiting policy, look for effects or consequences that will support your position.
b. Now strengthen your argument even more by using a definition argument.
c. Take the other side of the controversy. Find arguments against changing the present policy, using cause, effect, and definition.

2. Here's another campus issue. The student government has proposed that the dining halls remain open in the evenings as study centers. You can think of good arguments in favor of such a move: The overcrowding in the library will be alleviated; students will not have to cross campus at night, because the dining halls are in or adjacent to the dorms; students can develop better study schedules and habits because the dorms tend to be noisy.

a. The arguments given in favor of the dining/study centers are those of effects, or consequences. Can you think of any causal arguments to support the new policy? What definition arguments can you use?
b. Anticipate the opposition. How might they use cause and effect and definition to refute your arguments?

Likenesses and Differences. The third source of argument is probably less convincing in most cases than the other two. You argue from likenesses and differences when you compare your proposal or its outcome to another situation. An argument against sending American troops to Central America could compare the situation with that in Vietnam; an argument in favor could compare it with the European situation during World War II. In neither case, however, are the situations exactly the same, so the opposition can use the same arguments by showing how different they are—that is, by arguing the differences.

Here's another issue. Are the illegal immigrants from the Carib-

15.4

bean and Mexico comparable to the "boat people" of Indochina? You could argue for changes in our immigration policies by showing the likeness or differences. And how does the situation compare with the immigration from Europe in the nineteenth and early twentieth centuries?

In the preceding examples we have compared one war with another and one national group with another. But arguments from likenesses often draw analogies between things or situations that are not the same. Such analogies give the audience a new angle of vision. The analogy will be persuasive to the extent that the audience accepts the two situations as comparable. Consider the following arguments:

1. Bull fighting is illegal in the United States. Yet every year for the amusement of the public, countless rodeo animals are tortured with electric prods, genital straps, and ropes. These inhumane exhibitions ought to be outlawed.

2. Most modern parents probably can't understand the parents of centuries past who allowed their children to witness public hangings and whippings in the town square. But these same parents seem to have no qualms about letting their children witness barroom brawls, beatings, muggings, maimings, and murders on a daily basis in the privacy of their own living rooms. Public torture has been outlawed; television violence ought to be outlawed, too.

3. If cockfighting and dog fighting are illegal in public arenas, boxing ought to be illegal, too.

4. Construction workers are required to wear hardhats on the job. Motorcyclists should certainly be required to wear helmets on the highways.

FOR CLASS DISCUSSION

1. Find points of comparison in the foregoing situations to make the arguments as convincing as possible.
2. Refute the arguments by showing ways in which the situations are different.
3. In a letter to the editor of *The New York Times* (May 28, 1982), Jean Boddewyn used the analogy of the "last carriage":

To The Editor:
    There is some perverse logic in the argument used to justify raising the drinking age in New York State to 19 (news story May 27). It reminds

me of the story (apocryphal?) about the commission set up to investigate train collisions and derailments in Belgium. It turned out that most casualties occurred in the last carriage. So the commission recommended that the last carriage be eliminated.

15.4

The same faulty logic is being used in the drinking-age case. Assuming that the facts are incontrovertible, it goes like this: (1) car accidents are most frequent among 18-year-old drinking drivers; (2) 18 is when these youngsters reach the legal drinking age; (3) therefore, raising the drinking age to 19 will reduce the rate of car crashes involving 18-year-old drivers.

Right.

But it will always be the first age cohort to reach drinking age that will have the highest rate of casualties. Therefore, saving the lives of 18-year-old youngsters can be equally achieved by lowering the drinking age to 17, since that group would then be the first one to drink, drive and crash at an above-average rate.

The present bill will simply move the highest rate of drunk-driving casualties to 19-year-old people. Later on, this will logically suggest raising the drinking age to 20—and so on, ad nauseam. We'll be endlessly trying to eliminate the "last carriage."

One can only urge a veto of this ill-conceived, if well-intentioned, bill.

If possible, refute the author's argument by showing the weakness of the analogy.

4. Following is another argument using analogy:

> When mosquitos are a problem, it is standard practice to get rid of stagnant water and to cover windows with screens. Nobody calls that coddling mosquitoes. But when somebody proposes spending money to clean up slums, and to screen society from crime by building humane jails and by hiring many more honest, well-trained cops, the outcry against coddling criminals always kills the budget.
>
> —ROBERT SHERRILL, *Life* (November 13, 1970)

Restate Sherrill's point in a single sentence. Refute the argument by showing the weakness of the analogy, if possible.

External Arguments. The logical arguments we have looked at so far—definition, cause and effect, and likenesses and differences—are internal; they are drawn from the issue itself. Another way of persuading an audience is to call on outside authority by using the testimony of experts and/or statistics.

Such external arguments are regularly used in the debates of

15.4

legislative bodies at every level of government, from the city council to the U. S. Congress. Take, for example, the local planning commission's proposal for building a new parking garage. In order to convince the city council and the taxpayers to support the plan, the commission uses external arguments:

> The number of spaces now available is far below the generally accepted population/parking ratio that experts have established for cities of this size.
>
> The cost of a new building will be higher next year.
>
> The revenue expected from the users will offset the cost of maintenance and operation.

Certainly most decisions involving taxes—whether to raise them or to lower them or to spend them—require such data.

In an article exposing the influence of television on the eating and drinking habits of viewers, Susan Holden used data from researchers at several universities:

> For 16 years, Michael Morgan and his colleagues at the University of Pennsylvania's Annenberg School of Communications have examined the attitudes and habits television cultivates. Their recent analysis of nutrition messages in a typical week's prime time (8 to 11 P.M.) programs reveals that eating, drinking, or talking about food occurs an average of nine times per hour. Snacking accounts for 39 percent of these references to food.
>
> Such bombardment with televised images of snacking probably sends some viewers to the refrigerator, and aggravates obesity, says Michael Mahoney, a psychologist and authority on weight control at Pennsylvania State University.
>
> As disturbing as the enticement to eat is the televised fare itself. Lois Kaufman, a communications researcher at Rutgers University, noted references to eating, drinking, or talking about food in ten of the most popular prime-time shows aired during one week. Of those references, 34 percent were to alcohol, soda pop, or other beverages (excluding milk); 28 percent were to cakes, pies, cookies, chips, gum, candy, and ice cream; 12 percent were to meat, fish, and poultry; and a slender 13 percent were to fruits, vegetables, and grain and dairy products combined.
>
> —"Why Television is Fattening," *Nutrition Action* (May 1982)

In ruling against school officials who removed a book from a school library, Federal Judge Conrad K. Cyr of Maine called on the authority of the U.S. Constitution:

15.5

> Public schools are major marketplaces of ideas, and First Amendment rights must be accorded all "persons" in the market for ideas, including secondary school students.
>
> —*Slate* (May 1982)

FOR CLASS DISCUSSION

1. How would you characterize the internal sources of argument used in the foregoing quotations on television and book banning? Are they definition? Cause and/or effect? Likenesses and differences?

2. Look again at the examples of everyday arguments at the opening of this chapter. What appeals are they based on? What sources of argument do they use?

   "Come on. You'll enjoy yourself. Besides, it's too hot to work."

   "It's good—a lot like the early James Bond pictures."

   "The doctor says you need the exercise."

   "The leaks are ruining the insulation."

   "It's good for you."

   "It's nothing like spinach."

15.5 How Arguments Go Wrong

As you learned in the foregoing discussion, the "sources of argument" are ways of discovering arguments, procedures for finding evidence and for refuting the evidence of others. In using the sources, however, you must be wary of certain violations of logic known as *fallacies*. Fallacious reasoning will quickly destroy your credibility. All of your ideas could end up being suspect in the company of a fallacious argument. Understanding where the fallacies can occur will not only help you to avoid them in constructing your own arguments, it will help you to recognize weak spots in the arguments of others.

15.5

Some of our most common fallacies result from the misuse of the argument from consequences.

1. In the *post hoc* fallacy (short for *post hoc, ergo propter hoc,* or "after this, because of this"), an effect is erroneously attributed to an event that preceded it. For example, suppose the school's administration has recently allowed the sale of beer in the student union; shortly afterwards the library reports an increase in the number of weekend users. Is there a connection? Unless you can show a logical chain of events that would connect the two phenomena (and it seems highly unlikely in this case), you cannot argue that beer improves study habits.

Primitive beliefs and practices were, or are, often based on the doctrine of *post hoc:*

> A man harms his neighbor; this action causes his crops to fail.
>
> The tribe offers sacrifices to the gods; this action causes the harvest to be bountiful.

The *post hoc* doctrine is not limited to primitive cultures:

> Drop a fork and company will come.
>
> Touch a toad and warts will appear.
>
> Carry a rabbit's foot and your horse will finish in the money.
>
> Wear your lucky socks and the team will win.

The fallacy of the *post hoc* argument is not always so apparent; often the cause–effect relationship appears to be quite logical:

> After sex education is introduced into the junior-high curriculum, teenage pregnancy increases.
>
> After the number of women in the work force rises, schools report a rise in truancy.
>
> After pocket calculators become commonplace, the Scholastic Aptitude Test math scores drop.

But rarely is a single cause sufficient to bring about such complex social changes. You can refute such arguments by showing how other sufficient causes preceded the event.

2. The *non sequitur* ("it does not follow") is similar to the *post hoc* fallacy. Where the *post hoc* fallacy assumes unwarranted cause, the

non sequitur predicts effects or states conclusions that do not follow from the premises.
In some cases the *non sequitur* may be farfetched:

> If she's an airline stewardess, then she's obviously leading a wild life.
> If you're from California, then you probably know how to surf.

But often the *non sequitur* is hiding in what seems to be a reasonable conclusion:

> If this is a free country, and this is my property, then I have the right to raise chickens in the garage.
> If we would stop importing so much foreign steel, our domestic steel industry would become more competitive.
> If we turn the downtown area into a pedestrian mall, shoppers will come to the city instead of spending all their money in the suburban malls.

You can think of the *non sequitur* as an "if–then" statement in which the "then" is questionable. As a reader, you have the right to question such statements; as a writer, you have the responsibility to show how the conclusion follows logically from the premises.

3. Another common logical fallacy that often misuses consequences is the either–or argument, called the *false dilemma*. The phrase "on the horns of a dilemma" refers to the situation in which there are only two choices—and both appear to be equally negative:

> If I don't take my math requirement this semester, I won't graduate; if I do take it, I know my other grades will drop because math is hard for me and I'm already carrying a full load.

But in some cases the situation is not actually either–or, even though it may be stated that way; these are, in other words, false dilemmas:

> Either we pass this tax hike or we'll never get rid of the deficit.
> *Unstated alternative:* Why not cut spending?

> Either I join the sorority or I won't have any close friends.
> *Unstated alternative:* Why not join the glee club or the folk-dancing society to make friends?

Either I get this loan or I'll have to drop out of school.

Unstated alternative: Why not take a reduced course load and find a part-time job?

Some fallacies result from the misuse of the argument from definition.

4. One common fallacy, known as *begging the question,* assumes a definition that is not the nature of the thing, a definition that is itself arguable. An antihunting argument, for example, might beg the question of brutality:

How can a civilized society condone the *brutal* killing of animals?

We don't argue about the use of *civilized* as a modifier of *society;* here we would probably agree on the nature of society as civilized. But to say that "hunting is brutal" is itself an arguable proposition.

An argument against a proposed tuition hike might beg the question of necessity:

This *unnecessary* tuition hike will force many students to leave school.

The heat of legislative debates often includes question-begging terms:

This *discriminatory* change in the tax law will simply encourage cheating.

This *unfair* regulation will cause many small companies to go out of business.

Although the consequences predicted may be logical, the question-begging assumption in the subject of these statements makes them fallacious.

5. Another form of begging the question that misuses definition is *circular reasoning:*

Hunting is immoral because it is wrong to kill animals.

(This is simply another way of saying, "Hunting is immoral because hunting is immoral.")

The American diet, which is high in sugar and salt, is unhealthy because we eat too much sugar and salt.

Vegetarianism has increased in recent years because more and more people have stopped eating meat.

15.5

6. Another common fallacy is the *hasty generalization*, a statement in which the determiner *many* or *most* or *all* or *none* introduces an unsupported claim:

Most feminists are in favor of a military draft for women.

Most people would rather not pay taxes.

Many American cars are made with little thought for either workmanship or convenience.

The problem with such statements lies not only in their unsupported claims about many or most but also in their vagueness: What taxes would people rather not pay? Sales taxes? Property taxes? State income taxes? Which American cars? What kinds of poor workmanship? What inconveniences?

7. There are several types of fallacious arguments that attack people instead of issues: stereotyping, name-calling, and guilt by association. Whenever you call a person's character into question instead of concentrating on the issue, you are engaging in the fallacy of *ad hominem* ("to the person").

Senator Kidd's proposal to raise the gasoline tax may seem reasonable, but don't forget that he also wants us to deal with Communists. Just last week he voted to sell wheat to the Russians.

Such fallacies are perhaps more common in the heat of political speeches than they are in written arguments. But certainly they are abuses to understand and avoid.

FOR CLASS DISCUSSION

Identify any fallacies in the following statements:

1. You failed the exam, so you obviously didn't study.
2. The auto industry has not encouraged the law requiring airbags; they're simply not interested in safety.

15.5

3. If the government would get out of the agriculture business, our food prices would go down.

4. The abuses of big football schools in recruiting athletes would stop if TV would stop paying those colleges such huge sums for broadcast rights.

5. The wasteful expenditure of tax money on unprofitable and unnecessary railroads ought to be stopped.

6. Ross was just promoted to vice-president of the company. Either he's very lucky or he's got the right connections.

7. George and Margo dropped out of college; they were probably flunking.

8. Movie attendance is low because of all the undiscriminating people who would rather watch television.

9. The problem of juvenile delinquency in our country has decreased over the past few years because fewer young people under the age of eighteen are committing crimes.

10. Students in my first-period classes always get the best grades. I guess my lectures are more lively early in the morning.

11. I wouldn't lend Jake my money. He's a used-car salesman.

12. It's obvious that Senator Green is a racist. The Ku Klux Klan endorsed him.

13. If she was attacked in her own house, she was probably asking for it.

14. The ethical philosophy of the major networks can be relied on to regulate the level of violence on television.

15. The government has every right to withhold student loans from men who don't register for the draft. Why should taxpayers pay law breakers to go to school?

WRITING EXERCISES

In deciding on a *topic* for your persuasive essay, think about the arguable questions listed on pages 314–315:

- Questions of value and/or ethics.
- Questions of definition and explanation.
- Questions of policy.

Formulate your topic with a *purpose* in mind:

- To evaluate your position and/or to persuade others of its rightness (the positive argument).
- To argue for a course of action (the proposal argument).

15.5

In choosing your topic, also think carefully about your *audience:*

- Who wants to know your position?
- Whom should you persuade to adopt your point of view?

Or, in proposing a course of action,

- To whom should you address your proposal?

Following are some topics that you could argue either for or against:

1. College teachers have the right to express their political views in the classroom.
2. A community has the right to pass "blue laws" (laws that restrict businesses from being open on Sunday).
3. College athletes should share in the profits from gate receipts and TV contracts.
4. Students should have the same access to parking on campus as faculty members do.
5. Dormitory space should be allocated not on a first-come basis but on the basis of grade-point averages.
6. Drunk-driving convictions should carry a mandatory jail sentence, even for first offenders.
7. The names of juvenile offenders should be published in the local paper.
8. The philosophy of "Spare the rod and spoil the child" does more harm than good.
9. The federal government should pass a "bottle law" similar to those in Oregon and Michigan and Massachusetts.
10. The government should regulate the coverage of national elections by TV networks. (In 1980 Reagan was declared the winner and President Carter conceded before the polls had even closed in California!)

15.5

11. Major league baseball fields should be equipped with electronically monitored strike zones (or instant replays for umpires) so that decisions about strikes and balls will be objective and accurate.

12. We should have federal, rather than state, laws regarding divorce and child custody.

13. Adoption records should be readily available to both parents and children.

14. Communities should take the responsibility for regulating young people's access to public video games.

15. "Running computers" should be added as the "fourth R" to every public-school curriculum.

FOR CLASS DISCUSSION

The following proposal argument appeared as an editorial in *The New York Times* on November 17, 1982. As you read the argument, analyze its parts: What is the purpose of each paragraph? At what point does the writer propose a course of action? How has the writer prepared the reader to accept the proposal? Consider also the kinds of arguments used. Identify ethical, logical, and emotional appeals. Identify also the sources of logical arguments used.

1. Some people watch boxing to see skill, others just for blood. Far worse than the blood is the unseen damage. Retinas are dislodged, kidneys bruised and, after repeated pounding, the cerebral cortex accumulates damage to the higher functions of the brain, leading to loss of memory, shambling walk: the traits of the punch-drunk boxer. Can a civilized society plausibly justify the pleasure it may gain from such a sport?

2. Two unusually brutal melees last weekend attest to the violence. A 23-year old South Korean, Duk Koo Kim, now lies near death in Las Vegas after being bludgeoned unconscious under the auspices of the World Boxing Association. In Miami, Aaron Pryor, the association's junior welterweight champion, was allowed to pound away at Alexis Argüello's head 12 times after his opponent had lost the capacity to defend himself. Mr. Argüello afterward "sat there the way a piece of meat sits in your icebox," wrote Dave Kindred in The Times.

3. With pro football sidelined until now, boxing has been flourishing. But popularity by itself is no justification. The Colosseum was packed when the Romans sent gladiators to fight to the death for sport. Holding

that humans are more than meat, our age requires skill, not violence, to be the prime ability demonstrated in a sport.

15.5

4. Boxing has progressed only a little from bare-knuckled butchery to Queensberry rules and gloves. Football may cause more injuries, mountaineering and auto racing may claim more lives, but boxing is the only sport in which the explicit goal is to injure the opponent. Even people offended by cockfighting and bullfighting somehow accept the deliberate maiming of the human body, perhaps because the worst damage appears after the blood has been wiped away and the crowd has gone home sated.

5. If boxers choose freely to fight, and the public to watch, why should others interfere? Because the public celebration of violence cannot be a private matter. And the boxers' choice is not so free. Adulation and promoters' greed impel some to return to the ring against their best interests. Sugar Ray Leonard, luckily recovered from a detached retina, has resisted the temptation; Muhammad Ali did not.

6. Since boxing is not about to be banned, the first priority is to reduce injury. The most useful single step would be a national commission to set uniform standards of medical supervision. At present every state has differing, generally insufficient notions of how to prevent injuries.

7. New York's state athletic commission has led the way by insisting that brain-trauma kits be available at every match and requiring use of a thumbless glove to prevent eye injuries. Other reforms might include rigorous checks for neurological damage, and more authority for referees to stop fights at the earliest sign of slurred reflexes.

8. Even with moderation of its violence, a civilized society will hope for more: that boxing will eventually cease. The 21st century will surely appraise our coarseness of feeling with the same wonderment with which we contemplate the public hangings that were common in the 19th.

The following reply to the editorial was published in the "Letters to the Editor" column the following week:

To the Editor:
  Your Nov. 17 editorial on the brutality of boxing, although well-meant, was ill-conceived in analysis and proposals.
  First, the shift from London prize ring to Queensberry rules was not, as you suggest, progress. Gloves, while protecting the knuckles, added weight to the fists and expanded the area of the impacting surface,

15.5

thereby only facilitating and intensifying the role of aggressive punching within the fight.

The 10-second knockout rule had similar effects.

When a pugilist was knocked down under London rules, the round ended. Assisted back to his corner, he had 30 seconds to recuperate and return to "scratch." In the Queensberry system, a boxer had only 10 seconds to resume fighting and had to do so unassisted from where he fell. This not only made reciprocal aggression the only viable defense but also offered a great advantage to heavy hitters.

Similarly, the corollary rule that confined a bout to a limited number of finite rounds simply reduced the scope for caution and increased the utility of aggression.

In short, Queensberry gloves and rules tended to demand a more physically aggressive and structurally offensive style of boxing than the "bare-knuckled butchery" of the London ring.

Also, your call for better medical supervision, although laudable and desirable, is also less than a solution. A historical perspective or even a side-long glance at the rules for international amateur contests demonstrates that the level of violence and the frequency of injury can indeed be controlled, but only by redesigning the internal structure of the fistic exchange.

A national commission devoted to this more fundamental reform of the activity within the ring, in addition to improved oversight from its apron, is the only way to insure the survival of this sportive drama as a demonstration of skill.

—LEONARD ELLIS

Assess the writer's counterarguments. What kinds of proof has he used to refute the editorial? Has he shown to your satisfaction that the editorial was "ill-conceived" and that the proposal was "less than a solution"? Cast yourself in the role of the editor and refute this letter.

Part IV

The Writing Process

Now that you've made some decisions about the writing situation and have thought about the modes of discourse, it's time to turn to the writing process. To think of writing as a process might help you get over the notion that writing is a talent you were born with—or without. Writing is a learned ability, and, like other skills, it gets easier the more you practice. To think of writing as a process might also help you realize that good writers—even professional writers with many years of experience—don't just sit down at their typewriters and come up with a finished piece of writing. They proceed in stages—exploring ideas, writing notes, making plans, sketching outlines, arranging and rearranging. They write rough drafts, just as you will; they think about their paragraph structures, just as you will; they develop techniques for revising and editing, just as you will.

There is no one best writing process, no one right way of going from an idea to a finished essay. But there are certain steps that work for many writers, some tried-and-true techniques. The three chapters in this section contain practical suggestions for helping you develop your own personal, workable writing process.

Chapter 16 has some strategies for coming up with ideas, specific suggestions for the beginning, middle, and end of the essay. The discussions of paragraph structure and coherence in Chapter 17 should be helpful both in the composing and the revising stages of writing paragraphs. Chapter 18 encourages you to listen to your words and to be attentive to your personal voice. At the end of these chapters you'll find questions that will help you in your revision and editing stages. These chapters also demonstrate how a conscious understanding of grammar can be applied at all stages of the writing process.

As you read these chapters and as you go through your own writing process, don't be in a hurry. Remember that writing takes time. Be sure to give yourself enough time for all the stages of planning and writing and revising and editing and proofreading.

16

Planning and Writing the Essay

A finished piece of writing represents a great many choices made—choices about topic, audience, and purpose (as discussed in Chapter 11), and about many other factors as well. You must consider your attitude toward the topic; you must think about the opening and closing and about the arrangement of the parts. Some of these decisions come easily, almost automatically, given a particular writing situation; others require deliberate thought. In this chapter we will consider some of the choices you must make, along with some strategies to help you make them.

16.1 *Exploring the Topic*

By this time you have made some important choices: You have decided on your topic, your purpose, and your audience; and you have thought about them enough to come up with a thesis statement—a tentative one, at least. The next step in planning the essay is to look for ideas. Whether the information comes primarily from the library or from your own experience, you can generate ideas by asking questions. We'll let *T* stand for *topic:*

- What is T?
- How did it come about?

339

16.2

- What else was happening at the time?
- What larger unit is T a part of?
- What are its parts?
- What is T similar to?
- What is it different from?
- What is T's effect on people or its environment?
- What is the effect of people or the environment on T?
- How has T changed?
- What surprises me the most about T?
- What does the future hold for T?
- What do the experts say?

Obviously, not every question will apply to every topic and purpose. But some of the answers you come up with will apply; and others may trigger still further questions and ideas about your topic.

FOR CLASS DISCUSSION

Select a current issue from your campus or community—one concerned, for example, with dorm contracts or the drinking policy or discipline or schedules or parking—or even a national issue, such as draft registration; then generate ideas about the topic by asking the questions listed above.

16.2 *Exploring Attitudes*

Your thesis statement summarizes both your purpose for writing and your audience. It may or may not include your attitude. But before you begin to write, you must answer two more questions:

1. What is your attitude toward the topic?

Your own attitude will make a big difference in how you write the essay:

- Is it *serious*, as it would be in an argument for higher wages?
- Is it *serious* to the point of being *somber*, as it would be in a paper on world hunger or nuclear fallout?

- Is it *enthusiastic*, as it might be in an essay about the outlook for solar energy or wind power?
- Is it *light-hearted*, as it would be in a narrative about your most embarrassing moment or your first date?
- Is it *tongue-in-cheek*, as it might be in a survey of attitudes toward baldness or elbows?
- Is it *pessimistic*, as it might be about the economy or the effects of acid rain?
- Is it *optimistic*, as it might be in explaining how the pollution problems of the Willamette River or Lake Erie were solved?

Your own attitude toward the topic will affect your style of writing, your choice of words, and your tone of voice. And it will be apparent from the very first paragraph.

2. What is the attitude of your audience?

Although you can never know exactly what other people think, you must have a notion of their attitude about the topic; otherwise you won't know where to begin or where to go from there. Do you intend to reinforce their attitude, or are you and the audience on opposite sides? Is the audience skeptical? Is it supportive? Is the audience naive or knowledgeable about the subject? If naive, you must include adequate background information; if knowledgeable, you may need only to remind them of certain details.

16.3 Planning the Essay

The plan that emerges from your material—or, to put it another way, the plan you impose on your material—will depend on the particular writing situation. The importance of audience and purpose will become clear, for instance, when you try to decide where to begin:

- What does the reader already know?
- What does the reader need to know?
- Is the subject matter common knowledge, perhaps concerning a well-known issue or event?

16.3

• Is it technical or unusual or historical, something people haven't known before or haven't thought about for a long time?

There is obviously no one solution to the problem of planning.

In general, we can describe the essay as consisting of three parts: a beginning, a middle, and an end; or an introduction, a main body, and a conclusion. In the actual writing stage, you will probably want to have a general outline of your whole plan to work from, before you begin putting words on paper in paragraph form. For example, an essay on planning a bicycle trip directed to the Outing Club might look something like this in the initial planning stage:

Introduction: [My background as a cyclist, maybe?]
Body:
    Planning the route
    Estimating the time
      —for actual travel
      —for rest stops and meals
      —overnight
    Equipment needed
      —for traveling
        bike and parts
      —for safety
      —for emergencies [anecdote about farm in Iowa?]
      —for camping (sleeping and cooking)
    Getting in shape [include in intro, maybe]
    Clothing
      —comfort   [include with equipment?]
      —rain gear
    Costs [Maybe this should come right after the equipment discussion.]
    Conclusion (Payoff: exercise, fresh air, good company; cost per mile compared with cars, etc.)

With an informal outline such as this, you are beginning to make decisions about the content of the essay and the arrangement of the parts. Now you're getting anxious to start writing. But before you begin, take time to consider your point of view.

16.4 Establishing the Point of View

The term *point of view* refers to the relationship of the writer to the writing situation. Included in that relationship is your attitude, whether serious or light-hearted, pessimistic or optimistic. That attitude will have consequences for many of the decisions you make as you write, especially when it comes to vocabulary and sentence style. A tongue-in-cheek or humorous essay on working conditions in the dining hall, for example, would include language far different from that of an essay on mine safety.

The decision that the term *point of view* most often brings to mind is whether to use the first person or to stick strictly to third. In writing a narrative about a personal experience, you will probably use the first person, although in writing someone else's story, you would probably avoid *I*. Certainly other forms of discourse can also make good use of the first person. The bicycle trip, for instance, would undoubtedly include passages about the author's personal experiences—especially in the introduction and the conclusion. The writer of the bicycle essay would also be likely to address the reader in the second person, as "you":

> The first thing you'll want to do is to make sure that both you and your bicycle are in top working order.

This description of the point of view in the bicycle essay may sound inconsistent. And haven't you always been told to be consistent, to stick to one or the other, not to jump from the first person to the third and back to the second?

First of all, no writing is ever strictly first or second person. When judged from the standpoint of pronoun use, all writing will include third-person pronouns: *he, she, it, they,* and so on.

Haven't you also been told to avoid the first person most of the time in expository writing? That's probably bad advice, too, especially if you're avoiding *I* and *we* just for the sake of avoiding them. Later in this chapter, we will look at the introductions of two essays from *Smithsonian*, serious essays on natural science. Both are essentially in the third person, but in their introductions both writers include sentences in the first person:

> The idea of a cave as a habitat or ecosystem, as the home of a community of animals, seems a violation of what *we* think of as a law of nature. (Italics added.)
> —DONALD DALE JACKSON, "Close Encounters with the Creatures of Another World," *Smithsonian* (November 1982)

> For *my* own part, *I* am torn by ambivalence when it comes to the white-tailed deer. Walt Disney got to *me* early. (Italics added.)
> —JOHN G. MITCHELL, "Our Wily White-tailed Deer: Elegant but Perplexing Neighbors," *Smithsonian* (November 1982)

There are, of course, writing situations that call for the objectivity of the third person—and the third person only. In certain lab reports, business analyses, legal documents, and, always, news stories, the *I* or *we* of the author would be out of place. But in many essays an occasional reference to writer or reader is perfectly normal and acceptable.

Before leaving the subject of point of view, we should mention the use of *you*, the second-person pronoun. You'll notice that many of the sentences in the foregoing paragraphs, as well as the sentence you're reading now, include *you* as the subject. That *you*, of course, stands for you, the reader. But *you* does not always address the reader; it is often used in a more general sense, with a meaning more like that of the third person. Notice the use of *you* in this passage by Carl Sagan, describing an excursion into the back rooms of the Museum of Man in Paris:

> Most of the rooms were evidently used for storage of anthropological items, collected from decades to more than a century ago. *You* had the sense of a museum of the second order, in which were stored not so much materials that might be of interest as materials that had once been of interest. *You* could feel the presence of nineteenth-century museum directors engaged, in their frock coats, in goniometrie and craniologie, busily collecting and measuring everything, in the pious hope that mere quantification would lead to understanding. (Italics added.)
> —*Broca's Brain*

Here *you* takes the place of *one* or *a person;* it is not "you, the reader." In British English, *one* is commonly used in such contexts in both speech and writing; in American English, however, we tend to use the less formal *you*, even in writing. For American readers, *one* somehow calls attention to itself.

When you write your essay, don't worry about a polished point of view the first time through. Write in a personal voice, using *I* or *you* if it seems natural. You can always go back in the revising and editing stages and change any of those decisions.

16.5 *Writing the Essay*

The Beginning: Four Criteria

Once you have outlined the content of your essay and have decided on the point of view, you're ready to begin the actual writing. Where do you begin? Probably the best place is at the beginning, with the introduction. Although it's true that some writers don't worry about the introduction until they have finished writing the main body of an essay—and some books even offer that advice—you may feel more comfortable about the middle if you've already made some decisions about the beginning. Of course, you should always feel free to revise your opening—or to scrap it entirely—as the essay takes shape. But for some people the opening provides the impetus for writing the rest of the essay.

First impressions are important, both in person and on paper. To make that first impression a positive one, your introduction should

1. set the right tone for the essay;
2. introduce the topic;
3. establish your credibility;
4. arouse the reader's interest.

That list may seem like a tall order for just a paragraph or two. Making a good first impression is indeed a tall order—and it's not always easy. But you'll discover that a good beginning is worth the effort that it takes.

Following are some examples that illustrate how different writers, including student writers, have accomplished those goals. The

16.5

first is the opening of the article from *Smithsonian* by Donald Dale Jackson, one sentence of which we have already seen:

> Sunless, devoid of plants, cool and silent as the surrounding stone, a cave seems the very antithesis of life, a rockbound realm suitable only for the creatures that dwell in the human imagination. The idea of a cave as a habitat or ecosystem, as the home of a community of animals, seems a violation of what we think of as a law of nature. No light means essentially no vegetation, and no vegetation means an absence of the primary nourishment that rests at the base of the food web in any ecosystem. The uncompromising blackness of the cave's eternal night also means that the struggle for survival underground is a battle of the blind; eyesight, and thus the whole range of visual signals and clues that guide surface-dwelling species to their sustenance, is useless here.
>
> Yet the astonishing fact is that many caverns bustle with life. Almost everyone who has ventured beyond a cave entrance knows that bats are often in residence. The most visible cave-dwelling animals, bats are parttime occupants who use caves as bedrooms where they rest between nocturnal hunting forays or while hibernating in the winter. Bears, too, once commonly spent the winter in caves, and . . .

Let's examine this introduction in light of the aforementioned criteria:

1. What tone does it suggest? The first two sentences suggest a somewhat formal, scientific tone. Consider the author's choice of words: *devoid, antithesis, rockbound realm, habitat, ecosystem.* The structure of the first sentence—the opening string of adjectival phrases—adds to the formality. So do such phrases as "the uncompromising blackness of the cave's eternal night." But certainly, such a tone seems perfectly appropriate for the readers of *Smithsonian.*

2. Is the topic clear? The title and the accompanying pictures actually give the topic away, but even without those clues we know what the topic is before we reach the second paragraph, where it is clearly stated in the first sentence. In the first paragraph the verb *seems* alerts us not to be fooled by what "seems" to be true and prepares us for *yet* in the second paragraph.

3. Has the author established his credibility? If we know nothing about Jackson's credentials as a science writer, what makes us believe him here? First of all, his information rings true, and it squares with what we already know about caves and light. And of course, he is writing in *Smithsonian,* a magazine with a reputation for sound scholarship on subjects dealing with nature and the environment.

4. How does he arouse the reader's interest? The use of language is the first thing that we notice. If we let ourselves hear the words, we appreciate the somewhat dramatic opening, with its introductory series of adjectival phrases and alliteration, "silent as the surrounding stone." And he grabs us with that first idea—a cave's unsuitability for any but imaginary creatures; we can easily go along with that. Notice also how he strengthens his bond with the reader not only by using first person, as we mentioned earlier, but by including in simple terms some things that we, the nonexperts, know about caves—ideas that the readers and the expert share, for example, no light means no vegetation. And certainly if we have any interest in the subject at all, we're going to be grabbed by the outlandish notion presented in the second paragraph: that caverns "bustle with life."

Notice also the catchy title. Even though we suspect that the essay will be scientific and informative, we don't expect it to be ponderous with "close encounters" in the title.

FOR CLASS DISCUSSION

1. Following are several other introductions. The first is from another *Smithsonian* essay; the next three are from student essays. Read the title and the introduction; then evaluate how effectively the authors
   a. set the tone of the essay;
   b. introduce the topic;
   c. establish their credibility;
   d. arouse the reader's interest.

Our Wily White-Tailed Deer: Elegant but Perplexing Neighbors

Consider *Odocoileus virginianus*, the white-tailed deer. No other large mammal in America is so widely distributed, so devoutly admired, so eagerly sought in the hunt, so zealously protected, so destructive of overstocked range, so influential on the perceptions of those who value wildlife for whatever reasons, consumptive or otherwise. The whitetail is a creature of superlatives. Half a century ago, as the species began to bounce back from a long bout of slaughter and habitat deprivation, the naturalist Ernest Thompson Seton proclaimed it to be "the swiftest, keenest, shyest, wisest, most prolific and most successful of our Deer. . . . The whitetail is the American Deer of the past, and the American Deer of the future." Time has only strengthened that judg-

16.5

ment, though Westerners attuned to the mule deer, and Pacific-coast dwellers partial to blacktails, may heartily disagree.

For my own part, I am torn by ambivalence when it comes to the white-tailed deer. Walt Disney got to me early. I wept for Bambi when the huntsmen slew its mama; yet today I count deerslayers among my closest friends, and understand what drives them to it and bear no grudge and, in fact, occasionally join them afield, bearing arms. But I have never shot a deer, or at one.

The Big Gulp

The rabbit scampers nervously on the cold linoleum floor, its nose twitching, eyes searching, and ears at attention. Suddenly, the once harmless log comes alive and the rabbit realizes its fears. The rabbit is in the company of a snake, an Indian python. My pet strikes quickly, seizing the rabbit's head in its powerful jaws. The rodent hasn't a chance. The python quickly throws its thickly muscled coils around its prey; after a brief struggle, the victim suffocates. The snake may now relax its coils and begin to swallow.

The swallowing and digesting of food by a snake involves many simple but highly specialized organs. . . .

—PAUL CHRISTY

Christmas Vacation: One of the Main Causes of Mining Accidents?

In the past month or two we have been bombarded with news of coal mining accidents. Newspaper headlines like "Men Killed in Mine Disaster" have enlightened us on the many hazards of coal mining. To some these accidents may have no significance, but to those who belong to a coal mining family, such as myself, the recent disasters have made us wonder about their causes. Many causes are published and broadcast, but experts only speculate upon the actual cause. There were three mining accidents within five days during the three weeks before Christmas, which leads me to believe there might have been a common cause for the three accidents.

—DENISE ANDERSON

Checking in to "General Hospital"

It is 3 P.M. on any average weekday. College students across the country are witnessing murders, rapes, drug and alcohol abuse, divorces, seductions, and underworld dealings. No, American college campuses are not becoming dens of iniquity or great crime centers of the world. Rather, students are tuning in to view the continuing saga of the nation's top-rated soap opera, "General Hospital."

—CINDY RUNKLE

2. Check the introductions of magazine articles or of the essays in your reader. What opening strategies have the authors used?

3. Look again at the informal outline of the bicycling essay being planned in the previous section of this chapter. Imagine yourself—an experienced cyclist—as the author. Write an opening for the essay that will fulfill all the goals of an effective introduction.

16.5

The Middle

In the earlier section on planning, you saw the bicycling essay beginning to take shape in outline form with a list of ideas to be covered. Now try to figure out the best arrangement for those ideas by finding the most effective pattern of exposition to follow. (The patterns are discussed in detail in Chapter 14.)

Two patterns come to mind: division analysis and process. The other expository modes—comparison/contrast, classification, and definition—might come into the essay, but they wouldn't work well in governing the overall design. Both division and process are concerned with parts. Which way of looking at the parts would be more effective for your purposes in this paper? How important, for example, is chronology? Is there an order in which the various details of planning the bicycle trip should be presented? In other words, is it important for the reader to learn about equipment before thinking about time for traveling and camping? Should costs be discussed first? Last?

Certainly, the length of time involved in the trip will affect the equipment needed and the costs. But, in fact, the planning is really not controlled by steps; that is, one step in the planning process does not depend on the completion of previous steps. For that reason, you can reject process and assume that the more effective of the two patterns will be straight analysis, or division into parts—a pattern already suggested by the outline.

Now that you've made that decision, what next? Go back to the sketchy outline and fill it in with some specifics: What equipment? What clothing? How much money? How many miles per hour? What happens when it rains?

Next, decide on a logical order for explaining all of these details. Because a straight time order for planning the trip seems neither crucial nor really manageable, on what basis should you describe the parts of the planning task? Certainly, the first requirement for a

16.5

bicyclist planning a trip is a bicycle, and that, at the very least, is what all the audience would have in common. So why not start there—with the equipment? That discussion would naturally lead into the special equipment needed for this particular trip, and so on.

Paragraph Blocs. Each section of the middle will almost certainly cover a number of subtopics, so the paragraph will be grouped into what are sometimes called *paragraphs blocs.* The first bloc, covering equipment, might have four or more paragraphs:

$$
\begin{array}{ll}
\textit{Bloc 1} & \left\{ \begin{array}{l} \text{bicycle} \\ \text{emergency gear} \\ \text{camping gear} \\ \text{food and supplies} \end{array} \right. \\
\textit{Equipment} & \\[2em]
\textit{Bloc 2} & \left\{ \begin{array}{l} \text{time} \\ \quad \text{for traveling} \\ \quad \text{for eating} \\ \quad \text{for sleeping} \\ \text{road conditions} \\ \text{schedule} \end{array} \right. \\
\textit{Itinerary} &
\end{array}
$$

This kind of plan not only keeps you, the writer, on track, it helps you to recognize the places that require signals for the reader. In a long magazine article, as well as in a textbook such as this one, you generally find headings and subheadings that help the reader to follow the writer's plan. But in shorter works the writer generally signals the reader in other ways.

In the first paragraph bloc the reader expects each paragraph to discuss equipment, with the first sentence of each one introducing a new topic or subtopic on the subject. But when you've finished the discussion of equipment, you must let the reader know that a new topic is beginning. One way to do that is to use a short transition paragraph, perhaps only one or two sentences:

> Equipment is not the only aspect of the trip that will require careful planning. Consider the itinerary itself—the length of time, the miles to be covered, the route, the condition of the roads, and the facilities along the way. All of these aspects of the trip need to be thought about in advance.

This announcement of your intention for the paragraphs to follow in the second bloc is an outline of sorts for the reader. Moreover, it helps you by committing you to a plan.

The Ending

How should you conclude an essay? Again, there is no one answer. Generally speaking, you should stop when you've made your point, that is, when you've said what you had to say. But don't be too abrupt. We've all had the experience, while reading an article or story, of turning the page expectantly and finding no more. "Is that all?"

At the other extreme, perhaps, is the final paragraph that begins "In conclusion." Avoid that one most of the time. And don't simply summarize the main ideas of the essay. A summary may be useful in a long textbook chapter, but in an essay of eight hundred or a thousand words it's almost insulting to the reader's intelligence.

What do the pros do? Here are the final paragraphs of the two *Smithsonian* articles whose introductions we saw earlier. Note that both of them include quotations, one direct and one indirect.

Our Wily White-Tailed Deer: Elegant but Perplexing Neighbors

The whitetail does that sort of thing to all of us, one way or another. It curdles our emotions. It befuddles the brain. Its elegant presence convinces some folks that humankind is wrong to hunt; convinces others that the greater wrong would be to hunt not at all. Who knows? What worries me, as I gaze out the window and look beyond my whittled evergreens at the dark forest edge, is—how *do* we keep the balance? Like the man in Hartford was saying: there are more people who want deer than those who don't.

Close Encounters with the Creatures of Another World

The cave habitat, with its unique stability and simple food web, is as close to a self-contained ecosystem—saving only its dependence on outside sources for the first strand in the web—as any in nature. It is tempting to believe that the sturdy masters of making-do underground could better survive the various horrors that threaten the rest of us— toxic fumes, the exhaustion of our resources, nuclear war—even though they must retain their links to the outside world for air, water and food. It certainly seems possible that we can learn something from them "about population control," John Holsinger suggests, "or perhaps energy conservation." More generally, Holsinger observes, "We're going to have to evolve ways to get along with less"—a dilemma that cave creatures solved long ago.

The quotation is a common strategy for ending an article or essay, especially when the main body includes either reports about people and their activities or the testimony of authorities in a particular field. You can choose a quotation or an anecdote that reinforces your main idea.

One of the most common strategies is to speculate about the future. Notice that both of the *Smithsonian* conclusions include not only quotations but questions of the future. The student essay on "General Hospital" also ends with future prospects:

> Viewing "General Hospital" will remain a popular pastime with college students as long as the show continues to cater to their viewing needs and desires. If the cast stays young and the subject matter remains directed toward younger people, colleges across the nation will continue to tune in every day at 3 P.M.

Prospects for the future, with or without quotations, are almost inevitable in the conclusions of articles dealing with science and technology. Here are two more final paragraphs from the same issue of *Smithsonian* that the Jackson and Mitchell articles appeared in. The first is about molecular biology:

Mightier Machines from Tiny Atoms May Someday Grow

Expectations shape actions, and expectations rest on a view of the future. The idea of molecular technology brings a new view of the future, and with it a new view of the world and a new framework for action. If we stumble forward blindly, as if molecular technology were a mere idea about some stuff in a test tube, we will reap the benefits late, while risking destruction. We have little choice but to open our eyes, to think hard on what we see, and to act as wisely as we are able.

—Eric Drexler

The second is about wind power:

They're Harvesting a New Cash Crop
in California Hills

It seems likely, if the wind industry can overcome its start-up problems, that we will see large and small wind farms with increasing frequency. And perhaps, like the windmills of Rembrandt's landscape paintings and the clanking wind motors of the Great Plains, the sleek white wind turbines that are now new technology will someday become 20th-Century symbols of North America's windiest places.

—JANET L. HOPSON

Another place to look for ending strategies is in your introduction. Notice how the concluding paragraph of the deer article echoes the perplexity, the two-sided attitude, introduced in the opening. A carefully planned introduction can pay off.

You can also find strategies for conclusions—and for introductions as well—in the traditional modes of composition (discussed in Chapters 12 through 15). A brief narrative, for example:

> Is a bicycle trip really worth all the trouble? At an isolated farm in Iowa I learned the answer to that question. For an hour or so I had been looking for a good place to stop for the night. As far as I and my map knew, there were no towns within miles. I couldn't even find a tree to lean my bike against. . . .

A comparison or contrast:

> Is a bicycle trip really worth all the trouble? If you want to go somewhere, a bicycle is the only way: It's cheaper than driving a car— and a lot better exercise; it's faster than walking; safer than hitchhiking; and quieter than riding a motorcycle. You won't have to wait around a train station and you won't have to run through airports. Your bicycle is more reliable than a hot-air balloon. And don't forget: Even though you'll need lots of muscles and stamina to climb those hills, you'll get to coast all the way down the other side.

You can also bring in definition or straight description in your conclusion.

There is one caution you should exercise in writing your conclusion: Avoid introducing a new topic, even though that topic is related.

16.6

The following sentences at the end of the wind-power article would simply frustrate the reader:

> Alongside those sleek wind turbines, we can also expect to see equal numbers of solar collectors. Together these two untapped resources will contribute substantially to our energy needs in the next century.

16.6 *The Title*

Titles for essays range from single words to complete sentences; most are somewhere in between. Noun phrases and verb phrases are probably the most common:

> "Close Encounters with the Creatures of Another World" (NOUN PHRASE)
>
> "Our Wily White-Tailed Deer: Elegant but Perplexing Neighbors" (NOUN PHRASE FOLLOWED BY AN APPOSITIVE NOUN PHRASE)
>
> "Checking in to 'General Hospital'" (VERB PHRASE)

How do you come up with a good title? Sometimes you have one in mind right from the start, something catchy or intriguing. If you do, such a title may help you to write the conclusion. The opposite situation is also possible: If you don't have a title in mind, you can look for one in the conclusion. A good conclusion will almost always yield an appropriate title. Another place to look is in the quoted material you might have used in the article.

What should the title do? It should help the introduction to carry out one of its jobs, either by arousing the reader's interest or by introducing the topic; it can also help establish the tone.

FOR CLASS DISCUSSION

1. Rewrite the conclusion to the essay on "General Hospital" by adding a quotation.
2. Write a conclusion to the bicycling essay that would go along with the introduction you wrote for the earlier exercise.
3. Think of new titles for familiar books or essays or television shows and see if your classmates can identify them.
4. Study the conclusions in the essays you have read in class. What strategies have they used? Can you make suggestions for improvement?

17

Writing Effective Paragraphs

Paragraphs, like people and snowflakes, come in all shapes and sizes. In newspapers they tend to be short, usually only one or two sentences, whereas in such magazines as *The New Yorker* they often extend for one or two whole columns. And sometimes a writer will turn even a single word or phrase into a paragraph to make the reader stop short. Yet even with this variety, even without hard-and-fast rules, there are some general strategies that can be useful to follow in writing effective paragraphs.

17.1 *General-to-Specific Paragraphs*

In the general-to-specific pattern of development, a sentence stating the general idea opens the paragraph, followed by specific details that support it. Such paragraphs are common in the expository prose of textbooks and essays. Think of your own experience as a textbook reader. When you go back through your reading assignments to review for an exam, you probably skim through the pages quickly, reading the headings and the first sentence of each section or paragraph to help you recall the material. In fact, you may have underlined that first sentence or highlighted it with a yellow marker. Why? More often than not, that opening sentence summarizes the main idea of the passage that follows.

17.1

The following paragraph—actually a one-paragraph essay accompanied by photographs—exemplifies this general-to-specific strategy:

An Airy Frame

From the inside out, the skeletons of birds are natural marvels of flight engineering and structure. They combine lightness with strength, and in all their parts form beautifully follows function. In all birds that fly, the breastbone, though extremely thin and light, has a deep keel which not only makes it rigid, but, more importantly, provides a large surface for attachment of the powerful flight muscles. Many bones found in other higher vertebrates are missing in the birds, having been discarded in the evolutionary process of lightening the load; others normally jointed are fused for stress-resistance and for further lightness. Most bird bones are hollow and some of these are trussed inside to make them stronger while preserving their flexibility. The skeleton of a three-to-four pound frigate bird with a seven-foot wingspread may weigh as little as four ounces—less than the weight of the bird's feathers.

—ROGER TORY PETERSON, *The Birds*

The Opening Sentence

The opening sentence of every paragraph is, of course, important; it is especially important in general-to-specific paragraphs, such as "An Airy Frame," where it not only announces the topic but states the main idea as well; it acts as the controlling idea of the paragraph. Notice that this statement of the main idea—usually called the *topic sentence*—is an arguable proposition rather than a statement of fact. To call bird skeletons "natural marvels of flight engineering and structure" is to invite questions: "What do you mean by that?" or "For instance?" The reader expects those questions to be answered, and, sure enough, the rest of the paragraph answers them with specific supporting details.

Following are two more examples of general-to-specific paragraphs, both of which are from textbooks—one an instruction book for learning a computer language; the other, an introductory sociology text. Notice again the opening arguable proposition:

The most important reason computers are so widely used today is that almost all big problems can be solved by solving a bunch of little problems—one after the other. Moreover, solutions to these little

problems can be obtained using the very limited capabilities possessed
by all computers. For example, the problem of producing the federal
civil service payroll is indeed a big problem. But to solve that problem
we need only do the following kinds of things for each employee on the
payroll. First: Input information about the employee such as his wage
rate, hours worked, tax rate, past pension deductions, etc. Second: Do
some simple arithmetic and decision making. Third: Output a few
printed lines on a check. By repeating this process over and over again
the payroll will eventually be finished. Since computers can do all these
things accurately and at high speeds, the reason for using them is
obvious.

—JOHN B. MOORE and LEO J. MAKELA,
Structured Fortran with WATFIV

College students should find ethnocentrism easy to understand,
since they experience so much of it. They are subjected to a barrage of
ethnocentric cultivation from before they arrive until the moment of
graduation—when the alumni office takes over. College newspapers
and annuals, pep rallies, trophy cases, and countless "bull sessions" all
combine to convince the neophyte that Siwash U. has unique virtues
denied to all lesser institutions. Rush week reaches a high point in
ethnocentric indoctrination. An elaborate drama is staged to allow the
pledge to perceive how only this particular fraternity has the social
values, the illustrious membership, the burnished traditions, and the
shimmering prestige which make joining it a privilege. Other fraternities are counterfeits, to whose members one condescends; the
unaffiliated student one simply ignores. Without the successful cultivation of ethnocentrism, few fraternities could meet the payments on the
mortgage, and every college "homecoming" would be a flop!

—PAUL B. HORTON and CHESTER L. HUNT, *Sociology*

Both of these paragraphs open with general statements, just as
the bird paragraph does. And in each case the opening sentence
announces the topic, sets up expectations in the reader, and states
the paragraph's main idea. Another common characteristic of each
opening sentence is its focus on a particular aspect of the subject,
pointing the reader in a particular direction—in effect, controlling
the paragraph. The first one, for example, doesn't promise to tell the
reader everything about the problem-solving techniques of computers, only one aspect: the way in which the computer breaks down
big problems into little ones. The second defines ethnocentrism by
focusing on experiences of college life. And the opening sentence of
the bird paragraph doesn't promise to tell everything about bird

17.2

skeletons, only about their aerodynamic qualities. In summary, then, a good opening sentence of the general-to-specific paragraph has three main features:

1. It states a generalization (often in terms of an arguable proposition)—a statement that requires evidence.
2. In doing so, it introduces the topic in a focused way.
3. And it sets up expectations in the reader.

Before examining the relationships between the opening sentence and those that follow it in the paragraph, we will look at paragraphs that follow a different pattern of development, those in which the opening sentence is not the main idea.

17.2 *Specific-to-General Paragraphs*

Here are two paragraphs by Carl Sagan from the middle of a discussion of pseudoscientific phenomena; they follow a paragraph about pyramids and "pyramidology" that debunks recent claims about the relationship between "ancient astronauts" and the pyramids:

> The Bermuda Triangle "mystery" has to do with unexplained disappearances of ships and airplanes in a vast region of the ocean around Bermuda. The most recent explanation for these disappearances (when they actually occur; many of the alleged disappearances turn out simply never to have happened) is that the vessels sank. I once objected on a television program that it seemed strange for ships and airplanes to disappear mysteriously but never trains; to which the host, Dick Cavett, replied, "I can see you've never waited for the Long Island Railroad." As with the ancient-astronaut enthusiasts, the Bermuda Triangle advocates use sloppy scholarship and rhetorical questions. But they have not provided compelling evidence. They have not met the burden of proof.
>
> Flying saucers, or UFOs, are well known to almost everyone. But seeing a strange light in the sky does not mean that we are being visited by beings from the planet Venus or a distant galaxy named Spectra. It might, for example, be an automobile headlight reflected off a high-altitude cloud, or a flight of luminescent insects, or an unconventional aircraft, or a conventional aircraft with unconventional lighting patterns, such as a high-intensity searchlight used for meteorological observa-

tions. There are also a number of cases—closer encounters with some highish index numeral—where one or two people claim to have been taken aboard an alien spaceship, prodded and probed with unconventional medical instruments, and released. But in these cases we have only the unsubstantiated testimony, no matter how heartfelt and seemingly sincere, of one or two people. To the best of my knowledge there are no instances out of the hundreds of thousands of UFO reports filed since 1947—not a single one—in which many people independently and reliably report a close encounter with what is clearly an alien spacecraft.

—CARL SAGAN, *Broca's Brain*

In each of the preceding paragraphs, the opening sentence introduces the topic, so in one sense we could label it the *topic sentence*. But it is not a topic sentence in the traditional sense of that term: It is not the main idea of the paragraph, as the opening sentence of the general-to-specific paragraph is; it is simply a statement of fact. And in both paragraphs the author builds up evidence that leads the reader to a conclusion in the final sentence, a conclusion that states the main idea of the paragraph.

Following are two further examples of the specific-to-general pattern. In both of them, the opening sentence simply states a fact. But it also serves an additional important purpose: It acts as a bridge or tie from the previous text.

This paragraph is preceded by a discussion of Sir David Brewster, who invented the kaleidoscope in 1816:

In the early 19th century, science was aboil with new ideas about light. The undulatory, or wave, theory was eclipsing the corpuscular, or particle, theory. The phenomenon of polarization—in which light, suitably reflected or refracted, exhibits curious effects when again reflected or refracted—intrigued scientists, especially Brewster, who vehemently opposed the undulatory theory. He experimented with bouncing light between mirrors, theorizing that after a number of successive reflections the light particles would become more and more polarized. His work with adjoining mirrors formed the backbone of the kaleidoscope. The great leap came when "the idea occurred to me of giving motion to objects, such as pieces of coloured glass, &c. which were either fixed or placed loosely in a cell at the end of the instrument."

—JEANNE A. MCDERMOTT, "The Kaleidoscope, Magic in a Tube, Is Enjoying Revival," *Smithsonian* (November 1982)

The next example follows a description of the government's income-support policies:

> Between 1965 and 1972, the United States doubled its overall spending on social welfare benefits—that is, on service and transfer payments. The increase, however, had little if any effect on the children of poor to near-poor families, and subsequent developments have made no significant changes. Most of the increased government spending that puts cash into the pockets of the poor has gone to groups other than families with children, in particular to the aged. The result, as we have said, is that the families of over a quarter of American children are left without the chance to provide a decent home environment. Other beneficiaries certainly merit the help they receive, but policies that so neglect children and their families reflect a distorted sense of national priorities.
>
> —KENNETH KENISTON and the CARNEGIE COUNCIL ON CHILDREN,
> *All Our Children*

17.3 Reader Expectation

An important difference between the two patterns of paragraph development that we have examined is that of reader expectation or reader response. Here again are the opening sentences of the general-to-specific paragraphs:

1. From the inside out, the skeletons of birds are natural marvels of flight engineering and structure.
2. The most important reason computers are so widely used today is that almost all big problems can be solved by solving a bunch of little problems—one after the other.
3. College students should find ethnocentrism easy to understand, since they experience so much of it.

Such general, and arguable, propositions clearly call for evidence: "Prove it," or "Who says?" would be a normal reader response. Notice also that the general topic sentence includes the writer's attitude toward the subject, which adds to reader expectation. Now look at the openers of the specific-to-general paragraphs:

1. The Bermuda Triangle "mystery" has to do with unexplained disappearances of ships and airplanes in a vast region of the ocean around Bermuda.

2. Flying saucers, or UFOs, are well known to almost everyone.

3. In the early 19th century, science was aboil with new ideas about light.

4. Between 1965 and 1972, the United States doubled its overall spending on social welfare benefits—that is, on services and transfer payments.

These statements of fact produce quite different effects on the reader. The reader is more likely to respond, "Right," or "Yes, I know," or "Why are you telling me this?"

Although it's true that the reader of the specific opening sentence may already know or suspect the author's attitude from clues in the rest of the text—as we do when Carl Sagan writes about the Bermuda Triangle and UFOs—there is no clue to that attitude in the opening sentence itself. It's simply a statement of fact, something anyone might say; there's nothing to agree or disagree with. Indeed, an author with a different bias writing about the Bermuda Triangle and UFOs—one, say, who is a firm believer in unknown forces and extraterrestrial visitors—could easily write paragraphs beginning with the very same words that Sagan used. And knowing that author's bias, the reader could predict what direction the paragraph will take (just as we can predict Sagan's direction). But the clues that enable readers to make such a prediction lie outside the opening sentence. In contrast, in the paragraphs about birds and computers and ethnocentrism, the general opening statements themselves tell the reader what to expect; they make the author's opinion and/or attitude about the topic very clear.

17.4 *The Example Paragraph*

Another paragraph type—a variation of the general-to-specific paragraph—might be called the *example paragraph*. It opens with a topic sentence that states a fact rather than an opinion, and the remaining sentences provide examples to support that fact. Here, for instance, are two example paragraphs from an article about the Zapotecs of Mexico:

In the 16th century Zapotec society was divided into two classes that did not intermarry. The upper stratum consisted of the hereditary rulers (*coqui*) and their families, along with minor nobles (*xoana*). The lower stratum consisted of commoners and slaves. Great emphasis was put on the order of birth of noble children: rulers were frequently recruited from the elder offspring and priests from the younger. Military campaigns were fought by noble officers commanding commoner soldiers. Nobles frequently formed political alliances by marrying into the elite families of other communities; commoners usually married within their village. Royal ancestors were venerated and were thought to have considerable supernatural power over the affairs of their descendants.

The Zapotec of the 16th century kept two calendars, one secular and the other ritual. The secular calendar of 365 days (*yza*) was divided into 18 "moons" of 20 days and one period of five days. The ritual calendar of 260 days (*pije* or *piye*) was divided into four units of 65 days called "lightnings" (*cocijo*) or "great spirits" (*pitào*). Each 65-day period was further divided into five periods (*cocii*) of 13 days (*chij*).

—JOYCE MARCUS, "Zapotec Writing," *Scientific American*
(February 1980)

Even though the example paragraph begins with a statement of fact, it differs from the specific-to-general paragraph in that the opening sentence is the most general one. The remaining sentences list the specifics; they do not build to a conclusion. The example paragraph simply presents factual information in a clear and well-ordered fashion. Often it serves as a summary or an outline of the information to follow, as in the following list of cave inhabitants from the *Smithsonian* article referred to in Chapter 16:

Biologists divide cave fauna into three categories. Trogloxenes, or "cave visitors," such as bats, crickets and the cave-nesting birds, are temporary residents that go in and out. Troglophiles, or "cave lodgers," including several varieties of spiders and many insects, can go either way: some members of a given species live underground while others in the same species do not. Troglobites, or "cave dwellers," are hard-core, full-time, back-to-basics cave inhabitants rarely encountered outside.

—DONALD DALE JACKSON

An obvious difference between this paragraph and the general-to-specific pattern is the reader's response. Because the example paragraph begins with a statement of fact, the reader is not moved to say, "Prove it."

So far in this chapter we have looked at three ways of developing paragraphs—three paragraph types—all of which can be effective in developing the ideas that you, the writer, wish to communicate. All three types generally need topic sentences in order to be effective. In the next section we will take up the question of that requirement.

17.5

17.5 Must Every Paragraph Have a Topic Sentence?

The answer to this question is "No, but . . ." It is, of course, impossible to state rules for writing effective paragraphs that will apply in every situation; the writer's purpose, the mode of writing, and, probably most important, the context all make a difference. However, the three styles of paragraphs we have looked at illustrate the most common styles for expository writing, writing meant to inform (see Chapter 14), and they generally do have a topic sentence. But in narrative prose, which moves through time from event to event, the paragraphs are less likely to go from general to specific or from specific to general. The narrative is often paragraphed according to the sequence of time or of dramatic episodes or of shifts from one character to another (see Chapter 13). But narratives may also include whole paragraphs of description or exposition, and these are likely to be organized in the same way as the paragraphs we have seen, with a general idea at either the beginning or the end.

As mentioned in the opening of this chapter, the expository writing in newspapers is also different from that of most textbooks. The typical paragraph in a news story consists of a single sentence, sometimes two, rarely more than three. Of the 38 full paragraphs on the front page of a recent, and typical, issue of *The New York Times*, 24 were single sentences, 8 were two sentences, and 5 were three; only 1 was longer. This practice is used for visual reasons, to make the page more accessible to a wide audience, which is generally reading quickly for information.

Perhaps "No, but . . ." is not the best answer to the question posed at the beginning of this section. A better one might be "Yes, but . . ." After all, paragraphs without topic sentences are rare. Certainly they are rare in the expository prose of good writers. A good writer follows a plan; the topic sentences are the underpinnings of that plan; they are the guideposts that help the reader to understand the writer's intention and meaning.

17.6 Development of the Paragraph

How long should a paragraph be? What constitutes a "well-developed" paragraph? As you might expect, there's simply no single answer to such questions. Every situation is different, depending on the topic, the audience, and even the organization of the paragraph. Sometimes a single example may be enough to fulfill the readers' expectations; other situations may call for detail after detail. The authors of the computer paragraph offered a single example of a big problem broken down into smaller ones, and that one example does the job. The author of the bird paragraph needed more examples to prove his point: details about a specific bone (the breastbone), about the general characteristics of bones (hollowness, absence of joints, and trussing), and about a specific bird (the frigate). A single detail would not have been enough to convince the reader that bird skeletons are aerodynamic "marvels."

Levels of Generality

One tool that can be useful for both developing paragraphs and assessing them is an outline showing "levels of generality." The example paragraph is probably the clearest illustration of this notion of levels. Here is an outline of the paragraph about the Zapotec calendars quoted earlier:

> **Level 1:** The Zapotec of the 16th century kept two calendars, one secular and the other ritual.
>
> > **Level 2:** The secular calendar of 365 days (*yza*) was divided into 18 "moons" of 20 days and one period of five days.
> >
> > **Level 2:** The ritual calendar of 260 days (*pije* or *piye*) was divided into four units of 65 days called "lightnings" (*cocijo*) or "great spirits" (*pitào*).
> >
> > > **Level 3:** Each 65-day period was further divided into five periods (*cocii*) or 13 days (*chij*).

As the outline shows, sentences 2 and 3 occupy the same level of generality, and sentence 4 is at a more specific level than sentence 3.

This particular paragraph may strike you as poorly developed, having only four sentences and only one at the third level. But given the purpose of the paragraph and the purpose of the article, this spare outline of calendars is sufficient.

17.6

An outline like this is no doubt familiar to you; it looks like one you might write in planning an essay or in outlining a textbook chapter you're studying. If we use conventional outline form, rather than numbers to indicate levels, the outline would look something like this:

I. Sentence 1
   A. Sentence 2
   B. Sentence 3
      1. Sentence 4

The other paragraph about the Zapotecs provides a good illustration of how an outline of the levels of generality can be used to improve a paragraph's development.

> **Level 1:** In the 16th century Zapotec society was divided into two classes that did not intermarry.
>
> **Level 2:** The upper stratum consisted of the hereditary rulers (*coqui*) and their families, along with minor nobles (*xoana*).
>
> **Level 2:** The lower stratum consisted of commoners and slaves.
>
> **Level 3:** Great emphasis was put on the order of birth of noble children: . . .

The last sentence obviously belongs at Level 3 because it is a specific detail, but it is subordinate to sentence 2, not to sentence 3. Clearly, the author should have reversed sentences 2 and 3 in order to tie in the specific details about the upper classes that fill the rest of the paragraph.

Donald Dale Jackson's four-sentence paragraph about cave dwellers quoted earlier is another that in outline form looks poorly developed:

1.		I.
2.		A.
2.	*or*	B.
2.		C.

17.6 The paragraph includes only the barest of facts, a classification of the three categories of cave dwellers. However, its purpose is simply to provide a framework in which the reader can place the details that follow in the rest of the essay.

In the paragraph following the classification of cave dwellers, the author used the general-to-specific pattern of development. Notice his focus and attitude in the topic sentence and the clear relationship from sentence to sentence in terms of the levels of generality:

> **Level 1:** All true troglobites, including several types of salamanders, fish, insects, and crustaceans, are thoroughly cave-adapted and splendidly matched to their environment.
>> **Level 2:** They are sightless, though most of them retain some form of useless eye.
>> **Level 2:** They generally lack skin pigment or coloration, since they need no protection from the sun.
>>> **Level 3:** The loss of sight and pigment yield no obvious advantage in the underground struggle for survival and no disadvantage, but their other adaptations are clearly beneficial.
>> **Level 2:** The appendages attached to most troglobites—their legs, antennae and the like—are often longer than those of their outside cousins; this gives them a broader operating range in the constant search for food.
>> **Level 2:** Their metabolism is generally lower than that of surface creatures: this enables them to spend less energy and to use what they have more effectively—they need less and live longer.
>> **Level 2:** Their reproductive habits are similarly adapted to the limitations of the cave habitat: they produce fewer and larger eggs, and their newborn are consequently bigger and better equipped at birth.

Sentence 4, the only one at the third level, comments on both preceding Level 2 sentences and introduces the next three Level 2 sentences; it makes clear why the author arranged the details as he did. Notice, too, that each of the last three sentences contains two complete clauses and two levels of generality. A more accurate outline would show those levels within the sentences:

> **Level 2:** The appendages attached to most troglobites—their legs, antennae and the like—are often longer than those of their outside cousins;

Level 3: this gives them a broader operating range in the constant search for food.

17.6

A paragraph that can be outlined this neatly is undoubtedly one that will fulfill the reader's expectations. However, when the sentences of an example paragraph or the general-to-specific pattern do not have a clear relationship, those expectations may go unfulfilled. In the paragraph about Zapotec social classes the reader simply does not expect a specific detail about the nobles in sentence 4, having just read a more general statement about the lower classes. It is when the reader's expectations are thwarted that you are likely to encounter "awkward" or "lacks coherence" written in the margin—when the reader happens to be your composition teacher.

The specific-to-general paragraph is probably the least likely of the three forms to have this neat outline as a framework. Of course, each sentence will be related to the one that has come before, but the levels of generality are not as clear-cut; there is no neat hierarchy. Look again, for example, at the UFO paragraph (page 358) and at the one on spending policies (page 360). The sentences are all related, but terms like *subordinate* or *coordinate* would not apply as they do in the foregoing outlined general-to-specific and example paragraphs. Another kind of paragraph without such a hierarchy, as you might expect, is the narrative paragraph, in which the dominant relationship from sentence to sentence is that of time.

WRITING EXERCISES

1. Why do you suppose Carl Sagan chose the specific-to-general pattern for his paragraphs on the Bermuda Triangle and UFOs? Rewrite them, following the general-to-specific pattern.

2. Here is another paragraph from Sagan's *Broca's Brain*—this one from a series of paragraphs describing future space missions. This paragraph constitutes his complete description of Mars rovers:

Mars Rovers. Before the Viking mission, no terrestrial spacecraft had successfully landed on Mars. There had been several Soviet failures, including at least one which was quite mysterious and possibly attributable to the hazardous nature of the Martian landscape. Thus, both Viking 1 and Viking 2 were, after painstaking efforts, successfully landed in two of the dullest places we could find on the Martian surface. The lander stereo cameras showed distant valleys and other inaccessible vistas. The orbital cameras showed an extraordinarily varied and geologically exuberant landscape which we could not examine close up with the stationary Viking lander. Further Martian exploration, both geological and biological, cries out for roving vehicles capable of landing in the safe but dull places and wandering hundreds of thousands of kilometers to the exciting places. Such a rover would be able to wander to its own horizon every day and produce a continuous stream of photographs of new landscapes, new phenomena and very likely major surprises on Mars. Its importance would be improved still further if it operated in tandem with a Mars polar orbiter which would geochemically map the planet, or with an unmanned Martian aircraft which would photograph the surface from very low altitudes.

Imagine the information in the preceding paragraph as your response to the following essay-exam topic for your class in aerospace science or engineering:

Describe a mission that scientists hope to carry out in the not-too-distant future.

How would you reorder and/or rewrite the sentences, given this new purpose and audience?

3. With a particular audience and purpose in mind, write a description of a person or a place, following the general-to-specific form of development. Here are some possible topics:

   a. When you read a letter from your parents or from a close friend, you can picture the writer in a setting. Describe your room for someone who has never seen it so that person can picture you accurately.

   b. The secondary education department in your college has asked you to write a thumbnail description of your high school so that their education majors who are going there as student teachers will know what to expect. You decide what would be the most useful information for them to know.

   c. Your mother or father wants to know about your roommate— an understandable curiosity for a parent to have. Describe your roommate.

Remember, the topic sentence of the general-to-specific paragraph is a statement of opinion or an arguable proposition, a statement that requires evidence-for support.

FOR CLASS DISCUSSION

1. Read the introductory paragraph of a number of essays or of chapters in textbooks. What pattern do they follow? Why?

2. How would you characterize the pattern of development in the following paragraph? In what way does it differ from the example paragraphs we have seen?

> There are three essential qualities for vulture country: a rich supply of unburied corpses, high mountains, a strong sun. Spain has the first of these, for in this sparsely populated and stony land it is not customary, or necessary, to bury dead animals. Where there are vultures in action such burial would be a self-evident waste of labor, with inferior sanitary results. Spain has mountains, too, in no part far to seek; and the summer sun is hot throughout the country. But it is hottest in Andalusia, and that is the decisive factor.
> —JOHN D. STEWART, "Vulture Country," *The Atlantic Monthly*
> (August 1959)

3. Judge the effectiveness of the following sentences as paragraph openers. In which of the three patterns of development would you be likely to find them? Can you make them more effective? In answering the last question, think about your own response, your expectations, as a reader.

   a. New York City is a dangerous place to live.
   b. Coyotes are dangerous animals.
   c. Katherine Hepburn's fourth Oscar set a record.
   d. According to the latest census figures, Montpelier, Vermont, is the nation's smallest capital city.
   e. Beautiful peaks of the Cascade Range make the Portland, Oregon, skyline spectacular.
   f. The lemur, a shrewlike creature, is at home both on the ground and in the trees.
   g. Jogging is a popular sport.
   h. Jogging is boring.
   i. Italy is the world's largest producer of wine.
   j. Many of the world's languages have no written form.

17.7 *Coherence in Paragraphs*

The opening sentence of the paragraph, as we have seen, sets up expectations about the paragraph as a whole; it may also be tied to the preceding paragraph. Each succeeding sentence does the same, both fulfilling and setting up expectations in the reader. The extent to which those expectations are fulfilled has a great deal to do with the effectiveness of paragraphs and essays. In this section we will look at three aspects of writing that contribute to that effectiveness: semantic cohesion, grammatical cohesion, and lexical cohesion.

Semantic Cohesion

Semantic cohesion, which is closely related to reader expectation, involves ties of meaning that go across sentence boundaries. An understanding of these semantic relationships between sentences can help the beginning writer achieve coherence and unity in the paragraph. It can also aid invention, triggering ideas about what should come next.

Let's look again at the paragraph about bird skeletons. It begins with a *statement* of the main idea:

> From the inside out, the skeletons of birds are natural marvels of flight engineering and structure.

As a reader, you respond to that statement: "What do you mean?" or "What exactly is a marvel of flight engineering?" The second sentence then restates the idea in more familiar terms:

> They combine lightness with strength, and in all their parts form beautifully follows function.

Such *restatement* is one kind of semantic tie to what has gone before—a particular relationship of meaning.

Now, in your role as reader, how do you respond next? What do you think will follow the restatement? Well, so far the discussion has been fairly abstract. The ideas sound reasonable, but you're not an expert on either birds or bones, so you're waiting for a specific *example* or *illustration* of the flight-engineering idea, some sort of proof. The author, of course, knows that his readers are likely to be nonexperts, and so in the next sentence he provides an example of lightness and strength to illustrate his point:

> In all birds that fly, the breastbone, though extremely thin and light, has a deep keel which not only makes it rigid, but, more importantly, provides a large surface for attachment of the powerful flight muscles.

The fourth sentence of the paragraph illustrates yet another kind of tie, *contrast.* Instead of providing further examples of lightness and strength, it explains how the bones of birds differ from those of other animals:

> Many bones found in other higher vertebrates are missing in the birds, having been discarded in the evolutionary process of lightening the load; others normally jointed are fused for stress-resistance and for further lightness.

Each of these sentences, then, is tied in meaning, or tied semantically, to what has gone before—through restatement or example or contrast.

Transition Devices. Often such semantic ties are marked or signaled by transitional words or phrases. For example, a *restatement* may be introduced by "in other words" or "that is." An *example* is often marked by "for example" (as in the preceding sentence) or "for instance," and *contrast* by "on the other hand" or "instead." Other common semantic ties and some of their signals are

Addition: in addition; moreover
Similarity: similarly; likewise
Conclusion: in conclusion; thus; therefore
Concession: although; yet; however.

The signals, of course, help the reader to make the connection. In the paragraph about computers quoted earlier (page 356), sentences 2 through 7 are marked:

> The most important reason computers are so widely used today is that almost all big problems can be solved by solving a bunch of little problems—one after the other. (2) *Moreover* . . . (3) *For example* . . . (4) *But* . . . (5) *First* . . . (6) *Second* . . . (7) *Third* . . .

The decision about whether to include the transitional signal depends to a great extent on reader expectation. If the reader expects an example to come next, then "for example" may not be necessary. It follows that a sentence introducing a contrast is much more likely to need the signal. The decision to include or omit it may also depend on

17.7

the intonation of the sentence or possibly its pace. The writer may wish to shift or delay the main stress or to slow the reader down; an inserted word or phrase can sometimes accomplish that. This technique will be discussed further in Chapter 18, "Revision and Style."

FOR CLASS DISCUSSION

1. What transitional devices could the author of the bird paragraph have used to show the semantic ties of restatement, example, and contrast in sentences 2, 3, and 4? Would they have improved the paragraph's overall coherence?

2. Given the audience for a computer textbook, are all of the transition devices in the quoted computer paragraph necessary? Which, if any, could have been omitted?

WRITING EXERCISE

Write a seven-sentence paragraph in which the sentences have the following semantic ties:

Statement [TOPIC SENTENCE] → Restatement → Example →
Similarity → Contrast → Example → Conclusion.

Here is an example of such a paragraph. The writer's purpose was to make a Texan understand her fondness for New Hampshire:

> [STATEMENT] Winter is my favorite season in New Hampshire. [RESTATEMENT] Ever since I was small, I've preferred cold weather to hot. [EXAMPLE] Nothing can compare with the tranquil beauty of winter's first snowfall. [SIMILARITY] And there's nothing as refreshing as the crisp air of a bright December morning. [CONTRAST] But the muggy heat and dust of summer stifle my ambition and sap my strength. [EXAMPLE] My only accomplishment in August is a small success in swatting flies. [CONCLUSION] But winter in the North, with its log fires and downhill slopes and grand holidays, always makes me glad to be a Yankee.

Here are some possible topic sentences to start you off. Before you begin, be sure to have a specific purpose and reader in mind. As you compose, experiment, both with and without the semantic ties marked.

a. One of the big problems that high school students must deal with is peer pressure.
b. Many Americans are too well fed.
c. Traveling is the best kind of education.

Grammatical Cohesion

The term *grammatical cohesion* refers to certain features of the syntax that tie sentences together. The first one, parallelism, introduces an echo of sorts; the repetition recalls for the reader the earlier structure and acts as a structural tie. The second aspect of grammatical cohesion concerns the relationship established by known, or old, information.

Parallelism. In Chapter 6 we discussed the parallelism of pairs and series of words and phrases within sentences. Parallelism becomes an important cohesive tie when such structures are repeated from one sentence to the next. In the following paragraph, for example, the repeated series of traits ties together the beginning, middle, and end sentences into a unified whole:

> Why imagine that specific genes for *aggression, dominance, or spite* have any importance when we know that the brain's enormous flexibility permits us to be *aggressive or peaceful, dominant or submissive, spiteful or generous? Violence, sexism, and general nastiness* are biological since they represent one subset of a possible range of behaviors. But *peacefulness, equality, and kindness* are just as biological—and we may see their influence increase if we can create social structures that permit them to flourish. (Italics added.)
> —STEVEN JAY GOULD, *Ever Since Darwin*

In the following paragraph, the authors set up a series of positives and negatives as an introduction to certain questions, which they then go on to discuss:

> *Without* the automobile, the airplane, and electricity, ours would be a very different and less comfortable world. *But because of them* air

pollution has become a major problem. *Without* steel and cement and factories and tractors, the industrial development of the past century would have been impossible; *with them,* the volume of wastes discharged into water and air has grown to alarming proportions. Insecticides have increased agricultural production manyfold and virtually eliminated the dread diseases of malaria and cholera, but they have all but extinguished the peregrine falcon, endangered other species, including *Homo sapiens,* in ways not yet fully known, and biologically destroyed many lakes and streams. Is large-scale pollution the inevitable companion of economic growth? If it is, how much growth do we really want? If it is not, how can we ensure growth with less pollution? (Italics added.)
>   —RICHARD G. LIPSEY and PETER O. STEINER, *Microeconomics*

As the foregoing paragraphs demonstrate, parallel structures do more than strengthen the coherence of prose; they also add the kind of rhythm and movement that we more often associate with poetry than with prose.

Known Information. Although the coherence provided by parallelism is important, it is not an essential part of a paragraph; we can think of it as optional. However, there is a second, more important, kind of repetition that is required in a coherent paragraph: the pattern of known and new information that ties the individual sentence to the whole text.

In the passage that follows, from an article about the automobile industry in *The New York Times Magazine* (January 9, 1983), notice how smoothly we go from the main point of one sentence to the main point of the next:

> On the surface, Jennings Chevrolet, a small, profitable, family-owned concern in Glenview, Ill., looks much the same as any other car dealership. But these establishments have become, in effect, paved business battlegrounds where the decisions of thousands of average customers coming and going through the big glass doors will determine the future or demise of the American automobile industry. These days, that industry is mildly hopeful, fueled by the popularity of "bargain" 10.9 percent interest rates. Some segments of it—and Wall Street—are also buoyed by a determined new theme in automotive advertising, which has Detroit beginning to play down economy of operation in favor of the glamorization of technology.
>
>   —ANDREW H. MALCOLM

The ease with which we read that paragraph is due in great measure to the ties between known and new information. Generally the subject of the sentence is a repetition of the topic under discussion— that is, the known information; the predicate introduces new information:

17.7

Sentence 1:

Jennings Chevrolet looks much the same as *any other car dealership.*

Sentence 2:

These establishments . . . will determine the future or demise of *the American automobile industry.*

Sentence 3:

That industry is mildly hopeful . . .

Sentence 4:

Some segments of it . . .

Often you can use this feature of grammatical coherence to identify problems in your own paragraphs. Does known information connect each sentence to what has gone before? If so, the reader is likely to expect the next sentence as you have written it. That question of reader expectation revealed a problem with coherence in the following passage, part of a student's essay about laying a carpet:

> After the tack stripping has been placed correctly, the room is ready for padding. The pad, made of urethane, comes in rolls that are 6 feet wide and 120 feet long. The customer has his choice of what thickness he wants. There is regular padding, three quarters of an inch thick, and heavy padding, one inch thick. The pad is rolled out from wall to wall . . .
>
> —TODD LINDBERG

There is no problem with the general topic sentence; and the second sentence is tied to it by the known information in the subject: *the pad.* The reader expects *the pad* or *padding* to be the subject. But the third sentence introduces the idea of thickness, which is new information. Notice that the subject of the third sentence—*the customer*—is also new information. The reader probably didn't expect that change of topic. The lack of old information in the sentence should signal the writer of a possible trouble spot, a weakness in coherence.

Sometimes, in paragraphs filled with factual details, such as the dimensions of the carpet pad, you may be tempted to add variety by introducing a completely new idea. In this essay the idea of the customer is certainly relevant, because it is the customer who chooses the carpet and hires the mechanic to install it, but is this the best place in the description to introduce the customer? Probably not.

FOR CLASS DISCUSSION

Rewrite sentences 3 and 4 of the carpet passage to provide grammatical cohesion with the rest of the text. If you decide to leave the customer in the paragraph, try to find a way to suggest that women as well as men are carpet customers. (see pages 248–250 for suggestions on eliminating sexist language.)

Sentence Stress. The main stress of a sentence, the peak of loudness and pitch, usually falls on the new information. Every sentence has a purpose. That purpose is generally to add new information of some kind; sometimes, as we saw in the section on semantic cohesion, its purpose is to restate an idea or to introduce a contrast or to give an example. The main stress will generally be on the word or phrase that carries out that purpose—the new information or contrast.

English sentences have a fairly regular up and down rhythm— or, rather, down and up, as the main stresses tend to come toward the middle or end of a clause, where the new information is commonly introduced, rather than at the beginning. As we have seen, the opening slot, the subject, usually provides the grammatical tie to the previous sentence; that known information rarely carries the main stress.

Read again the paragraph about bird skeletons that we examined at the beginning of this chapter. This time read it aloud and listen for the rhythm pattern, paying particular attention to the peaks of stress, the word or words in each sentence that you speak with the loudest volume and the highest pitch:

> From the inside out, the skeletons of birds are natural marvels of
> flight engineering and structure. They combine lightness with strength,

and in all their parts form beautifully follows function. In all birds that fly, the breastbone, though extremely thin and light, has a deep keel which not only makes it rigid, but, more importantly, provides a large surface for attachment of the powerful flight muscles. Many bones found in other higher vertebrates are missing in the birds, having been discarded in the evolutionary process of lightening the load; others normally jointed are fused for stress-resistance and for further lightness. Most bird bones are hollow and some of these are trussed inside to make them stronger while preserving their flexibility. The skeleton of a three-to-four pound frigate bird with a seven-foot wingspread may weigh as little as four ounces—less than the weight of the bird's feathers.

—ROGER TORY PETERSON, *The Birds*

17.7

Chances are that the rhythm contours you heard were fairly regular, with the valleys at the beginning of the sentences, as expected, and the peaks toward the middle—that is, with old information in the valleys, in subject position, and new, stressed, information in the predicate peaks. But what happens when the writer wants to put the new information in the subject? Surely such variation must be possible in this versatile language of ours. If so, how does the writer signal the reader to put the stress on the subject and at the same time maintain the appropriate rhythm?

In the bird paragraph the author confronted that problem in sentence 3, where the subject, *the breastbone*, is new information. (Notice that in sentence 2, the subject, *they*, is old information referring to the already-mentioned "skeletons of birds.") Because we don't normally begin a sentence on a rhythm peak, the author inserted a valley of known information with that opening prepositional phrase:

In all birds that fly, the breastbone, though extremely thin and light, has a deep keel . . .

Notice, too, that in this sentence the comment about the breastbone, the predicate information, is also new information. Again, the author inserted a valley of old information, *though extremely thin and light*—information from sentence 2.

The following passage, also from *The Birds* by Roger Tory Peterson, illustrates another method of putting the main stress on the subject. Again, read the passage aloud and mark the peaks of stress.

17.7 (The sentences are numbered so that the discussion of them will be easier.)

(1) A bird's feathers have to do many things. (2) Not only must they provide lift surfaces for wings and tail, but they must protect the bird against the weather and insulate it against loss of heat. (3) Feathers come in almost infinite variety, but they fall into four main categories. (4) Most numerous are the contour feathers which coat the body, giving it a streamlined shape. (5) A house sparrow wears about 3,500 of these in winter, and they are so efficient at sealing in heat that it can maintain a normal temperature of 106.7° F. without difficulty in below-freezing cold. (6) Lying beneath them are the soft down feathers, also used for insulation. (7) Scattered among both types are the hairlike filoplumes which sometimes protrude from the coat and may serve as a kind of decoration, or possibly as sensory organs.

In sentence 4 you probably marked the word *contour* as the point of highest stress. Even though it follows the verb, *contour* is part of the subject noun phrase: *the contour feathers which coat the body, giving it a streamlined shape.* The author also faced the problem in sentences 6 and 7, where his new information is contained in the subject: *the soft down feathers* and *the hairlike filoplumes.* In all three sentences he solved the problem by reversing the subject and the predicate:

Sentence 4:

The contour feathers . . . are the most numerous [*of the feathers*]→ Most numerous are the contour feathers . . .

Sentence 6:

The soft down feathers . . . are lying beneath *them*→ Lying beneath them are the soft down feathers . . .

Sentence 7:

The hairlike filoplumes . . . are scattered among *both types*→ Scattered among both types are the hairlike filoplumes . . .

In each case the predicate of the underlying basic sentence, instead of introducing the new information, contains the old information, either stated or implied (italicized in the preceding sentences). In the published version, shown to the right of the arrow, the author has shifted the word order, opening the sentences not with the subject but with part of the predicate.

FOR CLASS DISCUSSION

1. Revise the following passages to improve their cohesion. First, read the passage aloud, marking the points of loudest stress as you read. Pay special attention to the second and subsequent sentences. Do the peaks of stress fall on the new information? Does the sentence include a bridge of known information? In deciding how the passages could be improved, consider also the reader's expectations. After reading one sentence, try to guess what the next sentence is about. You may want to subordinate some of the ideas.

   a. The space program finally went coed in 1983. Sally Ride teamed up with a crew of four men on the space shuttle Challenger.

   b. In Utah the floods of 1983 wiped out farmlands and homes, causing millions of dollars in damage. The irrigation system along the Colorado was all but devastated. Many reservoirs and dams collapsed under pressure from the unusually heavy snowmelt.

   c. The Gateway Arch at the edge of the Mississippi River in St. Louis is the world's tallest monument. Eero Saarinen designed the stainless steel structure that commemorates the Westward Movement.

   d. The relentless heat of California's great Central Valley makes the summer almost unbearable at times. Over 110° is not an unusual temperature reading from June through September. Bakersfield often records the hottest temperature in the valley.

   e. Psychologists believe that color conveys emotional messages. Advertisers routinely manipulate consumers using color psychology. The pure white backgrounds and bold, primary colors of detergent boxes are thought to influence buyers. Cleanliness and strength are associated with those colors.

2. Read the following paragraph about Saudi Arabia, paying particular attention to peaks of stress and the coherence provided by known information. Identify the techniques that the author has used to tie the sentences together. Do all the sentences fulfill your expectations? Can you suggest changes to improve the paragraph's coherence?

   At dawn, the sun over the Arabian Hejaz paints the stark craggy buttes and mesas jutting from the golden sand with delicate hues of rust and amber. Crossing this parched land of stunning, pristine vistas, the newly laid ribbon of asphalt leading north from the Saudi Arabian city of Median follows the old camel caravan route to Damascus. Alongside it runs the twisted remains of the famed Hejaz railway built by the Turks for the pilgrimage to Mecca and sabotaged by the Arab followers of Lawrence of Arabia. The highway passes countless tiny oases and villages strung close by the wadis, or river beds, that today, as in ancient times, form the loci of Arab life. Loping along the undulating sands are the ubiquitous camels, which, after millenniums of faithful service as the vehicles of the desert, are fast being replaced by the white Toyota and Datsun pickups that now bounce over the sands.

—ROBERT REINHOLD, "Uncovering Arabia's Past," *The New York Times Magazine* (August 23, 1981)

The Passive Voice. Another strategy for putting the old and new information where the reader expects them to be is the use of the passive voice. The passive transformation, as you'll recall from Chapter 3, shifts the direct object to the subject position; further, because the main stress of a sentence generally falls on the predicate, not the subject, the passive automatically puts that original object in a position of nonstress.

Notice in the following paragraph how the passive construction in sentence 4 contributes to coherence:

Since 1945, suburbanization has been the most significant fact of American social and political life. The compilers of the 1970 census caught its magnitude by observing that for the first time more people in metropolitan areas lived outside city limits than within them. The 1980 figures confirmed this trend and measured its acceleration. *Moreover, the suburban explosion has been accompanied by a marked decline in city populations.* The result has been a steady growth of suburban power in American politics. The changing numbers have made its dominance inevitable, but the fact that suburbanites register and vote in much larger percentages than city dwellers has accelerated the shift. (Italics added.)

—RICHARD C. WADE, "The Suburban Roots of the New Federalism," *The New York Times Magazine* (August 1, 1982)

The passive sentence provides a smooth cohesive link to bridge both the previous sentence and the one that follows:

The 1980 figures confirmed the trend and measured its *acceleration.*

Moreover, the suburban *explosion* has been accompanied by a marked

decline in city population. The result *[of the decline]* has been a steady

growth of suburban power in American politics.

Other Sentence Transformations. In addition to the shifts of subject and predicate that we've seen so far, the grammar system provides a number of delaying tactics, transformations that delay the subject when we want it to carry the main stress:

1. In the *there* transformation, the subject is delayed until after the expletive *there* and, usually, a form of *be:*

> A strange man is coming up the walk. → There is a strange *man* coming up the walk.

Notice that in the transformed version *man* gets both extra stress and extra length.

2. The "cleft" sentence allows almost any element in the sentence to carry the main stress. This transformation uses the "generalized" *it:*

> Susan wrecked her motorcycle in Phoenix during Christmas vacation. → It was *Susan* who wrecked her motorcycle in Phoenix during Christmas vacation.
>
> *or*
>
> → It was during *Christmas vacation* that Susan wrecked her motorcycle.
>
> *or*
>
> → It was her *motorcycle* that Susan wrecked . . .

3. Another cleft transformation that changes the stress makes use of *what:*

> Their positive attitude about grammar really delights me. → What really delights me is their positive attitude about grammar.

4. Modifiers in the subject noun phrase may also have the effect of putting stress in the subject half of the sentence. Compare A, below, with A1 and A2:

A. The new students should fill out the yellow form.
A1. Only the *new* students should fill out the yellow form.
A2. The students who arrived this *term* should fill out the yellow form.

Do experienced writers really think about old and new information while they're writing and then deliberately pick a strategy for getting the peaks of stress in the right places? Probably not. But you can be sure that they listen to their inner voices as they write their sentences. And they also draw on their intuitive understanding of language (which you have to guide you as well) and their conscious understanding gained from their experience as writers (which you are now working on and developing).

It's probably also accurate to say that all of the passages by experienced writers that we have looked at have undergone revision. Chances are, none looked or sounded in their first drafts as they do in their finished forms. Certainly the foregoing statements apply to all of the sentences and paragraphs in this book. (See Chapter 18 for revision techniques.)

FOR CLASS DISCUSSION

Think about reader expectation and grammatical cohesion as you read the following passages. Notice the ways in which the authors have provided known information to tie the sentences together. Have they used the passive voice effectively, or would active voice sentences have been better? Would you be tempted to change any of the actives to passives? You might find it useful to read the sentences aloud and at the end of each to guess what follows. Does the next sentence fulfill your expectations? What other devices, besides the passive transformation, have the writers of these passages used to make their sentence stress effective?

1. In their efforts to trace cancer to its source, researchers began to dissect our genetic machinery, and before long they uncovered one of nature's strangest paradoxes: Normal cellular genes within our bodies can quickly be changed into cancer-causing agents, known as oncogenes. Under ordinary circumstances, they lie peacefully in our cells.

Yet exposure to carcinogens (cancer-causing chemicals) and sometimes certain viruses can damage one of these genes, bringing on the unrestrained and often deadly cancer.

We all carry within us the seeds of destruction: Oncogenes appear to be normal genes that have been harmed during an individual's lifetime. At the same time, however, myriad other genes function to prevent this disease by directing the cell to produce defensive biochemicals. Thanks to genetic engineering, these natural anticancer drugs have become accessible for detailed study and further testing.

—SHARON MCAULIFFE and KATHLEEN MCAULIFFE, "The Genetic Assault on Cancer," *The New York Times Magazine* (Oct. 24, 1982.)

2. "Never before has such a terror appeared in Britain as we have now suffered from a pagan race, nor was it thought that such an inroad from the sea could be made." So commented Alcuin in 793 when he heard of the Viking raid on Lindisfarne. What at first amazed the English was the speed of the Vikings' operations. Their ships appeared out of nowhere and ran in through the surf on to the beach, so that warriors could leap straight into action—and then they departed again as quickly as they had come. Though such feats were not thought possible in western Europe in the last eighth century, it was soon widely discovered to be otherwise.

For Viking shipbuilders had perfected reliable sailing-ships that had no need of deep water, safe anchorages or quaysides. Their construction and shallow draught allowed them to use any sloping beach as their harbour and to manœver in waters unsuitable for most European vessels of that time. No wonder that surprise was felt, along with terror and rage, at such raids, for it was not just islands, like Lindisfarne, or coastal settlements that suffered at the hands of the Vikings. They rowed their ships up rivers that led them to rich inland cities and monasteries—up the Thames and the Annon, the Elbe and the Seine, the Loire and the Rhone, and many, many more. That the Viking Age in western Europe began when it did must be attributed largely to the development of such ships in Scandinavia during the eighth century.

—JAMES GRAHAM-CAMPBELL and DAFYDD KIDD, *The Vikings*

3. The current debate over the insanity defense will not be settled quickly or easily. It touches on deeply felt American attitudes toward crime, punishment and personal responsibility, and raises some of the most complex questions in criminal jurisprudence. But whatever changes are made should not be the result of an urge to punish a particular man. The principle behind the insanity defense—that individuals may take actions for which they cannot justly be held criminally responsible—should not be abandoned thoughtlessly.

17.7

The first point that needs to be understood is why an insanity defense is necessary at all. A time-honored idea in Anglo-American jurisprudence is that conduct should be punished only when it is blameworthy. Accordingly, a generally overriding condition of criminal liability has been the presence of a criminal "state of mind," which lawyers call *mens rea*. The essence of the *mens rea* requirement is the conscious choice to commit an act warranting moral blame and deserving of punishment.

—IRVING R. KAUFMAN, "The Insanity Plea on Trial," *The New York Times Magazine* (August 8, 1982)

Lexical Cohesion

The term *lexical cohesion* refers to the connecting threads in the text created by the words themselves. Repeated words, synonyms and related words, and especially pronouns tie the subject matter in each sentence to the subject matter in the preceding and following ones. Lexical cohesion can be thought of as a part of grammatical cohesion.

Pronouns. Pronouns are probably our most common method of connection between sentences. Luckily, for native speakers they are automatic; in fact, pronouns are required by the grammar, so we have no difficulty in coming up with them. For example, the rules of grammar require the reflexive pronoun *himself* in the following sentence:

Steve cooked a steak for Barbara and *himself.*

It would be ungrammatical to say, "Steve cooked a steak for Barbara and *Steve*," unless there were two Steves, in which case the speaker would have to identify them further.

Here's another sentence in which a pronoun—in this case *they*—is required:

Steve and Barbara decided that *they* would go to a movie.

It would simply be ungrammatical to say

Steve and Barbara decided that Steve and Barbara would go to a movie.

The preceding sentences illustrate the rules that regulate pronouns *within* the sentence; the following sentences demonstrate that pronoun rules also apply *between* sentences, that is, across sentence boundaries. Taken separately, the four sentences below are grammatical, but together, as a paragraph, they are not. No native speaker would say or write them:

> Steve and Barbara had steak for dinner. Afterward Steve and Barbara went to a movie. Steve and Barbara were surprised that they enjoyed the movie. Walt Disney was not usually Steve and Barbara's cup of tea.

Nor would a native speaker say or write the following:

> A large crowd of students gathered on the lawn in front of the administration building, chanting for the university president. Right on schedule, the university president came through the big doors, waved to the large crowd of students, and stepped up to the microphone to address the large crowd of students. The large crowd of students cheered.

No one talks that way, and, of course, we don't write that way either. Instead we use pronouns in reference to noun phrases that have gone before:

PROBLEM PRONOUNS. Although it's true that our use of pronouns in speech is automatic—almost unconscious, in fact—we can easily confuse the reader if the referent of a pronoun is not clear.

Look again at the paragraph about bird skeletons and notice how pronouns connect the sentences. The noun phrase "the skeletons of birds" in the first sentence provides the reader with a referent for *they* and *their* in the second:

> From the inside out, *the skeletons of birds* are natural marvels of flight engineering and structure. *They* combine lightness with strength, and in all *their* parts form beautifully follows function.

But sometimes noun phrases with more than one noun—such as "the *skeletons* of *birds*"—can trick the writer and thus confuse the reader. Imagine a different second sentence in the bird paragraph:

> From the inside out, the skeletons of birds are natural marvels of flight

17.7

engineering and structure. *They* fly with such strength and grace because of *their* efficient aerodynamic design.

Now what do *they* and *their* refer to? As a reader, you might keep going, but you would probably do so with a sense of uneasiness. More likely, you would stop, then go back to the first sentence and ask, "What does? What flies? Skeletons of birds?"

Remember, expanded noun phrases have many possibilities for including nouns that modify the headword. The reader—or listener—usually expects pronouns to refer to noun headwords rather than to modifiers within the noun phrase.

Of all the pronouns, *this* and *that* and *it* are probably the most troublesome for the writer—or, rather, for the reader. With them the breakdown in coherence can occur when the pronoun has no antecedent at all, no specific noun phrase or nominal to which it refers. For example, note the use of pronouns in the following passage:

> Last year my brother Chet designed and built his own house—a beautiful rustic log cabin heated by solar energy. It really amazed me, because when we were kids he did nothing but break things, including all of my toys. He was always in trouble because of that.

Altogether there are nine pronouns in those three sentences. *My* and *me* and *we* and *he* and *his* give us no problem at all, having clear referents: the writer and the writer's brother Chet. But what do *it* and *that* stand for? To what noun phrase or nominal do they refer? Because pronouns like *it* generally refer to nouns or noun phrases, chances are that at first glance the reader will interpret *it* as "a beautiful rustic log cabin." But that interpretation is wrong: Instead, *it* has what we call *broad reference*, standing not for a single noun phrase but for the whole idea in the first sentence, the fact that Chet designed and built his own house. And how about *that* in the last sentence? Here the referent is fairly vague. The reader can figure it out, certainly, but it's not really the reader's job to do the figuring; that's the writer's job.

Here's a revised version of the passage. It has little, if any, added information. The difference between the two versions is simply a difference in coherence:

> Last year my brother Chet designed and built his own house—a beautiful rustic log cabin, heated by solar energy. *His talent for building*

really amazes me, because when we were kids he did nothing but break things, including all of my toys. He was always in trouble because of *that destructive streak.*

17.7

An alternative to the second sentence would retain *it* as the subject and include a noun phrase as an appositive:

It really amazed me, *his talent for building,* because when we were kids . . .

(See also the discussion of the broad-reference clause on pages 118–119.)

FOR CLASS DISCUSSION

1. In the paragraph on page 386 beginning "Altogether there are nine pronouns," the subject of the last clause is *that.* Does it have a clear referent? Would you consider the *that* an example of a broad-reference pronoun?

2. Following is a paragraph about the use of computers in education. Identify a broad-reference pronoun. Is its referent clear enough? Would a specific noun phrase improve the coherence of the paragraph? Provide a noun phrase to do the job.

> Thus far most efforts by educators to come to grips with the computer revolution have been modest and tentative. This is understandable when one recognizes that the microcomputer—the relatively small, inexpensive machine that has made computing feasible in schools and homes—is barely seven years old. In his 1970 book, "Future Shock," Alvin Toffler did not even mention microcomputers!
>
> —EDWIN B. FISKE, *The New York Times*

3. In the paragraph about troglobites (page 366) you will find two instances of a broad-reference pronoun. Would the paragraph be clearer without them?

4. Identify the cause of your uneasiness as you read the following passages. In most cases you can clear up the confusion by substituting a noun phrase for any questionable pronoun:

   a. On our way home from school, we heard a strange whimpering sound. It was a little dog with a crushed paw, lying near the railroad tracks. It was covered with blood and obviously broken.

b. The variations in the sounds played on a trumpet are achieved by changes in the distance they travel. This is done by depressing the valves.

c. Mount St. Helens is part of a circle of known active volcanoes surrounding the Pacific Ocean. They are known as the "Ring of Fire."

d. Practically without warning, Mount St. Helens erupted on Sunday morning, May 18, 1980. It began with a gigantic explosion that hurled approximately one cubic mile of ash and pulverized rock almost fourteen miles into the atmosphere.

e. Traffic laws governing pedestrians are the best kept secrets in our town. They have the right of way in all marked crosswalks, but you'd never know it. Motorists pay no attention to people stepping off curbs; they sound their horns and bully their way through.

Vocabulary Choice. Another important source of lexical cohesion in the paragraph is the words themselves: the repetition of key words, the use of synonyms, and the use of related words. Look again at the paragraph on bird skeletons: In every sentence except the second, the noun *skeleton* or *bone* appears. And throughout the paragraph, there are words that relate to "flight engineering and structure," a phrase used in the topic sentence:

lightness and strength
form and function
thin, light, rigid
lightening the load
jointed, fused, stress-resistance, lightness
trussed, stronger, flexibility

The use of this rather specialized vocabulary ties the sentences together.

Even a paragraph that is weak in other ways often has strong vocabulary ties, simply because the subject matter from sentence to sentence is connected, with words from a common semantic field. However, as a writer you can strengthen a paragraph's effectiveness and coherence by making sure that the words and phrases you choose are precise and varied and fresh. (The effective use of words is discussed further in Chapter 8.)

17.8 *In Summary: Ten Questions to Consider* 17.8

1. Does the paragraph have a focused main idea?
2. Is that idea adequately developed and supported with specific details?
3. Does the paragraph follow a plan, either by opening or by closing with a topic sentence?
4. Do the sentences set up expectations in the reader?
5. Are those expectations fulfilled?
6. Do the sentences include cohesive features that effectively tie them together?
7. Are transitions marked, when necessary?
8. Does the main stress of the sentence fall on new information?
9. Does every pronoun have a clear referent?
10. Are the words that are used precise and varied?

18

Revision and Style

18.1 What Is Revision?

If you think of revision as a step you take only after the teacher has read your essay and marked it up and handed it back, then you're too limited in your definition. Revision is more than that. It is re-vision: looking again, looking back. Revision goes on all the time, at every step along the way. Here, for example, is what the opening sentence of this paragraph looked like in the first draft of this chapter:

If you think of revision as ~~something you do to an~~ *a step you take* ~~essay,~~ after the teacher has read ~~it~~ and marked it *only your essay* up and handed it back, then you're ~~only partially right~~. *too limited in your definition.*

Your own early drafts probably look like that, too, with false starts and deletions and additions. If they don't maybe it's because you're not sure how to go about improving your sentences and paragraphs once you've written them down. One purpose of this chapter is to help you learn what to look for in that process of "looking again."

18.2 *What Is Style?*

We all know the word *style* as it pertains to fashion and decor. When we say that a hat or a room "has style," we are judging it in a positive way, as appropriate and pleasing. We also use the word with modifiers: "1950s style" or "hippie style" or "L.L. Bean style" clothes; "Victorian style" or "early American style" or "late Salvation Army style" furniture. Such terms can be either positive or negative, depending on the writing or speaking situation.

What do we mean by style in writing? We don't say of a particular piece of writing that it "has style"; nevertheless, we do make judgments about the appropriateness of a certain style or about its clarity or its obliqueness. We also use the word *style* to characterize the writing of a particular author. The straightforward, seemingly simple prose of Ernest Hemingway, for instance—the "Hemingway style"—contrasts with the complex embeddings of William Faulkner, as the following passage from Faulkner's "Barn Burning" illustrates:

> The boy, crouched on his nail keg at the back of the crowded room, knew he smelled cheese, and more: from where he sat he could see the ranked shelves close-packed with the solid, squat, dynamic shapes of tin cans whose labels his stomach read, not from the lettering which meant nothing to his mind but from the scarlet devils and the silver curve of fish—this, the cheese which he knew he smelled and the hermetic meat which his intestines believed he smelled coming in intermittent gusts momentary and brief between the other constant one, the smell and sense just a little of fear because mostly of despair and grief, the old fierce pull of blood.

Such publications as *Time, The New Yorker,* and *National Geographic* are also known for a particular style. And certain professions produce a characteristic style: *Official style* and *bureaucratese* and *educationese* are terms used to characterize the dehumanized communications that so often emanate from government officials, social scientists, and educators. The word *style,* then, refers to certain features of the writing of individuals and groups.

What influences style? Every aspect of the writing situation does: the topic, the purpose, and the audience.

- Is the topic serious? Technical? Well known? Obscure?
- Is the purpose instructive? Entertaining? Inspiring? Persuasive?
- Is the audience well informed? Naive? Friendly? Hostile?

A scientist writing in a professional journal about a medical breakthrough will choose words with precise meanings that are shared by fellow scientists. A political columnist, on the other hand, would use quite different techniques. Newspaper columnists like to ask rhetorical questions, questions they don't expect to be answered: "Does Senator Brown really think the voters will go along with this unworkable scheme?" They also like to use analogies—even when the two situations compare only slightly. The scientist, in using an analogy, will be careful to point out the differences in the two situations as well as the similarities. Clearly, the styles of two such writers will be quite different. The writing situation makes the difference.

Is it possible to judge writing style for any useful purpose? Is it possible to improve our own writing style? Certainly. The process of revision and the acquisition of a clear and appropriate style go hand in hand; and both can be learned. In this chapter we will look at a few simple techniques to help you think objectively about revision and your own writing style. At the end of the chapter you will find a checklist of questions to encourage effective revisions and to help you develop your own way with words.

18.3 *Learn to Listen*

One of the most useful tools you can develop for revising and for improving your style in every writing situation is your listening ability. Read your sentences to yourself, emphasizing the peaks of stress and pitch and putting in pauses where they ought to be, as if you were saying them aloud. Listen to that inner voice of yours with your inner ear. At times, of course, you'll want to read your work aloud, but in the early stages of composition, learning to hear that inner voice will help you to develop fluency in writing. Remember, you're very fluent in speech; in conversations with friends you hardly ever get stuck for words. Plunge into your writing in the same way;

then let your inner voice and inner ear work for you as you write down your ideas.

18.4 *The Use of Your Personal Voice*

Probably the most important question you can ask yourself is one that concerns your "personal voice": "Does the language I'm using sound natural, like something I'd really say?"

You've probably had the experience, when reading a letter from someone you know well, of hearing that person's voice. That's the same experience you should have in reading your own writing: You should hear your own personal voice coming through. But if what you've written doesn't sound like you, like anything you'd ever say, then you should reconsider your choice of words or style of phrasing.

This is not to suggest that writing is exactly like speech; it's not, of course. In the first place, we can convey meaning with voice and gestures that simply can't be reproduced on paper; and in our everyday conversation with family and friends we use informal words and phrases that we rarely see in writing. Further, in writing we use certain modifiers, such as nonrestrictive clauses and absolute phrases, and transition words and phrases, such as the *further* at the beginning of this sentence, that we don't often use in speaking. But even when we include those structures, we should be able to recognize our writing as our own.

Using a personal voice does not necessarily mean using the first person, nor does it mean being informal or breezy. Rather, *personal* in this sense means "natural," language that a real person would use. We have all had the experience of reading legal language and various official pronouncements that sound anything but natural; we've come to expect that nonpersonal voice in certain kinds of documents. But we don't expect such "legalese" or "bureaucratese" in the essays and articles and stories we read; likewise, we shouldn't use it in the essays and articles and stories we write.

To hear the difference between the impersonal style and the "personal voice," compare the first sentence of the previous paragraph with the revision. Read both of them aloud:

Original:

> Using a personal voice does not necessarily mean using the first person, nor does it mean being informal or breezy.

Revision:

Utilizing a personal voice is not contingent upon the adoption of the first person in one's writing nor is it necessarily to be regarded as synonymous with a writing style that could be termed informal or breezy.

No one's "personal voice" sounds like that: People don't talk that way, and good writer's don't write that way. But inexperienced writers sometimes do. Here, for example, is the opening of a law school applicant's response to the question, "Why do you want to study law?"

It has long been a tenet of my value system that as a capable individual I have a social and moral duty to contribute to the improvement of the society in which I live. It seems that the way to make a valuable contribution is by choosing the means that will best allow me to utilize my abilities and facilitate my interests.

In spite of the first-person point of view—the use of *I*—there's nothing "personal" in those lines. If the author had been asked in a face-to-face interview why she wanted to go to law school, she certainly would not have begun her answer with, "It has long been a tenet of my value system." Never in her life has she begun a sentence that way. Instead, she would have said "I believe" or "I've always thought." But like many inexperienced writers, she associated formal writing with lofty phrases and uncommon words.

A "personal voice" does not, of course, preclude the use of big words or uncommon words. Nor does the term *big words* refer to the number of syllables. It means pretentious or fancy words, words that call attention to themselves. The word *tenet*, as used in the law school statement, is one such pretentious word; it's out of place. Why? Mainly because there's a common, everyday word that means the same thing: *belief*. Even the Declaration of Independence, with its formal, ceremonial language, uses the simple word *truths:*

We hold these truths to be self-evident.

Chances are that Thomas Jefferson didn't consider, even in his first draft,

We hold these tenets of our value system to be self-evident.

18.4

There are times, of course, when an uncommon word is called for, a word with the precise meaning you want. All of us have words in our reading and writing vocabularies that we rarely, if ever, use in speech. And using them when they're called for does not mean giving up our personal voice. The mere fact that a word is infrequent does not make it pretentious. In the opening sentence of the previous paragraph, for example, the verb is *preclude*. That's a word that I rarely use in speech, but there's certainly nothing fancy or pretentious about it. In fact, there's no other word that will do the job quite as precisely and clearly.

Perhaps an even greater problem than the use of so-called fancy words is the kind of word flabbiness that we get with such phrases as "utilize my abilities and facilitate my interests." English is a rich language, with a store of derivational endings that allow us to change the precise meaning of words and to shift words from one form class to another with ease, as we saw in Chapter 7:

Noun	Verb	Adjective	Adverb
legalization legality	legalize	legal	legally

Most of these shifts result in useful and efficient words; *legalize* and *legalization* have clear and precise meanings. But flabbiness results when that ending or that change from one word class to another detracts from precision. "To utilize my abilities and facilitate my interests" may sound impressive, but what does it mean? *Utilize* simply means "use": "to use my abilities." And what does "facilitate my interests" mean? *Facilitate* does not mean "to carry out," as the writer apparently assumed; it means "to make easier." So "facilitate my interests" is not only pretentious; it is meaningless.

FOR CLASS DISCUSSION

1. Here again is the paragraph from *The New York Times Magazine* about suburbanization that we examined in the discussion of the passive voice. Think about the author's choice of words as you read it. Art they plain or fancy? Precise or flabby?

> Since 1945, suburbanization has been the most significant fact of American social and political life. The compilers of the 1970 census

caught its magnitude by observing that for the first time more people in metropolitan areas lived outside city limits than within them. The 1980 figures confirmed this trend and measured its acceleration. Moreover, the suburban explosion has been accompanied by a marked decline in city populations. The result has been a steady growth of suburban power in American politics. The changing numbers have made its dominance inevitable, but the fact that suburbanites register and vote in much larger percentages than city dwellers has accelerated the shift.
—RICHARD C. WADE, "The Suburban Roots of the New Federalism"

2. What does *suburbanization* mean? Note its metamorphosis from noun to adjective to verb and back to noun:

suburb + an + ize + ation

Is it an efficient and useful word, or is it pretentious?
3. Imagine a conversation in which the author of this paragraph tells someone about suburbanization, using the same ideas he has written. What changes would there be? In other words, how might the written and spoken versions of this paragraph differ?

18.5 *The Grammar of Your Personal Voice*

Even though our sentences are based on a limited number of simple sentence patterns, we have a great many options for expanding and manipulating those patterns. Even the words themselves are capable of shifting roles with the addition of derivational endings, as we saw with the word *suburbanization* in the foregoing exercise. This versatility produces the unforgettable language of Shakespeare and Austen and Faulkner, but it can also lead to obfuscation and pretention, and it often does. You can avoid such problems—you can keep your personal voice coming through—with a lesson from the sentence patterns.

You'll recall from Chapter 1 that the six sentence patterns describe the underlying framework of most of our sentences. The slots in the patterns represent functions: *subject–transitive verb–direct object; subject–linking verb–subjective complement,* and so on. In most of the basic sentences we have looked at, the subject is the "doer" of the action, also called the *agent.* In most cases, the verb is the action word; and in a typical transitive verb sentence, the direct

18.5

object is the objective or goal of the action. These relationships are apparent in the following simple sentences:

Agent	Action	Goal
The committee	selected	Sandra.
Computer games	bore	me.

The basic sentences shown here describe someone (or something) doing something to someone (or something).

Now, what do the sentence patterns demonstrate about your personal voice? To begin with, you would probably agree that the voice you generally use when you are talking with friends and family is your natural, personal voice. Chances are that in a conversation with them your sentences will tend to follow the basic pattern of agent–action–goal. In discussing the action of the club's nominating committee, for example, you might say something like this:

> "I was surprised that the committee selected Sandra as the candidate. We didn't expect them to pick a woman, but everyone was glad that they did. She'll do a good job."

Notice that these are not all simple, single-pattern sentences; and even though they're short, they're actually quite complex, as spoken sentences often are, with embedded clauses and phrases. But notice, too, that in all of the clauses, the subject is also the agent, the actor:

Agent	Action
I	was surprised
The committee	selected
We	didn't expect
Everyone	was glad
She	will do

Nominalization

Now let's look at the way a written report of the event might differ from the spoken:

> The committee's selection of Sandra came as a surprise. They weren't expected to pick a woman, but this decision was greeted with unanimous approval.

One obvious change in this version is the absence of the first person, the elimination of *I*. There's nothing wrong with that change, of course; in fact, it's often necessary because the first person may not be appropriate in a written report. But notice what has gone along with that change in person: In the first sentence, the word *committee*, the word that names the actors in the event, is no longer the subject; it has become a modifier, the determiner for the noun *selection*, which itself has undergone the change from verb to noun.

This change from a sentence, "The committee selected Sandra," to a noun phrase, or nominal, "the committee's selection of Sandra," is called *nominalization*.

Is there anything wrong with such changes? Certainly there's nothing ungrammatical about the nominalized version of the sentence. But how effective or appropriate is it to report on a committee's action—that is, on the action of people—in a style that is completely depersonalized. Look again at the two versions of the first sentence:

> I was surprised that the committee selected Sandra.
>
> The committee's selection of Sandra came as a surprise.

The first version has two agent–action clauses, both of which have human agents:

> I (*agent*) was surprised (*action*)
>
> The committee (*agent*) selected (*action*)

It is bound to be more lively and personal than the version without a human subject:

> Selection (*subject*) came (*action*)

What's the alternative for the writer who doesn't want to use the first person? Ask yourself who is doing what; then simply eliminate the nominalization and stick to the original agent–action: "committee selected."

> The committee selected Sandra as the candidate.

To retain the emphasis on the idea of surprise, you may or may not

18.5

want to include who felt the surprise:

> In a surprise move the committee selected Sandra as the candidate for president.
>
> *or*
>
> The club members expressed surprise when the committee selected Sandra as the candidate.
>
> *or*
>
> The committee nominated Sandra for president, a surprise move.
>
> *or*
>
> The committee selected Sandra as the candidate for president, an action that surprised everyone.

In comparing these alternatives with the nominalized version, you'll probably hear a more personal voice.

The problem with the nominalized agent is similar to the problem we saw with the earlier impersonal examples. Compare the following:

> It has long been a tenet of my value system that . . .
>
> We hold these truths to be self-evident that . . .

In the Declaration of Independence, someone is doing something:

> We (*agent*) hold (*action*) these truths (*goal*)

The law school applicant has bent over backward, to avoid the "someone."

FOR CLASS DISCUSSION

Following is a rewritten version of the paragraph about suburbanization that you read earlier. Without looking at the original, revise this paragraph with the "agent-as-subject" principle in mind. Compare your revision with the published version.

> Since 1945, suburbanization has been the most significant fact of American social and political life. The people responsible for the compilization of the 1970 census caught its magnitude with the observa-

tion that for the first time more people in metropolitan areas resided outside the boundaries of cities than within them. The 1980 figures represent a confirmation of this trend and a measurement of its acceleration. Moreover, the explosion of the population of the suburban areas has been accompanied by a marked decline in the population of cities. The result has been a steady growth of suburban power in American politics. The changing numbers have made its dominance inevitable, but the fact that the participation of suburbanites in registration and voting produced a much larger percentage than did the participation of city dwellers has resulted in an acceleration of the shift.

The Passive Voice

The passive voice, or passive transformation, is common in both writing and speaking; it is probably used more often than most people realize. In fact, the clause you just read is passive. As you will recall from Chapter 3, in the passive sentence the goal (the original direct object), rather than the agent, fills the subject slot:

Active:

The committee selected Sandra.

Passive:

Sandra was selected by the committee.

In Chapter 17 we saw how the passive voice can contribute to sentence coherence by allowing the shift of old and new information. That shift is also the reason for the passive in the second clause in this paragraph:

it is probably used more often than most people realize.

The passive puts *it*, the old information, in the position of nonstress, the subject slot.

The passive voice serves other purposes as well, as we saw in Chapter 3: It deletes the agent, where the agent is either irrelevant or unknown; and it delays the agent to the end of the sentence, where certain kinds of modifiers can be added more easily. Well-written and well-chosen passive sentences, like well-written and well-chosen active ones, can enhance any piece of writing.

18.5

But the passive voice can also result in writing that is lifeless and stilted and wordy. In fact, a common result of the passive voice is prose that is so stilted that it lacks any resemblance to a human voice:

> It was reported today that the federal funds to be allocated for the power plant would not be forthcoming as early as had been anticipated. Some contracts on the preliminary work have been canceled and others renegotiated.

In such "officialese" or "bureaucratese" the nonhuman quality is almost inevitable, as the agent role has completely disappeared from the sentences. In the above example the reader does not know who is reporting, allocating, anticipating, canceling, or renegotiating.

This kind of agentless passive is especially common in official news conferences, where press secretaries and other government officials explain what is happening without revealing who is making it happen:

> Recommendations are being made to the Israeli government concerning the Middle East problem.
>
> A tax hike has been proposed, but several other solutions to the deficit problem are also being considered.
>
> The president has been advised that certain highly placed officials are being investigated.

The faceless passive does an efficient job of obscuring responsibility, but it is neither efficient nor graceful for the writing that most of us do in school and on the job.

Often the inexperienced writer resorts to the passive voice simply to avoid using the first-person point of view. Here, first of all, is a gardener's account of spring planting written in the first person (*we*):

> In late April, when the ground dried out enough to be worked, we planted peas and onions and potatoes and prepared the soil for the rest of the vegetables. Then in mid-May we set out the tomato and pepper plants, hoping we had seen the last of frost.

Certainly the first person as used here would seem to be the logical choice for such a passage; nevertheless some writers take great pains to avoid it (and, unfortunately, some writing texts, for no logical reason, warn against using the first person). The result is a gardener's passive account of spring planting—without the gardener:

> In late April, when the ground dried out enough to be worked, the peas and onions and potatoes were planted, and the soil was prepared for the rest of the vegetables. Then in mid-May the tomato and pepper plants were set out in hopes that the frost was over.

This revision is certainly not as stilted as the earlier examples of agentless prose, but it does lack the live, human quality that the active version has.

FOR CLASS DISCUSSION

1. Rewrite the original gardening paragraph, eliminating the first-person point of view but maintaining the active voice. (See pages 56–57 for examples of this technique.)

2. The writer of the following passage, in eliminating the first person in this description of the woods, has obliterated any resemblance to a personal voice with awkward passives. There must be a better way to avoid the first person. Find it. (*Hint:* Think about the agent as subject.)

> The woods in the morning seemed both peaceful and lively. Birds could be heard in the pines and oaks staking out their territory; squirrels could be seen scampering across the leaves that covered the forest floor. While in the branches above, the new leaves of the birches and maples were outlined by the sun's rays; the leaves, too, could be heard, rustling to the rhythm of the wind.

3. Think about the underlying sentence patterns as you revise the following sentences. Try to make the agent the subject; pay special attention to nominalizations—verbs that have lost their verbness—and ineffective passives.

   a. David's unexpected arrival for the holidays was a shock to his parents. His neglect in not letting them know that he was coming was particularly upsetting to his mother.

   b. The broadening of one's view of life and the establishment of worthy goals are both important aims of education.

   c. The encouragement of the thinking process is also an important

18.6

educational aim. Strategies should be developed by students for the understanding of problems and for their solution.

d. Foreclosures by banks and other lending institutions resulted in the loss of farms to many Midwestern farmers during the early 1980s. High interest rates and low farm prices have been blamed for the situation.

e. High unemployment is considered an unavoidable side effect in the reduction of inflation.

f. Unfortunately, permanent unemployment may be increased by factory closings during the recessionary periods.

18.6 The Use of Your Voice to Revise

Let's look again at the very first sentence in this chapter. Here's the original:

> If you think of revision as something you do to an essay after the teacher has read it and marked it up and handed it back, then you're only partially right.

It's a perfectly good sentence as is; certainly there's nothing ungrammatical about it. And in a conversation, no one would have noticed anything about it that called for revision. But remember, writing and speech are different. Once a sentence has been written down, it's there to be read over and over again, slowly and carefully.

When you use your ear, when you listen to that inner voice as you reread the sentence, you may notice what your author noticed: the rhyming sounds of "you do to." It seemed somehow inappropriate to have an "oo-oo-oo" rhyme in the middle of a perfectly serious sentence. So here's an edited version:

Revision 1:

> If you think of revision as a step you take after the teacher has read your essay and marked it up and handed it back, then you're only partially right.

That's better, but there's still something wrong. Remember, this sentence is the opening sentence of the paragraph. It's also the topic sentence, and you'll recall from Chapter 17 that one job of the topic sentence is to set up expectations in the reader. In a well-designed sentence those expectations will be the right ones, the ones that the writer had in mind. One of the most important considerations in setting up those expectations is sentence stress. However, in that opening sentence, there's no way for the reader to know where the main stress should fall: Is it on *revision* or *step* or *teacher* or *read* or something else?

18.6

Does it really matter which word gets the main stress? To answer that question, try an experiment. Read the opening *if* clause in those four different ways, putting your peak of stress on the word in italics; then ask yourself what the rest of the paragraph is about:

> If you think of *revision* as a step you take after the teacher has read your essay . . .
>
> If you think of revision as a *step* you take . . .
>
> If you think of revision as a step you take after the *teacher* has read your essay . . .
>
> If you think of revision as a step you take after the teacher has *read* your essay . . .

Recall what has been said about reader expectation: Every sentence sets up expectations about what is coming next. The opening topic sentence is an especially important predictor. When there are four or more ways to read a sentence, the odds are that the reader's expectations, or predictions, will be wrong. So what happens? After the second sentence, the reader must go back and reread the first one—and stop and think about it for a moment—to get the writer's intended meaning. It is that stopping and rereading that detracts from the coherence of a text. And it is that jumping back and forth, when the reader happens to be your composition teacher, that results in marginal notes that read "awkward" or "lacks coherence."

Getting back to that opening sentence, which of the four stress patterns is the right one? None. Every one is wrong. The idea that you, the reader, were supposed to understand from the opening sentence—and paragraph—is that revision goes on constantly, not simply as a final step. The word you were supposed to stress in that sentence is the word *after*. But because prepositions rarely carry the main stress in a sentence, how is the reader supposed to know that?

18.6

The addition of the word *only* will do the job quite well:

Revision 2:

> If you think of revision as a step you take *only* after the teacher has read your essay and marked it up and handed it back, then you're only partially right.

As you may recall from Chapter 7, words like *only* are called *qualifiers*. Other common ones are *very, extremely, rather, quite,* and *so*. Qualifiers (some of which are also known as *intensifiers*) mark or signal adjectives and adverbs. (In the sentence we are revising here, *only* marks an adverbial prepositional phrase, which is somewhat less common.) Almost invariably, the addition of a qualifier will add length and stress to the word it signals. Read the following sentences aloud; notice how the addition of the qualifier changes the focus of the sentence:

1. The steak was rare and delicious.

   The steak was *very* rare and delicious.

   The steak was rare and *extremely* delicious.
2. The passive voice is common in presidential news conferences.

   The passive voice is *extremely* common in every presidential news conference.

   The passive voice is common in *absolutely* every presidential news conference.

(Incidentally, retaining both qualifiers would probably result in a less effective sentence, because the sentence would no longer have a single point of focus.)

3. After the last performance, the producer explained the financial situation carefully.

   After the *very* last performance, the producer explained the financial situation carefully.

   After the last performance, the producer explained the financial situation *very* carefully.

Back to our revision. With the addition of *only* in the *if* clause, the *only* in the main clause now sounds repetitive. What can we do about that? We can't leave it out, because that second *only* puts the stress on *partially*, which is where we want it. (Without *only*, the stress would be on *right*.) We could substitute *just*—"Then you're just partially right"—but that doesn't sound as good. The new version—a complete rewrite of the main clause—is even better. Besides eliminating the repetition of *only*, this version adds the word *limited*, which provides a semantic tie to the idea of *only:*

Revision 3:

> If you think of revision as a step you take only after the teacher has read your essay and marked it up and handed it back, then you're too limited in your definition.

Every change made in that sentence came as a result of listening: first, the inappropriate rhyme of "you do to"; second, the lack of a signal for stress; third, the repetition of *only*. The actual revision didn't take long; and it happened right away, during the initial composition of that paragraph. The revision was actually a part of the composing process. When you learn to use that inner voice, such revisions come easily. With practice you'll find yourself doing them as you go along.

18.7 Grammar and Sentence Style

Learning to listen with that inner ear is one technique for becoming conscious of and improving your sentence style as you reread and revise your prose. Another is to apply what you know about sentence grammar. In Part I, you learned about a variety of ways to expand sentences using modification and coordination and subordination. In this section we will examine how deviations from the usual and expected sentence structure can affect a writer's style.

Word Order Variation

Variation from the standard subject-verb-object word order is fairly common in poetry; it can be effective in prose as well, partly because it is uncommon. In the following sentence, Charles Dickens varied his word order with good effect:

> Talent, Mr. Micawber has; money, Mr. Micawber has not.

18.7 Another fairly common rearrangement occurs when a clause as direct object opens the sentence:

> Which of these calls seemed more mysterious, it is not possible to say.
> —JAMES AGEE

Robert Frost used this variation, too, in the first line of his famous poem "Stopping by Woods on a Snowy Evening":

> Whose woods these are, I think I know.

Notice that all of these variations put special emphasis on the verb, the slot that usually gets rather weak stress when the sentence has a direct object.

The following sentence, written by Winston Churchill, illustrates another kind of shift in word order. Here the very last noun phrase in the sentence is the grammatical subject:

> Against Lee and his great Lieutenant [Stonewall Jackson], united for a year of intense action in a comradeship which recalls that of Marlborough and Eugene, were now to be marshalled *the overwhelming forces of the Union.*

When you read this sentence aloud, you can hear your voice building to a peak of stress on *overwhelming forces,* just as Churchill planned. In fact, it's hard to read the sentence without sounding Churchillian.

Ellipsis

Another fairly common stylistic variation is the use of ellipsis, where part of the sentence is simply left out, or "understood," usually for the purpose of avoiding repetition. In the following description of Stonewall Jackson, Churchill used ellipsis in both sentences. In the first, he left out the linking verb in all but the first clause:

> His character was stern, his manner [was] reserved and usually forbidding, his temper [was] Calvinistic, his mode of life [was] strict, frugal, austere.

> Black-bearded, pale-faced, with thin, compressed lips, aquiline nose, and dark, piercing eyes, he slouched in his weather-stained uniform a

professor-warrior; yet [he was] greatly beloved by the few who knew him best, and [he was] gifted with that strange power of commanding measureless devotion from the thousands whom he ruled with an iron hand.

18.7

—*The Great Democracies*

Notice also in the last sentence that in the clause after the semicolon both the subjects and the verbs are understood.

The following sentence, written by Joan Didion about Joan Baez, includes the same kind of ellipsis, the understood subject and verb in the second clause:

The roles assigned to her are various, but [they are] variations on a single theme.

And here's a sentence that includes both ellipsis and a shift in word order:

Of time, I have plenty; of money, no need.

The Coordinate Series

Many of the structural variations that writers use for special effects occur in connection with coordinate structures—pairs and series of sentences and sentence parts. One effective way of changing the emphasis in coordinate structures entails a small deviation from the usual way of using conjunctions. In a series of three or more structures, we generally use commas between the parts of the series, and we use a conjunction before the final member:

At the class reunion, we laughed, joked, sang the old songs, and reminisced.

Here are two variations. Read them aloud and listen to the differences.

At the class reunion we laughed and joked and sang the old songs and reminisced.
At the class reunion we laughed, joked, sang the old songs, reminisced.

18.7

The differences are subtle, but meaningful. The first variation puts emphasis on each verb with a fairly equal beat: ╱and ╱and ╱and ╱. It also puts a lilt in your voice. The second variation, the one without conjunctions, has an open-ended quality, as though the list were incomplete. The writer seems to be saying, "I could go on and on; I could tell you much more."

The first sentence in Churchill's description of Jackson includes that second technique. The phrases themselves have no conjunctions, as a regular series would, nor does the final series of adjectives:

> His character was stern, his manner reserved and usually forbidding, his temper Calvinistic, his mode of life strict, frugal, austere.

There's a hint of strictness and frugality in the style that echoes the words themselves. With conjunctions, the sentence would lose that echo:

> His mode of life was strict and frugal and austere.

The Introductory Appositive Series

You'll recall from your study of modifiers that the appositive is a noun phrase that renames another noun. In the following passages, the sentence opens with a series of noun phrases that act as appositives to the subject. In the first example, Churchill describes Queen Victoria:

> High devotion to her royal task, domestic virtues, evident sincerity of nature, a piercing and sometimes disconcerting truthfulness—all these qualities of the Queen's had long impressed themselves upon the mind of her subjects.

Often the noun phrase series is in apposition to a pronoun as subject:

> Political and religious systems, social customs, loyalties and traditions, they all came tumbling down like so many rotten apples off a tree.
> —WILLIAM GOLDING

Notice, too, in these examples that the series does not include a conjunction before the last member.

All of these variations in sentence grammar do more than simply add variety to a paragraph. Their special structure tells you that the writer crafted these sentences carefully. Such craftsmanship itself sends a message to the reader: "Pay attention! I wrote this sentence with special care. It's important."

18.7

SENTENCE PRACTICE

Look for examples of sentences in your own writing that could be improved by using the foregoing techniques of special emphasis. Then, using the following sentences as models, rewrite your sentences:

1. Shifted direct object:

   The glow of the flames, we could see for miles.

2. Shifted direct object, emphasizing a contrast:

   His voice, we could barely hear; his meaning, we understood at once.

3. Coordinate sentences with ellipsis:

   Youth is a blunder; manhood a struggle; old age a regret.

   —DISRAELI

4. Rhythmic repetition:

   With reasonable men, I will reason; with humane men, I will plead; but to tyrants I will give no quarter, nor waste arguments where they will certainly be lost.

   —WILLIAM LLOYD GARRISON

Notice that the last member of the series is expanded with a clause. This is a fairly common form in oratory. Try it also without the initial adverbial phrase:

   I will work; I will save; I will wait; I will recognize my chance when it comes.

5. Introductory series of noun phrases, in apposition to the subject:

   Snow, slush, ice-covered sidewalks—winter is certainly here.

18.8

Bearded zealots, sitting cross-legged on the ground, wallowing in Haiku poetry, Bhagavad-Gitas and Zen in an atmosphere saturated with the exoticisms of incense, opiates and lanterns—the "scene," in short, smacks of a Dr. Fu Manchu melodrama.

—F. M. ESFANDIARY

FOR CLASS DISCUSSION

Following is the complete paragraph about Joan Baez in which the earlier elliptical example appears. Listen with your inner ear as you read the paragraph. Notice a kind of crescendo, or peak, in the middle, with its use of repetition and ellipsis. Notice also how the sentence structure echoes the meaning. In what way is the last sentence different from the preceding ones? Why did the author change her style?

Joan Baez was a personality before she was entirely a person, and like anyone to whom that happens, she is in a sense the hapless victim of what others have seen in her, written about her, wanted her to be and not to be. The roles assigned to her are various, but variations on a single theme. She is the Madonna of the disaffected. She is the pawn of the protest movement. She is the unhappy analysand. She is the singer who would not train her voice, the rebel who drives the Jaguar too fast, the Rima who hides with the birds and the deer. Above all, she is the girl who "feels" things, who has hung on to the freshness and pain of adolescence, the girl ever wounded, ever young. Now, at an age when the wounds begin to heal whether one wants them to or not, Joan Baez rarely leaves the Carmel Valley.

—JOAN DIDION, *Slouching Towards Bethlehem*

18.8 *Grammar and Revision: Some Questions to Ask*

Question 1: Is *And* Effective and Accurate?

And seems like such a simple word, not a word to make mistakes with. But as we pointed out in Chapter 6, any technique we use as often as we do coordination has to be used carefully. A good question to ask yourself as you read over your essay is this: Is *and* accurate?

The *and* between the two halves of a compound sentence is the most easily misused. It will be accurate only if the two sentences are, indeed, equal in importance, that is, only if the sentence actually has two equal points of focus.

The writers of the following sentences should have asked themselves the question about *and:*

1. Picnic tables and grills are provided, and no matter where you are on the island you can see the lake.
2. Nature had provided a playground of trees and shady walks, and it had been taken away by modern machines and city planners.
3. The air inside the mine felt heavy, and it was filled with the tiny flecks of coal dust that seemed to be everywhere.
4. The fog shrouded the city, and even the tallest buildings were invisible.
5. After the lightning struck, we dashed out to look for damages, and we were shocked.
6. The shelves were made of polished walnut, and they extended the length of the room.
7. He shifted into high gear, and the car took off in a cloud of dust.
8. The Sunday paper sometimes weighs three pounds, and it is always more than I can read in a day.

In the foregoing sentences, the answer to the question of focus is probably obvious: One of the two clauses ought to be subordinated somehow. The context of the sentence will determine which is the main idea and which the subordinate.

In Chapter 6 we looked at the compound sentence with more than two clauses:

Blanche filled the bags with hot roasted peanuts, and I stapled them shut, and Oggie packed them in the cartons.

The question of focus applies here as well. Why would you want to join three short sentences in this way, using *and?* Isn't the result a rather boring sentence? Wouldn't it be more effective if one of the ideas were subordinated?

After Blanche filled the bags, Oggie and I stapled them shut and packed them in the cartons.

That revision is certainly just as grammatical as the original, but it has

18.8

changed the feeling that the sentence evokes. Read both versions aloud, listening for the peaks of stress and the intonation contours:

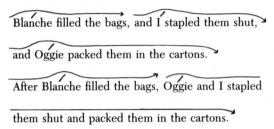

Your decision, of course, will depend on the context of the sentence and your purpose for writing it.

In the previous section on sentence style, we saw how deviations from conventional punctuation and syntax can enhance the meaning of a sentence. Here, however, the differences in focus and meaning are accomplished within the boundaries of conventional punctuation and sentence structure. For example, if you want to show the tedium involved in the peanut-packing job, then the / *and* / *and* / rhythm may be just right. The subordinated version seems to suggest a less boring, perhaps more efficient process. Further, sentences that are short and choppy often suggest speed or activity or excitement; they might also suggest unhappiness or despair. Long sentences may suggest thoughtful or leisurely or unhurried situations or feelings. And the variation in length can itself be used for special effects. A two- or three-word sentence in a paragraph of long sentences invariably calls attention to itself.

The Misuse of **Plus.** Before leaving the subject of *and*, we should mention a usage (or "misusage") that is becoming more and more common, especially in speech—the substitution of *plus* for *and:*

> I know we're having barbequed chicken at the picnic, *plus* I think we're having spareribs.
> In the graphics course we have daily drawing assignments *plus* a weekly design project.

The word *plus* is not a conjunction; it is a preposition used in arithmetic: Two plus two equals four. The use of *plus* to replace *and* is not only inaccurate, it calls attention to itself—a sure sign of a misused, out-of-place word.

Question 2: Is the Subordinate Clause Effective?

The question of appropriate subordination comes up not only with regard to compound sentences; it comes up in every sentence with a subordinate clause as well. Such openers as *because, although, since, if, when, even though,* and *as long as* signal a subordinate, not a coordinate, relationship of one idea to the other. As a careful writer you will want to pay particular attention to that relationship:

- Is the idea in the main clause really the main idea?
- Is the idea in the subordinate clause really the subordinate idea?

Answers to those questions, of course, depend on the writer's purpose. You cannot look at a sentence out of context and declare which idea is properly the main one and which the subordinate. Notice, for example, the second sentence in these two variations of a passage about the practice of footbinding:

> We like to think of carefree childhood days as something of a universal, a time for play and freedom that has always been a part of every culture. *But in China a girl was only a few months old* (MAIN CLAUSE) *when her mother began binding her feet* (SUBORDINATE CLAUSE), wrapping them with tight bandages day after day, to prevent their normal development. For centuries, the growing-up years of Chinese girls were years of pain.

> The practice in Chinese culture that Westerners probably understand the least is the centuries-old practice of footbinding. *When a little girl was only a few months old,* (SUBORDINATE CLAUSE) *her mother began binding her feet,* (MAIN CLAUSE) wrapping them with tight bandages day after day to prevent their normal development. Indeed, it must have been hard for the little girls themselves to understand why they were being tortured so.

In each case the first sentence of the paragraph sets up different expectations, so of course what follows has a different focus. Notice that the order of the two ideas in the second sentence is the same, but because a different idea is subordinate, the emphasis of each is different.

Because there are numerous ways besides the clause to subordinate ideas in a sentence, an equally important question is this:

- Is the clause the most effective subordinate structure for expressing the subordinate idea, or would another—such as a verb phrase, a prepositional phrase, or an absolute phrase—be better?

Here, for example, is a sentence with a subordinate clause, followed by three variations in which the subordinate structure is of a different form:

When classes were over for the term, we hitchhiked to Kansas City.

Variation 1: Participial phrase

Having finished classes for the term, we hitchhiked to Kansas City.

Variation 2: Prepositional phrase

At the end of the term, we hitchhiked to Kansas City.

Variation 3: Absolute phrase

Classes having ended for the term, we hitchhiked to Kansas City.

The answer to the question of effectiveness will, of course, be determined by the context, because in each case the stress and focus are different. The subordinate clause, with its complete subject and predicate, takes part of the focus from the main idea, because both clauses have intonation contours with similar peaks and comparable lengths:

When classes were over for the term, we hitchhiked to Kansas City.

So even though the first clause is subordinate in structure, there is a balanced feeling to the two ideas.

In the first alternative, the participial phrase puts emphasis on the verb *finished*, in that the participle shares the subject *we* with the main clause.

The prepositional phrase, having no verb, gets less stress; more than likely it constitutes a valley rather than a peak in the overall text. However, that quality could easily be changed with the addition of a qualifier or modifier, which would change the focus:

> At the very end of the term, we hitchhiked ...
>
> *or*
>
> At the end of a long, dismal term, we hitchhiked ...

The third alternative, with the absolute phrase, suggests both a cause–effect and a time relationship between the phrase and the main clause. The absolute phrase is a strong modifier that calls attention to itself. You'll notice, in reading it aloud, that the first three words are all given heavy stress; that attention invariably detracts from the idea in the main clause. (See pages 115–118 for further effects of the absolute phrase.)

Question 3: Is *But* Accurate?

The coordinating conjunction *but* has its problems, too, as in this sentence from *Time:*

> The changes had been rumored for months, but the timing came as a surprise.

Because *but* is a coordinating conjunction, just as *and* is, this sentence has two ideas that, by reason of its structure, can be considered only as equals. But are they? Here's another from the same page of *Time:*

> Political crisis is as familiar to Italians as pasta, as regular as a strike, but the latest parliamentary high-wire act in Rome had even seasoned observers worried.

Is the somewhat trivial comparison between crisis and pasta really equal in importance to the so-called high-wire act that has even seasoned observers worried? Probably not.

The problem with *but* sometimes becomes clear when you try to predict what's coming in the second clause. The *but* says that a contrast is coming. Try to predict the second clause in the first example—without looking back: *The changes had been rumored for months, but*—But what?

> The changes had been rumored for months, *but no one believed them.*
>
> *or*
>
> The changes had been rumored for months, *but they turned out to be untrue.*
>
> *or*
>
> The changes had been rumored for months, *but they never came about.*

We don't expect the sentence to say,

> The changes had been rumored for months, but the timing came as a surprise.

If you read the original sentence carefully, you'll discover that the first clause is clearly subordinate to the second; the sentence has only one main focus: the second clause. With the first clause subordinated, that focus is much clearer:

> Although the changes had been rumored for months, their timing came as a surprise.

In the second sentence from *Time,* again the culprit is *but.* The *but* clause is not simply a contrast, it is the main idea—the only main idea; the first clause needs to be subordinated:

> Although political crisis is as familiar to Italians as pasta, as regular as a strike, the latest parliamentary high-wire act in Rome had even seasoned observers worried.

Remember, a compound sentence has two points of focus that, in terms of structure, are equal. The compound sentence is effective only when that structure accurately reflects the relationship of the two ideas. If a single point of focus would be more accurate, then a subordinating conjunction should introduce one of the two ideas.

FOR CLASS DISCUSSION

1. Revise the following compound sentences to give them a single focus. Is the revision an improvement?

a. Coordinating conjunctions are common in both speech and writing, but they're not always easy to use accurately.

b. The knapsack fell down the steep bank into the river, and there was nothing I could do about it but watch it disappear.

c. The interest rates fell drastically during the last quarter, but government economists are still worried about high inflation and low productivity.

d. Long-distance telephone calls may be cheap, but I'd still rather get a letter.

2. Here is the final passage from Ernest Hemingway's short story "The Snows of Kilimanjaro." The woman is in a tent in an African hunting camp, her mortally wounded husband on the cot next to her. Why did Hemingway use *and* so often? What effect does it have? Rewrite the long paragraph, changing some of the coordinate structures into subordinate ones. Have you improved any of the sentences?

Just then the hyena stopped whimpering in the night and started to make a strange, human, almost crying sound. The woman heard it and stirred uneasily. She did not wake. In her dream she was at the house on Long Island and it was the night before her daughter's debut. Somehow her father was there and he had been very rude. Then the noise the hyena made was so loud she woke and for a moment she did not know where she was and she was very afraid. Then she took the flashlight and shone it on the other cot that they had carried in after Harry had gone to sleep. She could see his bulk under the mosquito bar but somehow he had gotten his leg out and it hung down alongside the cot. The dressings had all come down and she could not look at it.

"Molo," she called, "Molo! Molo!"

Then she said, "Harry, Harry!" Then her voice rising, "Harry! Please, Oh Harry!"

There was no answer and she could not hear him breathing.

Outside the tent the hyena made the same strange noise that had awakened her. But she did not hear him for the beating of her heart.

3. You may have heard or read the dictum, "Never begin a sentence with a conjunction." Collect samples of professional writing that contradict that statement. Explain why the writers made the choice they did. (One place to look is in this book.)

4. The following passage from *Invisible Man* by Ralph Ellison illustrates a dramatic use of *and:*

He was standing and he fell. He fell and he kneeled. He kneeled and he bled. He bled and he died. He fell in a heap like any man and his blood

18.9

spilled like any blood; red as any blood, wet as any blood and reflecting the sky and the buildings and birds and trees, or your face if you'd looked into its dulling mirror.

How would you characterize the effect of *and* in these sentences? How would the use of subordinate structures change that effect? Write a passage on another subject, using *and* as Ellison did. Here are some possible openings:

The starting gun sounded and the sprinters leaped.

The crowd was silent and the whistle pierced the air.

The woman leaned against his shoulder and then she slumped to the ground.

The knapsack rolled like a stone down the bank and it disappeared into the black water.

5. Look again at the paragraph by Joan Didion that you read earlier in connection with grammar and style (page 412). This time analyze the use of coordinate structures, of repetition, of ellipses, and of sentence length. Using its structure as a model, write a paragraph about someone you know well.

6. Is it possible for the main focus of the sentence to be carried by a subordinate structure? Try to find examples of sentences that appear to break the rule of "main idea in main clause." Do you understand the writer's strategy?

7. Contrast the styles of the excerpt from "Barn Burning" by William Faulkner at the beginning of this chapter with the Hemingway passage in Question 2 above. Notice especially the difference in how ideas are subordinated and coordinated. What is the effect on the reader? Think, for example, about the feelings and thoughts of the characters, their ideas, and their emotions. Imagine the styles of the two passages reversed. Try to rewrite the Hemingway passage in Faulkner style, and vice versa.

18.9 In Summary: Ten Questions to Consider

1. Do you feel comfortable in speaking aloud the words and phrases you have written?

2. Do any of your words call attention to themselves?

3. Have you avoided unnecessary repetition in your words and phrases?

18.10

4. Have you avoided the awkward passive structures and nominalizations that eliminate the agent for no good reason?
5. Are the parts of your coordinate structures of the same form— that is, are they parallel?
6. Do the main stresses in your sentences fall where they should, on the new information?
7. Are the ideas in the clauses of your compound sentences coordinate ideas? In other words, have you used *and* accurately?
8. Does *but* introduce an idea that is both contrasting and coordinate?
9. Are the ideas in your subordinate structures really subordinate ideas?
10. Does variation in your sentences—in their length and in their openers—contribute to sentence effectiveness?

18.10 Six Proofreading Questions

The last step in your job as editor is to proofread your work to make sure that the spelling and punctuation are accurate. The following questions pinpoint some common problems:

1. Have you used commas where you need them?
   • With the conjunction between two parts of a compound sentence.
   • After every introductory clause or verb phrase.
   • To set off nonrestrictive modifiers in the noun phrase.
2. Have you avoided using commas between the two parts of a compound structure within the sentence?
3. Have you taken advantage of the contribution that colons and semicolons make?
4. Are you sure of your decisions regarding capitalization, apostrophes, and quotation marks?
5. Have you checked the spelling of problem words, including such troublesome sound-alikes as *their/there/they're, accept/except, too/to/two,* and *your/you're?*
6. Have you made your corrections neatly?

Glossary of Mechanics and Punctuation

The conventions for mechanics and punctuation listed here (and used throughout this book) follow, for the most part, the recommendations of the University of Chicago Press as given in *A Manual of Style* (1982). For details of capitalization, abbreviation, and hyphenation of particular words, consult an up-to-date dictionary.

Abbreviations

1. Titles

When used with a name, the abbreviations *Dr.*, *Mr.*, *Mrs.*, and *Ms.* are standard:

Dr. White is in his office.

Also note:

I called the doctor today. (*Not* I called the dr. today.)

The titles *President, Senator, Governor,* and *Professor* are written in full (and capitalized) when used with a surname:

I really like Professor Brown's class.

With a full name, the title is usually abbreviated:

Prof. Betsy Brown
Gov. Mario Cuomo

The title *Reverend* is properly written with *the*, followed by a title (*Mr., Dr.*) and the name:

The Reverend Dr. Martin Luther King, Jr.
The Reverend Mr. Russell Bolm

Subsequent mentions can be, simply,

Dr. King
Mr. Bolm (*Not* Reverend Bolm or Rev. Bolm.)

In text, *Saint* and *Mount* are written out:

Saint Joan
Mount Rainier

However, in writing *Mount St. Helens, Saint* is often abbreviated. When *Saint* is part of a person's name, the individual's own usage is followed:

Yves Saint Laurent

2. Acronyms

Acronyms, initials that are pronounced as words, as well as other agency abbreviations, are generally written in capitals without periods. NATO, OPEC, UNESCO, USA, IRS, YMCA, CIA.

Unless the identification of the initials is obvious, as with USA or

USSR, the full name should be spelled out at first mention; in subsequent mentions use initials:

> When the representatives of the Organization of Petroleum Exporting Countries meet in Syria next week, their decision will have far-reaching effects on oil prices world wide, even for countries who refuse to buy OPEC oil.

3. Other Abbreviations

Other abbreviations that are standard in prose are B.C., A.D., A.M., and P.M. (sometimes written in lower case: a.m., p.m.). Do not abbreviate *street, avenue, boulevard,* and the like, even when used in proper names:

> I live on the corner of Water Street and Oak Avenue.

Do not use abbreviations in discussing *days* or *months* or *states:*

> From Maine to California, we vote on the first Tuesday in November.

Do not use abbreviations for course names, such as *psych* for *psychology, bio* for *biology,* or *chem* for *chemistry;* however, *math* is an acceptable shortened form of *mathematics.*

Apostrophe

1. Possessive Case

To show the possessive case, add *'s* to singular nouns, both common and proper:

> Bob's friend
> the ocean's deep blue color

Even when the noun ends with an *s*-like sound, add both the *apostrophe* and *s:*

> Kris's

(**Note:** Some writers omit the possessive *s.*)

Add only the apostrophe to the regular plural noun:

the cats' tails
the students' complaints

For irregular plurals, add 's:

the women's movement
the children's teachers

(A good rule of thumb for the addition of s is related to pronunciation: When you add the sound of s, add the letter; if you pronounce the possessive without adding an s sound, do *not* add the letter: Jesus' followers, Texas' laws, but Ross's friend.)

(See Rules 6, 7, and 8 in Chapter 9 for further discussion of the plural and possessive of nouns.)

2. Plurals of Words Other Than Nouns

In making words other than nouns plural, when the addition of s alone would be misleading, add an apostrophe:

A's and B's (but ABCs)
Ph.D.'s
p's and q's
do's and don't's

Numbers that name decades are generally written without the apostrophe:

1950s

3. Contractions

In writing contractions, use an apostrophe to replace the missing syllable or letter(s):

do not = don't
he will = he'll
it is = it's (Note: The possessive pronoun *its* has no apostrophe.)

it has = it's
cannot = can't

Brackets

1. Within Parentheses

Use for parenthetical material within parentheses:

The anthropologist who lived with the Iks in northern Uganda (reported by Lewis Thomas in *The Lives of a Cell* [1974]) apparently detested the tribe he was studying.

2. In Quoted Material

Use for interpolations or explanations within quoted material:

"Everyone close to the king surmised that she [Mrs. Simpson] would be nothing but trouble for the realm."

Capitals

1. Proper Nouns

Capitalize *proper nouns*—nouns that name a specific person, geographical location, or institution:

Reggie Jackson
Professor Corbett
Aunt Teresa
Central Park
Linfield College
Mount Sinai Hospital
the Washington Monument

a. Titles such as *aunt* and *professor* and nouns such as *park* and *lake* are lowercased when they are not part of a name:

Teresa is my aunt.
Dr. Corbett is my favorite professor.

The biggest park in the city is Central Park.
Linfield is a small college in McMinnville, Oregon.

b. Titles such as *president* and *governor* are capitalized only when used with a proper name:

After the president finished his speech, the audience gave him a standing ovation.
The governor announced his support for President Reagan.

c. Do not capitalize *mother* and *father* when they are used with a determiner:

I just spoke to my mother on the phone.

Usage is divided when *mother* and *father* are used as proper names; however, the tendency is to capitalize when the word is used as a proper name.

I called Mother last night.

2. Words Derived from Proper Nouns

Capitalize words derived from proper nouns:

Jacksonian
American
Reaganomics
Faulknerian
Americanize

3. Names of Groups of People

Capitalize names of groups of people:

the English	Lutheran	Indian
Caucasian	Mormon	Amerindian

Note that *black* and *white* in reference to race are lowercase.

4. Documents and Events

Capitalize well-known documents and events:

the Bill of Rights   World War II
the Gettysburg Address   the Korean War
the Battle of Hastings   the Marshall Plan

5. Calendar Terms

Capitalize months, days of the week, and holidays:

November   National Book Week   Passover
Thanksgiving Day Labor Day   Tuesday

Note that seasons are lowercase: fall, autumn, spring, summer, winter.

6. Titles

In titles of books, articles, plays, and other works of art, capitalize the first and last word, as well as all other form-class words (nouns, verbs, adjectives, and adverbs), pronouns, and long structure words. Do not capitalize short structure word, such as prepositions and conjunctions, except in opening and final position:

A Manual of Style
How to Find Treasures in Your Grandmother's Attic
Cooking Without Calories
Something to Live For

Note: On the first page or title page of your essay or story, write the titles as shown here, without quotation marks or underlines. See also Quotations.

7. In Quotations

In quotations, capitalize the first word, even when the quoted material is not a complete sentence:

The queen said, "Off with his head!"

I've always tried to follow Franklin's advice: "A penny saved is a penny earned."

When quoted material is integrated into your sentence, do not capitalize, even though the original is a complete sentence:

When Horace Greeley said to "go West, young man," he probably had no idea of the traffic problems he was creating for California freeways.

Even set off as a block, the integrated quote does not have to be capitalized, even when the original is a complete text:

Lewis Thomas, in *The Lives of a Cell,* argues that computers, no matter how many there are or how smart they become, will never equal the social collective nature of the human species. He firmly believes this because as human beings

we do a lot of collective thinking, probably more than any other social species, although it goes on in something like secrecy. We don't acknowledge the gift publicly, and we are not as celebrated as the insects, but we do it. (p. 112)

Colon

1. Appositives

Use the colon to introduce an appositive or a list of appositives:

The board appointed three committees to plan the convention: finance, program, and local arrangements.

Often such a list is introduced by "as follows" or "the following":

The three committees appointed to plan the convention are as follows: finance, program, and local arrangements.
The board appointed the following committees: finance, program, and local arrangements.

Note that a complete sentence precedes the colon; what follows the colon is an appositive. *Do not* put a colon between a linking verb and the subjective complement:

> *The committees that were appointed are: finance, program, and local arrangements.

(See Chapter 4 for a discussion of the colon in the punctuation of appositives.)

2. Conjunction of Sentences

Use a colon to join two sentences, where the second sentence completes the idea, or the promise, of the first:

> Only one obstacle lay between us and success: We had to come up with the money.

> We may as well face up to it: there is a highly visible difference between the pace of basic science and the application of new knowledge to common problems.
>
> —LEWIS THOMAS

Note that the convention of capitalizing a complete sentence following the colon is on the fence: Some publishers (such as Macmillan) always capitalize; others capitalize questions only; others capitalize only when what follows the colon is a direct quotation. Whichever method you follow, be sure to follow it consistently.

3. Introduction of Direct Quotation

Use a colon to introduce a direct quotation:

> Concluded a Western diplomat in Moscow: "The main impression Bush and Shultz had was of Andropov's great self-confidence and control."
>
> —*Time*

> Asked about the probable outcome, Huang replied: "I am optimistic."
>
> —*Time*

A comma can be used instead of the colon in these sentences.

4. Other Uses

Other uses of the colon include the following:

a. After the salutation in a letter:

Dear Mr. Jones:

b. In expressions of time:

12:15 p.m.

c. In biblical references and bibliographic information:

Matthew 2:11
Volume 36:2

d. In titles that include appositives:

Language and Composition: A Handbook and Rhetoric
The Cleanup of Lake Erie: An Environmental Success Story

Comma

1. Compound Sentences

Use a comma along with a coordinating conjunction between the parts of a compound sentence:

I didn't believe a word Phil said, and I told him so.

Note that the comma alone is inadequate; we need both the comma and the conjunction. (See also page 132.)

There's an exception to this rule. We can eliminate the comma between sentences when they are quite short and when the pause and pitch change indicated by the comma would weaken the effect. In the following sentences, for example, the lack of punctuation adds to the feeling of incessancy:

The rains came and the whole town worried.

The rain kept falling and the river kept rising.
The young folks filled the sandbags and the old folks prayed.

But such sentences are fairly rare; in most cases the comma is clearly called for, even when the sentences are short.

2. Lists

Use commas when listing a series of three or more sentence elements:

We gossiped, laughed, and sang the old songs at our class reunion.
We hunted in the basement, in the attic, and through all the storage rooms, with no results.

Note: Some publications mistakenly eliminate the comma before *and;* see page 126 for a discussion of its importance.

3. Introductory Clauses

Use a comma to set off an introductory subordinate clause or any phrase that contains a verb:

When the singing stopped, we went home.
After singing the old songs for hours on end, we finally called it a night.
Having reminisced for hours about the good old days at Silverton High, we called it a night.
To keep the guests laughing, Juanita brought out her photograph album.

4. Subordinate Clauses

Use a comma to set off a subordinate clause following the main clause if the clause has no effect on the outcome of the main clause:

We went to the picnic, even though we knew the rain would start any minute.

Note that in the following sentences the idea in the main clause will not be realized without the subordinate clause; therefore, we use no comma.

I'll go to the picnic if you will.

Wilma went to the picnic because Dave was planning to be there.

In general, *if* and *because* clauses are not set off; *although* and *even though* clauses are. See also page 112.

If you are in doubt about the punctuation of the clause following the main clause, shift it to the beginning of the sentence; there it will always be set off.

5. Sentence Modifiers

Set off words and phrases that function as sentence modifiers:

a. Adverbs:

Luckily, we escaped without a scratch.
We escaped without a scratch, luckily.
Bob decided, then, to hitch a ride to town.
Meanwhile, there was nothing for the rest of us to do but wait.

b. *Yes* and *no:*

No, I can't go.
Yes, he's the culprit.

c. Prepositional phrases:

In the meantime, there was nothing to do but wait.
We waited for two hours, in fact.

Note: Such words and phrases often provide a transitional tie to the previous sentence, which the comma emphasizes. They are also used to slow the reader down or to shift the point of sentence stress. See Chapter 17 for further discussion of cohesion and stress.

d. Absolute phrase:

The rain having stopped, we decided to go ahead with the picnic.
Dick relaxed in front of the fire, his feet propped on the coffee table.

6. Introductory Phrases

Use a comma to set off introductory adverbial phrases if they are long or if the absence of the comma would cause a misunderstanding:

> Toward the end of the semester, everyone in my dorm starts to study seriously.
>
> During the summer, vacation plans are our main topic of conversation at the dinner table.

7. Nonrestrictive Modifiers

Use commas to set off "commenting" (nonrestrictive) modifiers in the noun phrase. An adjectival is nonrestrictive when the referent of the noun it modifies is already clear to the reader—that is, if the noun has only one possible referent:

> Bill's roommate, a senior history major, spends every night in the library.
>
> My hometown, which relies on the lumber industry for its economic well-being, is always affected by fluctuations in the housing market.

(See Chapter 4 for further discussion of the punctuation of restrictive and nonrestrictive participial phrases, adjectival clauses, and appositives.)

8. Coordinate Adjectives

Use commas in the noun phrase between coordinate adjectives in preheadword position. *Coordinate* refers to adjectives of the same class—for example, subjective qualities:

> a tender, delightful love story
> a challenging, educational experience
> a dismal, completely depressing day

Other classes of adjectives include objective qualities, such as color, age, size, shape, and material:

> a tall young man
> a huge red ball

The adjectives in the preceding examples are from different classes, so we use no comma between them. Sometimes the string of adjectives includes both subjective and objective qualities:

> a splendid old table
> an ugly square concrete sculpture

A good rule of thumb for making a decision about commas between these prenoun modifiers is this: If you could insert *and* or *but*, use a comma:

> *an ugly and square concrete sculpture
> *a square and concrete building
> *a huge and red ball
> a tender and delightful story
> a beautiful but inexpensive necklace

See section 4.3 for further discussion of prenoun modifiers.

9. Nouns of Direct Address

Use a comma to set off nouns of direct address in either opening or closing position:

> Students, your time is up.
> Put your pencils down, everyone.
> Help me, dear.
> Bill, please open the door.

10. Direct Quotations

Use commas to set off direct quotations that fill the direct object slot after verbs such as *say* and *reply:*

> The waiter said, "Good evening; my name is Pierre."
> Harold replied, "I'm Harold, and this is Margaret."

When the quotation precedes the verb, the comma goes within the quotation mark:

I'll have the scampi," Harold told Pierre, "and Margaret would like the prime rib. But we'll begin with a bottle of Dom Perignon," he added, using his best French accent.

Direct quotations may also be introduced by colons.

11. State and Year

Use commas to set off the name of a state:

I found Cheyenne, Wyoming, a surprisingly small city.

Also set off the year in a complete date:

I remember where I was on November 22, 1963, when I heard the news of President Kennedy's assassination.

Note that we include commas both before and after the state name and the year.

Dash

To type the dash, use two hyphens with no space either before or after.

1. Interruptions Within a Sentence

Use a dash (or a pair of dashes) to set off any interrupting structure within the sentence or at the end:

Tim decided to quit his job—a brave decision—and to look for something new.
Tim decided to quit his job and look for another—a brave decision.

Note that when the interrupter is a complete sentence, it is punctuated as a phrase would be:

Tim quit his job—he was always a rash young man—to follow Horace Greeley's advice.

2. Appositives

a. Use dashes to call attention to an appositive:

> The microorganisms that seem to have it in for us in the worst way—the ones that really appear to wish us ill—turn out on close examination to be rather more like bystanders, strays, strangers in from the cold.
> —LEWIS THOMAS

b. Use a pair of dashes to set off a list of appositives that are themselves separated by commas (see also pages 86–88):

> All of the committees—finance, program, and local arrangements—went to work with real enthusiasm.

c. The list of appositives set off by a dash can also come at the beginning of the sentence when the subject is a pronoun referring to the list:

> The faculty, the students, the staff—all were opposed to the provost's decision to reinstate the old dormitory regulations.

d. *Namely* and *that is*, both of which are signalers of appositives, can be preceded by either a dash or a comma; the dash gives the appositive more emphasis:

> Some mammals have no hair—namely, the whales.
> Israel's policy in Lebanon brought out 400,000 antigovernment demonstrators—that is, one tenth of the population.

Ellipses

1. Omissions

Ellipses points (three spaced periods) are used to indicate words or sentences that have been omitted within a quoted passage. Here, for example, is an elliptical version of a longer passage by George Orwell:

> Gandhi's pacifism . . . was religious, but . . . it was . . . capable of producing desired political results.

To indicate an ellipsis at the end of a sentence, use four periods, the first of which is the period for the completed sentence. For example, if we were to add to the preceding elliptical quotation not the next sentence but the second following one, we would add three periods to the one after *results:*

> . . . capable of producing desired political results. . . . It entailed such things as civil disobedience, strikes, lying down in front of railway trains . . . and the like.

We generally do not use ellipses points at the end of the quoted material.

When quoting poetry, use a complete line of spaced periods to indicate an omitted line or lines.

2. Hesitation

Ellipses are sometimes used to indicate a hesitation or an unfinished thought, especially in dialogue:

> "You can get away with anything when you're dealing with a woman. If there were a man running this place . . ."
>   —FLANNERY O'CONNOR

Exclamation Point

1. Exclamatory Sentence

The exclamation point is the terminal punctuation for the exclamatory sentence, a transformation that changes the emphasis of a declarative sentence, usually with a *what* or *how* structure:

| We have a hard-working committee. | ⟶ | What a hard-working committee we have! |
| It's a gorgeous day. | ⟶ | What a gorgeous day it is! |

The exclamation point is actually optional in certain exclamatory sentences; in some cases it would probably be inappropriate:

> How calm the ocean is today.
> What a sweet child you have.

2. Emphasis

The exclamation point is used in sentences that call for added emotion; however, it should be used sparingly:

"Get out!" he shouted. "I never want to see you again!"
The history exam held a real surprise for me: I had studied the wrong assignment!
"Ouch! My shoe pinches."

Hyphen

1. Compound Words or Phrases

The hyphen expresses a compound word or phrase in prenoun position as a unit:

a two-inch board
a silver-plated teapot
a well-designed shoe
an out-of-work carpenter
the end-of-term celebration

Note that when they are not in prenoun position these modifiers are written without hyphens:

He is out of work.
The party was held at the end of the term.
The shoe was well designed.
The board is two inches wide.

When the modifier in prenoun position is an -*ly* adverb, the hyphen is not used:

a nicely designed house
a clearly phrased message

See also section 4.3.

2. Prefixes and Suffixes

a. For most prefixes and suffixes, the trend is away from hyphenation:

prefabricated	nonnative	microorganism
prewar	semicolon	extracurricular
superpower	intravenous	
pseudoscientific	coauthor	

Exceptions occur when (1) the base of the word is capitalized:

anti-Semitic	pre-Christmas	un-American

and (2) when the absence of the hyphen will cause a misreading or when the hyphenated phrase denotes a different meaning from the non hyphenated one:

> The *re-creation* of the actual battle was the highlight of our historical pageant.
> My principal *recreation* is playing darts.
> After I threw away an old chair, my neighbor *recovered* it from the trash pile and then *re-covered* it.

b. Hyphenate words formed with *self* (*self-contained*), *vice*, (*vice-president*), *half* (*half-grown*), and *elect* (*governor-elect*).
c. Words formed with *ex-* (meaning "former") and *pro-* (meaning "for") have retained the hyphen:

ex-husband
pro-union

d. Other exceptions to the trend away from the hyphen occur when the addition of a prefix or a suffix without the hyphen will cause problems of spelling and/or pronunciation:

shell-like
pre-emergent
co-op

Italics

In preparing a final essay, whether handwritten or typed, underline a word or phrase to indicate italics.

1. For Titles

Use italics for titles of books, plays, films, record albums (as opposed to single song titles), magazines, newspapers, and works of art (paintings and sculptures).

2. For Words Used as Words

Use italics for a word when you are referring to the word itself:

The word *fraternity* means more than weekend parties.
I always forget the difference between *judicial* and *judicious*.

3. For Foreign Words

Use italics for foreign words that are not Anglicized. If you are in doubt about the status of a foreign word, check a current dictionary.

I always feel a special *joie de vivre* when I am with Claudia.

4. For Stress

To indicate stressed words, use italics only sparingly:

Don't say you *have* to study grammar; say you *get* to.

You can usually make those same distinctions with variations in word order. For example,

Studying grammar is not something you have to do; it's something you get to do.

Numbers

1. Numbers of One or Two Words

Within your text, spell out any numbers of one or two words; use numerals for the others:

> There are 625 students in our dorm.
> On my floor there are twenty-two history majors.

Note that when a hyphenated number is connected to another word, the entire phrase is hyphenated:

> A sixty-two-year-old man not only started but also finished the Boston Marathon last year.

Numbers that are even hundreds, thousands, and so on, are written without hyphens—*one hundred, two thousand*—except when another word is part of the phrase:

> one-hundred-foot cliff
> six-million-dollar man

2. Numbers in Lists and Ranges

In a text that contains a list of numbers or a range of numbers, use numerals for all of them if any contain three or more digits:

> In just over five years, the Guardian Angels, a volunteer crime patrol in New York City, has grown from a band of 13 young men to over 4,500.

> We have 19 faculty members, 25 graduate students, and 320 undergraduate majors in our department.

3. Numbers at the Beginning of a Sentence

Spell out any number that begins a sentence:

> Nineteen seventy-six was a busy year for flag makers.

If the number is too large or awkward to spell out, find a way to reconstruct the sentence:

Flag makers had a busy year in 1976.

4. Numbers Used for Money

References to money can be either spelled out or expressed with digits and dollar signs:

a. Spell out isolated amounts according to the rules for all numbers:

The movies that cost twenty-five cents when I was a girl now cost five dollars.

b. Use numerals for exact sums that include both dollars and cents:

My new hat cost $16.25.

c. Do not mix the two:

The movies that cost 25¢ when I was a girl now costs $5.25.

d. Large sums of money given in round numbers are usually expressed in units written with a dollar sign:

The government plans to spend $3 billion on nuclear research for the U.S. Navy this year.

5. Other Numbers

Other numbers are written as follows:

Addresses and highway numbers:

321 North James Avenue; Highway 80.

Chapter and page numbers:

Chapter 6; pages 69–72.

Dates:

December 7, 1941, or 7 December 1941; 55 B.C., A.D. 1066.

(**Note:** B.C. follows the date; A.D. precedes it.)

Fractions and percentages:

one-half; 6½; 8½-by-11 inches; 6 percent; 40.5 percent.

(In a passage with a list of figures, be consistent: If any of them require digits, then use digits for all.)

Other measures:

20 cc.; 150°C, 6-point type; 45 mph.

Parentheses

1. Interruptions

Parentheses, in many cases, function just as dashes and commas do—to set off explanatory information or, in some cases, the writer's digressions:

> It is hard to remember, when reading the *Notebooks*, that Camus was a man who had a very interesting life, a life (unlike that of many writers) interesting not only in an interior but also in an outward sense.
>
> —SUSAN SONTAG

> I stopped her and put a five-sou piece (a little more than a farthing) into her hand.
>
> —GEORGE ORWELL

> A young Austrian named J.F. Voightländer (same family as the camera people), who was studying optics in London, took the idea home with him and started making monocles in Vienna about 1814. . . . There was always something about the monocle that intimidated (or provoked) the ordinary citizen.
>
> —DORA JANE HAMBLIN

Unlike dashes, which call attention to a passage, the parentheses generally add the information as an aside: They say, "By the way," whereas the dash says, "Hey, listen to this!"

2. Technical Information

Parentheses are also used to include technical information within a text:

> English poet William Cowper described the experience of tithing in "The Yearly Distress, or Tithing Time at Stock, in Essex" (circa 1780).
> For years I never missed an issue of *Astounding* (now published as *Analog*).

Note the punctuation of parenthetical structures: (a) A complete sentence added parenthetically within another sentence has neither an opening capital letter nor end punctuation:

> The long winters in North Dakota (newcomers quickly learn that March is a winter month) make spring a time of great joy.

(b) When a complete sentence is enclosed in parentheses—one that is not embedded in another sentence—the terminal punctuation is within the parentheses:

> I look forward to every month of the year. (February, I will admit, is short on saving graces, but at least it is short.) April is probably my favorite, with its clean spring air and promise of summer.

Period

1. Terminal Punctuation

Use a period as the terminal punctuation for declarative sentences and for exclamatory sentences that lack exclamatory force:

> We had a quiet afternoon. (declarative)
> What a quiet afternoon we had. (exclamatory)

2. Abbreviations

Use a period for certain abbreviations:

> Dr.   a.m.   A.D.
> Mr.   p.m.   M.A.

Mrs.	etc.	M.D.
Ms.	B.C.	Ph.D.

(See also *Abbreviations* and *Ellipses*)

Question Mark

1. Terminal Punctuation

Use the question mark as terminal punctuation in all direct questions:

Do you have anything to add?
What can you tell me?
He said what?

2. Quotations

In punctuating quoted questions, include the question mark within the quotation marks:

John asked, "What can you tell me?"

When a quotation is embedded in a question, the question mark is outside the quotation marks:

Who said, "Give me liberty or give me death"?

Note that the period is omitted from the quoted sentence.

When a quoted question is embedded in another question, only one question mark is used—and that one is inside the quotation mark:

Did he ask you straight out, "Are you a shoplifter?"

Quotation Marks

1. For Direct Quotations

Use double quotation marks to indicate another person's exact words, both written and spoken:

In 1943 Churchill told Stalin, "In war-time, truth is so precious that she should always be attended by a bodyguard of lies."

2. Within Direct Quotations

Use single quotation marks around quoted material within a quote:

> Describing the degeneracy of the nation in a letter to Joshua F. Speed, Lincoln wrote that "as a nation we began by declaring that 'all men are created equal.' We now practically read it 'all men are created equal except Negroes.'"

3. In Quotations in Block Form

A fairly lengthy quoted passage, one of several lines or sentences, is usually included in a text in block form. In typing a block quotation, indent the left margin five spaces, with paragraph indentations five additional spaces; the right-hand margin is also moved in five spaces; the quotation is single-spaced. Block paragraphs have no quotation marks; any quotes within them take the regular double quotation marks.

It's important that quotations of the same general length be treated consistently throughout the essay. If you use block style for one six-line quotation, do not use run-in style for another.

4. In Dialogue

In most passages of dialogue, each speaker's exact words are punctuated as a separate paragraph:

> "You seem excited," Raggie said. "What's up?"
> "Nothing." Phil had no intention of giving away the surprise he was working on in his shop, so he left the room before she could ask any more questions. "See you later."
> "Where are you going?"
> "Just down to the basement to putter."

Note that if the speaker's identity is clear, there is no need for "he said" or "she said" in every line.

5. For Special Uses of Words

Use quotation marks, but use them sparingly, to call attention to an ironic or special use of a word, as in the following excerpts from a *Time* report on the Soviet secret police, the KGB (February 14, 1983):

> Today more than four decades after the height of Stalin's reign of terror, many Soviets are still reluctant to call the organization [the KGB] by name, preferring such euphemisms as "the Committee," "the Office," or just an abbreviation, G.B.
>
> To Soviet agents in Ottawa, one Royal Canadian Mounted Police Officer, who remains anonymous, seemed an ideal "mole" for penetrating the Canadian security service.
>
> In the Andropov era, the KGB has apparently been careful not to soil its own hands with murders of revenge, political assassinations and other "wet" (bloody) affairs.

6. For Titles

Use quotation marks around titles of articles, poems, chapters of books, songs, and any title of a section of a larger work when including the title in a sentence. For titles in footnotes, endnotes, and bibliographies, see Chapter 20. For capitalization in titles, see *Capitals*.

Semicolon

1. As a Conjunction

Use a semicolon to connect sentences as a compound. You can think of the semicolon as having the connective force of the comma-plus-conjunction:

> The use of the semicolon indicates a close relationship; it gives the sentence a tight, separate-but-equal bond.

2. With a Conjunctive Adverb

Use a semicolon in a compound sentence that includes a conjunctive adverb:

> We worked hard for the Consumer Party candidates; however, we knew they didn't stand a chance.

3. With a Conjunction

You can also use the semicolon along with a conjunction:

> Great indeed is Fear; but it is not, as our military enthusiasts believe and try to make us believe, the only stimulus known for awakening the higher ranges of men's spiritual energy.
>
> —WILLIAM JAMES

(See also Chapter 6 for examples of compound sentences with semicolons.)

4. In the Separation of Series

Use semicolons to separate a series of structures with internal punctuation:

> The study of our grammar system includes three areas: phonology, the study of sounds; morphology, the study of meaningful combinations of sounds; and syntax, the study of sentences.

(See also page 86.)

Slash

In certain contexts the slash means "choose one" or "either–or":

> We can take some of our electives using the pass/fail system. (You will either pass or fail.)
> You can borrow the thesaurus and/or the dictionary. (You can borrow either one of them or both.)

Part V

Research

Whether or not you are ever assigned a formal "research paper," you will have many occasions to use the resources of the library. And no matter if your library is large or small, you'll discover that it's a treasure trove of information. You'll also discover that using the library has a kind of snowball effect: The more you learn about it, the more reasons you'll find to use it.

In this section we will follow a student as he explores the library in search of ideas and information for an essay on the subject of antinuclear protesting. That subject, you'll recall, is the one from the general area of energy that we zeroed in on in Chapter 11. Like many topics, however, it's not one that most people could write on without going beyond their own experience. But that "going beyond" can be challenging and educational and, yes, even fun.

In Chapter 19, then, we discuss the resources of the library and how to find and use them. In Chapter 20 we describe how the writer narrowed his topic and made use of the sources. Also included are two versions of his essay: the first, with comments and questions that a careful reader might ask, and a final draft, which incorporates the writer's revisions.

19

Using the Library

"The topic of antinuclear protesting sounds like a good one: It involves individuals and groups, the government, the power industry—all of us, in fact. Certainly the controversy over the use of nuclear power is not about to go away. But I know so little about the topic: Where do I begin?"

The place to begin, no matter what the topic, is with yourself. Think through the topic as thoroughly as possible. What do you know now about the protest movement? What would you like to learn? Why would anyone else be interested in the topic? As you brainstorm in this way, you may or may not find yourself moving toward a tentative thesis. Chances are that you do have opinions about the protest movement, even though they may not be based on clear evidence. So write down all your ideas and questions at the start.

There's a good reason for this preresearch step. When you finally get to the library and begin to read and take notes, it's easy to confuse your ideas and those of the authors you've consulted. In writing the first draft, you'll find yourself asking, "Let's see—did I read that somewhere?" Having an initial outline may help forestall such problems of documentation. You'll feel much more secure in stating ideas as your own and in knowing when to cite a source.

For many topics you write about, your library research will be quite limited. It may simply be a search for an authority or a statistic to back up your main thesis. Such research is like the icing on the cake—the finishing touch. But in the case of our student who has little more than curiosity and questions about the topic of antinuclear protesting, the library research will be quite a different undertaking. After brainstorming, then, it's time to go to the library. If you haven't been there before, go with a friend who knows the way around. You might also sign up for a tour; many libraries conduct them on a regular basis. Or just spend some time there on your own, exploring, discovering where the card catalog and reference area and periodicals are located. And by all means, ask the library staff for assistance when you're stuck. After learning your way around, then, you're ready to begin.

19.1 Step One: Identifying the Sources of Information

The first step in researching any topic is to figure out what the best sources of information are likely to be. For a topic like antinuclear protesting, the sources are certainly not the same ones you'd explore for, say, a report on the development of the atom bomb. Antinuclear protesting is not past history; it's happening now, so you need current sources.

1. **Newspapers.** Newspapers are the most current of the library's resources. Protests have been making the news recently, as well as during the past several years. Daily newspapers report them the day they happen, so *The New York Times* and *The Washington Post* would be excellent sources. Even the smaller dailies, papers from your own community or region, would cover protests that make the wire services. So yesterday's protests will be in the library today.

2. **Newsmagazines.** Weekly newsmagazines, such as *Time, Newsweek,* and *U.S. News and World Report,* also report current events, sometimes with more background information than the newspapers include. Last week's protests are in the library this week.

Another good source of world and national news available on a weekly basis, although not a newsmagazine, is *Facts on File: A Weekly Digest of World Events with Cumulative Index.* Many libraries subscribe to this loose-leaf publication.

3. **Other magazines and journals.** Popular magazines might

feature stories on the nuclear power industry, perhaps as it affects certain people or communities; and scholarly journals would also examine such an issue as it relates to science or social science or philosophy or history or health. Obviously, these sources are not as current as newspapers or newsmagazines; they often have a lag time of many months, even years. But because protesting has been going on for quite a few years now, both popular magazines and scholarly journals have had time to publish articles on the subject.

4. **Government publications.** Because the federal government has a great deal to do with the nuclear power industry, government publications would probably be a good source of information. Congressional hearing reprints provide reports of the experts who testify before congressional committees; and *The Congressional Record,* the daily reporting service of Congress, would also include current information. Publications put out by such agencies as the Nuclear Regulatory Commission would also be a likely source.

5. **Books.** Books would not be as up-to-date as the other kinds of publications, but chances are that many have been written on a variety of topics dealing with the nuclear power industry. Books would also be the source of any historical aspects of the topic. Looking at the issues of the past that brought out protestors may be one avenue worth exploring.

6. **Encyclopedias and encyclopedia yearbooks.** We don't usually think about encyclopedias as sources for current events—and, in fact, they're not good sources. But often overlooked are the yearbooks put out by the encyclopedias as supplements, which include summaries of the past year. Such yearbooks may, in fact, be a good place to get an overview of many current topics.

7. **Outside sources.** Going beyond the library's resources may sometimes be useful and even necessary. Outside agencies such as the local power company or the American Cancer Society are possible sources of information about the antinuclear topic. There may also be local people involved in the protest movement whom you might wish to interview—for instance, someone who may have taken part in protests.

Summary

The foregoing seven categories describe the resources that are the most likely to have information about antinuclear protesting.

They are arranged according to their currency, beginning with newspapers, the most current source. This arrangement is not meant to suggest that every researcher should begin with current sources—not at all. The specific topic will determine the best starting place. For an essay on the general area of civil disobedience, for example, you might think about famous protestors from our history, so checking out current newspapers and newsmagazines would obviously be a waste of time.

In Step One, then, you've determined what the best sources of information are likely to be; in Step Two, we'll discuss how to find those sources in the library.

19.2 Step Two: Finding the Information

1. **Newspapers.** The best place to begin looking for recent newspaper coverage of your topic is in one of the indexes to major newspapers, which most libraries have available. The index to *The New York Times,* which is published twice monthly with an annual cumulative index, lists the contents of the paper according to subject headings with summaries of the articles. Other widely used newspaper indexes are those of *The Washington Post, The Wall Street Journal,* and *The Christian Science Monitor.* The library generally stores back issues of newspapers on microfilm. Most libraries also subscribe to local and regional papers. Although these are not indexed, you can check their coverage on the dates given in the indexes of other papers. Sometimes in the days following a news event, the local paper will publish the reactions of local people, which may prove useful.

Another helpful index, one connected with news writing, is *Editorials on File,* which indexes and reprints editorials from U.S. and Canadian newspapers. Because editorials nearly always deal with controversial topics, you'll probably find this index especially useful for assignments dealing with argument and refutation. Your library may also have in its collection *Pulitzer Prize Editorials: America's Best Editorial Writing, 1917–1979)* (compiled by W. David Sloan).

The availability of these resources, like that of all of the publications mentioned in this chapter, will obviously vary from library to library.

2. **Newsmagazines.** The major newsmagazines are indexed in

Readers' Guide to Periodical Literature, an index of over 175 period- icals that every school library has, at least in abridged form. It is published twice in most months, with cumulative indexes every three months, as well as annually. The entries are listed alphabetically under both author and subject headings.

Another guide to popular literature that many libraries subscribe to is *Magazine Index*, in microtext format, which indexes over 350 periodicals.

3. **Popular magazines and scholarly journals.** Until you've spent some time exploring the library, you probably won't realize how many hundreds (thousands, even) of magazines and journals are published. It would be impossible for anyone to go through all of them—and libraries, of course, don't subscribe to all of them; that's where indexes become important.

The popular magazines that are likely to have feature articles on antinuclear protesting, such as *Atlantic* and *Harpers* and *Scientific American*, are indexed in both *Readers' Guide* and *Magazine Index*, just described.

The articles in the thousands of scholarly journals are compiled in literally hundreds of indexes, covering subject areas from A ("Agriculture") to Z ("Zoology"). You may want to ask the library staff for information on which indexes are available for your particular topic. Following are some of the most useful indexes for the general subject areas listed:

Agriculture

- *Animal Breeding Abstracts*, 1933 to date.
- *Bibliography of Agriculture*, 1942 to date.
- *Biological and Agricultural Index*, 1964 to date. (Formerly *Agricultural Index*, 1916–1964.)
- *Review of Applied Entomology*, 1913 to date.

Anthropology

- *Abstracts in Anthropology*, 1970 to date.

Architecture

- *The Architecture Index*, 1950 to date.
- *Architectural Periodicals Index*, 1972 to date.

19.2

Art

• *Art and Archaeology Technical Abstracts*, 1955 to date.
• *Art Index*, 1929 to date.

Astronomy

• *Astronomy and Astrophysics Abstracts*, 1969 to date.

Biography

• *Biography Index*, 1946 to date.

Biology

• *Biological Abstracts*, 1926 to date.
• *Biological and Agricultural Index*, 1964 to date. (Formerly *Agricultural Index*, 1916–1964.)
• *Bioresearch Index*, 1967 to date. (Formerly *Bioresearch Titles*, 1965–1966.)

Business

• *Accountants' Index*, 1912 to date.
• *Business Periodicals Index*, 1958 to date. (Formerly *Industrial Arts Index*, 1913–1957.)
• *Consumers Index to Product Evaluations and Information Sources*, 1973 to date.
• *F & S Index International: Industries, Countries, Companies*, 1967 to date.
• *F & S Index of Corporations and Industries*, 1960 to date.
• *Personnel Management Abstracts*, 1955 to date.

Chemistry and Physics

• *Chemical Abstracts*, 1907 to date.
• *Electrical and Electronics Abstracts*, 1903 to date. (Formerly *Science Abstracts*, 1898–1902.)
• *Physics Abstracts*, 1903 to date. (Formerly *Science Abstracts*, 1898–1902.)

Criminology

19.2

- *Abstracts on Criminology and Penology*, 1969 to date. (Formerly *Excerpta Criminologica*, 1961–1968.)
- *Abstracts on Police Science*, 1973 to date.
- *Criminal Justice Abstracts*, 1977 to date. (Formerly *Crime and Delinquency Literature*, 1968–1977.)

Ecology and Environment

- *Applied Ecology Abstracts*, 1975 to date.
- *Chicorel Index to Environment and Ecology*, 1975 to date.
- *Ecological Abstracts*, 1974 to date.
- *Environment Index*, 1971 to date.
- *MER* (Man, Environment Reference) *Environmental Abstracts*, 1974 to date.
- *Pollution Abstracts*, 1970 to date.
- *Selected Water Resources Abstracts*, 1968 to date.

Education

- *Business Education Index*, 1940 to date.
- *Current Index to Journals in Education (CIJE)*, 1969 to date.
- *Education Index*, 1929 to date.
- *Exceptional Child Education Abstracts*, 1969 to date.

Energy

- *The Energy Index*, 1973 to date.
- *Energy Information Abstracts*, 1976 to date.
- *Renewable Energy Bulletin*, 1974 to date.

Engineering

- *Engineering Index*, 1884 to date.

Ethnology

- *Abstracts of Popular Culture*, 1977 to date.
- *Index to Literature on the American Indian*, 1972 to date.
- *Index to Periodical Articles by and about Blacks*, 1960 to date.

19.2

Food Science and Nutrition

 • *Food Science and Technology Abstracts*, 1969 to date.
 • *Nutrition Abstracts and Reviews*, 1931 to date.

Forestry

 • *Forestry Abstracts*, 1939 to date.

Genetics

 • *Genetics Abstracts*, 1968 to date.

Geography

 • *Current Geographical Publications*, 1938 to date.
 • *Geo Abstracts*, 1972 to date. (Formerly *Geographical Abstracts*, 1966–1971.)

Geology

 • *Abstracts of North American Geology*, 1966 to date. (Formerly *GeoScience Abstracts*, 1959–1966.)
 • *Bibliography and Index of Geology*, 1933 to date.
 • *Offshore Abstracts*, 1974 to date.
 • *Petroleum Abstracts*, 1961 to date.

Health, Physical Education, and Recreation

 • *Abstracts on Hygiene*, 1926 to date.
 • *HPESR Abstracts*, 1966 to date.

History

 • *America: History and Life*, 1964 to date.
 • *Historical Abstracts: Parts A and B*, 1955 to date.
 • *Humanities Index*, 1974 to date. (Formerly *International Index*, 1907–1965, and *Social Sciences and Humanities Index*, 1965–1974.)
 • *Writings on American History*, 1902 to date.

Horticulture

 • *Horticultural Abstracts*, 1931 to date.

Human Resources

19.2

- *Human Resources Abstracts*, 1973 to date.
- *Humanities Index* (see listing under *History*).

Language and Literature

- *Abstracts of English Studies*, 1958 to date.
- *Essay and General Literature Index*, 1900 to date.
- *Humanities Index* (see listing under *History*).
- *MLA Abstracts of Articles in Scholarly Journals*, 1971 to date.

Law

- *Index to Legal Periodicals*, 1908 to date.
- *Index to Periodical Articles Related to Law*, 1958 to date.

Mathematics

- *Mathematical Reviews*, 1940 to date.

Medicine

- *Dental Abstracts*, 1956 to date.
- *Index Medicus*, 1960 to date.

Meteorology

- *Meteorological and Geoastrophysical Abstracts*, 1959 to date.

Microbiology

- *Microbiology Abstracts*, 1965 to date.

Military Science

- *Air University Library Index to Military Periodicals*, 1949 to date.

Music

- *Music Article Guide*, 1966 to date.
- *The Music Index*, 1949 to date.
- *Popular Music Periodicals Index*, 1973 to date.

Nursing

- *International Nursing Index*, 1966 to date.
- *Nursing and Allied Health*, 1977 to date. (Formerly *Cumulative Index to Nursing and Allied Health Literature*, 1956–1976.)
- *Nursing Studies Index*, 1970 to date.

Oceanography

- *Oceanic Abstracts*, 1966 to date.

Philosophy

- *Philosopher's Index*, 1967 to date.

Political Science

- *ABC Pol Sci*, 1969 to date.
- *International Political Science Abstracts*, 1951 to date.

Population

- *Population Index*, 1935 to date.

Psychology

- *Psychological Abstracts*, 1927 to date.

Public Affairs

- *Public Affairs Information Service Bulletin*, 1915 to date.

Religion

- *Catholic Periodical and Literature Index*, 1967 to date. (Formerly *Catholic Periodical Index*, 1930–1968.)
- *Christian Periodical Index*, 1958 to date.
- *Guide to Social Science and Religion in Periodical Literature*, 1964 to date.
- *Religion Index One: Periodicals*, 1978 to date. (Formerly *Index to Religious Periodical Literature*, 1949–1977.)
- *Religious and Theological Abstracts*, 1958 to date.

Science and Technology

19.2

- *Applied Mechanics Reviews*, 1948 to date.
- *Applied Science and Technology Index*, 1958 to date. (Formerly *Industrial Arts Index*, 1913–1957.)
- *Computer Abstracts*, 1957 to date.
- *Metals Abstracts Index*, 1968 to date.
- *Nuclear Science Abstracts*, 1948 to date.
- *Science Citation Index*, 1961 to date.

Social Science

- *Social Sciences Citation Index*, 1972 to date.
- *Social Sciences Index*, 1974 to date. (Formerly *International Index*, 1907–1965, and *Social Sciences and Humanities Index*, 1965–1974.)

Sociology

- *Sociological Abstracts*, 1952 to date.

Speech

- *DSH Abstracts*, 1960 to date.
- *Speech Abstracts*, 1970 to date.
- *Speech Communication Abstracts*, 1975 to date.

Statistics

- *American Statistics Index*, 1973 to date.

Theater

- *Guide to the Performing Arts*, 1957 to date.
- *The New York Times Theater Reviews*, 1920–1970, 1971.
- *Theater/Drama Abstracts*, 1974 to date.

Urban Affairs

- *Urban Affairs Abstracts*, 1971 to date.

Women

- *Women Studies Abstracts*, 1972 to date.

19.2

Zoology

- *Wildlife Review*, 1952 to date.
- *Zoological Record*, 1864 to date.

The foregoing list includes a number of indexes that would be likely sources for articles dealing with antinuclear protesting; those listed under "Ecology and Environment," "Energy," and "Public Affairs" would be a good place to start. There's another good way to find information: Check the bibiographies listed at the end of the articles you find. Often those references will lead you to articles you might have missed. Such bibliographies are themselves indexed in a useful reference guide called *The Bibliographic Index: A Cumulative Bibliography of Bibliographies* (1937 to date). In this index, bibliographies from books and magazines, as well as separately published bibliographies, are indexed according to subject. It is issued twice a year, with an annual cumulative index.

4. **Government publications.** Many libraries act as depositories for government documents, which range from Department of Agriculture bulletins to the *Congressional Record*. But other libraries, too—even small ones—have many government documents in their collections. Many government documents are indexed in the *Monthly Index to United States Government Publications*. Another helpful index is the *Index to U.S. Government Periodicals*. A good source of material on current topics is *The Congressional Service Index to Publications of the U.S. Congress*, which provides abstracts of committee hearings, reports, and other materials pertaining specifically to Congress.

Incidentally, government publications are not generally included in the library's card catalog; many times they are indexed separately, with a different numbering system, and are shelved in a separate area.

5. **Books.** The library's book collection is indexed on cards in the card catalog or, increasingly, on microfiche. For many topics the card catalog would be the likely place for the researcher to begin. You can look up the name of an author, a title, or a subject area—the three ways in which the card catalog indexes information. In some libraries all the cards are alphabetized together; in others they are separated.

Here, for example, is a book that was easy to find in the card catalog. The first stop was the subject heading "Nuclear Power."

Under that heading was the direction, "See Atomic Power." It was under the subject heading "Atomic Power—Law and Legislation—United States" that the following card was filed:

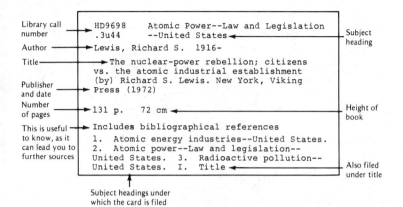

6. **Encyclopedias and encyclopedia yearbooks.** As mentioned earlier, for current topics such as antinuclear protesting encyclopedias would not be particularly useful, although for other topics they may, in fact, be a good place to start; you can get an overview of the topic that might be very helpful. Often overlooked, however, are the yearbooks of encyclopedias, which bring the encyclopedias up to date on a yearly basis.

Many encyclopedia entries are written by specialists in the field; such articles are generally signed. Following are some of the well-known encyclopedias. In addition to these, your library may have subject-area encyclopedias in its reference collection. Yearbooks will probably be shelved with the set.

General Encyclopedias

- *Encyclopaedia Britannica,* 15th ed., 30 vols., 1974.
- *Encyclopedia Americana,* 30 vols., 1975.
- *Collier's Encyclopedia,* 24 vols., 1976.

Shorter Encyclopedias

- *The Lincoln Library of Essential Information,* 1973.
- *The New Columbia Encyclopedia,* 1975.

19.3 *Step Three: Using the Resources*

You will save a great deal of time, frustration, and backtracking if you take careful notes as you do your library research. First, record the bibliographical information of each source accurately, using a 3-by-5-inch card: author, title (of both article and book), publisher, date, volume number, and so on. Check the sample bibliographical entries on pages 479–482 to be sure you record all the necessary information. In citing a newspaper article, for example, you'll need not only the author and the page number, but also the section number of the paper and the column number on the page.

These cards will be especially useful when it's time to type the bibliography. All you'll need to do is put them in the proper order and list them, following the bibliographical conventions. Also be sure to include the library call number on the card (even though it doesn't appear in the bibliography) so that you can easily find the publication in the library again, if necessary.

For taking notes on your reading, you'll probably want to use larger cards—4-by-6 or 5-by-7—or perhaps a special section in your notebook. As soon as you become familiar with your subject, start to identify topic headings for the cards, so that one card (or page) contains notes from several sources. Always identify the source of the notes, perhaps by reference to the bibliography cards. Also, be sure to include in your notes the page numbers from which you copied them; any references to the sources in your essay, whether or not you use a direct quote, require the exact page numbers.

There's a distinct advantage to using cards for note taking: You can spread them out in front of you to think about what you've found. And when you begin writing, you can put them in some sort of logical order.

As you take notes, it's probably a good idea to record the actual words from your sources, even for information that you plan to paraphrase rather than quote directly. And of course, to save time, instead of copying by hand you can spend five cents to use the library's copy machine. If you do reproduce pages by machine, be sure to write the source of the copy, including the page number, on the copy itself. Do it immediately—have your pen in hand right there at the copy machine. Nothing is more frustrating than to have to play detective looking for the source of that anonymous xeroxed page you stuck in your notebook last week. Incidentally, even for the articles and pages you make machine copies of, you should write down a brief summary on a card to keep with your other notes. You'll quickly discover that doing research is like following a branching path. One source leads to another—and that one to yet another. You'll find yourself going from article to bibliographical list to author and on to another article and back to the first path. It's important to keep track of where you've been and where you're going with a well-organized system of taking notes.

And by all means, give yourself time. Don't rush through a research project. You can't expect to make a quick trip to *Readers' Guide*, look up an article or two, and immediately start to write. A good research paper simply doesn't happen that way. You need time to mull over the topic, to think about the information you've gathered, to let it simmer—to somehow make it your own.

In the next chapter we'll follow our student writer as he works his way through the research and the writing of his essay on antinuclear protesting.

20

Writing the Research Paper

20.1 The First Step: Focusing

Paul, our student writer, discovered very soon after beginning his research that the newspapers and magazines and government publications of the past five years or so are filled with information about nuclear energy and the public's reaction to it. For example, *The New York Times Index* for 1978 lists at least 250 articles under the heading of "Atomic energy and weapons, United States, electric light and power," all of which deal specifically with power companies. And of these, several dozen deal with protests: the anniversary of the Seabrook demonstration; the Clamshell Alliance; arrests at nuclear plants in South Carolina, Louisiana, and California; efforts by seven Hudson Valley communities to stop the construction of a plant; convictions for trespassing at the Trojan plant in Oregon; the arrest of Dr. Spock and others at Seabrook; the success of the antinuclear movement in Hawaii; and on and on. So already Paul is overwhelmed with possibilities. And remember—these newsworthy events took place before Three Mile Island became a household word!

Readers' Guide brought to light a great many additional topics, especially in the newsmagazines. And, as it turned out, *Time* and *Newsweek* and *U.S. News and World Report* provided much of the

20.1

specific information on people and places that Paul cited in his finished paper, the essay reprinted on pages 494–506. *Readers Guide* also led him to the article that became the main focus of his essay. But perhaps even more interesting, it was the information in *Readers' Guide*—the nature of the citations themselves—that provided evidence for the prediction he made about the future of the nuclear protest movement, which you'll read in the last paragraph of his essay.

Before beginning his research, Paul had considered a number of possibilities as the focus of the essay: the pros and cons of the antinuclear protest movement, for example. What are the issues that the protestors raise? How does the industry answer them? Another possibility, one that sounded a little more demanding, would be to argue on one side or the other. However, neither of these approaches seemed very original; they had probably been used before, with much more authority than he could bring to them. Either one was likely to end up as a pastiche of other people's ideas.

For several days Paul thought about all the reading he had done—the all-important "simmering" period. Then he came across an article in *Society* called "From Elite Quarrel to Mass Movement" by Robert Cameron Mitchell. Here was an intriguing idea: the evolution of a protest movement, the steps that it goes through. Paul felt certain that he had found his focus.

> "How can I make something interesting out of this? Mitchell's article is a fairly limited treatment of the subject—and pretty dull. Maybe I could describe the evolution of a single protest in detail. Or maybe I could attack the topic in a comprehensive way."

Paul mulled it over. He recognized that here was the chance to educate himself—and others. He would take the idea of evolution and apply it to people—something that Mitchell hadn't really focused on. Who are the people involved in the various stages of the evolution? What moves them to action? Do all protest movements go through these stages with these kinds of people?

After making this decision, Paul could start making sense of his notes, first sorting them into chronological order. By this time he had gathered details of the various protests, starting in 1973 with the rally at Montague, Massachusetts. He reread the articles from the newsmagazines (most of which he had made copies of), this time with a specific goal: Who were the people involved? Why did they care? On the basis of the reading he had done, he came up with a plan in the form of an outline.

20.2 *The Informal Outline*

An outline—even an informal "scratch" outline—serves as a framework, a series of guideposts to keep you on track. And it refreshes your memory. It's surprisingly easy to forget what you were planning to say if you don't write it down. The outline is especially useful to have when you get stuck on a particular sentence or paragraph: You can always jump ahead to the next section when you know what the next section is going to be.

On page 472 is Paul's original scratch outline, which begins with a short summary of the Mitchell article, followed by the four phases of the evolution. Some of the details got cut from this plan before he finished, and several new sections were added. You can compare this one with the finished outline shown on page 495. Don't ever assume that you're somehow committed to an outline—after all, you, the writer, are the person in charge. You should always feel free to add or subtract whenever you think you can improve on the plan.

20.3 *Acknowledgment of Sources*

Some of the hardest decisions for writers to make concern the actual citation of sources in the essay. When should you quote directly? When should you paraphrase? How do you work in other people's ideas most efficiently? Which ideas should you footnote?

In the finished essay at the end of the chapter, you'll find four different ways in which Paul used his sources. They are listed here not necessarily in any kind of rank order; the context will determine which method works best. However, we can generalize somewhat about effectiveness: Probably the least effective use of a source is a quoted sentence or passage within a paragraph for which the reader has not been prepared at all. When you, as a reader, come to such a sentence, you may wonder why all of a sudden you're reading a quotation, so you look at the footnote or endnote for an explanation—which may or may not be there. Happily, Paul had none of these unexpected quotes in his finished essay.

ANTINUCLEAR PROTESTING

Summary of Mitchell's analysis

Analysis applied to the people involved in protests:

Local people expressing concern
Radicalization of the grass roots
  1973—Montague, Mass.
  1977—Seabrook, N.H.
  1977—Diablo Canyon, Calif.
  1977—Portland, Ore.

Deradicalization: The Big Event
TMI
After TMI

Political digestion by society
  Udall's committee—a moratorium
  Commoner's political party
  Jerry Brown et al.—motives?

Accomplishments of the movement
  Changes in attitudes and industry

Summary: Where do we go from here?

Here, then, are some effective ways to use sources:

1. In this example, Paul integrated a partial sentence, quoted directly, into a sentence of his own. In the previous sentence, he identified the source, so that the reader is prepared for the quotation:

> Phase one is characterized by "a small elite of knowledgeable insiders [scientists] who criticized the manner of technology's development by the Atomic Energy Commission, not the technology itself."

Obviously a long phrase like this required quotation marks. Not quite so obvious is the need for quotation marks around a short phrase or even a word. But, in fact, anytime you use someone else's words, you need to acknowledge the source. Farther on in that paragraph you'll find the words "direct-action phase" and "eclectic tactics" in quotes.

Notice also in the foregoing quoted sentence that Paul has added the word *scientists* as an explanation for the reader. Always use brackets with such additions.

2. A second method of using sources is to include in your paragraph a complete sentence in quotes. Again, be sure your reader is prepared. As explained previously, it is disconcerting to come up against quotation marks completely unprepared:

> Barry Commoner, a Washington University professor, agreed: "I was floored by the size of the demonstration. This issue has become a dominant, broad public issue for the first time."

3. On pages 501–502 Paul quoted fairly long passages by Thoreau and King. Because they run for more than four lines—and because he wanted to give them prominence—he set them off in a single-spaced block, indented five spaces on either side.

You can eliminate parts of quoted material by using ellipses, as you'll notice Paul did in the King quotation. In doing so, you must be careful to retain the author's intended meaning.

4. Sometimes you use another's idea without using the exact words, as Paul did on page 498, where he summarized details of some of the protests. Such occasions also require a footnote or endnote. Here it's fairly obvious that he got the information somewhere, because it includes dates and numbers. But even abstract or general ideas of another person need to be acknowledged.

20.4   A Word About Plagiarism

The name we give to the unacknowledged use of another's words and ideas is *plagiarism*, from the Latin word for "plunderer." The name applies not only to exact words that are plundered, but to ideas of a general nature as well. There is, of course, a great deal of general knowledge, ideas in the public domain that everyone knows; obviously we don't know the sources of all our ideas. But when you read background information on a particular topic that is presented in a new way, in a way that you hadn't thought about before, you must cite that source if you use those ideas in your writing. The most important characteristic of a good writer is honesty.

20.4 *The Typing of the Final Draft*

Begin with a *title page*, which will include the title of the essay and your name, along with any other information that your instructor requires, such as the course name and date.

If you include an *outline*, use the standard designations for the levels of information: Roman numerals; capital letters; Arabic numerals; lowercase letters. Paul's outline is on page 495.

The *first page* of your essay will have the title centered about three inches from the top. Leave margins of about 1½ inches on all sides; beginning on page two, number the pages with digits in the top right-hand margin; double space your paper.

The *citations* in the text itself can come either at the bottom of the page (footnotes) or at the end of the text (endnotes). Endnotes are more common and are certainly easier for the typist. Number the notes consecutively throughout the text by using a raised digit, always at the end of a sentence, never in the middle. In citing a direct quotation, put the digit at the end of the quotation.

Footnotes begin three spaces below the last line of text, with the first line indented five spaces. Number the footnote with raised a digit, with no space after it. Footnotes are single spaced, with double spacing between them.

Endnotes are typed on a page at the end of the text, with the title "Notes" centered two inches from the top. Leave three spaces between the title and the first note. The notes are indented five spaces and are numbered consecutively with a raised digit followed by a space. All lines are double spaced. For examples, see Paul's endnotes on page 505.

The *bibliography* is titled and spaced in the same way as the endnotes page. However, the indentation of the lines is the opposite: The first line of each entry is flush with the left-hand margin; all subsequent lines are indented five spaces. The bibliography is arranged alphabetically by the first author's last name. In works with more than one author, only the first author's name is reversed—last name first. Works without an author's name are included in alphabetical order according to title. Paul's bibliography is on page 506.

20.5 Documentation: Footnotes and Endnotes

The following list provides examples of the kinds of sources you are most likely to use as references in your research. The first citation of a reference always includes complete information; subsequent citations generally need only an identifying name and a page reference, such as

Haugen, p. 29.

If you have more than one source by the same author, the second and all subsequent references should clearly indicate which source is being cited; use both the name and the title, or abbreviated title, along with page numbers:

Roberts, Sentence Patterns, p. 14.

For information about the citation of sources in your essay, the use of notes, and the conventions of typing the citations, see the earlier sections of this chapter entitled "Acknowledgment of Sources" and "The Typing of the Final Draft."

The forms described in the lists that follow, for both notes and bibliography, are based on the *MLA* (Modern Language Association) *Handbook for Writers of Research Papers, Theses, and Dissertations* (New York: MLA, 1980) by Joseph Gibaldi and Walter S. Achtert.

20.5

1. A book with a single author:

   [1]Thomas Rogers, At the Shores (New York: Simon and Schuster, 1980), p. 22.

2. A book with more than one author:

   [2]Jeanne Fahnestock and Marie Secor, A Rhetoric of Argument (New York: Random House, 1982), p. 76.

(Where there are more than three authors, use only the first author's name, followed by "et al." or "and others.")

3. A work in more than one volume:

   [3]Robert Graves, The Greek Myths (Baltimore: Penguin, 1955), I, 114.

(When you include the volume number, designated here by the Roman numeral, you omit "p." or "pp." before page numbers.)

4. An edited work:

   [4]Jane Austen, Pride and Prejudice, ed. Donald J. Gray (New York: Norton, 1966), p. 49.

5. A work in a collection by different authors:

   [5]Jane Jacobs, "A Good Neighborhood," in The Little, Brown Reader, ed. Marcia Stubbs and Sylvan Barnet, 2nd ed. (Boston: Little, Brown, 1980), p. 151.

6. A compilation:

   [6]Richard Hofstadter, ed., The Progressive Movement: 1900–1915 (Englewood Cliffs, N.J.: Prentice-Hall, 1963), p. 3.

7. An encyclopedia article, unsigned:

[7]"Mandarin," <u>Encyclopedia Americana,</u> 1976 ed.

(In a work that is alphabetically arranged, volume and page number may be omitted unless the citation is of one page of a multipage article.)

8. An encyclopedia article, signed:

[8]Richard J.C. Atkinson, "Stonehenge," <u>Encyclo-paedia Britannica,</u> 1958 ed.

9. A government document:

[9]U.S. Bureau of Labor Statistics, <u>Productivity</u> (Washington D.C.: GPO, 1958), p. 10.

10. An unpublished dissertation:

[10]Betsy E. Brown, " 'Palliatives of Inarticulate Art': Narrative Technique in Valdimir Nabokov's English Novels," Diss. Ohio State University 1978, p. 32.

11. An article in a journal with page numbers that continue throughout the annual volume:

[11]James A. Berlin, "Contemporary Composition: The Major Pedagogical Theories," <u>College English,</u> 44 (1982), p. 767.

12. An article in a journal with separate page numbers for each issue:

[12]Ruth Thaler, "Art and the Written Word," <u>Journal of Basic Writing,</u> 2, No. 4 (1980), p. 73.

13. An article from a weekly magazine:

> [13]David M. Alpert, "Three Mile Island Legacy," Newsweek, 7 April 1980, p. 33.

14. An article from a monthly magazine:

> [14]John Morrison, "The Evolution of the Wine Bottle," Wines & Vines, March 1983, p. 33.

15. An unsigned editorial in a newspaper:

> "IDC Plays an Important Role," Editorial, Centre Daily Times, 4 April 1983, Sec. A, p. 4, cols. 1–2.

(A signed editorial would begin with the author's name, followed by the information as shown above.)

16. A signed article from a daily newspaper:

> [16]Howard Benedict, "Challenger Given OK for Lift-off," Centre Daily Times, 4 April 1983, Sec. A, p. 1, cols. 5–6.

17. A book review:

> [17]Mark Lilla, rev. of Philosophical Explanations, by Robert Nozick, The American Scholar, 51 (1982), p. 428.

18. A lecture:

> [18]Carol Gay, "Preparing Slides for the Electron Microscope," lecture for Physiology 545, The Pennsylvania State University, 11 February 1983.

19. An interview:

> [19]Telephone interview with Jane Barnard, Designer/ Editor, Hande Graphics, 14 October 1982.

20. A television or radio program:

20.6

> [20]Wall Street Week, host Louis Rukeyser, PBS, 1 April 1983.

20.6 *Documentation: Bibliography*

You'll notice that the main differences between the bibliographical format (given here) and the note citations (given in the previous section) are the use of periods between the sections in the bibliographical format, the absence of parentheses, and the reversal of the first author's name (last name first). Also, references to specific pages within the work are not included; where the work cited is a part of a larger publication, such as an article in a magazine, then the page numbers of the entire work are included. Note also the differences in margins and indentation.

When listing two or more works by the same author(s), give the name(s) in the first entry only. In subsequent entries, type ten hyphens in place of the name, as shown in the first entry. You can arrange several works by a single author either chronologically or alphabetically.

For information about the conventions of typing the bibliography, see the earlier section in this chapter entitled "The Typing of the Final Draft."

The following entries follow the MLA format:

1. A book with a single author:

> Rogers, Thomas. The Pursuit of Happiness. New York: New American Library, 1968.
>
> ----------. At the Shores. New York: Simon and Schuster, 1980.

(The hyphens stand for the full name in the preceding entry. When the second work has additional authors, those names will follow the hyphens.)

2. A book with more than one author:

> Fahnestock, Jeanne, and Marie Secor. A Rhetoric of Argument. New York: Random House, 1982.

20.6

(Note that only the first author's name is reversed; this order is used for the purpose of alphabetizing the entries.)

3. A work in more than one volume:

> Graves, Robert. The Greek Myths. Baltimore: Penguin, 1955. Vol. I.

4. An edited work:

> Austen, Jane. Pride and Prejudice. Ed. Donald J. Gray. New York: Norton, 1966.

5. A work in a collection by different authors:

> Jacobs, Jane, "A Good Neighborhood." In The Little, Brown Reader. Ed. Marcia Stubbs and Sylvan Barnet. 2nd ed. Boston: Little, Brown, 1980, pp. 151–154.

6. A compilation:

> Hofstadter, Richard, ed. The Progressive Movement: 1900–1915. Englewood Cliffs, N.J.: Prentice-Hall, 1963.

7. An encyclopedia article, unsigned:

> "Mandarin." Encyclopedia Americana. 1976 ed.

8. An encyclopedia article, signed:

> Atkinson, Richard J.C. "Stonehenge." Encyclopaedia Britannica. 1958 ed.

9. A government document:

> U.S. Bureau of Labor Statistics. Productivity. Washington, D.C.: GPO, 1958.

10. An unpublished dissertation:

20.6

> Brown, Betsy E. " 'Palliatives of Inarticulate Art': Narrative Technique in Vladimir Nabokov's English Novels." Diss. Ohio State University 1978.

11. An article in a journal with page numbers that continue throughout the annual volume:

> Berlin, James A. "Contemporary Composition: The Major Pedagogical Theories." College English, 44 (1982), 765–77.

12. An article in a journal with separate page numbers for each issue:

> Thaler, Ruth. "Art and the Written Word." Journal of Basic Writing, 2, No. 4 (1980), 72–81.

13. An article from a weekly magazine:

> Alpert, David M. "Three Mile Island Legacy." Newsweek, 7 April 1980, pp. 33–34.

14. An article from a monthly magazine:

> Morrison, John. "The Evolution of the Wine Bottle." Wines & Vines, March 1983, p. 33.

15. An unsigned editorial in a newspaper:

> "IDC Plays an Important Role." Editorial. Centre Daily Times, 4 April 1983, Sec. A, p. 4, cols. 1–2.

16. A signed article from a daily newspaper:

> Benedict, Howard. "Challenger Given OK for Liftoff." Centre Daily Times, 4 April 1983, Sec. A, p. 1, cols. 5–6.

20.7

17. A book review:

> Lilla, Mark. Rev. of Philosophical Explanations, by
> Robert Nozick. The American Scholar, 51 (1982),
> 426–32.

18. A lecture:

> Gay, Carol. "Preparing Slides for the Electron Micro-
> scope." Physiology 545 lecture, The Pennsylvania
> State University. 11 February 1983.

19. An interview:

> Barnard, Jane. Designer/Editor, Hande Graphics. Tele-
> phone interview. 14 October 1982.

20. A television or radio program:

> Wall Street Week. Host Louis Rukeyser. PBS, 1 April
> 1983.

20.7 *Two Drafts of Paul's Essay*

The marked copy of Paul's essay on the following pages is a rough draft, but it is by no means his first draft. Most sections of this version went through several revisions before reaching this stage. Paul also followed a good practice in typing this working draft. You'll find that it's much easier to evaluate the strengths and weaknesses of your sentences and paragraphs and ideas if you see the essay in typed form. To go through all these stages— including two typed drafts— does, of course, take time. It's obvious that Paul's work was not a last-minute, rush job.

You will find it useful to read the comments in the margins and then compare this version of the essay with the final copy, which follows it, to see how Paul responded to the suggestions. The comments and questions focus on issues that apply to every writing situation.

Understanding Protest

in Contemporary America

Popular protest and civil disobedience are the
hallmarks of a vigorous democracy, replacing armed
conflict with nonviolent intellectual confrontation.
A common tendency is to view protest movements
separately, each as a separate body of individuals
addressed specifically to its single-issue orientation
and lacking any broader role in the evolution of
American society. But actually the protest movements
that have grown and caught national attention in the
last thirty years have been part of America's
comprehensive evolution as a society, and all of these
movements, civil rights, the Vietnam war protest, and
the nuclear power protest, display similar
characteristics.

The nuclear-power protest movement is the most
recent of the movements, It provides a convenient
vehicle for analyzing the growth pattern of contemporary
protest. Robert Cameron Mitchell offered an excellent
starting point for an analysis of a contemporary
protest with his identification of four distinct
phases in the nuclear-power protest movement.[1]
Phase one is characterized by "a small elite of

Who is your audience? What do most people think of in connection with protest? The 1960's, maybe? Your intro should help establish a bond with the reader.

This appositive series gets lost in the commas; use dashes.

This linking be signals a spot for an appositive. Try combining sentences.

Who is he?

Repeated from previous sent.

2

*who are the
insiders?*
Help the reader.

knowledgable insiders who critized the manner of

technology's development by the Atomic Energy

Commission, not the technology itself." Phase two,

*Those pairs
are clues to
wordiness: try
to tighten.*

he maintained, consists of the grass-roots organizing

of ordinary citizens, who organized into groups that

*The point to stress
here is legally.
Give it a whole
phrase, not just
a word.*

challenged nuclear power legally. These groups

usually focus on environmental impact studies and

other environmental concerns. Phase three (is) what

*Another
linking be.*

Mitchell called the "direct-action phase," (This)

involves civil disobedience in the form of disruptive

*who does They
refer to?*

demonstrations. The groups also attempt *and* to occupy

nuclear power installations. Then (they) *also* enlarged the

scope of address to include the technical aspects of

nuclear power generation along with other, broader

social issues. The fourth phase (is) not clearly

*Do phases
"stand"?*

defined, standing *is labeled* rather amorphously under the title

"eclectic tactics."

Mitchell's tactical analysis is valuable as a

model for looking at the evolution of contemporary

what idea?

American protest movements. Adopting this idea, and

rewrite

substituting the nature of a movement's participants

*Help your
reader see the
focus on
people rather
than tactics.*

for the concern with tactics, shows a clear four-phase

model that fits not only the nuclear power protest

movement but other protest movements as well.

*Oppose what?
Study, maybe?*

In phase one, a group of people band together to

study
oppose a matter of mutual, local concern. This *phase*

*Awkward
noun phrase*

corresponds with the *development of the* nuclear-power protest movement's

3

Put stress on the "great social issues."

What's a "specific town"?

development] in the 1960s. During a decade when ~~the~~ *were* great social issues ~~were~~ [racial equality and the war in Vietnam,] citizens who felt threatened by nuclear reactors being constructed in their ~~specific towns~~ *own communities* expressed their concern by forming autonomous protest groups independent of the protest establishment.

Wordy

That's an appositive; it needs commas.

What are frameworks?

In the 1970's [As the decade of the 1970s came on,] however, a second phase, or radicalization, overcame this grass— roots autonomy, generating nationwide organiz~~ational~~ *ed* *support* frameworks and leading the movement into alliances with the Union of Concerned Scientists, Ralph Nader's Critical Mass organization, the Clamshell Alliance, Friends of the Earth, Environmental Action, and a plethora of similar groups. These new participants

"Doing" what? Believing?

espoused ~~believed in~~ civil disobedience and extralegal measures of protest, and in so doing they radically altered the

This idea needs main focus, not a subordinate clause

nature of the movement, attracting a new constituency~~,~~ *O. Such was the case* ~~as~~ in 1973 when the announcement of plans for a nuclear power plant in Montague, Massachusetts, brought ~~a~~ *out* group of local residents that "included a number of refugees from the radical sixties who settled there in order to create an alternative rural lifestyle."[2]

"Brought to bear" loses its meaning when separated by such a long phrase.

This specific information needs more explanation — or perhaps to be deleted.

It was these veterans of the Vietnam war protest *then used* movement who ~~brought~~ their skills in civil disobedience ~~to bear~~ against the nuclear power industry, beginning with [Sam Lovejoy's destruction of a weather tower] at Montague in 1974 and culminating with over

4

1,500 arrests of protestors at the Seabrook, New

Hampshire, reactor site on April 30, 1977.

This radicalization was not confined to the east

Is this ~~it~~
compound verb
accurate?   coast, ~~(but)~~ spread across the country, reflecting the

Let the   national coordination of the antinuclear power
reader know
that you're   movement. San Luis Obispo, California, and Portland,
going from   *In fact,*
specific to   Oregon, were both targets of protests in 1977. During
general.   the first eight months of 1977, more than 120
repetitive
movements?   demonstrations, rallies, and plant occupations had
                                    nationwide
                   occurred across the country.[3] Clearly, the protest's

                   constituency had radically changed by that time.

                   Phase three in a protest movement's evolution, the

                   deradicalization phase, is by far the most important

Awkward   because (it is at this time that what had) hitherto been

                   considered somebody else's problem becomes generally
Which of these   *Although*
ideas should   recognized as everybody's problem. ~~However,~~ radical
get the main
focus? ie, is   demonstrations and ~~civil~~ disobedience attract media
but accurate?
                   attention and thus bring an issue before the American
To focus stress
on the B E,   public, (but) this force is insufficient for pushing
shift it to the   *is*
predicate.   a movement into phase three. Instead, the Big Event
Another link-
ing be.   (is) the catalyst required for deradicalization. ~~The~~
                   ~~Big Event is,~~ that often unplanned incident that

                   raises the consciousness of the general public,

                   particularly the middle class, causing them to ponder

                   seriously what they had previously considered a local

Semicolons   or radical issue. The civil rights movement had the
would show
this as a series march on Washington; the war protest had the North
of related
sentences

5

Try a colon for
emphasis!   Vietnamese Tet offensive; In the case of nuclear power,

                      the Big Event occurred on March 28, 1979: It was the
Leave TMI to
the end for *at*   Three Mile Island accident.
emphasis.
                      This near-meltdown of a reactor near Harrisburg,

                      Pennsylvania, the "worst nuclear accident in the

                      U.S. since utilities began producing electricity

                      from the atom more than 30 years ago, exposed many

                      glaring weaknesses in the operation and maintenance

                      of nuclear plants."[4] Suddenly, while sipping their

                      morning orange juice and glancing over the paper,

                      Americans were jolted by terrifying headlines that

                      caused them to reconsider their attitude toward

That prep. phrase   nuclear power. For some concern centered on plain
needs a comma.
                      physical safety, whereas others saw the dream of low-cost

                      electricity replaced by staggering construction and

                      cleanup costs.

Remind the   Regardless of motivation, the demographics of the
reader of   protest movement changed sharply after TMI, becoming
phase three.   entering phase three, deradicalization.
                      deradicalized through the mass change in American

                      public opinion. Writing in Newsweek one year after TMI,
                      David M. Alpera pointed out this very fact:
                          In the year since the accident, public
                      opposition to nuclear power has risen despite
                      numerous safety improvements mandated for
                      nuclear plants. Many ordinary Americans have
                      joined the anti-nuclear activists who no
                      longer trust the nuclear industry or its
                      government regulators. "These Middle Americans
                      give a kind of respectability to the movement,"
                      said the organizer of one protest last week.
                      "The public now realizes that this is not the
                      normal run of agitators and malcontents."[5]

6

Lead in
with this.
When was
this written?

Is this
info'
subordinate?

Nothing could better point out the change that had
taken place in the constituency of the protest movement
than the use of the words "ordinary Americans." in the
above quotation from Newsweek, written by David M. Alpern.
This deradicalization, initiated by the Big Event
of TMI, was completed by the time of the May, 1979,
with a demonstration in Washington, D.C., which attracted
over 70,000 people and displayed the broad base of
support enjoyed by the antinuclear power movement.
Lorna Salzman, who represented Friends of the Earth
at the rally, said, "What we have here is a grass
roots movement, one that includes students, farmers,
engineers and the middle class."[6] Barry Commoner, a
Washington University professor, put the event in
perspective: "I was floored by the size of the
demonstration. This issue has become a dominant,
broad public issue for the first time."[7] Such is the
result of deradicalization in phase three.

In

agreed

vague!

Even as Commoner spoke with reporters, the movement
was entering its fourth and final phase, that phase in
which the dominant issue, be it civil rights or nuclear
power, is politically digested by the society.
Congressman Morris Udall noted this in commenting on
the Washington demonstration: "The potential is there
for making nuclear power the centerpiece of politics
in 1980. It has an intensity of its own."[8] And he
was right. His own House Interior Committee, in a

Put the stress
on politically.

This seems an
unnecessary
interruption
of the
Commoner
info. Can you
delay-or delete?

7

rare bipartisan display, voted a six-month moratorium
on all new nuclear plant construction or licensing.

Transition is missing! That digestion was speeded up by Commoner himself, who ∧ ~~Barry Commoner~~ formed his own political party and ran

for president on the antinuclear power platform. ~~Time~~ ∧

Transition needed. Help the reader see this as another example of "digestion." Others at the demonstration were ~~ran a picture of~~ ∧ Jerry Brown, ∧ Jane Fonda, and Tom pictured in Time Hayden, ∧ watching the Washington demonstration from a
balcony, each perhaps wondering how this new movement
(new at least to them) could be turned to political
advantage. Later, Jerry Brown, (then governor of

Identify JB at his first mention, above. → California,) told reporters: "I'm at the forefront of
the antinuclear movement."⁸

The reactions cited above are all symptomatic of
an open society digesting a protest movement, of an
ungainly democracy gathering an issue to its bureaucratic
bosom. When people like Barry Commoner, Jane Fonda, and
Jerry Brown coopt the issue, the movement's evolution
is complete: from a matter of local, small-group
concern to an organized national political issue,

This what? complete with its own constituency. (This) has become the evolution ∧

How about a contrast for dreams? American way of protest. What began with one person's nightmares fears of radiation evolved into another person's dreams
of the presidency.

It is far too easy to view this process cynically

Right word? skeptically, to construe its outcome negatively when
compared with the pure, honest passion of those who Such cynicism

What is this? first raised the issue. This would be a grave error
in light of the historical context of popular protest.

8

Henry David Thoreau, writing at the time of the Mexican

War, pointed out the value of such protest and its

place in the American democracy: "If we were left

solely to the wordy wit of legislators in Congress

This could be
indented and
single-spaced   for our guidance, uncorrected by the seasonable

for emphasis.   experience and the effectual complaints of the people,

America would not long retain her rank among the

nations."[109] A hundred years later, Martin Luther King,

Jr., articulated how the people's complaints were to

be delivered by bringing about what he called tension:

> Nonviolent direct action seeks to create
> such a crisis and foster such a tension that
> a community which has constantly refused to
> negotiate is forced to confront the issue.
> . . . I have earnesly opposed violent
> tension, but there is a type of constructive,
> nonviolent tension which is necessary for
> growth. Just as Socrates felt that it was
> necessary to create tension in the mind so
> that individuals could rise from the bondage
> of myths and half-truths to the unfettered
> realm of creative analysis and objective
> appraisal, so must we see the need for . . .
> the kind of tension in society that will
> help men rise . . . to the majestic heights
> of understanding and brotherhood.[110]

So, in view of this historical context and the fact

that the antinuclear issue is now being digested by the

American society as a whole, what has the tension of

this particular protest movement accomplished? Aside

from the fact that simply reaching this fourth phase

of evolution is no small success in itself, there has

been a great shift in the way Americans think about

nuclear power and a concomitant effect on the nuclear

What is the   *it was reported in 1982,*
two-year span   power industry. "In the last two years, 23 plants have
covered? We
need a date.

9

been canceled and not one started. Part of the fallout
from Three Mile Island was tighter regulation and more
frequent lawsuits, which have aggravated delays and
cost overruns at the 76 plants still under construction."¹²//

In addition, "An accident at the Ginna nuclear plant
near Rochester, N.Y., in late January [1982] spotlighted
a little-known problem: At least 39 of the nation's
72 operating nuclear plants are plagued with deteriorating
tubes in steam generators. Officials warn that similar
accidents are likely in the future."¹³ This demonstrated

A paragraph break would help the reader here.

vulnerability to mechanical and construction deficiencies
is ~~also~~ *clearly* affecting the industry. "The NRC [Nuclear

Is "also" accurate?

Regulatory Commission] recently shut down Pacific Gas &
Electric Company's controversial Diablo Canyon plant on

This long quote should be in block form like your other long ones.

the central California coast after utility officials
acknowledged that the wrong blueprints were used to
build earthquake-safety supports. The 2.3 billion-dollar
project already is seven years behind schedule."¹⁴/³

It was this very plant that demonstrators tried to
close down in 1977, and at that time they were arrested
for their efforts. But that was in the radical stage
of the movement's evolution. Five years later,
however, the society had digested the issue; (and) the

Is that an effective and? *Make the sentence stress exact.*

federal government did *exactly* what those original protestors
intended.

Everything is a function of time, and protest
movements are no exception. Having achieved its

10

Tell the reader to expect a contrast.

desired effect, the antinuclear power movement might be expected now to disappear. *But* ∧ ~~S~~uch is not the case, not with this protest nor with any of the other protests mentioned, for the key to understanding protest movements in contemporary America is to see that although each movement may begin with an issue such as nuclear power, *y* no movement stands alone in

A "quarter century" sounds like a long time!

In just twenty-five years

the evolutionary continuum of American democracy. (Just in the last quarter-century) we have seen the civil rights movement grow to embrace and energize the antiwar movement, contributing its wealth of knowledge and experience to the newer cause. And, as pointed out above, it was veterans of the war protest movement *who* ~~that~~ brought direct action and national organization to the nuclear power issue. What does

What is the antecedent of this?

experience

this ∧ say about the future? Harvey Wasserman has pointed the way: "We inherited a lingering worry about radiation from the ban-the-bomb movement and revived it to the point where a reborn disarmament campaign can pursue its cause with a vastly expanded base in the 1980s."~~15~~ [14]

This?

rebirth

Already this ∧ is happening; those people involved in the nuclear power issue are now funneling into a renewed protest against nuclear weapons. A glance at any index of periodicals will show that whereas

Listen to the string of s's! (Switch coupled and associated.)

always

five years ago the word antinuclear (was almost ~~solely~~

coupled

~~associated~~) with power, it is now ~~coupled~~

associated

in nearly

11

Unnecessary repetition of is.

points to

Try a semicolon.

every citation with <u>weapons</u>. This (~~is~~) ~~strong~~ evidence
~~that~~ a new movement (is) building in America. ~~and~~ as

this movement begins evolving through the four

phases of protest, it should be critically evaluated,

not shunned in fear, it should be intellectually

challenged, not emotionally rejected. For the surge

and ebb of popular protest is the heartbeat of a

vital democracy. As one popular 1960s song put it:

"The beat goes on."

Understanding Protest

in Contemporary America

by

Paul Hutchison

English 150

Professor Martha Kolln

May 17, 1983

i

Understanding Protest

in Contemporary America

I.   Protests: A part of America's evolution as a democracy.

II. Mitchell's tactical analysis of the nuclear power protest.

    A. Phase one: inside criticism.

    B. Phase two: grass-roots organization.

    C. Phase three: direct action.

    D. Phase four: eclectic tactics.

III. Analysis of the people involved in the four phases.

    A. Grass roots: local citizens.

    B. Radicalization.

        1. Support from organized groups.

        2. Arrests of 1960s radicals.

        3. Nationwide coordination.

    C. Deradicalization.

        1. The Big Event.

        2. Concern with TMI.

        3. Support of citizenry: march on Washington.

    D. Political digestion.

IV. Historical context of popular protests.

    A. Thoreau's philosophy.

    B. King's introduction of tension.

ii

V.   Accomplishments of the movement.

     A.   Shift in thinking by ordinary people.

     B.   Shifts in policies by industry and government.

VI. The next phase.

     A.   Continuation of the evolution.

     B.   Evidence of change.

Understanding Protest

in Contemporary America

Faculty and students who remember the campus protests of the

late 1960s tend to do so either with nostalgia about the good old

days or with despair about the sorry state of affairs brought on by

those antiwar hippies. "Wasn't that a time!" both groups declare.

But what about today? Are the protests over? Have young people

nothing to protest anymore? No cause to rally around?

The campus is quieter, certainly, than it was during the years

of the Vietnam war. But protest movements never really end. Indeed,

popular protest and civil disobedience are the hallmarks of a

vigorous democracy. In fact, protest movements are a vital part of

America's evolution as a society, and all of these movements--civil

rights, the Vietnam war protest, and the nuclear power protest--

display similar characteristics.

The nuclear-power protest movement, the most recent of the

movements, provides a convenient vehicle for analyzing the growth

of contemporary protest. Writing in Society, Robert Cameron Mitchell

offered an excellent starting point for an analysis with his

identification of four distinct phases in the nuclear-power protest

movement.[1] Phase one is characterized by "a small elite of

knowledgeable insiders [scientists] who criticized the manner of

technology's development by the Atomic Energy Commission, not the

technology itself." Phase two, he maintained, saw the grass-roots

organization of ordinary citizens into groups who challenged nuclear

2

power through legal means by focusing on environmental impact studies
and similar concerns. Phase three, which Mitchell called the
"direct-action phase," involves civil disobedience in the form of
disruptive demonstrations and the occupation of nuclear power
installations. The demonstrators also enlarged their scope of address
to include the technical aspects of nuclear power generation along
with other, broader social issues. The fourth phase, not clearly
defined, is labeled rather amorphously "eclectic tactics."

Mitchell's tactical analysis is valuable as a model for looking
at the evolution of contemporary American protest movements in
general--not only the protest against nuclear power. But instead of
analyzing tactics, as Mitchell did, we will examine the participants.
Who are these protestors? And how do the groups differ in the
different phases of the movement?

In phase one, a group of people band together to study a matter
of mutual, local concern. This phase corresponds with the development
of the nuclear-power protest movement in the 1960s. During a decade
when racial equality and the war in Vietnam were the great social
issues, citizens who felt threatened by nuclear reactors being
constructed in their own communities expressed their concern by
forming autonomous protest groups independent of the protest
establishment.

In the 1970s, however, a second phase, or radicalization,
overcame this grass-roots autonomy, generating nationwide organized
support and leading the movement into alliances with the Union of
Concerned Scientists, Ralph Nader's Critical Mass organization, the
Clamshell Alliance, Friends of the Earth, Environmental Action, and
a plethora of similar groups. These new participants espoused civil

3

disobedience and extralegal measures of protest, and in so doing
they radically altered the nature of the movement, attracting a new
constituency. Such was the case in 1973 when the announcement of
plans for a nuclear power plant in Montague, Massachusetts, brought
out a group of local residents that "included a number of refugees
from the radical sixties who settled there in order to create an
alternative rural lifestyle."[2] It was these veterans of the Vietnam
war protest movement who then used their skills in civil disobedience
against the nuclear power industry, beginning with the Montague
protest in 1974 and culminating in over 1,500 arrests of protestors
at the Seabrook, New Hampshire, reactor site on April 30, 1977.

This radicalization was not confined to the East Coast; it
spread across the country, reflecting the national coordination
of the antinuclear power movement. San Luis Obispo, California, and
Portland, Oregon, were both targets of protest in 1977. In fact,
during the first eight months of 1977, more than 120 demonstrations,
rallies, and plant occupations had occurred nationwide.[3] Clearly,
the movement's constituency had radically changed by that time.

Phase three in a protest movement's evolution, the
deradicalization phase, is by far the most important. In phase three,
what had hitherto been considered somebody else's problem becomes
generally recognized as everybody's problem. Although demonstrations
and disobedience attract media attention and thus bring an issue
before the public, this force is insufficient for pushing a movement
into phase three. Instead, the catalyst required for deradicalization
is the Big Event, that often unplanned incident that raises the
consciousness of the general public--particularly the middle class--
causing them to ponder seriously what they had previously considered

a local or radical issue. The civil rights movement had the march
on Washington, D.C.; the war protest had the North Vietnamese Tet
offensive; in the case of nuclear power, the Big Event occurred on
March 28, 1979: the accident at Three Mile Island.

This near-meltdown of a reactor near Harrisburg, Pennsylvania,
the "worst nuclear accident in the U.S. since utilities began
producing electricity from the atom more than 30 years ago, exposed
many glaring weaknesses in the operation and maintenance of nuclear
plants."[4] Suddenly, while sipping their orange juice and glancing
over the morning paper, Americans were jolted by terrifying
headlines that caused them to reconsider their attitude toward
nuclear power. For some, concern centered on plain physical safety,
while others saw the dream of low-cost electricity replaced by
staggering construction and cleanup costs.

Regardless of motivation, the demographics of the protest
movement changed sharply after TMI, clearly entering phase three--
deradicalization. Writing in Newsweek one year after TMI, David M.
Alpern pointed out this very fact:

> In the year since the accident, public opposition
> to nuclear power has risen despite numerous safety
> improvements mandated for nuclear plants. Many
> ordinary Americans have joined the anti-nuclear
> activists who no longer trust the nuclear industry or
> its government regulators. "These Middle Americans
> give a kind of respectability to the movement," said
> the organizer of one protest last week. "The public
> now realizes that this is not the normal run of
> agitators and malcontents."[5]

Nothing could better illustrate the change that had taken place in
the constituency of the protest movement than Alpern's use of the
words "ordinary Americans."

In May 1979, over 70,000 ordinary Americans displayed the broad
base of support enjoyed by the antinuclear power movement with a

5

demonstration in Washington, D.C. Lorna Salzman, who represented
Friends of the Earth at the rally, said, "What we have here is a
grass roots movement, one that includes students, farmers, engineers,
and the middle class."[6] Barry Commoner, a Washington University
professor, agreed: "I was floored by the size of the demonstration.
This issue has become a dominant, broad public issue for the first
time."[7] Such is the result of deradicalization in phase three.

Even as Commoner spoke with reporters, the movement was entering
its fourth and final phase, that period in which the dominant issue,
be it civil rights or nuclear power, gets digested politically by
the society. That digestion was speeded up by Commoner himself, who
formed his own political party and ran for president on the antinuclear power platform. Others at the Washington demonstration were
Jerry Brown, then governor of California, Jane Fonda, and Tom Hayden,
who were pictured in Time watching the demonstration from a balcony,
each perhaps wondering how this new movement--new at least to
them--could be turned to political advantage. Later Jerry Brown told
reporters: "I'm at the forefront of the antinuclear movement."[8]

The reactions cited above are all symptomatic of an open society
digesting a protest movement, of an ungainly democracy gathering an
issue to its bureaucratic bosom. When people like Barry Commoner,
Jane Fonda, and Jerry Brown coopt the issue, the movement's evolution
is complete: from a matter of local, small-group concern to an
organized national political issue, complete with its own constituency.
This evolution has become the American way of protest. What began with
one person's nightmares of radiation evolved into another person's
dreams of the presidency.

It is far too easy to view this process cynically, to construe
its outcome negatively when compared with the pure, honest passion of

6

those who first raised the issue. Such cynicism would be a grave
error in light of the historical context of popular protest. Henry
David Thoreau, writing at the time of the Mexican War, pointed out
the value of such protest and its place in the American democracy:

> If we were left solely to the wordy wit of legislators
> in Congress for our guidance, uncorrected by the
> seasonable experience and the effectual complaints of
> the people, America would not long retain her rank
> among the nations.[9]

A hundred years later, Martin Luther King, Jr., articulated how the
people's complaints were to be delivered by bringing about what he
called "tension":

> Nonviolent direct action seeks to create such a crisis
> and foster such a tension that a community which has
> constantly refused to negotiate is forced to confront
> the issue. . . . I have earnestly opposed violent
> tension, but there is a type of constructive, nonviolent
> tension which is necessary for growth. Just as Socrates
> felt that it was necessary to create tension in the mind
> so that individuals could rise from the bondage of myths
> and half-truths to the unfettered realm of creative
> analysis and objective appraisal, so must we see the need
> for . . . the kind of tension in society that will help
> men rise . . . to the majestic heights of understanding
> and brotherhood.[10]

So, in view of this historical context and the fact that the
antinuclear issue is now being digested by the American society as
a whole, what has the tension of this particular protest movement
accomplished? Aside from the fact that simply reaching this fourth
phase of evolution is no small success in itself, there has been a
great shift in the way Americans think about nuclear power and a
concomitant effect on the nuclear power industry. "In the last two
years," it was reported in 1982, "23 plants have been canceled and
not one started. Part of the fallout from Three Mile Island was
tighter regulation and more frequent lawsuits, which have
aggravated delays and cost overruns at the 76 plants still under

7

construction."[11] In addition, "an accident at the Ginna nuclear plant

near Rochester, N.Y., in late January [1982] spotlighted a little-

known problem: At least 30 of the nation's 72 operating nuclear plants

are plagued with deteriorating tubes in steam generators. Officials

warn that similar accidents are likely in the future."[12]

This demonstrated vulnerability to mechanical and construction

deficiencies is clearly affecting the industry:

> The NRC [Nuclear Regulatory] Commission recently shut
> down Pacific Gas & Electric Company's controversial
> Diablo Canyon plant on the central California coast
> after utility officials acknowledged that the wrong
> blueprints were used to build earthquake-safety
> supports. The 2.3 billion-dollar project already is
> seven years behind schedule.[13]

It was this very plant that demonstrators tried to close down in

1977, and at that time they were arrested for their efforts. But that

was in the radical stage of the movement's evolution. Five years later,

however, after society had digested the issue, the federal government

did exactly what those original protestors intended.

Everything is a function of time, and protest movements are no

exception. Having achieved its desired effect, the antinuclear power

movement might be expected now to disappear. But such is not the case,

not with this protest nor with any of the other protests mentioned,

for the key to understanding protest movements in contemporary America

is to see that although each movement may begin with an issue such as

nuclear power, no movement stands alone in the evolutionary continuum

of American democracy. In just twenty-five years we have seen the

civil rights movement grow to embrace and energize the antiwar

movement, contributing its wealth of knowledge and experience to the

newer cause. And, as pointed out above, it was the veterans of the

war protest movement who brought direct action and national

8

organization to the nuclear power issue. What does this experience
say about the future? Harvey Wasserman has pointed the way: "We
inherited a lingering worry about radiation from the ban-the-bomb
movement and revived it to the point where a reborn disarmament
campaign can pursue its cause with a vastly expanded base in the
1980s."[14]

   Already this rebirth is happening; those people involved in
the nuclear power issue are now funneling into a renewed protest
against nuclear weapons. A glance at any index of periodicals will
show that whereas five years ago the word antinuclear was almost
always coupled with power, it is now associated in nearly every
citation with weapons. This evidence points to a new movement
building in America. As this movement begins evolving through the
four phases of protest, it should be critically evaluated, not
shunned in fear; it should be intellectually challenged, not
emotionally rejected. For the surge and ebb of popular protest is
the heartbeat of a vital democracy. As one popular 1960s song put
it: "The beat goes on."

9

Notes

[1]Robert Cameron Mitchell, "From Elite Quarrel to Mass Movement," Society, July/August 1981, pp. 76-84.

[2]Mitchell, p. 81.

[3]Mitchell, p. 82.

[4]Kenneth R. Sheets, "Is Nuclear Power Finished in the U.S.?" U.S. News & World Report, 29 March 1982, p. 59.

[5]David M. Alpern, "Three Mile Island's Legacy," Newsweek, 7 April 1980, p. 33.

[6]"'Hell No, We Won't Glow,'" Time, 21 May 1979, p. 18.

[7]Time, 21 May 1979, p. 18.

[8]Time, 21 May 1979, p. 18.

[9]Henry David Thoreau, "Civil Disobedience," in Walden and "Civil Disobedience" (New York: Airmont, 1965), p. 253.

[10]Martin Luther King, Jr., "Letter from Birmingham Jail," in The Norton Reader, ed. Arthur M. Eastman (New York: Norton, 1980), pp. 472-73.

[11]Peter W. Bernstein, "A Nuclear Fiasco Shakes the Bond Market," Fortune, 22 February 1982, p. 100.

[12]Sheets, p. 59.

[13]Sheets, p. 59.

[14]Harvey Wasserman, "The Industry That Couldn't," Progressive, April 1982, p. 66.

10

Bibliography

Alpern, David M. "Three Mile Island's Legacy." <u>Newsweek</u>, 7 April 1980,

   pp. 33-34.

Bernstein, Peter W. "A Nuclear Fiasco Shakes the Bond Market."

   <u>Fortune</u>, 22 February 1982, pp. 100-115.

"'Hell No, We Won't Glow.'" <u>Time</u>, 21 May 1979, pp. 17-18.

King, Martin Luther, Jr. "Letter from Birmingham Jail." In <u>The Norton</u>

   <u>Reader</u>, ed. Arthur M. Eastman. New York: Norton, 1980, pp.

   470-84.

Mitchell, Robert Cameron. "From Elite Quarrel to Mass Movement."

   <u>Society</u>, July/August 1981, pp. 76-84.

Sheets, Kenneth R. "Is Nuclear Power Finished in the U.S.?" <u>U.S. News &</u>

   <u>World Report</u>, 29 March 1982, pp. 59-60.

Thoreau, Henry David. "Civil Disobedience." <u>Walden and "Civil</u>

   <u>Disobedience</u>." New York: Airmont, 1965.

Wasserman, Harvey. "The Industry That Couldn't." <u>Progressive</u>, April

   1982, p. 66.

21

Special Writing Situations

Chances are that most of the writing you've done lately has been part of your composition class—a class for improving your writing skills. You've probably written more words for your assigned essays than you've done in all of your other classes put together.

But certainly formal essays are not your only writing tasks. Both in other classes and in situations outside of school you use your writing skills. And when you do, remember that the principles described in the preceding chapters apply not only when you write formal essays; they apply to all of your writing. Whatever the writing situation may be, you will take purpose and audience into account; you will select words for their effect; you will connect the ideas logically and smoothly; and you will think about your personal voice.

In this chapter we will look at three particular writing situations that come up from time to time. The first you've probably encountered many times already: the essay examination. The second is a writing task that will come up for a variety of reasons as your world expands beyond the campus: the business letter. The third, a more specialized writing task, is one that you will face when it's time to apply for a job: the résumé.

21.1   21.1 *The Essay Examination*

- Analyze Thomas Jefferson's contribution to American architecture.
- Explain the effects of the railroad on the development of the western United States.
- Discuss the importance to Greek life of the Agora of Athens.
- Contrast the narrative technique, the treatment of the supernatural, and the establishment of mood in the tales of Hawthorne and Poe.

Writing an essay in response to such directions differs in two important ways from the writing of other essays and of term papers. First, of course, your time is limited. You can't mull over the topic for a day or two, then write a first draft and let it simmer, then think it all through again, revise, and rewrite. In other words, the process is different. The second difference, however, eliminates the need for some of that mulling over: The writing situation is specified, with topic, purpose, and audience all given.

1. The topic, obviously, is the examination question itself. (Notice, incidentally, that the foregoing "questions" are not questions at all; they are directions in the form of imperative sentences, or commands. In this discussion, however, we'll refer to them as questions.)
2. The audience is your instructor—or, perhaps, an assistant who does the grading.
3. Your purpose has several layers: to develop the thesis or prove the point asked for in the question and thus to demonstrate your understanding of the subject matter; and also to prove that you deserve the C or B or A you're hoping for.

With the writing situation established, then, your first step is to read the question carefully, paying particular attention to the imperative verb: *describe, analyze, explain, compare, contrast, discuss*. You'll also want to pay attention to other key words in the question:

Analyze . . . *contribution* . . .
Explain the *effects* . . .

Discuss the *importance* . . .

Your strategy for carrying out that task will be very much like the strategies you use when writing other compositions. First, come up with a thesis statement or main idea that you want to support. This step—the real planning stage for the essay—will take time. Before you can formulate your idea, you must think through the topic. For example, the question "Analyze Thomas Jefferson's contribution to American architecture" calls for analysis. As you would do in an analysis, or division, essay, you will think about the *parts* of Jefferson's contribution. You might begin by jotting down in the form of a scratch outline the buildings that Jefferson designed. As you plan your answer, always keep in mind the key word in the question—in this case, *contribution.* You might focus on the unique contribution of individual buildings, or identify a theme that runs through all the work, or show how one building—Monticello, for example— represents Jefferson's main contribution. After jotting down details, formulate your main idea. Then arrange the details to support it. The amount of detail you include will depend partly on how much time you have for the essay. Your plan for a fifteen-minute essay will obviously be different from that for a forty-minute or hour-long essay.

The opening statement for your essay will be much like the topic sentence of a general-to-specific paragraph. It should include (1) the point or idea you plan to prove and (2) your attitude or opinion or focus. Your best strategy is to get right to the point:

> Thomas Jefferson's contributions to architecture are best illustrated in his innovative designs for the University of Virginia and his beloved Monticello.

Then set about proving that point with specific, supporting evidence.

This opening strategy illustrtes another important difference between the examination essay and the general essay: You don't need a formal introduction. In the general essay, you'll recall, there are goals for the introduction that go beyond the topic itself: to gain the reader's attention and to establish your authority. You may take a whole paragraph or more to do that—relating an anecdote, narrating an experience, quoting an expert, or in some other way introducing yourself and the topic to your readers. The reader of the examination

21.1

essay, however, is ready and waiting, already primed for the topic. So get right to the point—the sooner, the better.

Here are some further suggestions for making your answer as effective as possible:

1. Write in the third person. Don't begin your essay with "I believe" or "I feel." To announce that what you are writing is your own opinion or belief is simply unnecessary. With the third person you're much more likely to use the actual topic of the sentence as the sentence subject.

2. Don't pad your answers with superfluous phrases or with a needless repetition of key words from the question. Graders of essay exams have a great deal of reading to do; they appreciate concise prose and specific information.

3. Keep your reader on track with transition words and parallel structures wherever they are helpful:

> *One important contribution* is the Rotunda . . .
>
> *Another influence* Jefferson had . . .
>
> Probably his *most lasting influence* has been . . .

In answering a question about a process—for example, one tracing the development of the railroad or showing the process of cell division—make the steps or time divisions clear:

> The *first* step . . .
>
> *Next* . . .
>
> *After* the initial steps . . .
>
> *In the years that followed* . . .
>
> *Finally* . . .

For the comparison/contrast essay, make your strategy clear—either the part-to-part or the whole-to-whole plan. In the case of the Hawthorne and Poe question, for example, because it asks you to show the contrasts of three different aspects of their writing, your outline would probably look like this, organized into three paragraphs:

> I. Narrative technique
>   A. Poe
>   B. Hawthorne

II. Supernatural
   A. Poe
   B. Hawthorne
III. Mood
   A. Poe
   B. Hawthorne

21.2

4. Close the essay with finality. For most short exam essays, that conclusion will be a single sentence:

> Indeed, Jefferson's contributions as an architect rival his contributions as a statesman.

or

> Even the glass and steel skyscrapers of our time have not surpassed the beauty and functionalism of Jefferson's designs.

The point is to make sure that your reader knows that the answer is complete. Nothing is more frustrating than to turn a page with expectations and find it blank. Remember, your reader is poised with pen in hand, ready to write a comment and put a grade on your essay. A thoughtful and clear conclusion will leave the reader with a positive feeling.

In summary, then, the most important differences between the examination essay and other essays are the writing situation, which is already specified, and the limited time: (1) Use the time well by planning ahead carefully; there will be no time for rewriting and very little for proofreading; (2) get right to the point with clearly stated ideas, supported by specific evidence; (3) assist the reader by using transitions; and (4) make the ending clear.

21.2 The Business Letter

You needn't work in an office to have occasion for writing business letters, and you needn't be a business major. The term *business letter*, as used here, actually refers to form rather than content. The writing situation that calls for this form could be a letter of protest to your professor about a grade, a letter to the editor of your

21.2

local paper, a letter of inquiry about a mail order, or that important job-application letter.

Like every writing task you undertake, the business letter requires that you consider the writing situation carefully: the occasion for the letter, the audience, and the purpose. Whatever that situation might be, there are some general guidelines for you to follow:

- *Get to the point.* Let your reader know the reason for the letter in your first paragraph.
- *Be tactful and courteous.* Even when you're mad about something—a jade pendant you ordered that turned out to be plastic or a pair of gloves for two left hands—use tact in expressing yourself, including the polite conventions of "Dear_____:" "Thank you," and "Sincerely."
- *Use your personal voice.* If you wouldn't say "enclosed herewith please find . . . ," then don't write it. You can be businesslike without being pretentious or stuffy.
- *Put yourself in your reader's place.* Consider what the reader knows and needs to know of you and your situation. Provide all the necessary background information.
- *Make your letter look businesslike.* Type neatly, using one side of standard 8½-by-11-inch typing paper; make sure that all corrections are unobtrusive.

The sample letter given here shows the six standard sections that every business letter should have. It also illustrates a helpful general rule:

- Single space within the parts.
- Double space between the parts.

Here are some further details about the six sections:

1. *The heading.* This includes your address and the date. Position the heading to line up approximately with the letter's right-hand margin. If you are using a printed letterhead, you would include only the date, either centered or lined up with one of the margins,

(1) 10 Chesapeake Drive
San Jose, CA 95126
November 9, 1983

(2) Sales Department
Clites Printing Company
321 North James Avenue
Silverton, OR 97381

(3) Dear Sales Department:

At the recent Collegiate Conference in Livermore, we received a sample of your custom-printed tote bags, which we find to be exceptionally sturdy and attractive. Our organization is interested in selling the bags at our spring carnival next April.

(4) Would you please send us information on size and prices. Also, is it possible to have the bags printed in two colors?

We will appreciate hearing from you soon.

(5) Sincerely,

Chris Judy

(6) Chris Judy, Chairman
The Horticulture Club

21.2 depending on the letterhead's design. Here are some other conventions to note:

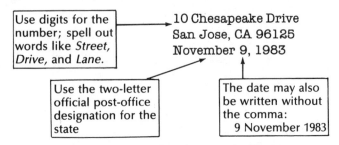

Use digits for the number; spell out words like *Street, Drive,* and *Lane.*	10 Chesapeake Drive San Jose, CA 96125 November 9, 1983

Use the two-letter official post-office designation for the state	The date may also be written without the comma: 9 November 1983

2. *The inside address.* This appears at the left margin, from two to six spaces below the date, depending on the space needed for the body of the letter. Use the same conventions for spelling the street and the state as in the heading. Always use a courtesy title before the name of a specific person: Use abbreviations for *Mr., Mrs., Ms.,* and *Dr.;* spell out completely the title *Professor.* If you don't know a woman's marital status, use *Ms.* Also us *Ms.* if the woman herself signs her name in that way, even when you know her marital status.

3. *The salutation.* Begin one double space below the inside address. The standard convention is to use the word *Dear*—yes, even for perfect strangers!

Professor Charles Rhodes
Department of History
Slippery Rock State College
Slippery Rock, PA 16011

Again, *Professor* is spelled out; use a colon after the name.

Dear Professor Rhodes:

Probably more problems arise with the salutation than with any other part of the letter. As in the sample letter shown, you don't always have a name. In such cases some writers still use the single-sex form of *Dear Sir* or *Gentlemen.* Most people, however, try to find an alternative that includes the possibility that there are women in the company. The salutation used in the example, *Dear Sales Department,* is one solution. Another solution is *Dear Ladies and Gentlemen,* although to some people that sounds much too formal, almost like a graduation speech. Another solution, now being encouraged, is either to eliminate the salutation altogether or to substitute an "attention" line, such as the following:

```
Clites Printing Company
321 North James Avenue
Silverton, OR 97381

Attention: Sales Department

    At the recent Collegiate Conference ...
```

Of all the possibilities, *Dear Sir* and *Gentlemen* are the most likely to give offense.

4. *The body.* Single-space the letter, beginning one double space below the salutation. You can either indent the paragraphs, as in the example, or keep all the lines flush with the left-hand margin. Double-space between paragraphs. Paragraph unity is important, of course, but so is ease of reading, so try to keep your paragraphs reasonably short. Single-sentence paragraphs in opening and closing position are fairly standard in business letters.

5. *The complimentary close.* This appears one double space below the last line of the body. Begin approximately in line with the heading, making adjustments for the length of your name and title. The word or phrase you use in the closing will depend on your relationship to the person addressed. You might close with *Regards* or *Warm regards* to a business associate you know well; in a letter to an anonymous sales department, *Yours truly* or *Sincerely* is standard. In a two-word close, such as *Yours truly* or *Sincerely yours*, only the first word is capitalized.

6. *Signature block.* Always type your name about four spaces below the complimentary close. Include your title, if any. Depending on length, you can use one or two lines, or even three, if you include the name of the organization you represent:

```
Sincerely,                    Yours truly,



Chris Judy, Chairman          Christopher K. Williamson
The Horticulture Club         Editor-in-Chief
                              The Collegian Magazine
```

21.3 The Résumé

Among the most important single writing projects you will undertake within the next few years will be your personal résumé, the statement that sums up for strangers who you are, to help them foresee the employee you could become. The kind of job you are seeking will make some difference in the way you write your résumé, of course; the application for a summer job or a part-time job, for instance, would be different from a career application. But in general the following guidelines apply for presenting yourself on paper for a potential employer:

Step 1: Analyzing Yourself

The first step is to write down all of the experiences you have had that matter, or might matter, to that potential employer. Brainstorm with yourself:

1. *List your interests and activities.* What hobbies do you have? Do you like the outdoors? Do you play an instrument? Are you good with your hands? Do you like crafts or woodworking? Are you a tinkerer with engines?

2. *List the organizations you are affiliated with.* Do you belong to clubs at school or church or in the community? Are you a member of a fraternity or sorority? Are you in the band? A debater? A thespian? An athlete? Have you held office in student government? In your fraternity? Have you acted in plays? Built sets? Worked for the school newspaper? The yearbook?

Write down everything about yourself that you can think of. Obviously all of this won't be appropriate in your résumé, but just thinking through your interests and activities and accomplishments may trigger ideas you have forgotten—experiences that just might be important.

3. *Summarize your education.* Take a look at your college transcript. Write down the courses that a potential employer might want to know about. For some employers your Spanish courses and your electives in Latin American studies might be significant; others may be more interested in your psychology or labor studies or economics courses. Maybe your math and computer science electives will make an impression, even for nontechnical jobs.

4. *Summarize your work experience.* Make a list of all the jobs you've had, from delivering papers to delivering pizza. Think about the kinds of skills and commitments they required. What did you learn from those jobs? Were you on your own or closely supervised? Did you make decisions? Did you deal with the public? Did you handle money or accounts? Were you rehired the next summer?

21.3

Remember, potential employers are not necessarily looking for someone experienced at a particular job, although in some cases they may be; often they are looking for someone capable of learning it, a person who will be right for the company and the job. So assess yourself as carefully as you can at this stage, thinking about the kind of person you are and the experiences you have had that will communicate your strong points.

Step 2: Condensing and Organizing Your Data

The sample résumé at the end of the chapter illustrates the format for presenting your information. In the explanation below you'll note that some of the information is described as optional. Every résumé, however, should include Section 1 (identification), Section 3 (education), Section 4 (work experience), and Section 7 (references). The others—career objectives, other activities, and personal data—are optional, but they are certainly appropriate in most cases.

Try to limit the résumé to a single page, if possible. Obviously, you can't always do that, so a second page might be required, if, for example, you have a long list of jobs. Completeness is certainly more important than brevity.

Do not use complete sentences in presenting the information. Use either noun phrases or verb phrases, whichever work best, but be consistent.

1. *Identification.* Include your name, address, and telephone number. If you're using a school address, it's a good idea to include your home address as well, especially if the school year is almost over.

2. *Career objective(s).* This statement can include both long-range and short-range goals. Don't be vague and don't try to impress the reader with lofty phrases, such as "I want a career that will challenge and stimulate my creative abilities and contribute to humankind." If you are preparing the résumé for a specific company,

you should know enough about that company to state your goals quite specifically:

> To gain experience in all phases of accounting so that I can eventually specialize in financial planning and management.
>
> To begin as a management trainee, eventually to become a manager in the field of fashion design.

Your library is a good source of information about specific companies. Look for such publications as *Standard and Poor's* or *Moody's* manuals, which detail the history and the current operations of most large companies. If the library doesn't have these references, a local stockbroker's office probably will. In addition, companies often make the news, so the periodical indexes in the library may be a source of information.

(Note: This background information about a company is especially important when you go for a personal interview.)

3. *Education.* For most students this is the most important section, the one you have been working on for the past several years. Always begin with your most recent school. If you expect a degree at the end of the semester or the school year, make that clear. Also mention specific courses that you have taken in your major (the advanced ones), as well as related courses that have pertinence to the job. If your grade average is impressive—a strong B or higher—mention it.

4. *Experience.* If some of your jobs are related to the job you're applying for and others are not, it's probably a good idea to separate them into two groups, listing the related ones first. Be sure to include special skills that the job required or that you learned while working on it if those skills are relevant to the job you're applying for.

5. *Other activities.* Include a section on your extracurricular activities if those activities say something important about you: positions of leadership in student government, for example, or in the dorm or the sorority; staff positions on the school paper or yearbook; participation in varsity athletics, in drama, in music. Include any scholastic honors and awards, as well as membership in honor societies. Also include any experience doing volunteer work.

6. *Personal data.* In general, you need offer no personal data. In fact, the law forbids employers to ask about religion or race or marital status. Your height and weight are also irrelevant to most jobs,

unless, perhaps, strength is important. But certainly you can include such information. You could also include your age if you are older than the usual college student and if that information is not apparent from the data already shown. For some jobs your maturity might be an asset. In this section you can also include your military record.

7. *References.* Most prospective employers want three or four references. If you are sending your résumé to a company in response to an advertisement or to a request, list the names and addresses and business telephone numbers of your references. If you are sending your résumé to a long list of companies, you should probably state "References furnished on request" rather than listing the names. The people who agreed to write reference letters for you (and, of course, you have asked them and received their permission to use their names) should not be inundated with requests unless the job possibility is a good one.

The best references are job- or school-related. The listing should make clear to the prospective employer your relationship to the person. If it isn't clear, from either the person's title or address, explain in a parenthetical note who the person is.

Summary

The purpose of a résumé is to open the door for you, to help you get a personal interview, so introduce yourself in writing as effectively as possible.

In general, give prominence to the important information, emphasizing the details of school, work experience, and other activities that will count the most with the prospective employer. Present the information clearly and neatly, using an open, easy-to-read format with a lot of white space. Confine your résumé to a single page, if possible.

Barbara DiClemente
7104 Ruskin Lane
Plainsboro, PA 18221
(214) 616-4340

CAREER
OBJECTIVE

To enter the computer field as a programmer; to use and improve my programming skills.

EDUCATION

1982–84

Delaware County Community College, Media, PA. Major: Data Processing. Associate in Arts and Science Degree to be awarded, June 1984 (GPA 3.74 on a 4.00 scale).

Professional courses: Cobol, Advanced Cobol, OS/JCL (IBM), Assembler (IBM 370), Basic, RPG II, Systems and Procedures, Statistics, Accounting, Finite Mathematics.

WORK
EXPERIENCE

Summer
1982–84

Cashier, A.P. Fisher, Inc. (sheet metal fabricators). Handled accounts receivable and petty cash. Used telex machine.

Summer
1979–81

Cashier, Gardenside Theatre, Plainsboro, PA.

OTHER
ACTIVITIES

Advertising manager for campus semiweekly newspaper for three semesters. Supervised sales staff of six (monthly billing: $7,800); directed ad layouts.

REFERENCES

Mr. A.P. Fisher
A.P. Fisher, Inc.
2101 North Elm Street
Plainsboro, PA 18221
(214) 662-8117

Mr. John Sharp, Manager
Gardenside Theatre
East Main Street
Plainsboro, PA 18221
(214) 680-4666

Professor Richard Devon
Department of Computer Science
Delaware County Community College
Media, PA 18823
(210) 707-6722

Index

A

A, an
    with countable nouns, 161,
        195
    as determiners, 61, 173
Abbreviations, 423–25
    acronyms formed from,
        424–25
    for names of courses, 425
    standard forms of, 425
    of titles, 423–24
Absolute adjectives, 169
Absolute phrases, 115–18
    defined, 139
    effective use of, 416–17
Abstract nouns, 160–61
    in noun hierarchy, 195
Abstracts, indexes to, 457–64
Accept, except, 251
Acknowledging sources, 472–74
Acronyms, 424–25
Active voice, 47
    defined, 139
    in revision, 402–4

Addresses
    in business letters, 514
    numbers in, 444
Ad hominem argument, 331
Adjectival clause, 75–81
    defined, 139
    punctuation of, 79–81
    relative pronoun omitted in,
        76, 80
Adjectivals, 59–97
    adjectives as, 61–64
    appositives as, 81–92
    defined, 139
    multiple postnoun, 92–93
    nouns as, 61–64
    participial phrases as, 66–75
    postnoun, 65–97
    prepositional phrases as,
        65–66
    relative clauses as, 75–81
Adjectives, 11, 165–69
    in absolute phrase, 116
    compound, 124
    defined, 139
    degree of, 166–68

Adjectives (cont.)
    derivational suffixes of, 165
    inflectional suffixes of, 166
    as prenoun modifier, 61–64
        classes of, 62–63
        commas with, 62
        hyphens with, 63–64
    subclasses of, 168–69
        absolute, 169
        attributive, 168
        predicative, 168–69
Adjective-test frame, 11, 168–69
Adverbials, 13
    clauses as, 14, 110–15
    defined, 140
    of manner, 23, 169–70
        defined, 144
    noun phrase as, 13
    of place, 23
    prepositional phrase as, 13
        compound, 124
    of reason, 24
    in split infinitive, 243–44
    of time, 23
    verb phrase as, 13–14,
        72–73
Adverbs, 169–71
    defined, 140
    degree of, 166
    derivational suffixes of,
        169–70
    flat, 170
    hyphens with, 63
    inflectional suffixes of, 170
    manner, 169–70
    relative, 78–79
    as sentence modifier, 110–11
Affect, effect, 251
Affix, 156–58
    defined, 140
Agent
    defined, 140
    in passive voice, 48, 53
    in revision, 398–404
    of transitive verb, 9
Aggravate, irritate, 252
Agreement. *See* Pronoun–

antecedent agreement;
    Subject–verb agreement
All
    as determiner, 173
    subject–verb agreement
        with, 162
All right, alright, 252
Almost, most, 252–53
Alot, 253
Alright, 252
Ambiguity
    in elliptical comparison,
        113–14
    of postnoun modifiers, 92–93
    in sentence patterns, 19
Among, between, 253
Amount of, number of, 195, 253
Analogy, as evidence in argument,
    323–25
Analysis. *See* Division
And, 179
    accuracy of, 412–15
    in compound sentence,
        132–33
    with semicolon, 135
    within sentence, 124–30
    in series, 125–26
    style of, in published works,
        419–20
Animate nouns, 196
Ante-, anti-, in spelling, 231
Antecedent
    of broad-reference pronouns,
        187–88
    of indefinite pronouns,
        245–50
    of personal pronouns, 181–83
Anti-, ante-, in spelling, 231
Anymore, as regionalism, 253
Anyways, 253
Apostrophe, 425–27
    with contractions, 426–27
    misuse with *its,* 259
    with plurals, 426
    with possessive case, 227–29,
        425–26
Appeals of argument, 318–27

emotional appeals, 320–21
ethical appeals, 318–20
logical appeals, 321–27
Appositives, 81–92
  colon with, 84–86
  dashes with, 86–88
  defined, 140
  gerund as, 101–2
  infinitive as, 104
  introductory, 410–12
  punctuation of, 83–92
  and style, 410–12
Argumentation, 266, 313–36
  appeals of, 318–27
    emotional, 320–21
    ethical, 318–20
    logical, 321–27
  audience in, 316
  fallacies in, 327–32
  parts in essay of, 316–18
  topics for, 314–15
  writing assignments for,
    333–34
Arrangement
  in argument, 316–18
  in descriptive essay, 281
  in essay planning, 342
Article, definite/indefinite
  with countable and
    noncountable nouns, 161,
    195
  as determiner, 61, 173
Article, in journals and magazines
  form for bibliography, 481
  form for notes, 477–78
As well as, 33
Attitude
  exploring, 340–41
  of writer, 202–3
Audience
  in argument, 316
  for description essay, 280–81
  effect of word choice on, 194,
    203, 209
  in writing situation, 269–70
Authority of writer, 319–20
Auxiliaries, 25–31, 173–75

defined, 140
meaning of, 41–42
modal, 35–37
modal-like, 174
Awhile, a while, 254

B

Background in argument essay,
  317
Base form of verb, 26–28
  defined, 141
  irregular, 43–46
  in subjunctive mood, 39
Base morpheme of word, 155–57
  defined, 140
Be
  appositive as alternative to, 82
  as auxiliary with -*ing* verbs,
    29–31
  forms of, 27
  as intransitive verb, 17n
  as linking verb, 17–18
  in passive transformation,
    47–57
Begging the question, 330
Beginning point in narrative,
  291–93
Beside, besides, 254
Between, among, 254
Bibliography
  form of, 479–82
  typing of, 475
Body of business letter, 515
Book review
  form for bibliography, 482
  form for notes, 478
Books
  form for bibliography,
    479–80
  form for notes, 476
  using in research, 455,
    464–65
Brackets
  for additions to quoted
    material, 427

Brackets (cont.)
within parentheses, 427
British English
spelling, 221n, 222n
use of *one*, 345
Broad reference
clause, 141
pronoun, 188, 386
in relative clause, 118–19
Business letter, 511–15
facsimile, 513
Bust, burst, 255
But
with compound modifier, 124
in compound sentence,
131–32
inaccurate focus with 131,
417–18
with semicolon, 135

C

Capitals, 427–30
with calendar terms, 429
with documents and events,
429
with names of groups of
people, 428
with proper nouns, 427–28
in quotations, 429–30
in titles, 429
with words derived from
proper nouns, 428
Card catalog in library, 464–65
Case. *See also* Possessive case
defined, 141
of personal pronouns, 183–84
errors with, 184
of *who/whom,* 76
Cause and effect, as evidence in
argument, 322–23
Center around, 255
Circular reasoning, 330–31
Citations
form of, 475–79
typing of, 474
Cite, sight, site, 255

Classification, as expository mode,
307–10
Clause. *See also* Subordinate
clause
nominal, 104–10
as postnoun modifier, 64,
75–81
Cleft sentence, 381–82
Coherence in paragraphs, 369–88
Cohesion
grammatical, 373–84
lexical, 384–88
semantic, 370–73
vocabulary choice in, 388
Collective nouns, 162–63
Colon, 430–32
with appositives, 84–86,
430–31
in compound sentences,
88–89
at conjunction of sentences,
431
with direct quotation, 431
errors with, 89–91
Comma, 432–37
with absolute phrase, 115–17
in compound sentences,
132–33, 432–33
with conjunctive adverb, 134
with coordinate adjectives, 62,
435–36
with direct address, 436
with direct quotations,
436–37
with introductory clause, 108,
433
in error between sentence
slots, 19–20
in error within nominal
clause, 107–9
with introductory phrase, 435
with list, 433
with nonrestrictive modifier,
68–71, 79–81, 435
with parenthetical
expressions, 111
with prenoun modifiers,
62–64

with sentence modifiers,
110–11, 434
with series, 125–27
with state and year, 437
with subordinate clause, 108,
433
Comma splice, 132–33
Common nouns, 195
Comparative degree, 166–68
defined, 141
with *more*, 167
Comparison/contrast
in conclusion of essay, 353
as evidence in argument,
323–25
as expository mode, 303–7
using metaphor in, 205
Complement. *See also* Direct
object; Indirect object;
Objective complement;
Subjective complement
defined, 141
in sentence patterns, 9–12,
17–18
Complimentary close in business
letter, 515
Compound. *See* Coordination
Compound sentence, 129–36
with *and*, 130, 412–14
with *but*, 131–32, 417–18
with colons, 88–89
punctuation of, 132–36
with comma-plus-
conjunction, 132–33
with semicolon, 133–35
Conclusion
avoiding new topic in,
353–54
using comparison/contrast, 353
in narratives, 288–89
using narrative, 353
using quotation, 351–52
Concrete nouns, 160–61
in noun hierarchy, 195
Conditional mood, 37
defined, 141
Conjunctions, 178–79
in compound structures, 123–38

defined, 141
effective use of, 412–15
subclasses of, 179
Conjunctive adverb, 179
in compound sentences,
134–35
defined, 141
Connotation, 192–94
in description, 282–84
semantic features and,
195–97
semantic reaction, 198
Contractions
apostrophes in, 426–27
levels of usage, 255–57
Contrast, as semantic feature of
paragraphs, 370–73
Coordinating conjunctions, 179.
See also And; But
in compound structures,
124–32
in revision, 412–20
Coordination, 123–38. *See also*
Compound sentence
defined, 141
effective use of, 412–15
and style, 409–10
within the sentence, 124–29
punctuation of, 125–27
punctuation of series,
125–26
Correlative conjunction, 179
in compound structures,
127–29
parallel structure with,
127–28
subject–verb agreement
with, 128–29
Could of, 257
Countable nouns, 195–96
with *amount of/number of*,
253
determiners with,
195
with *fewer/less*, 258
Credibility of writer
in argument, 318–20
in introduction, 345–47

D

Dangling gerund, 102–3
Dangling infinitive, 14
Dangling participle, 73–75
Dash, 437–38
  with appositives, 86–88, 438
  with sentence interrupters,
    437
Declarative sentence, defined, 142
Definition
  as expository mode, 310
  as logical proof, 321–23
  of words, 193–94
Degree
  of adjectives, 166–68
  of adverbs, 166
  defined, 142
  with *more* and *most*, 167
  of preposition *near*, 166–67
Demonstrative pronouns, 187–88
  with broad reference, 188,
    386
  as determiners, 60, 173
  as nominals, 187–88
Denotation, 192–94
Derivational affixes, 142, 157–58
Derivational suffixes, 157–58
  of adjectives, 165
  of adverbs, 169–70
  of nouns, 159–60
  of verbs, 163–64
Description, 266
  arrangement in, 281
  point of view in, 281–82
  as rhetorical mode, 279–85
  word choice in, 282–84
  writing assignments for,
    284–85
  writing situation for, 280–81
Determiners, 59, 172–73
  defined, 142
  subclasses of, 173
Dialects, 237–39
Dialogue
  level of contractions in, 256
  in narrative, 293–95
  punctuation of, 448

Diction
  appropriate, 237–39
  dialect differences in, 238–39
  euphemism, 208–9
  figurative language, 203–8
  Glossary of Usage, 251–63
  levels of, 199–202, 237–39
    in contractions, 255–57
  personal voice and, 201–2,
    394–404
  predictability and redundancy
    in, 209–13
  pretentious, 201, 394–97
  standard written English,
    defined, 238
Different from, different than, 257
Direct address, 436
Direct object
  defined, 142
  gerund as, 101
  infinitive as, 104
  in passive transformation,
    47–51
  in transitive-verb patterns,
    9–12
Direct quotation
  acknowledging source of, 473
  in block form, for lengthy, 448
  brackets for additions to, 427
  colon before, 431
  compared with indirect,
    294–95
  effective use of, 473
  in narrative, 293–95
  nominal clause as, 106
  omissions in, ellipses for, 438
  paragraphing of, in dialogue,
    448, 473
  punctuation of, 19n, 448
  in writing conclusion, 351–52
Dissertation
  form for bibliography, 481
  form for notes, 477
Division
  in essay, 349–51
  as expository mode, 300–303
Do, as auxiliary, 40
Documentation, 475–82

bibliography, 479–82
footnotes and endnotes,
    475–79
Dominant order, in description,
    281
Doubling consonants, in spelling,
    220–21

E

-*ed* form of verbs, 26–28
    irregular, 43–46
Editorial
    form for bibliography, 481
    form for notes, 478
Editorials on File, for use in
    research, 456
-*eed*/-*ede*, in spelling, 223
Effect, affect, 257
Ellipsis
    for hesitation, 439
    for omissions, 438–39
    and style, 408–9
Elliptical clause, 113–14
    defined, 142
Emotional appeals, in argument,
    320–21
Emphasis
    with exclamation point, 440
    with italics, 442
    in sentences and paragraphs.
    See Stress in sentences
Emphatic reflexive pronoun. *See*
    Intensive pronoun
-*en* form of verbs, 26–28
    irregular, 43–46
encyclopedias
    form for bibliography, 480
    form for notes, 477
    listed, 465
    using in research, 455
Ending of essay, 351–54. *See also*
    Conclusion
Endnotes, typing of, 474–75
Essay examination, 508–11
Ethical appeals, in argument,
    318–20

Everybody, everyone, referent of,
    245–46
Evidence, in argument, 317
ex-, with hyphen, 441
Example, as semantic feature of
    paragraphs, 370–73
Example paragraph, 361–63
    topic sentence in, 362–63
    levels of generality in,
        364–65
Except, accept, 257
Exclamation point, 439–40
    for emphasis, 440
    with exclamatory sentence,
        439
Exclamatory sentence, 142,
    439
Expanded forms
    of passive verbs, 51–53
    of verbs, 28–31
Expectation. *See* Reader
    expectation
Explanatory appositive, 83,
    181
Expletives, 8, 180–81
    defined, 142
    it, 180, 381
    or, 83, 181
    that, 104–10, 181
    there, 7, 181, 381
Exposition, 266, 297–312
    classification, 307–10
        writing assignments for,
            309–10
    comparison/contrast, 303–7
        writing assignments for,
            305–7
    definition, 310–12
        writing assignments for,
            312
    division (analysis), 300–303
        writing assignments for,
            302–3
    process, 298–300
        writing assignments for,
            299–300
External arguments, as logical
    proof, 325–27

F

Fallacy in argument, 327–32
  ad hominem, 331
    guilt by association, 331
    name-calling, 331
    stereotyping, 331
  begging the question, 330
  circular reasoning, 330–31
  false dilemma, 329–30
  hasty generalization, 331
  non sequitur, 328–29
  post hoc, ergo propter hoc,
    328
False dilemma, as fallacy in
  argument, 329–30
Farther, further, 257
Fewer, less, 195, 258
First person
  as point of view
    in exposition, 343–44
    in narration, 290
  and passive voice,
    55–56, 402–3
  auxiliaries and, 32
  form of *be* with, 27
  of pronouns 183, 185
Flat adverbs, 170
Flaunt, flout, 258
Focusing, on research topic, 469–71
Footnotes
  form of, 475–79
  typing of, 474
For-, fore-, 231
Foreign words, italics for, 442
Form of modals, 36
Form-class words, 154, 158–71.
  See also Adjectives; Adverbs;
  Nouns; Verbs
    defined, 143
Frequently misspelled words,
  233–35
Function words. *See*
  Structure-class words
Functional order, in description,
  281
Further, farther, 258
Fused sentence, 132–33

G

Gender
  as feature of nouns, 196
  of pronouns, 183
    with unknown referent,
      246–50
General-to-specific paragraph,
  355–58
  levels of generality in,
    366–67
  topic sentence of, 356
Gerund, 99–103
  dangling, 102–3
  defined, 143
  functions of, 101–2
  subject of, 100–101
Glossary of Grammatical Terms,
  139–49
Glossary of Mechanics and
  Punctuation, 423–50
Glossary of Usage, 251–63
Goal (direct object), 9
"Good English," 237–50
Government documents
  form for bibliography, 480
  form for notes, 477
  using in research, 455–64
Grammar of sentences, 1–138
  and revision, 412–20
  questions for revision of, 412,
    415, 417
  and style, 407–12
Grammatical cohesion, 373–84
Guilt by association, as fallacy, 331

H

Had better, 258
Hasty generalization, as fallacy,
  331
Heading for business letter, 512,
  514
Headword of noun phrase, 59–61
  defined, 143
Hierarchy of nouns, 195–96
Human, as noun feature, 196

Hyphens, 440–41
  in compound words or
    phrases, 440
  with prefix, 441
  with prenoun modifiers, 63
  with suffix, 441

I

ie/ei, in spelling rule, 220
Illustration, as semantic feature of
  paragraph, 370–73
Imperative sentence, 8
  defined, 143
Imply, infer, 258–59
Inanimate nouns, 196
Indefinite pronouns, 188–89
  antecedents of, 245–50
  expanded forms of, 189
  as headwords, 162–63
  number of, 189, 245–46
  relative, 77–78
  subject–verb agreement
    with, 162–63
  they as, 247–48
Indefinite relative pronoun,
  77–78
Indexes, as research tools
  to newspapers, 456
  to periodicals, 457–64
Indicative mood, 38
  defined, 143
Indirect discourse, nominal clause
  as, 106–7
Indirect object, 11–12
  defined, 143
  in passive transformation, 50
Indirect quotations, compared with
  direct, 294–95
Indirect question, 106–7, 180
Infer, imply, 258–59
Infinitive
  as adverbial, 13–15
  dangling, 14–15
  defined, 143
  as nominal, 103–4
  split, 242–44

Inflectional suffixes
  of adjectives, 166
  of adverbs, 170
  defined, 143
  of nouns, 160
  of verbs, 26–28, 164
Information
  in library, 454–67
  in sentences, known and new,
    374–76
-ing form of verbs, 26, 29–31
Inside address for business letter,
  514
Intensifier. *See* Qualifier
Intensive pronouns, 186–187
Inter-, intra-, in spelling, 231
Interjection, defined, 144
Interrogative pronouns, 190
  in nominal clauses, 104–5
Interrogatives, 179–80
  defined, 144
  in nominal clauses, 104–5
  as question words, 179
Interview
  form for bibliography, 482
  form for notes, 478
Intonation pattern. *See also* Pitch
  of voice; Stress in sentences
  defined, 144
  of restrictive and
    nonrestrictive clauses, 69
  of sentence series, 413–14
  of subordinate clause, 416
Intra-, inter-, in spelling, 231
Intransitive verb, 16–17
  defined, 144
Introduction, of essay, 345–49
Invention techniques
  appeals of argument as,
    318–27
  in exploring topics, 339–40
  in finding topics, 270–77
Irregular noun plurals, spelling of,
  224–27
Irregular verbs, 26–28
  defined, 144
  listed, 43–46
Irritate, aggravate, 252

It
  in cleft sentence, 381
  as expletive, 180
  as personal pronoun, 182–84
Italics
  for foreign words, 442
  for stressed word, 442
  for titles, 442
  underlining, in typing, 442
  for words used as words, 442
Its, it's, 259
-ize/-ise, in spelling, 222–23

J

Job résumé. *See* Résumé
Journals
  indexes to, 457–64
  using in research, 454, 457

K

Kind of, sort of, type of, 259
Known information, 374–76

L

Lay, 259
Leave, let, 259–60
Lecture
  form for bibliography, 482
  form for notes, 478
Less, fewer, 195, 260
Let, leave, 260
Levels of diction, 199–202
  with contractions, 255–57
  informal, 200–201, 237–39
  pretentious, 199–202,
    394–96
Levels of generality in paragraphs,
  364–69
Lexical cohesion, 384–88
Library
  card catalog in, 464–65

encyclopedias in, 465
information in, 454–55
finding, 456–65
use of, 453–67
Lie, 260
Likenesses and differences, as
  evidence in argument, 323–25
Linking verb, 17–18
  defined, 144
Listening, the importance of,
  393–94
Logical appeals in argument,
  321–27
  cause and effect as, 322–23
  definition as, 321–23
  external evidence as, 325–27
  likenesses and differences as,
    323–25

M

Magazines, indexes to, 457–64
Main verb of sentence patterns,
  5–24
Manner adverbs, 23, 169–70
  defined, 144
Maybe, may be, 260
Meaning, 191–92
  categories of, 194–97
  of form and structure words,
    153
Metaphors, 204–8. *See also*
  Analogy; Comparison/contrast
  mixed, 205
Middle of essay, 349–51
Might of, 260
Misplaced modifiers, 92–97
Misspelled words, listed, 233–35
Mixed metaphor, 205
MLA style
  in bibliography, 479–82
  in notes, 475–79
Mnemonic devices, in spelling,
  232–33
Modal auxiliaries, 35–38
  defined, 144
  form of, 36–37

meaning of, 37–38
Modal-like auxiliaries, 174
Mood, 37–40
 conditional, 37
 defined, 145
 indicative, 38
 subjunctive, 38–40
Morphemes, 155–57
 defined, 145
Morphology, 155
 defined, 145
Most, almost, 260
Movable participle, 71
 compared to adverbial,
  72–73
Multiple modifiers, 92–97
Must of, 260

N

Name-calling, as fallacy, 331
Narration, 266, 287–96
 beginning point in, 291–93
 components of, 288
  conclusion, 288–89
  movement through time,
   288
  setting the scene, 288
 in conclusion of essay, 353
 point of view, 290–91
  first person, 290
  third person, 290–91
 quotations in, 293–95
 as rhetorical mode, 287–96
 writing assignments for, 296
 writing situation in, 289
Narrowing topic, 271–72, 276
 in research paper, 469–71
Newsmagazines, in research, 454,
  456–57
Newspapers, in research, 454, 456
 indexes to, 456
Nominal, 99–110
 clause as, 104–10
 defined, 145
 gerund as, 99–103
 infinitive as, 103–4

Nominal clause, 104–10
 as indirect question, 180
 punctuation of, 107–10
Nominalization of verbs, 398–401
Nominative absolute. *See* Absolute
 phrase
 defined, 145
Noncountable nouns, 195–96
 with *amount of* and *number
  of,* 253
 determiners with, 195
 with *fewer* and *less,* 258
Nonhuman, as noun feature, 196
Nonrestrictive modifier
 appositive as, 83–84
 clause as, 79–81
 defined, 145
 participial phrase as, 68–71
 punctuation of, 28–71, 79–81
Non sequitur, as fallacy, 328–29
Note taking in research, 466–67
Noun clause. *See* Nominal clause
Noun phrase, 6, 59–97
 as adverbial, 13
 appositive, 81–83
 defined, 145
 as device for narrowing topic,
  271, 276
 modifiers in. *See* Adjectivals
 multiple modifiers in, 92–93
 as object of preposition, 13,
  177
 in sentence pattern formulas,
  9–18
Nouns, 158–63
 collective, 162–63
 concrete/abstract, 160–61
 defined, 145
 derivational suffixes of,
  159–60
 as headwords of noun phrases,
  61–62
 inflectional suffixes of, 160
 noncountable, 160–61
 plural-only forms, 161–62
 as prenoun modifiers, 61–64
 referents of, 9
 semantic features of, 195–97

Number
  defined, 145
  of demonstrative pronouns,
    187
  of indefinite pronouns,
    162–63, 245–46
  of nouns, 160
    collective, 162–63
    plural-only forms,
      161–62
  of reciprocal pronouns, 187
  of subject, 33
Number of, amount of, 195, 253
Numbers, 443–45
  address and highway, 444
  chapter and page, 444
  dates, 444
  as determiners, 173
  fractions, 445
  percentages, 445
  in lists and ranges, 443
  for money, 444
  of one or two words, 443
  as sentence openers, 443–44

O

Object of preposition, 13, 177
  gerund as, 101
Objective case
  of pronouns, 183–84
  errors with, 184
Objective complement, 10–11
  defined, 145
  in passive transformation, 50
Observation, spelling and,
  230–32
Old information, 374–76
Omission
  of conjunction in series,
    409–10
  in elliptical clauses of
    comparison, 113
  of expletive *that* in nominal
    clause, 106–7
  indicated by ellipses, 438–39

  of needed comma in series,
    126
  that produces ambiguity,
    113–14
  of *whom* and *that* in relative
    clause, 76
  of words for stylistic variation,
    408–9
One, to replace *you,* 345
Opening sentence of paragraph,
  356–58
Optional slots in sentence
  patterns, 12–16
Outline
  of essay, 342–43
  of final draft, 471–72
  informal, 471–72
  of paragraph, 365–67
  typing of, 474
Outside sources, using in research,
  455

P

Paragraph
  blocs, 350–51
  coherence in, 369–88
  development of, 364–69
  grammatical cohesion in,
    373–84
  known information in,
    374–76
  lexical cohesion in, 384–88
  parallelism in, 373–74
  questions to consider, 389
  semantic cohesion in,
    370–73
  sentence stress in, 376–79
  transition, 350–51
  transition in, 371–73
Paragraph blocs, 350–51
Paragraph development, 364–69
  blocs, 350
  levels of generality in,
    365–67
  semantic features of

contrast, 370–73
  example, 370–73
  illustration, 370–73
  restatement, 370–73
  statement, 370–7,3
Parallel structure, 127–28
  defined, 145
Parallelism, as cohesive device in
  paragraphs, 373–74
Parentheses, 445–46
  for interruptions, 445
  in sentence pattern formulas,
  17
  for technical information, 446
  in verb-expansion rule, 34
Parenthetical expressions, 111
Participial phrase
  as adverbial, 73
  defined, 145
  effective use of, 416–17
  in opening position, 71
  as postnoun modifier, 64,
  66–75
  punctuation of, 68–71
Participle
  in absolute phrase, 115–18
  dangling, 73–75
  defined, 146
  form of, 66
  nonrestrictive, 68–71
  as postnoun modifier, 66
  as prenoun modifier, 63, 75
  restrictive, 68–71
Parts of speech, 153–90. *See also*
  Form classes; Pronouns;
  Structure classes
  listed, 154
Passive voice, 47–57
  as cohesive device, 380–81
  defined, 146
  focus of, 53
  in revision, 401–4
  use and misuse of, 55–57,
  402–3
Past tense
  defined, 146
  of modal auxiliaries, 36–37
  of verbs, 26–28, 41, 34–35

Perfect verb forms, 41–42
Period
  with abbreviations, 446–47
  as terminal punctuation, 446
Periodicals, indexes to, 457–64
Person. *See also* First person;
  Second person; Third person
  auxiliaries and, 32
  defined, 145
  as a feature of personal
  pronouns, 183
  as a feature of reflexive
  pronouns, 185
Personal pronouns, 182–85
  case of, 183–84
Personal résumé. *See* Résumé
Personal voice
  grammar of, 397–404
  importance of, 394–97
  in revision, 404–7
Personification, 203
Phrasal preposition, 177–78
Phrasal verbs, 177, 240–41
Phrases
  absolute, 115–18
  appositive, 81–92
  dangling
    gerund, 102–3
    infinitive, 14
    participle, 73–75
  introductory
    participial, 71
    sentence modifiers,
    111–12
  for shifting stress,
    376–78
  prepositional, 13, 64–66
  restrictive and nonrestrictive,
  68–70, 83–84
  transitional, 371
Pitch of voice, in series, 125–26.
  See also Intonation pattern;
  Stress in sentence
Place, adverbials of, 23
Plagiarism, 474
Planning the essay, 339–45
Plural
  as feature of nouns, 195

Plural (cont.)
    collective nouns, 162
    plural-only forms, 161
    as feature of pronouns
        demonstrative, 187
        indefinite, 162–63,
            245–46
        personal, 183
        reciprocal, 187
        reflexive, 185
Plural-only nouns, 161–62
Plus, 261
    misuse of, 414–15
Point of view, 343–45
    in description, 281–82
    in narration, 290–91
Positive degree, defined, 146
Possessive case
    apostrophe with, 227–29,
        425
    defined, 146
    with gerunds, 100–101
    of pronouns, 183–84,
        228–29
        in spelling, 228–29
        as determiners, 173,
            183–84
    in spelling, 227–29
Post hoc, ergo propter hoc, as
    fallacy, 328
Postnoun modifiers, 64–67. *See
    also* Adjectivals
Predicate, 5–8
    defined, 146
Predictability, 209. *See also*
    Reader expectation
Prefix, 156
    defined, 146
Prenoun modifiers, 61–64
    adjectives and nouns, 61–64
    commas with, 62–63
    hyphens with, 63
    phrase as, 63
    participle, 75
Prepositional phrase
    in absolute phrase, 115–18
    adjectival, 64–66
    adverbial, 13

    defined, 146
    effective use of, 416–17
    for shifting sentence stress,
        376–78
Prepositions, 13, 176–78. *See
    also* Prepositional phrase
    defined, 146
    degree in *near,* 166–67
    at sentence end, 239–42
    shifted, 241–42
    simple, 177
    phrasal, 177–78
Present tense of verbs, 26–28, 41
    defined, 147
Prewriting, 273–77
Principal, principle, 261
Pro-, with hyphen, 441
Process
    as expository mode, 298–300
    an individual's writing,
        337–38
    writing as, 337–421
Progressive verb forms, 41–42
Pronominal, 182
Pronoun–antecedent agreement
    defined, 140
    of demonstrative pronoun,
        187–88
    with *everyone* and *everybody,*
        245–50
    of personal pronouns, 182–83
    of reflexive pronouns,
        185–86
Pronouns, 181–90. *See also*
    Pronoun–antecedent
    agreement; Reference of
    pronouns
    broad-reference
        of demonstrative, 188,
            386
        of relative, 188–19, 141
    defined, 147, 154
    demonstrative, 187–88
        with broad reference,
            188, 386
        as determiners, 60
        as nominals, 187–88
    errors with, 184–85, 186

gender of unknown referent,
246–50
indefinite, 188
number of, 189, 245–46
intensive, 186–87
interrogative, 104–5, 190
in lexical cohesion, 384–88
personal, 182–85
number of, 183
person of, 32, 183
possessive case, 183–84,
228–29
as determiners, 60, 173,
183–84
spelling of, 228–29
problems with, 385–88
reciprocal, 187
referent of, 245–50
reflexive, 185–86, 384
relative, 189
in adjective clauses, 75–81
with broad reference,
118–19, 141
Pronunciation, spelling and, 232
Proofreading, 421
Proper nouns
determiners and, 60
in noun hierarchy, 195
punctuation of modifiers with,
80–81
Proposal argument, 333, 334–36
Proximity, as feature of
demonstrative pronouns, 187
Punctuation. *See also front*
endpaper for list of punctuation
marks
of adverbial verb phrase,
72–73
of appositives, 83–92
of coordinated parts, 125–27
of direct quotations, 19n, 448
of nominal clause, 107–10
of opening adverbs, 110–11
of parenthetical expressions,
111
of participial phrases, 68–73
of prepositional phrases, 21,
111

of relative clauses, 79–81
restrictive/nonrestrictive,
68–71, 79–81
of sentence modifiers, 20,
110–13
of sentence openers, 20–22,
110–13
of sentence slots, 19–20
of subordinate clauses, 21,
108–10, 112–13
Purpose, 267–70
in description, 280–81
in narration, 289
in writing situation, 269–70

Q

Qualifier, 175–76
defined, 147
in revision, 406–7
Quantifiers, 188
as determiners, 173
Question mark
with quotations, 447
as terminal punctuation, 447
Questions, 7
essay, for examination,
508–11
punctuation of, 447
quoted, within question, 447
that result in end
prepositions, 241–42
words indicating, 179
Questions of argument, 314–15
Quotation marks, 447–49
in dialogue, 448
for direct quotations,
447–48, 473
within direct quotations, 448
in quotations in block form,
448
for special uses of words, 449
for titles, 449
Quotations. *See also* Direct
quotations
in narrative, 293–95
use of, 473–74

Quotations (cont.)
    in writing conclusions,
        351–52

R

Radio program
    form for bibliography, 482
    form for notes, 479
Reader. *See* Audience
Reader expectation, 360–61
    and grammatical cohesion,
        376–81
    redundancy and, 211–12
*Readers' Guide to Periodical
    Literature,* using in research,
    457
Really, overuse of, 244
Reason, adverbials of, 24
Reason is because, 261
Reciprocal pronouns, 187
Redundancy, 209–13
    of cliches, 212–13
    as unnecessary repetition,
        211–12
Reference of pronouns
    to clause or sentence. *See*
        Broad reference
    everyone and *everybody* as
        plural, 245–46
    of personal pronouns, 182–84
    of reciprocal pronouns, 187
    of reflexive pronouns,
        185–86
    of relative, in clauses, 75–81
    unknown gender of, 246–50
Referent
    defined, 147
    of indirect object, 12
    of noun phrase, 9
    of objective complement, 11
    of subjective complement, 18
Reflexive pronoun, 185–86
    for lexical cohesion, 384
Refutation, in argument essay,
    317–18

Regular noun plurals, spelling of,
    223–24
Regular verb, defined, 147
Relative adverb, 78–79, 179
Relative clause, 75–81
    with broad reference, 118–19
    defined, 147
    punctuation of, 79–81
    with *whom,* 76–77
Relative pronoun, 75–81, 179,
    189
Repetition
    as cohesive device, 388
    of old information, 374–76
    redundant, 212–13
    rhythmic, as style feature, 411
Research, 451–520
Research paper, 469–505
    draft with comments, 483–93
    final draft, 494–506
Restatement, as semantic feature
    of paragraph, 370–73
Restrictive modifier
    adjectival clause, 79–81
    appositive, 83–84
    defined, 147
    participle, 68–71
Résumé, 516–20
    facsimile of, 520
Revision, 391–421
    personal voice in, 404–7
    qualifiers in, 406–7
    questions to consider,
        420–21
    stress in, 405–7
    using voice in, 404–7

S

-*s* form of verbs, 26–28
Salutation for business letter,
    514–15
Second person
    auxiliaries with, 32
    as point of view in essay,
        343–45

of pronouns, 183, 185
Self-, with hyphen, 441
Semantic cohesion, 370–73
Semantics, 191–92
Semicolon, 449–50
  in compound sentence, 133
  as a conjunction, 449
  with a conjunction, 135, 450
  with a conjunctive adverb,
    134–35, 449
  in the separation of series, 450
Sentence fragments, 112
Sentence, fused, 132–33
Sentence modifier, 110–21
  adverbial as 110–11
  defined, 147
  parenthetical expression as,
    111
  subordinate clause as, 111–15
Sentence patterns, 5–24
Sentence style. *See* Style
Sentence transformations
  cleft, 381–82
  exclamatory, 142
  interrogative, 144
  passive, 47–57
  there, 7, 148, 381
Series, and style, 409–10
Set, 261
Sexist usage, 246–50
Silent *e* rule, in spelling, 221–22
Simple past, 41
Shifted preposition, 241–42
Sight, site, cite, 261
Signature block for business letter,
  515
Simile, 204
Singular
  as feature of nouns, 195
    collective, 162
    plural-only forms, 161
  as feature of pronouns
    demonstrative, 187
    indefinite, 162–63
    personal, 183
    reciprocal, 187
    reflexive, 185

Sit, 261
Site, sight, cite, 261
Slang. *See* Levels of diction
Slash, 450
Sort of, kind of, type of, 261
Sources
  acknowledgment of, 472–74
  of argument. *See* Appeals of
    argument
Spatial order, in description, 281
Special writing situations, 507–20
  business letter, 511–15
  facsimile, 513
  essay examination, 508–11
  résumé, 516–20
  facsimile, 520
Specific-to-general paragraph,
  359–61
Specifiers, 188
  as determiners, 173
Spelling, 215–35
  British, 221n, 222n
  observation and, 230–32
  pronunciation and, 232
  reform of, 218–19
  rules of
    doubling consonants,
      220–21
    -eed/-ede, 223
    ie/ei, 220
    irregular noun plurals,
      224–27
    -ize/-ise, 222–23
    possessive case, 227–29
    regular noun plurals,
      223–24
    silent *e*, 221–22
  spelling tricks, 232–33
Split infinitive, 242–44
Standard written English, 238–39
Statement, in paragraph
  development, 370–73
Statistics, as evidence in
  argument, 325–26
Stereotyping
  as fallacy in argument, 331
  word association and, 199

Stress in sentence. *See also*
Intonation pattern; Pitch of
voice
with cleft transformation,
381–82
as cohesive device, 376–79
on italicized words, 442
with restrictive and
nonrestrictive clauses, 69
as revision tool, 405–7
in sentence series, 413–14
with *there* transformation, 381
Structure-class words, 172–81.
See also entries for subclasses
defined, 147
list of subclasses, 154
Style, 392–421
of appositives, 410–11
of coordinate series, 409–10
defined, 392
ellipsis as variation in, 408–9
grammar and, 407–12
of nominalization, 398–400
of passive voice, 401–4
questions to consider,
420–21
word order variation, 407–8
Subject of sentence, 5–8
as agent, 9, 53, 397–98
defined, 148
infinitive as, 103
in passive voice, 48–55
Subjective case, of pronouns,
183–84
Subjective complement, 17–18
compound, 124
defined, 148
gerund as, 101
infinitive as, 104
phrase as, 64
Subject–verb agreement, 8,
31–33, 61
with *as well as,* 33
with collective nouns,
162–63
with compound subjects,
128–29

with correlative conjunctions,
128–29
defined, 140
errors of, 8, 32–33
with plural-only nouns,
161–62
in *there* transformation, 7
Subjunctive mood, 38–40
defined, 148
Subordinate clause, 14
defined, 148
effective use of, 415–17
punctuation of, 21, 108–10,
112–13
as sentence fragment, 112
as sentence modifier, 111–15
Subordinating conjunctions, 179
in subordinate clauses, 14,
111–13
Subordinator, 14. *See also*
Subordinating conjunction;
Subordinate clause
defined, 148
Suffix, 155–58. *See also*
Derivational suffixes; Inflectional
suffixes
defined, 148
of form-class words, 157–58
Superlative degree, 166–68
defined, 148
with *most,* 167
Syntax, 155

T

Television program
form for bibliography, 482
form for notes, 479
Tense
defined, 148
meanings of, 41–42
of modal auxiliaries, 36
in verb-expansion rule,
34–37
of verbs, 26–27

Testimony, as evidence in
argument, 325–27
That
as demonstrative pronoun,
173, 187–88
with broad reference,
188, 386
as expletive in nominal clause,
104–6
omission of, 106–7
in indirect discourse, 106–7
as relative pronoun in
adjectival clause, 75–77
omission of, 76, 80
Their, there, they're, 262
There transformation, 7, 381
defined, 148
Thesis statement, 274–77
They
as indefinite pronoun,
247–48
as personal pronoun, 182–84
Third person
auxiliaries and, 32
in exposition, 343–45
as feature of pronouns, 183,
185
in narrative, 290
with -*s* form of verb, 27
Time
adverbials of, 23
movement through, in
narrative, 288
Title
finding an appropriate, 354
quotation marks for, 449
Title page, facsimile, 494
To, too, two, 262
Tone, of essay, 345–47
Topic
exploring, 339–40
finding, 270–72
focusing, in research paper,
469–71
list of, 277
narrowing, 271–72, 276
Topic sentence, 356–58

in example paragraph,
362–63
in general-to-specific
paragraph, 356–58
importance of, 363
in specific-to-general
paragraph, 359–60
Topics for argumentation, 314–15
Transition devices, 371–73
Transition paragraph, 350–51
Transitive verbs
defined, 149
passive voice of, 47–57
sentence patterns with, 9–12
Try and, 262–63
Typing the final draft, 474–75

U

Underlining to indicate italics, 442
Unique, absolute meaning of, 169
Usage, 237–50. *See also* Diction
Glossary of, 251–63
sexist, 246–50

V

Vague reference of pronouns. *See*
Broad reference
Verbals. *See* Gerund; Infinitive;
Participle
Verb-expansion rule, 29–31,
34–37
defined, 149
Verb phrase
as adverbial, 13–14, 72–73
compound, 124–26
defined, 149
in sentence patterns, 9–18
Verbs, 25–46, 163–65
adverbials with, 41–42
agent of, 48
agreement with subject,
31–33
errors in, 32–33

Verbs (cont.)
    auxiliaries with, 25–26,
      28–31, 34–38
    defined, 149
    derivational affixes of,
      163–64
    expanded forms of, 28–31,
      34–37, 40–43
      passive voice of, 51–53
    forms of, 26–28
      meaning of, 40–43
    inflectional suffixes of,
      164–65
    intransitive, 16–17
    irregular, 26, 43–46
    linking, 17–18
    modal auxiliaries with, 35–38
    moods of, 37–38
      conditional, 37
      indicative, 38
      subjunctive, 38–40
    passive voice of, 47–57
    phrasal, 177, 240–41
    regular, 26–27
      formula for expanded,
        29–31, 34–37
    tense of, 34–35
    transitive, 9–12
      passive voice of, 47–57
Vocabulary choice, as cohesive
    device, 388

W

What, in cleft sentence, 381
Which clause
    with broad reference, 118–19
    punctuation of, 80

Who, whom
    in adjectival clause, 76–77
    in nominal clause, 105
Who's, whose, 263
Word choice, 282–85
Word order, and style, 407–8
Words, 151–263. *See also* Diction
    frequently misspelled,
      233–35
    italics with, 442
      foreign, 442
      stressed, 442
      used as words, 442
    meaning, 191–92
    morphemes in, 155–57
    parts of speech, 153–90
      form classes, 158–71
      pronouns, 181–90
      structure classes, 172–81
    power of, 197–98
      in advertising, 198–99
    pretentious, 201, 394–97
    quotation marks for special
      uses of, 449
    semantic features of, 195–97
Writing situation, 267–77
    defining, 269–70
    in narration, 289
    summary of, 276–77

Y

Yet
    as conjunctive adverb,
      134–35
    as coordinating conjunction,
      124
You're, your, 263

Part I The Grammar of Sentences

1. **Sentence Patterns   5**
   1.1   The Two-Part Sentence
   1.2   The Six Basic Patterns
   1.3   Punctuation and the Sentence Slots
   1.4   Punctuation of Sentence Openers
   1.5   Summary

2. **Expanding the Verb   25**
   2.1   The Verb Forms
   2.2   The Expanded Forms
   2.3   The System of Expansion
   2.4   Subject–Verb Agreement
   2.5   Addition of Tense to the Verb String
   2.6   The Modal Auxiliaries
   2.7   The Moods of the Verb
   2.8   Summary of Verb Forms
   2.9   The Irregular Verbs

3. **The Passive Voice   47**
   3.1   A Three-Step Transformation
   3.2   Transformation of Expanded Verbs
   3.3   Use of the Passive Voice
   3.4   Misuse of the Passive Voice

4. **Expanding the Noun Phrase: Adjectivals   59**
   4.1   The Determiner
   4.2   The Headword
   4.3   The Prenoun Modifiers
   4.4   The Postnoun Modifiers

5. **Nominals and Sentence Modifiers   99**
   5.1   Nominals
   5.2   Sentence Modifiers

6. **Coordination   123**
   6.1   Coordination Within the Sentence
   6.2   Coordination of Complete Sentences

Glossary of Grammatical Terms   139

Part II Words

7. **The Parts of Speech   153**
   7.1   Morphemes
   7.2   The Form Classes
   7.3   The Structure Classes
   7.4   Pronouns

8. **Using Words Effectively   191**
   8.1   The Meaning of Words
   8.2   Denotation and Connotation
   8.3   Categories of Meaning
   8.4   Levels of Diction
   8.5   The Writer's Attitude
   8.6   Figurative Language
   8.7   Euphemism
   8.8   Predictability and Redundancy

9. **Spelling   215**
   9.1   Spelling Rules
   9.2   Spelling Tricks
   9.3   Frequently Misspelled Words

10. **What Is "Good English"?   237**
    10.1   Can Sentences End with Prepositions?
    10.2   Can We Split Infinitives?
    10.3   Are *Everybody* and *Everyone* Really Singular?
    10.4   Should Indefinite Antecedents Always Be *He*?

Glossary of Usage   251

Part III The Whole Theme

11. **The Writing Situation: Topic, Audience, and Purpose   267**
    11.1   Defining the Writing Situation
    11.2   Finding a Topic